# Counseling and Psychological Services for College Student-Athletes

*Second Edition*

# Counseling and Psychological Services for College Student-Athletes

*Second Edition*

Mary Jo Loughran, Editor
Chatham University

PUBLISHING

A Division of the International Center for Performance Excellence
West Virginia University
375 Birch Street, WVU-CPASS
PO Box 6116
Morgantown, WV 26506-6116

Library of Congress Card Catalog Number: 2019932507

ISBN: 9781940067377

Cover Design: Wendy Lazzell
Cover Photos: ID 648945988 © SolStock | Istockphoto.com
Production Editor: Kassi Roberts


10 9 8 7 6 5 4 3 2 1

FiT Publishing
A Division of the International Center for Performance Excellence
West Virginia University
375 Birch Street, WVU-CPASS
PO Box 6116
Morgantown, WV 26506-6116
800.477.4348 (toll free)
304.293.6888 (phone)
304.293.6658 (fax)
Email: fitcustomerservice@mail.wvu.edu
Website: www.fitpublishing.com

# Contents

# Acknowledgements

I'm one of those people who usually reads the *Acknowledgements* sections of books because I like to think that the individuals named therein deserve my thanks for their contributions to the work. If you are of such a mind, I invite you to add your own good wishes to the people I'm about to mention.

To Ed Etzel, where to even begin? Your earlier versions of this book had a prominent place on my bookshelf well before I met you. I am honored that you entrusted me with taking your handoff, and I am hopeful that I did the project justice. You are a generous colleague, a wise mentor, and a good friend.

To the 26 authors who contributed their time, expertise, knowledge, and hard work to create this book, I say thank you. Thank you for meeting deadlines, for your quick turnarounds, for considering my suggestions, and for sharing your approach to this work. You made my job easy.

To Barbara Ridenour Dalton and Kassi Roberts of FiT Publishing & International Center for Performance Excellence, I wish to express my thanks for your guidance and assistance throughout this process. It was tremendously reassuring to know that both of you were only a phone call or an email away.

To my graduate assistant, Meredith Deal, thank you for making such good use of your fine-tooth comb. Your diligence in looking at the trees allowed me to tend to the forest. I am also grateful to Anthony Isacco, Leigh Skvarla, and Maxine Kane for making editorial suggestions on the chapters I authored or coauthored.

I am grateful to my students and colleagues at Chatham University for sharing your teaching and learning space with me. I like to think that I'm a better psychologist because of our interactions. I know I'm a better person.

I want to express my love and gratitude to my family, all 45 of you. Thanks for making home into an idea that transcends time and space. To Max, that goes double for you.

Finally, to the countless collegiate student-athletes who entrust helping professionals every day with your struggles, your successes, your frustrations, and your dreams, thank you from all of us. It is an honor to know you.

**—Mary Jo Loughran**

# Foreword

The work of mental health professionals, including counselors, psychologists, social workers, and psychiatrists, in the realm of intercollegiate athletics has been expanding for the past three plus decades. For some time, organizations like the National Collegiate Athletics Association (NCAA) and individual institutions paid relatively little attention beyond lip service to the developmental and mental health issues impacting athletes' lives. Recent changes, primarily supported by the NCAA, have gradually transformed this area of practice into an evolving specialty field.

Thus, growing numbers of providers appear to be interested and involved in assisting collegiate athletes with their academic, personal-social, and health-related challenges. Today, providers work in counseling centers, some independently, and others as imbedded staff members within departments of intercollegiate athletics. Whatever one's professional background or situation may be, today's helping professional must be exceptionally well-prepared to work with these active young people from their later teens to early adulthood, within a self-described 'industry', employing a set of nearly incomprehensible rules that are unlike any other on campus.

The effective provision of helping services to college athletes is one that not only entails a passion to work with college students, who are also athletes, but also requires multiple competencies, including those of a fundamental clinical, consulting, and experiential nature. Providers must be able to bring a wide range of skills and abilities to their formal and informal interactions with clients and other stakeholders (e.g., administrators, coaches, academic advisors, and sports medicine professionals), who typically have very different backgrounds and perspectives on the biopsychosocial needs and health of today's student-athlete.

Perhaps as much as these prerequisites, mental health professionals must possess considerable 'cultural competence'—an in-depth understanding of the stressful context within which college students who are also athletes live and work. Providers must have a strong sense of what is ethical, both personally and professionally. They must also understand how these beliefs can impact practice: how they agree with the law, the values, and standard practices within the unique culture of intercollegiate athletics—because they often do not.

How then does the professional interested in working with this diverse population in this complex and challenging milieu become proficient and maintain her/his skills, abilities, and moral compass to do so? The answer to this question is not so simple. Nevertheless, a book like the one you are now holding, reading, and studying will be useful to this path in the short and long run.

This edition's editor, Dr. M. J. Loughran, has assembled a range of experienced professionals who share their insight and experiences about the myriad factors that impact effective, holistic work with college athletes as we approach the year 2020. Also presented are numerous, modern best practices that the reader and/or student-trainees can learn about and hopefully put into practice. I believe you will find this book personally meaningful and useful to your work in this regularly rewarding and frustrating realm of practice.

**—Edward F. Etzel, EdD**
*Professor/Licensed Psychologist*
*College of Physical Activity and Sport Sciences*
*West Virginia University*

# Consultation in Collegiate Athletics: Best Practices

*Doug Hankes and Deborah Roche*

## Introduction

The previous version of this chapter (Roche & Hankes, 2009) provided a detailed explanation of various models of consultation and described the structure, organization, and culture of intercollegiate athletic departments. Although this information is important, there are already many published descriptions of consultation models. This updated chapter focuses instead on specific factors and realities to consider when consulting within an intercollegiate athletic department. As noted elsewhere in the chapter, the process of consultation can be notably influenced by numerous variables, including the type and scope of services offered (e.g., mental health-focus versus performance excellence/enhancement), the relationship between the provider and the athletic department (e.g., embedded versus external), and, for external providers, the location of practice (e.g., university counseling center versus private/community practice). Further, the size and budget of the athletic department will impact the realities of consultation services. For example, a power five university—a member of one of the five major Division I conferences (ACC, Big Ten, Big 12, Pac-12, and SEC)—can provide substantially greater financial support compared to smaller Division I, Division II, or Division III institutions.

## Consultation versus Collaboration

Consultation and collaboration are often used interchangeably, however, professionals in the field are passionate about delineating the differences and identifying each as separate processes. One definition of consultation is

> *a voluntary problem-solving process that can be initiated and terminated by either the consultant or consultee. It is engaged primarily for the purpose of*

> *assisting consultees to develop attitudes and skills that will enable them to function more effectively with a client, which can be an individual, group, or organization. Thus, the goals of the process are two-fold: enhancing services to third parties and improving the ability of the consultee to function in areas of concern to them. (Brown, Pryzwansky, & Schulte, 2011, p. 1)*

In other words, the consultant is the expert and the consultee is the recipient of that expertise.

Collaboration, on the other hand, involves a process in which both parties work together to identify a problem, target a solution, and implement strategies toward the problem resolution (Pryzwansky, 1977). The assumption in collaboration is that it involves all participants being active in all phases of the change process.

In many ways, collaboration is a basic element of the counseling or therapy process. The therapy process can be explained to new clients as a collaboration. The collaborative process in therapy assumes that both parties utilize their knowledge and expertise in their work. The helping professional brings expertise in mental health issues and the change process, or at least, that is typically the assumption and hope of the client when seeking assistance. The client brings knowledge and expertise about themselves and their perceptions of the world, even if they are accompanied by distortions or confusion. Together, the counselor and client make decisions about changes that will help the client get better and function more effectively.

By definition, the concept of collaboration seems to be a better fit for what actually occurs when working in the highly competitive culture of an athletic department, as compared to the more commonly used term, consultation. Regardless of terminology, however, there is a cautionary note for helping professionals seeking to work in this environment. Facilitating change via a collaborative process frequently takes time and patience, neither of which is plentiful in the intercollegiate athletic environment. Athletic administrators pay helping professionals to come into their organization to address a problematic situation and are likely to expect the consultant to take on the expert role in implementing change, especially in a culture that typically expects that everything should have happened yesterday. Lip service to the process of change easily falls to the realities of needing solutions to problems immediately, or at least, the optic that an issue is being addressed. That said, a helping professional who spends more time in the expert role runs the risk of the client never developing the skills necessary to function independently. It is a noble goal to facilitate the process of creating competence (or even expertise) in the client, but, in the fast-paced reality of college athletics, this may be challenging to accomplish within the expected short time period allotted for this process.

## Intercollegiate Athletic Department Environment

It is still a commonly held belief that college athletics is an environment where student-athlete welfare is paramount, that important life skills and values are learned and reinforced, and that competition brings out the best in all who are involved. This is the case for the majority of cases. Unfortunately, given recent scandals in the headlines, in some instances it can be difficult to describe working in college athletics as anything different than "swimming in polluted waters" (Hankes, 2013). Andersen (2005) described the college sport environment as often being "deeply pathogenic places where people learn really horrible lessons that twist their views of the world and themselves" (p. 289). Perhaps even more damning, Etzel (personal communication, 2018) bluntly stated,

> *One could certainly drown in those murky waters—and/or at least be tempted to compromise personal/professional values under duress [i.e., from athletic administrators], when tempted through identification with teams and athletes, ego and self-promotion, getting and keeping a job, and/or a naive lack of awareness (impairment) of the potential harm that can occur to our clients when working in this setting.*

Recent high profile scandals include child sexual abuse, academic fraud, sexual assault, illegal recruiting and player payment, and widespread corruption/organized cheating. There is no basis in reality to ignore that college athletics is big business involving astronomical amounts of money in which collegiate student-athletic performances can have significant financial repercussions (Etzel & Watson, 2007; Sperber, 2000). While the largest scandals make the headlines, many individuals working in intercollegiate athletic departments are aware of any number of "mini-scandals" that do not quite rise to a level of crisis that results in public awareness. Both large-scale scandals and mini-scandals seem to be occurring on an increasingly frequent basis. This is the environment that any helping professional—whether housed internally or based externally, focused on performance enhancement versus mental health-related issues, or addressing individual versus organizational issues—must face. The helping professional who ignores these realities risks ineffectiveness at a minimum, and, in a worst-case scenario, can themselves become part of the scandal.

## Perceptions of Sport Psychology and Sport Psychology Professionals

It is important to acknowledge the elephant in the room. Not only are the financial stakes increasing in collegiate athletics, so are the number of opportunities for others to profit in support of the athletic industry. Helping professionals do not work for free and, in fact, can frequently make large sums of money, particularly in the higher echelons of competitive, high-profile intercollegiate athletics. It may be tempting for sport psychology professionals to compromise their professional and personal ethics in an effort to gain or accommodate work in this industry.

The above-mentioned financial incentives, coupled with the status associated with high profile intercollegiate athletic programs, creates the risk of attracting unscrupulous individuals to this field who may portray themselves or their credentials inaccurately. Although the term psychologist is restricted to those holding a state-issued license to practice, other terms such as sports counselor, mental trainer, or performance consultant can be used by anyone, regardless of their education or professional credentials (or lack thereof). Both the American Psychological Association (APA) and the Association for Applied Sport Psychology (AASP) have attempted to address this by issuing guidelines outlining the necessary preparation to enter this area of practice. Nonetheless, the lack of standard, codified preparatory requirements has tarnished sport psychology's reputation.

Athletic departments and universities risk incurring liability when they retain unvetted practitioners to work with their student-athletes. For example, unqualified individuals have been found providing mental health-related services without the appropriate state license. In other reported examples, student-athletes have been badgered to purchase products such as books, apps, visualization scripts, and confidence nuggets. These practices run afoul of the ethics codes of APA, AASP, and other related helping professions (For a more detailed discussion of these issues, see Chapter 15).

## Vetting External Sport Psychology Consultants

An important and prudent risk management tool for intercollegiate athletic departments is the vetting of outside consultants who work with their student-athletes and teams. It can be difficult for someone not familiar with the field of sport psychology to evaluate individuals who use a myriad of self-defined titles that do not require any specific training, certification, or licensure. Some examples of these self-defined titles include mental toughness coach, performance enhancement specialist, mental coach, and peak performance coach. The helping professional embedded in an athletic department is likely to have the most knowledge to assess the outside consultant's competency and credibility. If another athletic department administrator is tasked with the vetting process, the embedded helping professional might share the following questions to assist in evaluating the outside consultant's competency to provide their services and lessen the liability risk for the athletic department and university.

1. Does the consultant have a state recognized license?

2. If licensed, has the consultant been approved by the relevant state board to provide services across state lines?

3. Is the consultant registered as a business with appropriate liability insurance to cover their scope of practice?

4. Has a background check been done on the consultant? If not, why not?

5. If the consultant is focused solely on performance enhancement, do they hold a nationally recognized certification (e.g., Certified Mental Performance Consultant through AASP)? If they do not hold a nationally recognized certification, what is their explanation for not doing so?

6. What is the consultant's training for the services they are purporting to offer?

7. How does the consultant demonstrate their success in consulting beyond anecdotal reports?

8. What does the consultant promise or guarantee? Do they offer unique, revolutionary, or groundbreaking interventions that only they possess (Meichenbaum & Lilienfeld, 2018)?

9. Does the consultant imply or directly state that a previous consulting relationship ensured the organization's success (e.g., conference and/or national championships)? Does the consultant acknowledge any failures or lack of success with an organization? If not, why not?

10. Does the consultant drop the names (casually or directly) of famous, successful athletes and teams with whom the consultant has had contact?

In general, outside consultants should be appropriately credentialed, have a transparent rubric for measuring their effectiveness, and should be sparing in the credit they take for specific athletes' or teams' successes.

## Navigating Expectations in Sport Psychology Consultation

Effective consultation is a complex process. Some of that complexity can be decreased if the helping professional strategically educates and prepares the student-athlete for working together. Early and frequent bidirectional communication about expectations, objectives, and goals is critical. An oft-cited successful strategy is for the helping professional to ask themself who the client is. This question then guides them to make effective, sensitive, and ethical decisions in their interventions with student-athlete clients, coaches, teams, sports medicine personnel, athletic trainers, strength and conditioning coaches, and athletic department administrators.

Applied sport psychology consultation is notable for the numerous boundary crossings and multiple relationships that are typically avoided in more traditional psychological practices (Hankes, 2012). Given the number of individuals invested in a student-athlete's success, C. B. Fisher (2014) has offered a different, more nuanced question to ask when there are conflicts between ethical responsibilities and organization demands: what are the ethical responsibilities to each of the parties involved? This approach makes the informed consent process even more critical. Since many services in the consultation process can involve multiple parties in an athletic department, all participants should know and understand their priorities and commitments in advance to prevent misunderstandings. Fisher's (2017) ethical practice model of protecting confidentiality rights for use in agencies and organizations provides a detailed model that can guide the helping professional in avoiding the many potential pitfalls in a "murky" athletic department.

## Peer-to-Peer Consultation

### *Peer Consultation Components*

The importance of peer-to-peer consultation cannot be overstated, whether a practitioner is in early career or is a seasoned clinician. Practicing in a vacuum is not only lonely, it can be dangerous and far less effective. Peer consultation activities' aims cover a broad spectrum, including to improve and optimize clinical service delivery, to validate treatment interventions, and to clarify ethical dilemmas. In addition, peer consultation is considered one of the three primary elements of risk management principles, along with informed consent and documentation (Bennett et al., 2006).

### *The Big Sky Sport Psychology Retreat*

The two major associations available to professionals who provide counseling and psychological services to student-athletes are the American Psychological Association (APA) Division 47 (Society for Sport, Exercise, and Performance Psychology) and the Association for Applied Sport Psychology (AASP). Membership in either or both of these organizations provides practitioners with access to the necessary resources (e.g., conferences and journals) to achieve and maintain the level of competence required to do their work effectively. Both associations disseminate findings regarding best practices for helping professionals. Further, both associations have published ethics codes to guide the decision-making process in clinical practice and professional interactions.

Another resource available to sport psychology professionals who specialize in work with collegiate student-athletes is the informal Big Sky Sport Psychology annual retreat. This group, founded by Dr. Chris Carr, began as a gathering of 18 licensed psychologists affiliated with collegiate athletics and has organically grown to nearly 250 members. Over time, the annual gathering was moved to Big Sky, Montana, where it is held simultaneously with the meeting of the Big Sky Athletic Training Sports Medicine Conference (BSATSMC). The meeting's format is intentionally one of a retreat with an emphasis on discussion and collaboration rather than lecture. In addition to the annual retreat, the group serves as a supportive pool of consultants to utilize year round in times of professional complexity, confusion, and distress.

The Big Sky Sport Psychology Retreat has a primary focus on student-athlete mental health rather than athletic performance enhancement. There is, however, a full appreciation of the integrative approach that includes athletic performance-specific interventions. The retreat has steadily grown from its grass roots origins and now includes other licensed mental health professionals (e.g., counselors and social workers) in addition to licensed psychologists.

## NCAA Recommendations for Student-Athlete Mental Health and Wellness

Dr. Brian Hainline joined the National Collegiate Athletic Association (NCAA), the governing body for intercollegiate athletics, as its first chief medical officer in 2013. In 2014 at the Big Sky Sport Psychology Retreat, Hainline stated, "When I was hired, I thought the most important medical issue facing the NCAA was concussion. I was wrong. It is student-athlete mental health."

Since 2009, the NCAA has released two documents that have had a significant impact on sport psychology consultation on college campuses. The first publication, entitled *Mind, Body and Sport: Understanding and Supporting Student Athlete Mental Wellness*, was "designed to help athletics departments, campus mental health providers, and all sport stakeholders promote and develop effective strategies to understand and support student-athlete mental wellness" (National Collegiate Athletic Association [NCAA], 2014, p. 7). This resource provides institutions with critical information necessary to develop protocols to meet the mental health and wellness needs of their student-athletes. The document outlines common issues confronting student-athletes, including eating disorders, mood disorders and depression, substance abuse, concussion, and injury. Also included are descriptions of models for providing services to student-athletes on college campuses (NCAA, 2014).

In 2016, the NCAA published an additional resource, entitled *Mental Health Best Practices—Inter-Association Consensus Document: Best Practices for Understanding and Supporting Student-Athlete Mental Wellness*. This document provides recommendations and best practices to institutions for the provision of student-athlete mental health care (NCAA, 2016). The document's contributors established four key standards of care that are crucial to the understanding and support of college student-athlete mental wellness:

1. clinical licensure of practitioners providing mental health care,

2. procedures for identification and referral of student athletes to qualified practitioners,

3. pre-participation mental health screening, and

4. health-promoting environments that support mental well-being and resilience (NCAA, 2016, p. 6).

With these two publications, the NCAA highlighted that student-athletes have mental health needs requiring a unique protocol compared to those of their non-athlete peers. In addition, the NCAA strongly recommended that each campus identify specific providers to evaluate and treat their student-athletes and specified that these individuals have specialized training and licensure to accomplish best practices for providing such services (NCAA, 2014; 2016). The specified qualified practitioners include clinical/counseling psychologists, psychiatrists, clinical social workers, psychiatric nurses, and primary care physicians with core competence in mental health issues (NCAA, 2016). Ideally these individuals should be trained and competent to appreciate the culture of athletics and college-aged clients (NCAA, 2016). These recommendations created a tremendous demand for sport psychology consultants meeting these qualifications. Previously, colleges made independent decisions regarding whether and how to provide clinical and sport psychology services to their student-athletes and coaches; however, with these recommendations, the NCAA encouraged every campus to have a practitioner meeting the above-mentioned qualifications available to their student-athletes. It is not surprising that shortly after the Best Practices publication was released, Division I institutions responded by posting an abundance of full-time position advertisements for individuals possessing this unique skill set, training, and expertise.

This is a very exciting development for the field of sport psychology for a variety of reasons. Student-athletes mental health needs have been recognized and thoughtful guidelines put forth to effectively treat them. Also, there is finally a recognition that sport psychology services need to be available in some form for all student-athletes, resulting in an increase in available campus resources. This will likely result in timely mental health evaluations for student-athletes in distress being more readily available. Fifth, athletic departments will be more likely to find resources to pay for these services. Finally, the NCAA has outlined the best practices for all college student-athletes. They encourage pre-participation screening and other health promoting efforts to reach student-athletes and the athletic community (NCAA, 2016). Also, delineated as best practices for this population are services like stress management, as well as outreach efforts within the community and increased collaboration among the entities who work with athletes in order to facilitate the awareness of services. These recommendations validate the worth of the standards that conscientious helping professionals have followed for years.

## Models for Sport Psychology Services on College Campuses

Universities have a wide range of resources available to provide psychological services to student-athletes. The above-mentioned NCAA publications recommend, whenever possible, for helping professionals to work within the existing system on campus to develop a sport psychology mental health services program. Carr and Davidson (2014) identified the three most common models: (1) the full time athletics department sport psychologist, (2) the part-time consultation model, and (3) the referral model.

In our experience, the full time athletics department practitioner model usually falls into two categories. In the first scenario, the provider resides in the athletic department and often reports to the athletic director or a member of the administrative staff (Chamberlain, 2007). Alternatively, the helping professional may be a member of the multidisciplinary sports medicine team. Hack (2007) referred to this as a part-time model; however, recently many of these positions have transitioned from part-time to full-time.

Where the helping professional is housed can entail important differences in terms of reporting lines, documentation for contacts with student-athletes and other personnel, and provision of services to the athletic community. In the full-time model, the helping professional provides individual counseling, coordination of eating disorder and substance abuse treatment, team consultations (performance and clinical), staff education and consultation, and consultation to the athletics community on sport psychology related issues (Carr & Davidson, 2007).

In the part-time consultation model, an external helping professional or a staff member at the university's counseling center is identified to provide services to student-athletes (Carr & Davidson, 2014; Flowers, 2007). This individual provides the same service outlined above; however, their weekly time commitment is usually between 10–30 hours rather than the 40–50 hours of their full-time counterparts (Carr & Davidson, 2014).

Many university athletic departments use the referral model for student-athlete mental health services (Carr & Davidson, 2014). In this model, the athletic department "does not employ or retain an 'in-house' provider; rather, it identifies a specific provider within the community or counseling center who will take referrals for student-athlete psychological issues" (Carr & Davidson, 2014, p. 19). One challenge accompanying this model is that the provider may not be as accessible to the athletic community as they would be in either the full-time or part-time models (Carr and Davidson, 2014). Additionally, the external provider model limits the availability of prevention or educational services and instead utilizes more of an intervention strategy (Carr & Davidson, 2014). Another challenge associated with this model is the provider being perceived as 'an outsider'. The lack of day-to-day or casual contact can create challenges to effective communication and collaboration with the athletic department personnel (Carr & Davidson, 2014). Researchers have found that student-athletes and members of the athletic community often fear that providers will not understand their struggles (Lopez & Levy, 2013; Hack, 2007). When there is a significant physical separation, such as the student-athlete having to go off-campus, it is possible for this perception to increase. Similarly, establishing trust and rapport may take longer if the helping professional is not embedded on campus.

## Additional Considerations

Athletic administrators seeking to address student-athletes' mental health needs should consider the provider's office location, regardless of the service model being used. The provider may or may not have an office in the athletic department's complex, with pros and cons associated with each option. For example, student-athletes spend tremendous amounts of time in the athletic department and having the resource available there can make it easier for them to see a provider. However, a disadvantage of this arrangement could be that privacy or perceived privacy may be jeopardized. Depending upon where the office is located, coaches, trainers, athletic directors, and sports media could see when student-athletes seek help. Several researchers have found this to be a barrier to utilization of sport psychology services (Lopez & Levy, 2013; Gulliver, Griffiths, & Christensen, 2012).

Another variable to consider when developing the provider role regards the reporting line. For example, a licensed mental health professional reporting directly to the athletic director will have professional and ethical responsibilities that may or may not be within the knowledge base of the supervisor. On the other hand, if the provider is a member of the counseling center staff, it is important to clarify whether they report to the counseling center director, an athletics department administrator, or both. These details are vital to establish prior to offering services to student-athletes or the athletics department as a whole. Defining the reporting lines prior to providing services allows for clear communication of the legal and ethical responsibilities to the athletic community being served. Additionally, this a priori clarification of responsibilities provides all concerned parties with a shared understanding of how potentially confusing or conflictual issues will be managed, including confidentiality, legal issues, and crisis situations. Each design for consultation offers pros and cons for the helping professional and the athletic community. Ultimately, it is paramount that the sport psychology provider be familiar with the campus and be able to determine the best design given the resources for that college or university.

To summarize, the primary goal for those involved in arranging mental health services for student-athletes is to build a model that is effective for that community. This decision has many variables for consideration, including fiscal issues, space issues, reporting lines, as well as other factors that may be unique to that particular campus community. Beyond the systemic considerations are those pertaining to individual helping professionals. These recommendations are presented in the next section.

## Recommendations to Enhance Success

The role for sport psychology providers on college campuses is growing rapidly. To meet the numerous needs on campus, below are several specific recommendations providers should keep in mind to be maximally effective.

**Practice within your scope.** Whether you are trained as a licensed mental health provider or exercise physiologist, be sure the services you provide are within your area of expertise. Even within each of these disciplines there are treatment modalities for which one may or may not have training. For example, biofeedback is a common technique used with student-athletes in performance and clinical work. It is incumbent upon each helping professional to obtain the necessary training and expertise to practice specific techniques.

**Consult with supervisors or peers.** Having a group of professionals with shared background and training to consult when confronted with ethical and other treatment challenges is crucial to successful practice. While many universities are creating full-time sport psychology provider positions, these may be single positions expected to manage the needs of the entire athletic community. Chamberlain (2007) argued that although this job is fulfilling, it is also demanding and comes with many challenges, including long hours, managing dual roles, and ethical dilemmas. AASP, Division 47 of APA, and the Big Sky Retreat are all resources to help the provider create a helpful network of colleagues.

**Manage expectations.** Although the primary duty of the provider is to work with student-athletes, the role also includes interactions with coaches, trainers, counseling center staff members, outside clinical providers, drug and alcohol facilities, sports medicine providers, etc. As discussed earlier, explaining the parameters of practice to these entities will help minimize confusion, disappointment, or the creation of dual roles. It is impossible to predict every possible scenario; however, by explaining the limitations of confidentiality (e.g., the duty to report abuse), having the necessary paperwork for informed consent, explaining to coaches the hours available to see clients, coverage for emergencies, etc., many misunderstandings and conflicts can be avoided. For example, coaches often request helping professionals' attendance at practice, competitions, and early morning meetings. Although these may be valuable activities, it is not always feasible to attend all of these events. Explaining to coaches the provider's limits regarding time and allocated financial resources can help manage the expectation of 24 hour-per-day availability.

**Reduce stigma.** It is well documented that student-athletes and the athletic community frequently do not seek services (Lopez & Levy, 2013; Flowers, 2007; Carr & Davidson, 2014; Zillmer & Gigli, 2007; Hack, 2007; Gulliver et al., 2012). Carr and Davidson (2014) described how the expectation of mental toughness among student-athletes, fear of rejection by teammates, and other misperceptions may interfere with seeking treatment. Outreach and prevention programming can serve the dual purpose of introducing the provider to the community and reducing the stigma associated with help-seeking.

**Accessibility.** Being available and accessible is crucial to building rapport and helping reduce stigma. Several practitioners have discussed the importance of attending practices, dropping by the training room, fostering relationships with sports medicine and athletic training staff members (Hack, 2007; Flowers, 2007; Zillmer & Gigli, 2007). Being available and visible may serve to foster trust that is vital to providing mental health services to the athletic community.

**Establish a professional, ethical identity.** Zillmer and Gigli (2007) and Chamberlain (2007) discussed the importance of doing the right thing, which may not be the popular thing. Helping professionals are privy to a lot of sensitive information and find themselves in delicate or ethically complicated situations. Establishing and maintaining boundaries, honoring commitments, and remaining professional in and out of the office are key ingredients to forging trust and respect in the athletic community, as well as the campus community at large. Hack (2007) described the conflict a helping professional can experience when determining how to manage conflicting agendas from sources in the athletic community. D. Klossner (2005, personal communication) recommended, "the student-athletes [must] always be considered the client to assure that the sport psychologist is always acting in the client's best interest." When this standard is observed, the helping professional's role becomes clear, and it is easier to determine the professional thing to do.

## Conclusion

Complicated, complex, murky. These words and other synomyms have been used to describe the relationship of a sport psychology provider to a college athletic department since the inception of the role. Significant changes have occurred in athletics in the ten years since our last edition. As we discussed, several helpful resources for the development of mental health services for athletes are now available. In addition, there is recognition that this is a unique population who need a specialized provider to support them. Although these are positive changes from the past decade, there are also negative changes, including occasional corruption and business practices with young people who are too inexperienced to truly appreciate the ramifications of these protocols.

To do this work, one must constantly be considering M. A. Fisher's (2014) question—what are the ethical considerations for each of the parties involved—and, when considering that question, consultation with colleagues who have likely been in similar predicaments is the best strategy. In many ways our profession is in a position to promote positive change, educate all parties about mental health, and protect the young athlete from abuses of power. It is a massive task, but one that can be performed effectively and ethically by a helping professional with the appropriate level of education and training. Under these circumstances, it is also work that is enjoyable and satisfying.

# References

Andersen, M. B. (2005). Coming full circle: From practice to research. In M.B. Andersen (Ed.), *Sport Psychology in Practice* (pp. 287–298). Champagne, IL: Human Kinetics.

Bennett, B. E., Bricklin, P. M., Harris, E., Knapp, S., VandeCreek, L., & Younggren, J. N. (2006). *Assessing and managing risk in psychological practice: An individualized approach*. Rockville, MD: The Trust.

Brown, D., Pryzwansky, W. B., & Schulte, A. C. (2011). *Psychological consultation and collaboration: Introduction to theory and practice (7th Edition)*, Upper Saddle River, NJ: Merrill.

Carr, C., & Davidson, J. (2014). The psychologist perspective. *Mind, body, and sport: Understanding and supporting student athlete wellness*, 17–20.

Chamberlain, R. B. (2007). Sport psychology in a collegiate athletic department setting. *Journal of Clinical Sport Psychology 1*, 281–292.

Etzel, E. F., & Watson, J. (2007). Ethical challenges for psychological consultations in intercollegiate athletics. *Journal of Clinical Sport Psychology 1*, 304–317.

Fisher, C. B. (2014). Multicultural ethics in professional psychology practice, consulting, and training. In F. T. L. Leong, L. Comas-Díaz, G. C. Nagayama Hall, V. C. McLoyd, & J. E. Trimble (Eds.), *APA handbooks in psychology. APA handbook of multicultural psychology, Vol. 2. Applications and training* (pp. 35–57). Washington, DC: American Psychological Association.

Fisher, M. A. (2014). Why "who is the client" is the wrong ethical question. *Journal of Applied School Psychology 30*(3), 183–208.

Fisher, M. A. (2017, October). *The ethics of conditional confidentiality in college counseling centers*. Workshop presented at the meeting of the Association for University and College Counseling Center Directors, Denver, CO.

Flowers, R. (2007). Psychologist-sport psychologist liaison between counseling and psychological services and intercollegiate athletics. *Journal of Clinical Sport Psychology, 1*, 223–246.

Gulliver, A., Griffiths Kathleen, M., & Christensen, H. (2012). Barriers and facilitators to mental health help-seeking for young elite athletes: A qualitative study. *BMC Psychiatry, 12*(1), 157. doi:10.1186/1471-244X-12-157

Hack, B. (2007). The development and delivery of sport psychology services within a university sports medicine department. *Journal for Clinical Sport Psychology, 1*, 247–250.

Hainline, B. (2014, August). *Introductory remarks*. Workshop presented to the Big Sky Sport Psychology Retreat, Big Sky, MT.

Hankes, D. M. (2012). Sport and performance psychology: Ethical issues. In Murphy, S.M. (Ed.), *The Oxford Handbook of Sport and Performance Psychology* (1st edition, pp. 46–61). New York, NY: Oxford University Press.

Hankes, D. M. (2013, February). *There but for the grace of God go I: Ethics in sport psychology overview*. Paper presented at the 9th annual meeting of the Big Sky Sport Psychology Retreat: Student-Athlete Psychological Issues, Big Sky, MT.

Lopez, R. L., & Levy J. J. (2013, April 16). Student athletes' perceived barriers to preferences for seeking counseling. *Journal of College Counseling*, 19–31.

Meichenbaum, D., & Lilienfeld, S.O. (2018). How to spot hype in the field of psychotherapy: A 19-item checklist. *Professional Psychology: Research and Practice, 49*(1), 22–30.

NCAA. (2014). *Mind, body and sport: Understanding and supporting student-athlete mental wellness*. Retreived from https://www.ncaapublications.com/p-4375-mind-body-and-sport-understanding-and-supporting-student-athlete-mental-wellness.aspx

NCAA. (2016). *Mental health best practices—Inter-association consensus document: Best Practices for understanding and supporting student athlete mental wellness*. Retrieved from http://www.ncaa.org/sites/default/files/HS_Mental-Health-Best-Practices_20160317.pdf

Pryzwansky, W. P. (1977). Collaboration or consultation: Is there a difference? *Journal of Special Education, 11*, 179–182.

Roche, D. N., & Hankes, D. M. (2009). Consultation in intercollegiate athletics. In E. F. Etzel (Ed.), *Counseling and Psychological Services for College Student-Athletes* (3rd edition, pp. 51–84). Morgantown, WV: FIT Technologies.

Sperber, M. (2000). *Beer and circus: How big-time college sports is crippling undergraduate education*. New York: Holt.

Zillmer, E., & Gigli, R. W. (2007). Clinical sport psychology in intercollegiate athletics. *Journal of Clinical Sport Psychology, 1*(3), 210–222.

# 2

# Counseling Collegiate Student-Athletes: Developmental Considerations

*Deanna Hamilton*

## CASE STUDY: STEVEN

Steven is a 20-year-old sophomore student-athlete at Bigtime University. He identifies as male, straight, cisgender, and Latino. He scheduled an appointment at the university counseling center after overhearing one of his swimming teammates positively describe his own counseling experience, which was mandated after a substance use honor code violation. Steven had a difficult time pinpointing exactly why he made the appointment other than to report having a hard time balancing his academic responsibilities with the demands of swimming. During his intake appointment, Steven stated that he only felt like himself in the pool. Steven has never sought counseling before. When recounting his life prior to arriving at Bigtime U, he described moving through high school fairly easily. He did fine academically, had a few close friends, but devoted most of his time and energy to swimming. Though athletes were celebrated at his high school, swimmers were relatively "ignored," as compared to the soccer or basketball players.

Similarly, Steven reported that his first year of college went as well or even better than he expected. Academically, most of his classes were at the introductory level and not all that different from his high school classes. In swimming, Steven found that he was able to contribute to the team to a degree that pleased his coaches. Although he struggled with the rigorous training, travel, and competition levels, Steven enjoyed the novelty of these new experiences. Socially, Steven spent most of his free time with his teammates and felt comfortable having a ready-made social group.

Much to his surprise, when he began his sophomore year in college, Steven found himself feeling much less confident than ever before. His classes required much more reading and paper writing than he was accustomed to doing, and he quickly fell behind and missed several assignment deadlines. Though Steven was the first member of his family to attend college, his parents put a high value on education and he worried about disappointing them. Steven's roommate Mark—also a member of the swim team—was a pre-med major and talked frequently about his excitement to become a physician like both of his parents. Steven was an undecided major, and he had a hard time imagining himself in a career of any kind.

Socially, Steven continued to spend most of his time with his teammates, but he found himself feeling "out of sync" with many of them. Many of the swim team parties involved drinking and drug use. Steven had experimented a few times with alcohol and marijuana during his first year, but he didn't enjoy the feelings of being out of control and he felt that his swimming suffered for several days afterward.

The novelty of the first year's travel experiences had worn off by this time in his second year. Steven found himself feeling tired of the long bus rides, hotel rooms, and restaurant food. In the pool, Steven worked harder than ever, but his finish times didn't reflect his efforts. This year, there were two new distance swimmers on the team, and his coaches had begun hinting that Steven's scholarship might be in jeopardy if his times didn't begin to improve.

---

Collegiate student-athletes face the same developmental concerns and issues as nonathletes, so it is appropriate to situate their concerns within existing models of development. Simultaneously, it is important to recognize the unique challenges faced by student-athletes, including the need to balance their athletic and academic lives. This chapter will briefly review developmental theories of psychosocial and cognitive development for college students, as well as describe some of the research related to issues, tasks, and challenges faced by student-athletes as they transition into and out of the developmental period of young/emerging adulthood. It will begin by reviewing research and theory related to the transition to college for student athletes and follow with a brief overview of theories of development related to young and emerging adulthood. While there are certainly aspects of development that vary according to factors such as which NCAA Division the school competes in or the role that the student athlete has on the team (i.e., team captain), this chapter will consider development for all student-athletes across all sports in all NCAA divisions.

Participation in organized athletic activity occurs throughout the lifespan. Rate of team sport participation is highest among those aged 15–24 (Woods, 2017). For many sports, young adulthood and collegiate athletics/teams represent the pinnacle of elite athletic participation. Participation in NCAA athletic activity takes between 28–40 hours per week (median across all sports and divisions), which represents an increase from 2010 across all divisions (National Collegiate Athletic Association [NCAA], 2016). Though many college student-athletes are at their peak in terms of physical development, the vast majority of college student-athletes are in the emerging / young adulthood age range, and wrestling with development tasks in the cognitive and psychosocial domains. As noted by others (Valentine & Taub, 1999; Dorsch, Lowe, Dotterer, & Lyons, 2016), while the development of college student-athletes is similar to that of nonathletes (including the transition to college), there are also important differences, and it is important to consider them within the larger developmental framework.

College student-athletes must confront challenges related to time commitments involved in sports participation, and must also balance the other social and academic requirements of college. In addition, they face pressures to succeed on an individual, team, and university level. For example, the increased athletic time commitment was accompanied by increases in academic work across all divisions (median of nearly 40 hours per week) (NCAA, 2016). As a result, student-athletes reported difficulties with time and energy related to their involvement with sports (Wylleman & Lavallee, 2004). Further, some studies have found that student-athletes across all divisions demonstrate an increased likelihood of engaging in risky behaviors (e.g., substance use, binge drinking, unprotected sex, and sexual coercion) (Taylor, Ward, & Hardin, 2017; Yusko, Buckman, White, & Pandina, 2008; Hainline, Bell, & Wilfert, 2014; Young, Desmarais, Baldwin, & Chandler, 2017). Some studies have found increased rates of mental health related issues (e.g., anxiety, depression) among college student-athletes (Gill, 2008; Watson & Kissinger, 2007; Maniar, Chamberlain, & Moore, 2005), while other work has found rates of depression similar to those of nonathletes (Wolanin, Hong, Marks, Panchoo, & Gross, 2016). Whether or not disparities exist, the stressors involved in collegiate sports may contribute to an increased risk for the development of mental health issues (Sudano, Collins, & Miles, 2017). A recent review of the literature showed that, while student-athletes report they are willing to seek mental health or support services, they also perceive many barriers (e.g., stigma, availability of services) impacting the likliehood of actually receiving treatment (Moreland, Coxe, & Yang, 2018). While there is data connecting negative outcomes to college athletic participation, others have found benefits to playing collegiate sports. Ferrante and Etzel (2009) pointed out the ways in which athletic participation in college can help to ease the transition to college and contribute to greater overall satisfaction with the college experience. Melendez (2006; 2016) pointed to differential retention rates among minority and female student-athletes who have been graduating at higher rates than nonstudent-athlete peers and found that student-athletes reported higher levels of academic adjustment, as well as higher institutional attachment, than nonathlete students. Further, it should be noted that, in recent years, the mental health of college student-athletes, as well as availability of supports and services, has received greater attention from athletic departments and the NCAA—which produced a best practices document related to mental health support for student-athletes in 2016.

## College Student-Athletes and the Transition to College

In addition to the various ways attending college serves as a catalyst for developmental change (Arnett, 2016), so too does the very transition into college impact many students, including college student-athletes. Several authors have written about the transition to college as unique to the college student-athlete experience. For example, Gayles and Baker (2015) noted that for many student-athletes, the transition begins years before their first year of college as part of the recruitment process. The recruitment process includes consideration of where to attend college related to the athletic program, but also involves consideration of academic opportunities, financial implications, and desired distance from home. Further, pressure to perform well in high school athletics in order to continue participation at the collegiate level may also be heightened for the aspiring collegiate athlete.

The transition from high school to college is just one of the many transitions specific to college student-athletes over the course of their college careers. In addition, they may experience reductions in the amount of competitive playing time they experience as compared to high school (Gayles & Baker, 2015; Howard-Hamilton & Sina, 2001), transitions to working with a new coach, transitions in leadership roles within their team (Gayles & Baker, 2015; Howard-Hamilton & Sina, 2001), and transitions into retirement at the end of their collegiate careers (Miller and Kerr, 2002). Schlossberg's Transition Theory (1981) provides a useful framework for understanding the experience of college student-athletes. According to Schlossberg (1981), there are factors both external and internal to the individual that affect how one responds to transition. Specifically, the internal characteristics of the individual—e.g., age, health, race, socioeconomic status, social skills, the pre-transition and post-transition environment (such as level of support and the perception of the particular transition including whether the onset was gradual/sudden or experienced as positive/negative)—all impact how the individual experiences the transition.

While the impact on retirement from collegiate athletics has received a great deal of attention (see Chapter 4), the transition into collegiate athletics has received less focus, though this seems to be changing as colleges and universities develop programming to assist with the transition across different domains including athletic, social, and academic (Saxe, Hardin, Taylor, & Pate, 2017). In a qualitative study, Giacobbi et al. (2004) found that first year female athletes on the swim team experienced stress in areas ranging from athletics (training intensity and performance expectations) to the more psychosocial aspects of being away from home and developing relationships, and to meeting academic demands. Others (Papanikolaou, Nikolaidis, Patsiaouras, & Alexopoulos, 2003) have identified the various aspects of integrating onto a new team with a new coach, new roles, and new routines to be primary stressors during the transition. Female athletes in a study by Saxe et al. (2017) described "freshmen year blues," which included various aspects of struggle related to transition stress such as considering transferring to a different school or quitting sports participation. The athletes in this study went on to describe "senior year blues," which dealt with stressors related to retirement from collegiate athletics. Broughton and Neyer (2001) pointed to Parham's (1993) work, which explored areas that prove challenging for college student athletes. The six areas identified as points for attention within counseling and advising relationships include balancing the student/athlete roles; finding time and opportunity for social and athletic activities; developing a sense of mental balance; physically engaging in sport in a healthy way despite injuries; the relational, social demands placed on athletes (by coaches, team members, fans); and the end of one's athletic career.

## Psychosocial Development in College Students

### Erikson's Psychosocial Theory

Erikson's psychosocial stages of development (1963) expanded earlier models, including Freud's psychosexual stages, by describing development across the lifespan and acknowledging the social and cultural aspects of development. Each of Erikson's eight stages, which range from infancy to late adulthood, identifies the major theme or crisis for that stage, beginning with basic trust versus mistrust, which is the foundation of development and attachment in relationships in infancy, to integrity versus despair, which captures the primary issues as one approaches end of life. Each stage emphasizes developmental change with regard to relationships or connection to others or to one's self. The two stages in Erikson's model that are most relevant for understanding development of most typical college age students are identity versus role confusion in late adolescence and the intimacy versus isolation of young adulthood (ages 20–40).

In the identity versus role confusion stage, Erikson saw adolescence as a moratorium or time out to explore various aspects of identity (Broderick & Blewitt, 2015). It is through this exploration that adolescents come to develop a sense of fidelity to vocation, romantic relationships, and beliefs. Marcia (1966) developed a system to categorize the process of exploration and commitment across various domains. The identity statuses include moratorium (active crisis and exploration, not yet committing), achievement, foreclosure (arrived at a decision without crisis or exploration), and diffusion (not yet explored or committed). One issue faced by college student-athletes is a lack of time and opportunity for exploration given the extent of their athletic obligations and demands on their time.

While the basic idea of identity exploration has been written about in relation to racial and cultural identity development (Sue & Sue, 2013; Helms, 1995; Ferdman & Gallegos, 2001; Horse, 2005), career development (Holland, 1997), and sexual identity (McCarn & Fassinger, 1996; Bilodeau & Renn, 2005), it is unclear how identity exploration is impacted by the primary place that athletic identity holds for many college student-athletes. Further, it is important to acknowledge that identity development for students at colleges and universities in the United States is occurring within systems of historic and current marginalization and oppression. Thus, moving through the stages of racial identity development involves challenges and complexities not faced by majority or privileged groups. For example, two thirds of college students who identify as Black males do not graduate, which has been attributed to racial injustice, discrimination, and micro-macro aggressions (Harper & Quaye, 2007). Depending on the racial identity of team members, college student athletes who are racial minorities may feel more or less supported in all aspects of identity development. The NCAA reported, "Division I student-athletes graduate at a higher rate than the student body in nearly every demographic," including African American student athletes (Hosick & Durham, 2017). The reason cited for the increase in graduation rates is a shift in NCAA academic policies, increased support for academic success among athletes, and more accurate tracking of graduation rates. However, a report from the University of Southern California Race and Equity Center examined 65 of the most dominant Division I universities (schools in the power five conferences) and found that Black male athlete graduation rates (55.2% within six years) were lower than the overall student body (76.3%) and lower than Black male students who were not collegiate athletes (60.1%) for the period of 2013–2016 (Harper, 2018). Although there was a 2.5 percentage point increase in graduation rates for Black male athletes across the 65 schools studied over the past two years, there was actually a decrease in graduation rates among Black male athletes in 40% of the schools studied (Harper, 2018). Clearly the balance and integration of identity development for college student athletes is something that needs further research and attention among those who work with student-athletes from minority backgrounds.

A discussion of identity development among college student-athletes would be incomplete without considering the role of athletic identity in relation to over-all development. The findings related to athletic identity development and various aspects of the college experience have been both positive and negative. Brewer, Van Raalte, and Linder (1993) described athletic identity as a self-schema or aspect of self-image that is related to how highly invested or how strongly identified an indi-vidual is with the role of athlete. There are cognitive, social, emotional, and behav-ioral elements involved in athletic identity, thus, it can be influenced by and have an influence on social relationships and connections (Melendez, 2006). Positive outcomes include identity/sense of self, the ability to problem-solve and manage life, and intrinsic motivation as it relates to sport. The negative associations include difficulties with injuries, career development, and termination of athletic career (Brewer, 1999; Brewer, Van Raalte, & Petitpas; 2000). Differences in the role that athletic identity plays in development have been reported in relation to race/eth-nicity, gender, and academic status (first year-senior) (Brewer, 1999; Miller & Kerr, 2003; Melendez, 2009).

The other Erikson stage that corresponds to the age group often involved in collegiate athletics is the intimacy versus isolation stage of young adulthood (age 20–40). The process of exploring romantic relationships and ultimately commit-ting to one partner is the psychosocial task of young adulthood. Though Erikson (1963) focused on intimate romantic relationships at this stage, supportive connec-tions and bonds via friends, family, and teammates serve a crucial function in suc-cessfully navigating young adulthood. Researchers have explored the importance of social relationships among college student-athletes and their peers. Miller & Kerr (2002), as well as Melendez (2008), found that the social connections occurring among collegiate athletes serve as a primary mechanism for decreasing experiences of loneliness and increasing social networks. These connections in turn contribute to some college student athletes having an easier time adjusting to college (Melendez, 2006), as well as greater attachment to their universities (how connected they feel to the institution) compared to nonathletes. The degree to which participating in college sports promotes a positive transition may be especially true for minority student athletes by providing an increased sense of belonging on campuses that are primarily White (Bimper, Harrison, & Clark, 2013). Melendez (2016) reported a positive relationship between college athletic participation and social adjust-ment among commuter students attending college in an urban setting. Despite the positive association between athletic participation and certain aspects of social development, there are still difficulties with social connections and relationships with the university for many college student-athletes. Melendez (2008) examined the experiences of Black football players on a predominately White campus via qualitative analysis where players described feeling "mistrustful, isolated, and misunderstood…" (p. 442). Bimper, Harrison, and Clark (2013) employed qualitative methods to study the experience of Black male athletes who were high achieving in both their sport and the classroom. These student-athletes reported that recognizing and attending to the complexities involved in intersections of their athletic, academic, and racial identities was crucial to their success, particularly in relation to the assumptions (e.g., "they'd be less committed to their student role"), stereotypes (e.g., "'dumb' jock"), and prejudices (e.g., "they must play a sport because of their race") they experienced. Further, identifying and utilizing a supportive community was seen as beneficial. Finally, a feeling of empowerment to overcome stereotypes and get the most out of all aspects of their college education was a common factor among participants (Bimper, Harrison, & Clark, 2013).

## Arnett, College Students, and Emerging Adulthood

While Erikson's psychosocial theory continues to provide a focus for understanding personality development in young adulthood, typically described as ages 20–40 (Broderick & Blewitt, 2015) a new developmental stage, emerging adulthood, has been described and researched beginning with Arnett's research (Arnett, 2000; Arnett, Žukauskienė, & Sugimura, 2014). Since Arnett's initial work, emerging adulthood has been recognized in many venues including developmental textbooks, manuscripts published in various outlets, and an entire journal, *Emerging Adulthood*, devoted to the topic. Spanning the 18–29 age range (Arnett, Žukauskienė, & Sugimura, 2014), emerging adulthood is defined by transition and exploration and represents the age group to which most college student-athletes in the United States belong. According to Arnett (2016), college and university campuses provide the ideal setting for the exploration related to career, romantic relationships, and beliefs/worldview that is synonymous with the stage (2016).

Arnett argues that the period from 18–29 is "neither adolescence nor young adulthood but is theoretically and empirically distinct from them both" (Arnett, 2000, pg. 2; Arnett, Žukauskienė, & Sugimura, 2014). The primary characteristic of the stage is the variability and transition that cuts across developmental domains, including work, relationships, and living arrangements. Arnett specifies that, in the United States, there are five features that are common to the stage regardless of whether one is in school, working, or doing some combination of the two. The five features described by Arnett are identity explorations, instability, self-focus, feeling in-between, and possibilities and optimism. While Arnett and colleagues have identified mental health implications related to each of the five areas (e.g., confusion and anxiety related to identity exploration, emotional adjustment, and support required from instability), similarities and differences for college student-athletes have not been researched. For example, while the self-focus of emerging adulthood refers to the relatively small number of obligations those in the stage have, as well as freedom and independence (as compared to the years that follow), college student-athletes report overwhelming levels of obligation to their role as athletes, even in institutions identified as placing emphasis on the student versus athlete commitments (Hatteberg, 2017). Arnett described cultural shifts including delays in setting into stable careers and relationships, along with increased time in postsecondary education that make the 18–29 timeframe different from the young adulthood period that follows (Arnett, 2007). He also pointed out that the stage of emerging adulthood is dependent on the culture. That is, there are some cultures where it is not possible to have a stage in between adolescence and adulthood. The roles that sport involvement and athletic identity each play in emerging adulthood is an area for future research.

## Development Tasks of College Students

Perhaps the most well-known work related to developmental tasks of college students is the seven vectors of development model (Chickering, 1969; Chickering & Reisser, 1993). The seven vectors are developing competence, managing emotions, moving through autonomy toward interdependence, developing mature relationships, establishing identity, developing purpose, and developing integrity. Moving through the vectors is not a linear process, rather there are intersections and layering among the vectors that happen as students move through the college experience across intellectual, physical, and interpersonal domains. According to this model, all students are experiencing growth and transition across the vectors. Developing competence occurs across three domains ranging from the intellectual challenges of their course work, to participation in athletic activity, to meeting new people. Managing emotions and emotion regulation pertain to all aspects of the college experience, including the transition to college life and the successes, failures, and growth that go along with change. Moving through autonomy toward interdependence recognizes the balance required to both take responsibility for one's life and to be self-sufficient while also fostering connections and being able to ask for help when needed. Developing mature interpersonal relationships that involve intimacy in terms of physical and emotional closeness, establishing identity via experimentation with different attitudes, characteristics, and beliefs, and developing a sense of purpose and integrity that will facilitate development throughout the lifespan make up the seven vectors. It is important to note that Chickering (1969; Chickering & Reisser, 1993) emphasized the importance of the environment in which students are engaging the seven vectors. The college environment refers to everything from the size of the institution to faculty-student relationships, and student support services. The environmental components provide the foundation and framework for students' experiences.

## College Students—Cognitive Development

According to the Piagetian model (Inhelder & Piaget, 1958), cognitive development advances through a series of stages as the individual assimilates and accommodates information in ways that are increasingly complex. Beginning with the sensorimotor stage of infancy, where knowledge comes from acting on the word, cognitive development ends with the formal operations stage in adolescence. Cognitive development at the formal operations stage reflects the ability to engage in logical and systematic hypothetical-deductive reasoning, and the ability to consider information in the abstract as well as the concrete here and now (Piaget & Elkind, 1967). Perry (1970); Kitchener and King (1981); and Kitchener, King, Wood, and Davison (1989) described aspects of postformal thought that recognize continued cognitive development into young adulthood. A hallmark of postformal thought is the ability to integrate logical responses/problem solving with contradiction. Sinnott (1998) emphasized the relativistic nature of thought in young adulthood as reflective of the postformal stage—that is, the ability to recognize that there is more than one truth and more than one solution to a problem. It should be noted that some theorists (Schaie, 1978) disagreed that there is a stage beyond formal operations and, instead, see the different types of thinking and problem solving of young adulthood as representative of the different situations experienced as they move into adulthood.

Perry et al. (1986) interviewed hundreds of undergraduate students as they moved through the start of college to graduation. Review of the transcripts revealed nine developmental stages that moved from dualistic (right/wrong) thinking to the development of and commitment to individual belief systems—wrestling with diverse thoughts, ideas, and interpersonal experiences throughout college promotes more sophisticated thinking. Though Perry's ideas were not specifically connected to college student-athletes, it seems likely that the experiences they have as part of their team, travels, and competition contribute to the evolution of meaning making across Perry's stages. Similarly, the boundaries of how student-athletes consider challenges and ideas may be challenged more or less depending on the contexts and situations they are exposed to outside of the arena of sport.

The more sophisticated cognitive development of college students combined with the new environment (even those students who commute or live at home spend a great deal of time in their University community) provides a prime situation for considering developmental aspects of moral development (Reysen, Perryman,

& Phipps, 2017). In addition to the rules, honor code, or health and wellness policies that apply to a university community, there are athlete codes of conduct that provide guidelines to the moral behaviors, rules, or expectations that are expected to frame college life (i.e., a student-athlete handbook or student-athlete code of conduct). Code of conduct transgressions not only threaten student involvement in the classroom or in the dorm, but can also impact a student-athlete's ability to participate in sport. The most well-known theory of moral development, Kohlberg (1966) used responses to hypothetical moral dilemmas to categorize responses in one of six stages across three levels of increasing moral complexity—pre-conventional, conventional, and post-conventional (Kohlberg & Hersh, 1977). Not only did the higher levels of moral development require logical thinking, they also required moving from the pre-conventional stage, where the driving factor in moral or ethical decision making has to do with perceived consequences, to the conventional stage, where social input/perspective is key. The final move from the conventional to the post-conventional stage requires individuals to be able to recognize their own moral values and beliefs within reigning social and political systems and to discern that certain rules or laws might not be appropriate or applicable in every single case. Carol Gilligan (1982) articulated concern about the gender bias in Kohlberg's theory, that is whether or not one's response to moral dilemmas was seen as advanced or mature (post-conventional) had to do with privileging and individualistic framework above what she referred to as an "ethic of care" that recognized the importance of taking others into account when making moral or ethical determinations. More recent works (Fisher, 2016; Fisher, Shigeno, Bejar, Larsen, & Gearity, 2017) have called for exploring what models of care look like within collegiate athletics, and promoting models of moral development that emphasize connection and support as a way to dismantle the problematic messages and abusive behaviors that have been perpetuated in recent years.

## *Bronfenbrenner Bioecological Model*

The idea that there are multiple interacting systems that influence development is captured by Bronfenbrenner's theory. That is, in order to understand individual development, the dynamic and reciprocal influence of the systems in which the individual lives must also be considered. Often described as concentric circles, with the individual and traits of the individual at the center circle, Bronfenbrenner described proximal and distal processes that impact individual development (1986; Bronfenbrenner & Ceci, 1994). The circle of influence immediately surrounding the individual microsystem is referred to as the mesosystem. The mesosystem includes the systems that have direct influence on the individual (e.g., the family system, the school system) and, integral to Bronfenbrenner's model, the interactions between those mesosystems influence each other and exert influence on the individual. Surrounding the mesosystem layer is the exosystem, including the world of employment and the larger community, which is surrounded by the macrosystem, including the culture of origin, social movements, and religious belief systems. Notably, rather than simply thinking in terms of chronological age as the dimension, Bronfenbrenner (1986) also referred to the chronosystem, an acknowledgment that the particular time or period of history in which one is developing has influence on all the systems. When considering development of college student athletes, Bronfenbrenner's model is particularly useful in calling attention to the role that the athlete's family, coaches, teams, neighborhood, athletic department, athletic conference, university, and larger cultural messages about sports play in their developmental trajectories.

## Conclusion

Given the variety of challenges faced by college student-athletes, as well as the unique developmental trajectories faced by each athlete, it is important that those who provide counseling services have a developmental frame to guide their work. While some student-athletes may be "hyper" developed or advanced in some aspects of development (e.g., physical development, time management skills, social relationships with teammates, and/or family members who support their athletic endeavors), there may be other areas that are "hypo" or underdeveloped as a result of the time, energy, and effort devoted to sport (e.g., romantic relationships, vocational or career goals, political/community involvement). Further, given the transitional nature of emerging adulthood, sensistivity to the developmental "normalcy" of exploring various aspects of the self is an important aspect of working with college student-athletes. It is crucial to locate the student-athlete in the context of the various systems in which they are embedded, both for the sake of promoting student-athlete self awareness as well as assisting the helping professional in understanding the multiple factors interacting with and impacting the student-athlete. Finally, it is important to acknowledge the various systems impacting the helper herself. The college/university, athletic department, counseling/health and wellness center, acadmic departments, students' families, athletic culture of the college/university, the larger community/culture, and historical era will all play a part in the student-athlete's perceptions of health seeking behavior, as well as their commitment to and engagement in the work of counseling or therapy.

## Discussion Questions

1. Steven experienced a relatively smooth transition during his first year of college. What resources might have made this possible? For example, Steven's

classes during the first year had much overlap with those he had taken in high school. This may have helped Steven by saving him time he would have had to spend studying if this were not the case.

2. In what ways does Steven fit the description of an emerging adult?

# References


Arnett, J. J. (2000). Emerging adulthood: A theory of development from the late teens through the twenties. *American psychologist, 55*(5), 469.

Arnett, J. J. (2007). Emerging adulthood: What is it, and what is it good for?. *Child development perspectives, 1*(2), 68–73.

Arnett, J. J., Žukauskienė, R., & Sugimura, K. (2014). The new life stage of emerging adulthood at ages 18–29 years: Implications for mental health. *The Lancet Psychiatry, 1*(7), 569–576.

Arnett, J. J. (2016). College students as emerging adults: The developmental implications of the college context. *Emerging Adulthood, 4*(3), 219–222.

Bilodeau, B. L., & Renn, K. A. (2005). Analysis of LGBT identity development models and implications for practice. *New directions for student services, 111*, 25–39.

Bimper Jr, A. Y., Harrison Jr, L., & Clark, L. (2013). Diamonds in the rough: Examining a case of successful Black male student athletes in college sport. *Journal of Black Psychology, 39*(2), 107–130.

Brewer, B. W. (1999). Causal attribution dimensions and adjustment to sport injury. *Journal of Personal and Interpersonal Loss, 4*(3), 215–224.

Brewer, B. W., Van Raalte, J. L., & Linder, D. E. (1993). Athletic identity: Hercules' muscles or Achilles heel? *International Journal of Sport Psychology, 24*(2), 237–254.

Broderick, P. C., & Blewitt, P. (2015). *The Life Span* (4th ed.). Upper Saddle River, NJ: Pearson.

Bronfenbrenner, U. (1986). Ecology of the family as a context for human development: Research perspectives. *Developmental Psychology, 22*(6), 723.

Bronfenbrenner, U., & Ceci, S. J. (1994). Nature-nuture reconceptualized in developmental perspective: A bioecological model. *Psychological Review, 101*(4), 568.

Broughton, E., & Neyer, M. (2001). Advising and counseling student athletes. *New Directions for Student Services, 2001*(93), 47–53.

Chickering, A. W. (1969). *Education and identity*. San Francisco, CA: Jossey-Bass.

Chickering, A., & Reisser, L. (1993). The seven vectors: An overview. *Education and Identity*, 43–52.

Dorsch, T. E., Lowe, K., Dotterer, A. M., & Lyons, L. (2016). Parent involvement in young adults' intercollegiate athletic careers: Developmental considerations and applied recommendations. *Journal of Intercollegiate Sport, 9*(1), 1–26.

Erikson, E.H. (1963). *Childhood and society* (2nd ed.). New York: Norton.

Ferdman, B. M., & Gallegos, P. I. (2001). Racial identity development and Latinos in the United States. In C.L. Wjeyesinghe & B.W. Jackson III (Eds.), *New perspectives on racial identity development: A theoretical and practical anthology* (pp. 32–66). New York: New York University Press.

Ferrante, A. P., & Etzel, E. F. (2009). College student-athletes and counseling services in the new millennium. In E. F. Etzel (Ed.), *Counseling* and *psychological services* for *college student-athletes* (pp. 1–49). Morgantown, WV: Fitness Information Technology.

Fisher, L. A. (2016). "Where are your women?" The challenge to care in the future of sport. *Sex Roles, 74*(7-8), 377–387.

Fisher, L. A., Shigeno, T. C., Bejar, M. P., Larsen, L. K., & Gearity, B. (2017). Caring practices among US National Collegiate Athletic Association Division I female and male assistant coaches. *International Journal of Sports Science & Coaching*, 1–14. Retrieved from http://journals.sagepub.com/doi/pdf/10.1177/1747954117743114

Gayles, J. G., & Baker, A. R. (2015). Opportunities and challenges for first year student athletes transitioning from high school to college. *New Directions for Student Leadership*, (147), 43–51. doi:10.1002/yd.20142

Giacobbi Jr, P. R., Lynn, T. K., Wetherington, J. M., Jenkins, J., Bodendorf, M., & Langley, B. (2004). Stress and coping during the transition to university for first-year female athletes. *The Sport Psychologist, 18*(1), 1–20.

Gill, E. L. (2008). Mental health in college athletics: It's time for social work to get in the game. *Social Work, 53*(1), 85–88.

Gilligan, C. (1982). *In a different voice.* Cambridge, MA: Harvard University Press. Retrieved from https://www.insidehighered.com/news/2015/05/08/college-athletes -say-they-devote-too-much-time-sports-year-round

Hainline, B., Bell, L., & Wilfert, M. (2014). Mind, body, and sport: Substance use and abuse. *NCAA.* Retrieved from http://www.ncaa.org/sport-science-institute/mind-body-and-sport-substance-use-and-abuse

Harper, S. (2018). Black male student-athletes and racial inequities in NCAA Division I sports. *USC Race and Equity Center.* Retrieved from https://race.usc.edu/wp-content/uploads/2018/03/2018_Sports_Report.pdf

Harper, S. R., & Quaye, S. J. (2007). Student organizations as venues for black identity expression and development among AfricanAmerican male student leaders. *Journal of Student College Development, 48*(2), 127–144. Retrieved from http://repository.upenn.edu/gse_pubs/166

Hatteberg, S. J. (2017). Under surveillance: Collegiate athletics as a total institution. *Sociology of Sport Journal*, 1–34.

Helms, J. E. (1995). An update of Helm's White and people of color racial identity models. In J. G. Ponterotto, J. M. Casas, L. A. Suzuki, & C. M. Alexander (Eds.), *Handbook of multicultural counseling* (pp. 181–198). Thousand Oaks, CA: Sage Publications, Inc.

Holland, J. L. (1997). *Making vocational choices: A theory of vocational personalities and work environments.* (3rd ed.). Odessa, FL: Psychological Assessment Resources.

Horse, P. G. (2005). Native American identity. *New Directions for Student Services, 109*(1), 61–68.

Hosick, M. B., & Durham, M. (2017). D1 African American athletes graduate at record rates. *NCAA.* Retrieved from http://www.ncaa.org/about/resources/media-center/news/di-african-american-student-athletes-graduate-record-rates

Howard-Hamilton, M. F., & Sina, J. A. (2001). How college affects student athletes. *New Directions for Student Services, 2001*(93), 35–45.

Inhelder, B., & Piaget, J. (1958). *The growth of logical thinking from childhood to adolescence.* New York: Basic Books.

Kitchener, K. S., & King, P. M. (1981). Reflective judgment: Concepts of justification and their relationship to age and education. *Journal of Applied Developmental Psychology, 2*(2), 89–116.

Kitchener, K. S., King, P. M., Wood, P. K., & Davison, M. L. (1989). Sequentiality and consistency in the development of reflective judgment: A six-year longitudinal study. *Journal of Applied Developmental Psychology, 10*(1), 73–95.

Kohlberg, L. (1966). Moral education in the schools: A developmental view. *The School Review, 74*(1), 1–30.

Kohlberg, L., & Hersh, R. H. (1977). Moral development: A review of the theory. *Theory into Practice, 16*(2), 53–59.

McCarn, S. R., & Fassinger, R. E. (1996). Revisioning sexual minority identity formation: A new model of lesbian identity and its implications for counseling and research. *The Counseling Psychologist, 24*(3), 508–534.

Maniar, S., Chamberlain, R., & Moore, N. (2005, November 7). Suicide risk is real for student-athletes. *NCAA News, 42*(23). Retrieved from https://www.ncaa.org/sites/default/files/suicide.pdf

Marcia, J. E. (1966). Development and validation of ego-identity status. *Journal of Personality and Social Psychology, 3*(5), 551.

Melendez, M. C. (2006). The influence of athletic participation on the college adjustment of freshmen and sophomore student athletes. *Journal of College Student Retention: Research, Theory & Practice, 8*(1), 39–55.

Melendez, M. C. (2008). Black football players on a predominantly White college campus: Psychosocial and emotional realities of the Black college athlete experience. *Journal of Black Psychology, 34*(4), 423–451.

Melendez, M. C. (2009). Psychosocial influences on college adjustment in Division I student-athletes: The role of athletic identity. *Journal of College Student Retention: Research, Theory & Practice, 11*(3), 345–361.

Melendez, M. C. (2016). Adjustment to college in an urban commuter setting: The impact of gender, race/ethnicity, and athletic participation. *Journal of College Student Retention: Research, Theory & Practice, 18*(1), 31–48.

Miller, P. S., & Kerr, G. (2002). The athletic, academic and social experiences of intercollegiate student-athletes. *Journal of Sport Behavior, 25*(4), 346.

Moreland, J. J., Coxe, K. A., & Yang, J. (2018). Collegiate athletes' mental health services utilization: A systematic review of conceptualizations, operationalizations, facilitators, and barriers. *Journal of Sport and Health Science, 7,* 58–69.

National Collegiate Athletic Association. (2016, January). NCAA GOALS study of the student-athlete experience: Initial summary of findings. Retrieved from http://www.ncaa.org/sites/default/files/GOALS_2015_summary_jan2016_final_20160627.pdf

NCAA Sport Science Institute and the NCAA. (2016, January). Mental health best practices: InterAssociation consensus document: Best practices for understanding and supporting student-athlete mental wellness. Indianapolis, IN. [Data file]. Retrieved from http://www.ncaa.org/sites/default/files/HS_Mental-Health-Best-Practices_20160317.pdf

Papanikolaou, Z., Nikolaidis, D., Patsiaouras, A., & Alexopoulos, P. (2003). The freshman experience: High stress-low grades. *Athletic Insight: The Online Journal of Sport Psychology, 5*(4), 1–8.

Parham, W. D. (1993). The intercollegiate athlete: A 1990s profile. *The Counseling Psychologist, 21*(3), 411–429.

Perry, W. (1970). *Forms of intellectual and ethical growth in the college years.* New York: Holt, Rinehart, and Winston.

Perry, B., Donovan, M. P., Kelsey, L. J., Paterson, J., Statkiewicz, W., & Allen, R. D. (1986). Two schemes of intellectual development: A comparison of development as defined by William Perry and Jean Piaget. *Journal of Research in Science Teaching, 23*(1), 73–83.

Piaget, J., & Elkind, D. (1967). *Six psychological studies.* New York: Random House.

Reysen, R., Perryman, M., & Phipps, R. (2017). Theories of moral development. In W.K. Killam & S. Degges-White (Eds.), *College Student development: Applying theory to practice on the diverse campus* (pp. 65–74). New York: Springer.

Saxe, K., Hardin, R., Taylor, E. A., & Pate, J. R. (2017). Transition blues: The experience of female collegiate student-athletes. *Journal of Higher Education Athletics & Innovation, 1*(2), 25–48.

Schaie, K. W. (1978). Toward a stage theory of adult cognitive development. *The International Journal of Aging and Human Development, 8*(2), 129–138.

Schlossberg, N. K. (1981). A model for analyzing human adaptation to transition. *The Counseling Psychologist, 9*(2), 2–18.

Sinnott, J. (1998). *The development of logic in adulthood: Postformal thought and its applications.* New York: Springer Science & Business Media.

Sudano, L. E., Collins, G., & Miles, C. M. (2017). Reducing barriers to mental health care for student-athletes: An integrated care model. *Families, Systems, & Health, 35*(1), 77–84.

Sue, D. W. & Sue, D. (2013). *Counseling the culturally diverse: Theory and practice* (6th ed.). New York, NY: Wiley.

Taylor, E. A., Ward, R. M., & Hardin, R. (2017). Examination of drinking habits and motives of collegiate student-athletes. *Journal of Applied Sport Management, 9*(1), 56–77.

Valentine, J. J., & Taub, D. J. (1999). Responding to the developmental needs of student athletes. *Journal of College Counseling, 2*(2), 164–179.

Wolanin, A., Hong, E., Marks, D., Panchoo, K., & Gross, M. (2016). Prevalence of clinically elevated depressive symptoms in college athletes and differences by gender and sport. *Br J Sports Med, 50*(3), 167–171.

Watson, J. C., & Kissinger, D. B. (2007). Athletic participation and wellness: Implications for counseling college student athletes. *Journal of College Counseling, 10*(2), 153–162.

Woods, R. A. (2017, May). Sports and exercise. *U.S. Bureau of Labor Statistics.* Retreived from https://www.bls.gov/spotlight/2017/sports-and-exercise/pdf/sports-and-exercise.pdf

Wylleman, P., & Lavallee, D. (2004). A developmental perspective on transitions faced by athletes. In M. R. Weiss (Ed.), *Developmental sport and exercise psychology: A lifespan perspective* (pp. 503–523). Morgantown, WV: Fitness Information Technology.

Young, B. R., Desmarais, S. L., Baldwin, J. A., & Chandler, R. (2017). Sexual coercion practices among undergraduate male recreational athletes, intercollegiate athletes, and non-athletes. *Violence Against Women, 23*(7), 795–812.

Yusko, D. A., Buckman, J. F., White, H. R., & Pandina, R. J. (2008). Alcohol, tobacco, illicit drugs, and performance enhancers: A comparison of use by college student athletes and nonathletes. *Journal of American College Health, 57*(3), 281–290.

# 3

# Assisting the First-Year Student-Athlete

*Samantha Monda and Paul Downey*

## CASE STUDY: TONY

Tony is a first year student from out-of-state who is undecided about his major. He is male, African-American, a first generation college student, and a member of the football team. Tony arrived 10 minutes late for his 1 p.m. session. He apologized and said he just got out of class and needed to eat lunch before practice. Tony was referred for counseling because he was caught cheating on a history exam last week (held the Monday morning after an away football game). The team won and returned at midnight Saturday from their trip. Tony indicated that he was caught cheating on his test because he did not have time to study and expressed feeling upset with his professor because "he just doesn't understand what I'm going through." Tony explained that his grades have not been very good even though he goes to every class, just like in high school. He complained that his high school teachers would give him a study guide before each test but none of his professors now give him a study guide. He indicated that he didn't expect college to be this hard. Rather, he expected to go to class and the grades would take care of themselves.

Tony reported that he studies with teammates or a friend in the dorm because they have classes together. He reported that they typically talk more than anything because none of them have read the book. Only one member of the group takes class notes, which he shares with the others. Tony was visibly frustrated, and continued by saying that he was not feeling good the day before the test, so he did not go to the study session in the dorm. He reported that he was hungover from going out on Saturday night after the team got back from their big road win. The other guys on the team wanted to celebrate and invited Tony to come because he had made the game-clinching tackle. Since that game Tony had been promoted to practice with the first string defense. He went on to reveal that he only goes to class because attendance is mandatory and if he misses class without an excuse, he and his position group would be punished with extra running. Tony reported that he does not want to upset his teammates and therefore attends class, but went on to state that he never takes notes, can barely stay awake, and often spends the class session browsing social media on his phone. Tony then looked at his phone and stated that he had to leave because practice started at 2 p.m. The counselor made arrangements to meet again at the same time next week.

The first year of college for student-athletes may be one of the most influential during their time at a university. The experience of adjusting to a new academic, athletic, and social environment often lays the foundation for student-athletes' continued success and well-being over the duration of their college careers. Assisting individuals toward the goal of academic success is a common task for helping professionals working with this population. This chapter will provide insight into common issues that affect first-year student-athletes' academic development, inform helping professionals about academic requirements that student-athletes must meet, and offer best practices and ways to support this population on campus.

## Adjusting to College

Entering college is considered to be a transitional period for young adults where students are working toward achieving the developmental goals of establishing identity, developing competence, and becoming autonomous (Astin, 1999; Arnett, 2000; Chickering & Reisser, 1993). Once on campus, they are expected to adjust to a number of new and unfamiliar experiences (Petitpas, Brewer, & VanRaalte, 2009). Some may be living away from home for the first time and must discern how to live independently and cope with potential homesickness. Academically, college may involve an increased workload and greater classroom demands. Socially, students must make new friends and establish support systems on campus. Student-athletes also contend with additional transitions relating to their athletic role. They may be expected to give greater time commitments to their sports, adjust to a higher level of play where they may no longer be the most talented players, navigate new team dynamics with coaches and teammates, and accommodate their schedules for increased travel. While each of these experiences are manageable on their own, many student-athletes describe the accumulation of these adjustments to be challenging (Monda, Etzel, Shannon, & Wooding, 2015).

Balancing the dual roles of student and athlete is a unique yet important developmental task for student-athletes to achieve in order to be successful in college. Student-athletes have a limited amount of time and energy and must negotiate balancing the demands placed upon them by each role (Comeaux, Speer, Taustine, & Harrison, 2011). On an average day, it is not uncommon for student-athletes to rise at 5 a.m. for morning practice or weightlifting before classes begin, make a visit to the training room to rehab an injury, attend a full day of classes followed by a second workout, and then come home to eat, study, and recover for the next day. This schedule can be compounded on weekends or weeknights, where student-athletes may spend six to eight hours competing and multiple days traveling to and from away games. While the majority of student-athletes learn to successfully navigate the responsibilities of their dual roles during the first year, student-athletes as a whole are considered to be at-risk for adjustment issues during this time (Pascarella & Terenzini, 2005). Poor adjustment has been linked to retention risk as approximately 27–36% of first-year students in the general population withdraw from school after the first year (ACT, 2017).

Participation in a collegiate sport can pose challenges for first-year student-athletes but it also has the potential to buffer adjustment difficulties. Research in the general student population has shown that developing a social niche with peers and faculty can foster positive first-year adjustment and mental wellness (Azmitia, Syed, & Radmacher, 2013). Similarly, in the student-athlete population, participation in intercollegiate athletics can help reduce feelings of isolation and stress through bonding with teammates (Melendez, 2006). Student-athletes often begin building this social niche during the recruiting process when they form relationships with coaches and fellow student-athletes prior to coming on campus. They may be welcomed into an existing support system on the team and placed into a set of ready-made friends with similar interests and concerns. Knowing people on campus can help to reduce the anxiety of a new beginning and provide resources for issues that might arise during the first few months. Additionally, some student-athletes may ease into the adjustment of living on their own by moving onto campus during a summer session to begin pre-training workouts or take classes. This approach is commonly used by universities that have created summer bridge programs as a way to improve student engagement and student success outcomes (Lytle & Gallucci, 2015). Many athletic departments have also developed their own versions of summer bridge programs that allow student-athletes the experience of moving on campus early to familiarize themselves with their new environment and develop habits and support systems without the cumulative stress of their full-time academic and athletic responsibilities.

## Academic Development

The quality of student-athletes' educational experiences have been highly debated in both the media and in academic circles. Concerns over low graduation rates, academic integrity, and the degree of academic engagement among student-athletes has led to a discussion about ways to facilitate positive academic development in this subpopulation (Bowen & Levin, 2003; Love, Watkins, & Kim, 2017; Wolverton, 2015). While student-athletes share many similarities with general first-year students, they also have distinct needs that need to be taken into account by helping professionals.

Adjusting to the academic demands of college is often challenging to any first-year student regardless of whether he or she is an athlete or plays a high profile sport. They may encounter an increased amount of work in their classes, be required to think more critically, and be expected to function as autonomous learners (e.g. overcome procrastination and self-manage deadlines) (Pascarella & Terenzini, 2005). In order to keep up, first-year students often have to adapt their study habits and improve their self-regulation skills. For student-athletes, balancing the time demands and physical fatigue of sport can compete with the increased expectations of school, creating a sense of role conflict between their identities of athlete and student (Jayakumar & Comeaux, 2016). A seminal study by Adler and Adler (1987) captured the essence of this experience among high profile collegiate men's basketball players, an account still relevant to student-athletes today. Their exploration found that student-athletes often begin college with positive expectations and goals of achieving a degree but also possess an overly ideal impression about the ease and skills needed to succeed in the academic role. They started out by engaging in positive academic behaviors during the first year, but when the pressures of their sports increased and role conflicts arose, they were forced to make choices about how to allocate their time and energy. This led the athletes to invest more into their athletic role, often at the expense of their academic role, reducing their initial optimism about academics. While this study was conducted with high-profile basketball players, a more recent study indicated that a large percentage of student-athletes from all sports believed that their GPAs would have been higher had they not participated in a sport (Potuto & O'Hanlon, 2007). Although it is debatable whether their GPAs would actually have increased if they had less sport responsibility, this finding shows that student-athletes perceive their academics to be affected by the constraints of their athletic role.

The consequences of role conflict may have more of an effect on student-athletes who matriculate with less academic preparation, a weak academic identity, or less defined career goals (Jayakumar & Comeaux, 2016; Menke, 2015). A key developmental task of the first year is to identify an academic major and begin planning for a potential career. Instead, the athletic identity literature indicates that student-athletes are likely to focus heavily on athletics during the early stages of their college career (Lally & Kerr, 2005; Miller & Kerr, 2003). A strong athletic identity at the exclusion of a strong academic or professional identity has been linked to negative educational outcomes such as career immaturity and lower GPA, particularly among black male student-athletes (Cooper, Davis, & Dougherty, 2017; Linnemeyer & Brown, 2010). First-year student-athletes who are more focused on athletics and struggle to negotiate the demands of dual roles may be less likely to engage in educationally purposeful activities. This may be particularly true for student-athletes who enter college with less academic preparation. When the optimism about their initial academic goals begins to wane, they may focus their attention on athletic tasks that bring a greater sense of competency. Student-athletes have the additional pressure of meeting an NCAA requirement to declare a major by the time they start their third year of full-time enrollment (National Collegiate Athletic Association [NCAA], 2017a). While this requirement could create an opportunity to accelerate the development of academic identity, some critics suggest that it can lead to behaviors such as clustering into academic majors that are easier or more compatible with athletic responsibilities (Huml, Hancock, & Bergman, 2014). To the benefit of the student-athlete, the literature suggests that a reconnection with the academic role often occurs in the later years of student-athletes' college careers, as they begin to develop a multi-faceted identity and make an investment into educationally purposeful activities and a post-sport career (Miller & Kerr, 2003).

Being involved in educationally purposeful activities has been identified as one of the most influential factors leading to the academic success of college students (Astin, 1999; Gaston-Gayles & Hu, 2009; Pascarella & Terenzini, 2005). College sports are often criticized for interfering with student-athletes' ability to engage in sound educational practices, however, some studies have shown that student-athletes reported faring surprisingly well in comparison to nonathletes on certain academic measures such as interacting with faculty, engaging in active and collaborative learning, being academically challenged, and feeling as though they are on a supportive campus environment (Rettig & Hu, 2016; Umbach, Palmer, Kuh, & Hannah, 2006). Engagement in these positive educational experiences has been shown to be particularly strong for female student-athletes, who have reported greater educational outcomes than nonathletes. Additionally, the latest NCAA graduation rate data shows that student-athletes as a whole graduate at a slightly higher rate than the general student body (NCAA, 2017a). This finding challenges the perception that student-athletes are less academically engaged than their nonathlete counterparts and suggests that collegiate sport participation can be beneficial to student-athletes' academic and personal growth. In addition, a 2016

NCAA/Gallup survey found that former student-athletes scored higher than non-student-athlete peers on measures of purpose as well as physical, social, and community well-being (NCAA, 2016).

Student-athletes are often labeled with the stereotype of the "dumb jock," which may contribute to the perception of a lack of academic engagement. There is great diversity, however, in student demographics in this population (type of sport, division level, gender, race, international status, revenue-producing sport status, first-generation college student, family background, educational preparation, etc.) (Comeaux & Harrison, 2011). A number of highly motivated student-athletes with well-defined career goals populate both sports with limited professional opportunities and Division III institutions where there is greater balance between academics and athletics (Comeaux et al., 2011; Gaston-Gayles, 2004). As Gaston-Gayles (2004) noted, high academic motivation is a strong predictor of academic success, regardless of the degree of athletic motivation. Student-athletes who are highly engaged in their athletic role have the potential for academic success if they also exhibit an equal or greater level of academic motivation. Additionally, student-athletes' sport experience may provide them with opportunities to engage in the campus and greater community. Sport provides an environment to interact with a diverse group of people, and teams often participate in meaningful service activities, contributing to this sense of engagement (Rettig & Hu, 2009). At the Division I level, institutions often employ staff members in athletics who specifically work with student-athletes on academic and personal development issues. Astin (1999) has indicated that academic advisors play an important role in connecting students with academic opportunities on campus.

While most student-athletes indicate that they are satisfied with their overall college experience (Potuto & O'Hanlon, 2007), other studies show that subgroups of student-athletes are disadvantaged on important educational outcomes, such as academic grades and overall satisfaction with their college experience (Bowen & Levin, 2003; Cooper, Davis, & Dougherty, 2017; Rettig & Hu, 2016; Umbach et al., 2006). In particular, this effect is most robust for male athletes, black athletes, and athletes participating in high-profile sports such as men's basketball, football, and baseball. The distinction between high profile and low profile sports is supported by analyses conducted at highly selective Division III institutions (Bowen & Levin, 2003) as well as by NCAA Division I graduation rates, which indicate that men's basketball and football players consistently graduate at lower rates than their nonathlete counterparts (NCAA Research Staff, 2017). Compared to other student-athletes, the experiences of this group may be qualitatively different in the amount of time spent in sport, the perceived pressure from coaches and important others and the degree of visibility and public scrutiny they receive (Rettig & Hu, 2009; Cooper, Davis, & Dougherty, 2017; Menke, 2015).

While headlines suggest that student-athletes may be uninterested or unprepared for college, the reality is that there are a number of factors that impact the academic success and failure of student-athletes. The diversity within this population suggests the academic performance of student-athletes is multifaceted, just as it is for the general student population. Both individual and organizational factors that contribute to these outcomes must be considered when devising best practices.

## Academic Requirements

Over the past 25 years, the NCAA has established and refined measures to ensure that student-athletes are making adequate progress toward degree completion. These comprise a number of academic benchmarks that student-athletes must meet in order to maintain eligibility to play their sport. To assist first-year student-athletes academically, helping professionals should have a basic understanding of the external requirements that differentiate the experience of a student-athlete from the average college student.

Bylaw 14 of the NCAA Division I Manual (NCAA, 2017b) describes the legislative principles and thresholds that govern initial and continuing academic eligibility for student-athletes. Continuing eligibility is determined by the number of credits earned in the previous semester as well as the cumulative grade point average. All student-athletes must earn six degree-applicable credits each semester or quarter, with the additional stipulation that they must complete 18 semester hours or 27 quarter hours across the preceding year. First year student-athletes are required to earn 24 semester hours or 36 quarter hours of credit prior to the start of the second year of enrollment. Beyond the semester and yearly requirements, student-athletes must meet a specified percentage of degree requirements before the start of their third, fourth and potentially fifth years with 40%, 60%, and 80% thresholds. Furthermore, student-athletes must maintain a cumulative grade point average in order to maintain eligibility. This begins at the start of the second year when student-athletes must have a GPA equal to 90% of the institution's overall cumulative GPA required for graduation. Although this standard varies among institutions, the most frequent cumulative GPA at graduation is 2.00, making the requirement for student-athletes 1.80 (90% of 2.00). Student-athletes must have 95% of the graduating GPA by the start of their third year and 100% by the start of their fourth year and beyond.

Members of the general student body do not have to meet these same conditions, though they have some federally mandated and university mandated requirements. The most well-known requirements of students receiving federally funded financial aid is to satisfactorily complete 67% of enrolled classes and maintain a 2.00 cumulative grade point average. If these requirements are not met, the student would no longer receive federal financial aid, but could conceivably continue at the institution. Student-athletes also can continue to enroll at the school should they not meet eligibility thresholds, but they may not be allowed to compete again until they regain eligibility. Student-athletes in Divisions I and II put their athletic scholarships at risk if they are deemed ineligible for competition, which may preclude their continuation at the university due to the cost of out-of-pocket attendance. Student-athletes receiving federal financial aid and an athletic scholarship must abide by both sets of regulations.

The NCAA Academic Performance Program (APP) was the most recent addition to the academic reform efforts of the NCAA and its member institutions in Division I. Beginning in the fall of 2003, institutions were required to report on the eligibility and retention of each student-athlete who received athletically-related financial aid for each semester. In essence, by maintaining continuing eligibility and returning to school each semester, each scholarship student-athlete can earn two points per semester (one point for eligibility and one point for retention) and four points for the year (NCAA, 2003; 2014). These points are accumulated and an academic performance rate is developed. Institutions and teams who do not meet academic performance benchmarks are at risk for contemporaneous penalties, such as loss of scholarships, practice time, and opportunities for post-season competition. Most recently, in order to compete in NCAA championships, individual teams must meet a four year combined academic performance score equal to 93%, or more universally known as 930.

The APP also created the metric of graduation success rate for each team, which is defined as a six-year proportion of graduating student-athletes on athletically-related aid to those who entered an institution (NCAA, 2014). As opposed to the federal graduation rate, this metric is preferred by the NCAA, because it accounts for student-athletes who transfer into an institution. It also discounts student-athletes who withdraw from the institution and would have been academically eligible to compete had they returned. The academic performance score of 930 is known to loosely translate to a graduation success rate of 50% (NCAA, 2014). Academic performance and graduation success rates are not collected for Division II and III institutions, although Division II institutions use a similar academic metric called the academic success rate (Cooper, Davis, & Dougherty, 2017).

Beginning with the 2019–2020 academic year, the collective academic performance of student-athletes provides Division I institutions with an additional incentive to ensure their student-athletes are succeeding in the classroom. For the first time, revenue distribution from the NCAA is based on the academic performance of student-athletes using an Academic Distribution Unit (Hosick, 2016). It is estimated that between 2020 and 2030, over $1.4 billion will be distributed (Hosick, 2016). On one hand, this measure may help to highlight the importance of academics in the lives of student-athletes, lending more attention and resources to their academic development. On the other hand, some scholars suggest that a financial incentive may put additional pressure on administrators, coaches, and student-athletes to perform in the classroom at any cost, leading to behaviors that may undermine the quality of student-athletes' educational experiences—e.g., academic fraud, clustering, and low autonomy (Gurney et al., 2017).

## Facilitating Positive Academic Development

Empirically-based interventions that support the growth of the whole person have been found to most effectively prepare individuals for life and careers beyond college athletics (Navarro, 2014). In recent years, the NCAA and athletic departments have made significant investments in student-athlete support services, with much attention focused on academic and learning support. Regardless of their degree of involvement with the athletic department, helping professionals who engage with student-athletes can assist them in exploring their academic identities and in identifying resources in and out of the athletic realm. To do so, helping professionals should work in collaboration with various campus professionals to engage students in educationally purposeful experiences.

## Best Practices for Helping Professionals

Helping professionals will most likely encounter student-athletes who feel overwhelmed by the demands placed on them academically, athletically, and socially. Counselors and psychologists can promote better adjustment to college by preparing incoming student-athletes for what to expect upon their arrival. Many student-athletes (particularly those competing in fall sports) start living on campus prior to other students' arrival. They may be unable to attend the university's general new student orientation programs because of their athletic responsibilities. Because athletic department personnel and other university professionals typically have contact with incoming athletes prior to matriculation, helping professionals may have the opportunity to develop a transition program for first year students or to provide materials to familiarize student-athletes with the roles and responsibilities of college life. For example, a helping professional may work in conjunction with a team to develop a brochure with tips and advice written from the team themselves about what to expect during their first year. This brochure can be mailed to incoming first year student-athletes prior to their arrival on campus, providing a welcoming and informative tool to help them shape expectations.

Formal transition programs also provide effective ways to help student-athletes adjust to their new environments (Finch, 2009; Browning, 2015). Prior to 2010, many institutions offered transitional programming through the NCAA CHAMPS/ Lifeskills program, which focused on academic support, athletic support, career development, personal development, and service to the community. The NCAA restructured the national CHAMPS/Lifeskills program in 2010, and in 2016, the NCAA teamed with the National Association of Academic Advisors (N4A) to oversee lifeskills services for member institutions (NCAA, 2017c). Helping professionals would be wise to assess existing programs and identify gaps in services. In addition to commonly covered topics such as orientation to campus, coping with homesickness, maintaining health and wellness, and demonstrating effective study skills, it would be useful to cover issues specific to the student-athlete experience. Topics such as balancing school and sport, establishing an academic identity/major, managing stereotypes and/or cultural differences, developing realistic expectations of future careers in sport, and connecting with nonathletic resources on campus would all be beneficial in facilitating positive academic development.

Chickering and Gamson (1987) advanced seven principles that they argued to be key to effective undergraduate education. Briefly, these principles are

1. encourage student-faculty contact,

2. encourage cooperation among students,

3. encourage active learning,

4. give prompt feedback,

5. emphasize time on task,

6. communicate high expectations, and

7. respect diverse talents and ways of learning.

With these principles in mind, helping professionals can guide student-athletes toward using any and all of the seven best practices emphasized throughout higher education. Helping professionals can bridge the gap between the athletic and the academic worlds by encouraging social and academic interaction with nonathlete peers and faculty. Research indicates that developing relationships with nonathlete peers who display strong academic motivation can have a positive influence on the academic outcomes of student-athletes (Comeaux & Harrison, 2011; Gaston-Gayles & Hu, 2009). While student-athletes have been shown to have strong relationships with athletic peers and staff, these relationships can negatively influence student-athletes' academic performance if it is perceived that their teammates do not value academics (Levine, Etchinson, & Oppenheimer, 2014) or if there are subtle signs that the organizational subculture of the athletic department does not support academics (Jayakumar & Comeaux, 2016). While student-athletes have limited time to engage in extracurricular activities outside of athletics, small gestures of engagement such as sitting with nonathlete peers in class, developing relationships with fellow students in one's major, creating mixed study groups, joining a student organization, or engaging in university-wide community service can facilitate this goal.

Helping professionals can be invaluable in assisting student-athletes to integrate all aspects of their multifaceted identities. In an effort to prevent identity foreclosure and low career maturity, helping professionals can encourage student-athletes to build the foundation of a strong academic identity early in their college careers and teach them how to manage the challenges of role conflict. These goals can be accomplished through the exploration of potential career goals, the identification of strengths and interests outside of athletics, and the navigation of the academic barriers resulting from their dual roles of student and athlete. Additionally, introducing students to positive examples of student-athletes who have been successful in both academics and sport (preferably those who played their sport or share similar demographic characteristics) and encouraging student-athletes to form mentoring relationships with high achievers are other effective strategies.

## Academic-Athletic Student Support Services

In 1991, the NCAA mandated academic counseling and tutoring services for all Division I institutions and in 2002, the NCAA permitted member institutions to provide whatever academic-support services they deemed appropriate and necessary (Meyer, 2005). Institutions may provide varying levels of academic support for student-athletes depending on their size, division level, and financial resources. Some institutions collaborate with campus units serving the general student population, while larger Division I institutions may tailor independent, "one-stop-shop" services specifically to student-athletes. When helping professionals observe the need to refer a student-athlete for additional academic support, familiarity with the campus resources inside and outside of athletics is essential. Because academic-athletic support staff are often the providers of learning support and interventions for this population, it can be beneficial for counselors and psychologists to develop relationships with these campus colleagues to cooperate in creating holistic plans for student-athletes in need.

The emphasis on the academic performance rate metric has led many institutions to develop academic performance centers or resources specifically for student-athletes. This is the case even at institutions that are not considered to be top tier Division I institutions. The professional staff that are employed in these centers provide services to student-athletes similar to those found in a university learning resource center, such as providing guidance on principles related to time management, organization, prioritization, study skills, and study habits. Many of these units offer tutoring services and provide academic mentors who meet one-on-one with student-athletes to review calendars and plan assignment completion to meet standards and deadlines. Some centers may also employ learning specialists who assist the student-athlete with achieving mastery within their personal learning style. Most centers provide multiple computers, a quiet study space, and campus Wi-Fi access to facilitate and enhance student-athletes' academic performance.

First year transitioning student-athletes are often required to meet on a regular and frequent basis with their advisors, who can help identify campus opportunities and resources as they move through the matriculation process. One of the main goals of athletic academic support staff members is to promote the complementary value of academics and athletics and to encourage the transfer of lessons learned from one domain to the other. This assistance may help to promote student-athletes' engagement in the academic community and contribute to more positive educational outcomes. The methods used to achieve this engagement mirror the seven practices described by Chickering and Gamson (1987) to promote learning and are highlighted in the following section. However, it is of note that these services and interventions have largely been based on anecdotal evidence of what is effective in facilitating student-athlete academic development. Many services that have become known as best practices involve professionals spending a significant amount of time providing individualized attention to student-athletes to meet their needs.Comeaux (2012) found that few Division I programs measure the impact of interventions on learning outcomes and subsequently, calls have been made to utilize empirical data to ensure that practices being used are evidence-based (Navarro, 2014).

**Evaluation.** The best practices of providing services to the transitioning student-athlete start with a systematic approach that allows for collaboration among athletic department stakeholders and the university as a whole. Starting with admissions and evaluation, it is important to collect relevant academic (e.g., high school GPA, ACT/SAT scores, specific coursework) and demographic (e.g., first generation in college status and markers of socioeconomic status) information about incoming student-athletes. In 2009, the NCAA introduced a metric known as the Graduation Risk Overview (GRO), which attempts to identify the factors that may place a student-athlete at risk for not graduating. Once this information is collected, it can be combined with an assessment of learning styles (Kolb & Kolb, 2013; Fleming & Baume, 2006), athletic identity, and anecdotal information from coaches and others closely involved in recruiting the student-athlete. This anecdotal information can include observations of motivation, quality of previous education, and likelihood of competing and contributing to the team during the first year on campus. Johnson (2013) referred to this as "intimate knowledge of the student-athlete." This information provides a snapshot of the individual student-athlete, which can be helpful during the initial transition. These elements can be used to determine the specific approach and services provided to the student-athlete. This approach mirrors Chickering and Gamson's (1987) principle of respecting diverse talents and ways of learning.

Most NCAA Division I programs assist incoming student-athletes in adjusting to a more challenging academic environment, the increased sport-related time demands, and university and athletic department cultures. This is most often accomplished through a combination of group training sessions and individual meetings between the student-athlete and the academic support professional. The training sessions cover topics including study skills, planning for assignments, and strategies to engage faculty and classmates in preparation for assignment completion. The individual meetings should include establishing goals and creating a plan to meet those goals. This programming supports Chickering and Gamson's (1987) best practices of encouraging contact between students and faculty and encouraging cooperation among students.

**Skill development.** The value of establishing and maintaining a routine schedule cannot be overstated for the transitioning student-athlete. Creating a weekly routine that includes classes and training for sport allows student-athletes to see the open hours of their schedules. The helping professional can then encourage efficient use of the limited hours that are not already occupied. These hours can be used for purposeful studying, meeting with faculty, cocurricular opportunities, or necessary recovery. The focus of work during this skill development phase is on fostering the principles of active learning, prompt feedback, and time on task (Chickering & Gamson, 1987).

During the weekly meetings that occur in transition to the university, athletic academic support professionals should gauge the incoming student-athletes' existing skills and habits and teach those skills that are lacking, including time management, organization, prioritization, syllabus breakdown, and use of a calendar system. Of particular interest for student-athletes is the ability to work efficiently considering their mandatory training schedule and the fatigue that accompanies their workouts. For this reason, the principles of assignment awareness are crucial: what assignment is due, when is it due, what resources will be needed to complete it, and how long will it take to complete. A realistic assessment of the student-athlete's assignment awareness is indicative of their ability to manage day-to-day commitments. If a student has trouble with any one element, the helping professional will spend additional time teaching that element. Use of a calendar that identifies all assignments and competitions throughout the course of an entire semester allows the student-athlete to see conflicts and busy periods in the semester. Similar to nonathlete students, planning and prioritization must be mastered in order to avoid procrastination and cramming. Further, stress levels can be controlled when assignment details are known as opposed to sneaking up on the unprepared student.

**Monitoring.** Given the eligibility requirements that must be met by student-athletes, the university's academic support staff also monitors course-by-course progress of transitioning student-athletes. These staff members often know the details of the schedule for the student-athlete as well as or better than the student-athlete. By monitoring each course, they can gauge the academic skill set of the student, assignment awareness, and class attendance, and teach skills that the student does not yet possess. Through monitoring, the professional is able to provide prompt feedback (Chickering & Gamson, 1987). In many cases, the support staff member submits a weekly report that highlights and describes the behaviors, assignments, and accomplishments of each student-athlete for the week. This is distributed to respective coaches and other members of the academic support staff, leading to further prompt feedback. Many universities also use a version of early alert or progress reports that allow instructors to indicate how a student is performing in a course while there is still time to make adjustments. Support staff often have access to these reports and will use them to determine appropriate intervention needs.

## Tailored Interventions and Individualized Attention

As the first semester progresses, the support services provided to student-athletes may become more individualized as information becomes available. Staff members may conduct an ongoing needs assessment of the student-athlete based on grades, time management, observed/reported stress levels, and assignment awareness to determine what tailored interventions would produce the most desirable results. Common barriers to academic success include poor or nonexistent study habits, an inability to adjust study habits/styles for various forms of examinations, failure to prioritize assignments, procrastination, perfectionism, poor class attendance, poor classroom behavior, an inability to take relevant notes, academic misconduct, test anxiety, and educational disabilities such as ADD/ADHD or other learning disorders.

Helping professionals use a wide variety of tailored interventions to address student-athletes' individual needs. These may include assignment checklists with step-by-step instructions, teaching a variety of study skills connected to specific learning styles, offering a structured schedule of study hall hours, an objective-based study hall, constructing daily and weekly calendars, goal setting, and monitoring class attendance. Students are often encouraged to meet with their instructors to preview assignments before completion and review them after completion. Tutoring to supplement, re-explain, and provide repetition of information is a valuable tool for student-athletes, particularly if their travel schedules necessitate the missing of classes. If available, academic mentors and learning specialists may be assigned to meet with the student to address reading comprehension, time management, concentration strategies, and other skills related to preparing and completing assignments.

# Conclusion

First-year student-athletes share a number of characteristics with their nonathlete counterparts; however, helping professionals also should be aware of their unique needs. Assisting student-athletes in managing their academic responsibilities among the athletic and physical demands of sport is a common task for those working with this population. Facilitating positive academic development involves having an understanding of student-athletes' needs and the academic requirements placed upon them. Best practices for work with first year student-athletes include shaping academic expectations, offering transitional programming, fostering the development of academic identity, and identifying ways that a student can become academically engaged. Since institutions provide varying levels of academic support for student-athletes, helping professionals may benefit from assessing services offered, working collaboratively with academic support staff, and promoting skill development, monitoring, and individually tailored interventions.

# Discussion Questions

1. Describe Tony in the context of this chapter and your personal history working with student-athletes.

2. What are the main issues in this case? How would you prioritize them?

3. What are some possible reasons for Tony's poor performance in the classroom?

4. As a helping professional, what recommendations would you make to assist Tony?

5. Design at least three ideas that could help Tony adjust to his new role as student and contributor to his football team.

   a. How feasible are each of these ideas?

   b. What campus resources could you use to build a plan to assist Tony?

   c. Who would you involve in Tony's plan? If you included athletic-academic support staff or coaches, would you speak to them before meeting with Tony again? Would you get his permission to speak to them? Why or why not?

# References

ACT. (2017). National collegiate retention and persistence-to-degree rates. Iowa City, IA.

Adler, P., & Adler, P. A. (1987). Role conflict and identity salience: College athletics and the academic role. *The Social Science Journal, 24*(4), 443–455.

Astin, A.W. (1999). Student involvement: A developmental theory for higher education. *Journal of College Student Development, 40*(5), 518–529.

Arnett, J. J. (2000). Emerging adulthood: A theory of development from the late teen through the twenties. *American Psychologist, 55,* 469–480.

Azmitia, M., Syed, M., Radmacher, K. (2013). Finding your niche: Identity and emotional support in emerging adults' adjustment to the transition to college. *Journal of Research on Adolescence, 23*(4), 744–761. doi:10.1111/jora.12037

Bowen, W. G., & Levin, S. A. (2003). *Reclaiming the game: College sports and educational values.* Princeton, NJ: Princeton University Press.

Browning, A. (2015) Bridging the gap: Academic support for entering special-admit college athletes. In E. Comeaux (Ed.), *Making the connection: Data-informed practices in academic support centers for college athletes* (pp. 109–125). Charlotte: NC: Information Age Publishing.

Chickering, A. W., & Reisser, L. (1993). *Education and identity* (2nd ed). San Francisco: Jossey-Bass.

Chickering, A. W., & Gamson, Z. F. (1987). Seven principles for good practice in undergraduate education. *American Association of Higher Education Bulletin, 39,* 3–7.

Comeaux, E. (2012, April). The role and influence of support service practitioners and big-time college head coaches: An academic-athletic priority collision. Paper presented at the annual meeting of the American Educational Research Association, Vancouver, BC.

Comeaux, E., & Harrison, C. K. (2011). A conceptual model of academic success for student-athletes. *Educational Researcher, 40,* 235–245.

Comeaux, E., Speer, L., Taustine, M., & Harrison, K. (2011). Purposeful engagement of first-year Division I student-athletes. *Journal of the First-Year Experience & Students in Transition, 23*(1), 35–52.

Cooper, J. N., Davis, T. J., & Dougherty, S. (2017). Not so black and white: A multi-divisional exploratory analysis of male student-athletes' experiences at National College Athletic Association (NCAA) institutions. *Sociology of Sport Journal, 34,* 59–78.

Finch, L. (2009). Understanding and assisting the student-athlete-to-be and the new student-athlete. In E.F. Etzel (Ed.), *Counseling and psychological services for college student-athletes* (pp. 349–378). Morgantown, WV: Fitness Information Technology.

Fleming, N., & Baume, D. (2006) *Learning styles again: VARKing up the right tree! Educational developments, 7*(4), 4–7.

Gaston-Gayles, J. L. (2004). Examining academic and athletic motivation among student-athletes at a Division I university. *Journal of College Student Development, 45*(1), 75–83.

Gaston-Gayles, J. L., & Hu, S. (2009). The influence of student engagement and sport participation on college outcomes among Division I student athletes. *The Journal of Higher Education, 80*(3), 315–333.

Gurney, G., Lopiano, E., Snyder, D., Willingham, M., Meyer, J., Porto, B., Ridpath, D. B., Sack, A., & Zimbalist, A. (2017). *The Drake Group position statement: Why the NCAA Academic Progress Rate (APR) and Graduation Success Rate (GSR) should be abandoned and replaced with more effective academic metrics* (revised). Retrieved from https://the-drakegroup.org/2015/06/07/drake-group-questions-ncaaacademic-metrics/

Hosick, M. B. (2016, October 27). DI to distribute revenue based on academics. *NCAA*. Retrieved from http://www.ncaa.org/about/resources/media-center/news/di-distribute-revenue-based-academics

Huml, M. R., Hancock, M. G., & Bergman, M .J. (2014). Additional support or extravagant cost? Student-athletes' perceptions of athletic academic centers. *Journal of Issues in Intercollegiate Athletics, 7*, 410–430.

Jayakumar, U. M., & Comeaux, E. (2016). The cultural cover-up of college athletics: How organizational culture perpetuates an unrealistic and idealized balancing act. *The Journal of Higher Education, 87*(4), 488–515.

Johnson, J. (2013). Assessing academic risk of student-athletes: Applicability of the NCAA Graduation Risk Overview model to GPA. *NACADA Journal, 32*(2), 76–89.

Kolb, D., & Kolb, A. (2013). The Kolb Learning Style Inventory 4.0: A comprehensive guide to theory, psychometrics, research on validity and educational applications. Experience based learning systems.

Lally, P. S., & Kerr, G. A. (2005). The career planning, athletic identity, and student role identity of intercollegiate athletes. *Research Quarterly for Exercise and Sport, 76*(3), 275–285.

Levine, J., Etchinson, S., & Oppenheimer, D. M. (2014). Pluralistic ignorance among student-athlete populations: A factor in academic underperformance. *Higher Education, 68*(4), 525–540.

Linnemeyer, R. M., & Brown, C. (2010). Career maturity and foreclosure in student athletes, fine arts students, and general college students. *Journal of Career Development, 37*(3), 616–634.

Love, A., Watkins, J., & Kim, S. (2017). Admissions selectivity and major distribution in big-time college football. *Journal of Issues in Intercollegiate Athletics, 10*, 1–16.

Lytle, L., & Gallucci, R. (2015). An evaluation of the University of California, Santa Barbara's freshman summer start program: Impact on students and campus. *Summer Academe*, 2–19.

Miller, P. S., & Kerr, G. A. (2003). The role experimentation of intercollegiate student athletes. *The Sport Psychologist, 17*, 196–219.

Melendez, M. C. (2006). The influence of athletic participation on the college adjustment of freshmen and sophomore student athletes. *College Student Retention, 8*(1), 39–55.

Menke, D. J. (2015). The 3-I advising process and athletes with foreclosed identity. *NACADA Journal, 35*(1), 22–28.

Meyer, S. K. (2005). NCAA academic reforms: Maintaining the balance between academics and athletics. *Phi Kappa Phi Forum, 85*(3), 15–18.

Monda, S. J., Etzel, E. F., Shannon, V. R., & Wooding, C. B. (2015). Understanding the academic experiences of freshman football athletes: Insight for sport psychology professionals. *Athletic Insight, 7*(2), 1–14.

National Collegiate Athletic Association. (2003, October). *NCAA Division I Academic reform: Overview*. Retrieved from http://www.sc.edu/faculty/PDF/DivisionIAcadReform.pdf

National Collegiate Athletic Association. (2014). *NCAA Division I academic performance program manual*. Retrieved from https://www.ncaa.org/sites/default/files/201415%20 APP%20Manual%20with%20Appendices%2011-17-14.pdf

National Collegiate Athletic Association. (2016). *Understanding life outcomes of former NCAA student-athletes. The Gallup-Purdue Index report*. Retrieved from https://www.ncaa. org/sites/default/files/2016_Gallup_NCAA_StudentAthlete_Report_20160503.pdf

National Collegiate Athletic Association. (2017a). *Overall Division I graduation rates*. Retrieved from https://web3.ncaa.org/aprsearch/public_reports/instAggr2017/1_0.pdf

National Collegiate Athletic Association. (2017b). *2017–18 NCAA Division I manual, operating manual*. National Collegiate Athletic Association. Indianapolis, IN.

National Collegiate Athletic Association. (2017c). *Life skills*. Retrieved from http://www. ncaa.org/about/resources/leadership-development/life-skills

Navarro, K. (2014). A conceptual model of Division I student-athletes' career construction processes. *College Student Affairs Journal, 32*(1), 219–235.

NCAA Research Staff. (2017). *Trends in graduation success rates and federal graduation rates at NCAA Division I institutions*. Retrieved from http://www.ncaa.org/sites/default/ files/2017D1RES_Grad_Rate_Trends_FINAL_20171108.pdf

Pascarella, E. T., & Terenzini, P. T. (2005). *How college affects students: A third decade of research*. San Francisco, CA: Jossey-Bass.

Petitpas, A. J., Brewer, B., & Van Raalte, J. L. (2009). Transitions of the student-athlete: Theoretical, empirical, and practical perspectives. In E.F. Etzel (ed.), *Counseling and psychological services for college student-athletes* (pp.283-302). Morgantown, WV: Fitness Information Technology.

Potuto, J. R., & O'Hanlon, J. (2007). National study of student-athletes regarding their experiences as college students. *College Student Journal, 41*, 1–25.

Rettig, J., & Hu, S. (2016). College sport participation and student educational experiences and selected college outcomes. *Journal of College Student Development, 57*(4), 428–446.

Umbach, P. D., Palmer, M. M., Kuh, G. D., & Hannah, S. J. (2006). Intercollegiate athletes and effective educational practices: Winning combination or losing effort? *Research in Higher Education, 47*(6), 709–733.

Wolverton, B. (2015). NCAA says it's investigating academic fraud at 20 colleges. *Chronicle of Higher Education, 61*(20), A13–A13.

# 4

# Transitioning out of Athletics: Career Counseling with Student-Athletes

*Ryan M. Sweeny*

## CASE STUDY: JAN

Jan was a member of the women's basketball team on full scholarship at Great State, a large public Division I university. Both of her parents were teachers, one at the elementary school level and the other at the high school level. As with most Division 1 student-athletes, Jan had shown athletic promise at an early age and had devoted her athletic life solely to basketball beginning in elementary school. In high school she led her team to the state championship in both her junior and senior years. She was highly recruited by several universities and made her college decision based primarily on her positive impression of Great State's women's basketball program and the promise that she would likely get plenty of playing time as early as her first year.

Jan had entered the university with some general, but nonspecific ideas about her future. She wanted most of all to play in the WNBA, but knew she faced long odds of making it to this level even if she worked hard and stayed healthy throughout her college career. She also knew she did not want to be a teacher like her parents but couldn't imagine what other types of careers might interest her. In high school her favorite classes had been physical education and biology. Jan matriculated as an undeclared major. The academic advisor in the athletic department recommended that Jan register for courses in the communications program because those classes did not conflict with the basketball practice or game schedules. Jan noticed that many of the students in her classes were also student-athletes. Although she achieved good grades throughout college, Jan did not especially enjoy the communications classes.

During her time at Great State, Jan participated in required career and life-skills programming offered by the athletic department but did not make an appointment at the university's career center until the fall of her senior year. As she was entering her final season of basketball, she was on track to graduate in four years, and had begun to worry about her career future.

During the first session with Dr. Nagel, her assigned counselor, Jan agreed to commit to several meetings if they could be arranged around her basketball and class schedules. They discussed her academic progress to date and began to explore some of her career thoughts and ideas. Jan reported having spoken with a few employers in the communications field at one of the mandatory career fairs she had attended during her sophomore year but stated that she could not picture herself doing well nor succeeding at any of the jobs mentioned. Jan was clearly discouraged.

Dr. Nagel asked Jan about her basketball career. Jan reported that she had performed well during her first year and earned a starting position by the end of her first season. The next two seasons also were very strong, and in her junior year the team finished as the runner-up in the conference championship game and earned an at-large bid to the NCAA tournament. During the final practice prior to their Round 1 tournament appearance, Jan landed awkwardly during a routine jump shot and felt something pull in her knee. Although she managed to start the game, she had considerable pain and had to sit out for most of the second half. After the season ended, Jan had knee surgery to repair a torn meniscus, followed by months of physical therapy and rehab. Her recovery progressed well, and Jan reported that her surgeon and physical therapist told her that she would be able to play her final season. Nonetheless, Jan shared with the counselor that her dreams of playing professionally were now highly unlikely to come to fruition. Dr. Nagel offered Jan the opportunity to take a career interest inventory. Jan readily agreed.

In their second meeting, Dr. Nagel reviewed the results of the assessment with Jan and encouraged her to use the results as a starting point for her investigation of possible career areas that aligned with her interests. They also talked in greater depth about Jan's experience of being injured and the disappointment that accompanied her realization that she would most likely never play basketball professionally. Dr. Nagel asked Jan if she had noticed any positive outcomes to this experience. After pausing to think about this, Jan replied that she had enjoyed the physical therapy sessions that followed her surgery because she liked the process of setting the goal of strengthening her knee and using the assigned exercises to work toward that goal. Jan also mentioned having enjoyed her conversations with Amy, her physical therapist.

Dr. Nagel invited Jan to think about how she might use her injury experience as an opportunity for exploration. Together, they discussed Jan's interest in her own rehabilitation, coupled with her memory of having enjoyed her high school biology class. She wondered aloud if physical therapy might be a potential career for her. Dr. Nagel asked Jan to set a goal for taking an action step prior to their next meeting. Jan said she would plan to talk with Amy during their next appointment about the process of becoming a physical therapist.

Jan emailed Dr. Nagel the following week with the news that she and Amy had talked about physical therapy as a career. She also reported having requested application information for several programs within a two-hour radius of her hometown. Finally, she mentioned having made an appointment with her academic advisor to talk about rearranging her class schedule to begin to tackle the prerequisite courses for most physical therapy programs.

During their next meeting, Jan and Dr. Nagel discussed the concrete steps that Jan would need to take to continue to pursue physical therapy as a career option. Dr. Nagel noticed that Jan spoke with excitement in her voice about her plan. They agreed to meet again if Jan felt the need to do so during the application process.

Two years after she graduated from Great State, Jan emailed Dr. Nagle to say thanks for working with her. She reported that she had spent a year following her graduation taking prerequisite courses in anatomy and physiology and had received an admission offer from two of the physical therapy programs to which she applied. Now in her first semester of study, Jan told Dr. Nagel that she knew that this was a good career choice for her.

Student-athletes at the college level devote an incredible amount of their lives to their athletic pursuits. At the most basic level are the time, physical, and mental energy requirements demanded by athletic competition. On a deeper level, there is the personal identity of being an athlete that most have adopted from a very young age. As their college athletic careers come to an end, student-athletes are faced with the daunting task of transitioning into a completely new life devoid of the student-athlete identity. Even transitioning to a sports-related career such as coaching or broadcasting poses many challenges. This chapter explores common challenges facing student-athletes in their career development and outlines a career counseling model to assist during the transition from student-athlete to post-graduation.

Student-athletes face many pressures related to their sport, including time practicing and competing, off-season preparation, competition success (or failure), and the reality that their participation will one day end. The process of exploring, selecting, and preparing for a career after the end of athletic participation can be a daunting task for student-athletes. Research indicates that student-athletes tend not to utilize career resources or engage in career-related activities (Sowa & Gessard, 1983; Tyrance, Harris, & Post, 2013), therefore, their overall career development is negatively impacted (Kennedy & Dimmick, 1987). By not utilizing career resources, student-athletes set themselves up for increased difficulties as they try to transition out of athletics and into the world of work.

## Career Preparation Challenges Facing Student-Athletes

### Time Spent in Athletics

The first significant challenge facing college student-athletes is the amount of time that is required. The NCAA strictly regulates the time that student-athletes can spend engaged in sport-related activities, both in-season and out-of-season. In general, across Divisions I, II, and III, student-athletes are limited to spending 20 hours per week on countable activities—e.g., practice, competition, and mandatory training sessions during the season. There is, however, no limit to the number of hours spent on noncountable activities—e.g., injury treatments, compliance meetings, community service projects, and travel to/from competitions (National Collegiate Athletic Association [NCAA], 2009). Division I has an eight-hour countable time limit during the off-season and the summer, Division II has an eight-hour countable time limit during the off-season but not the summer, and Division III prohibits mandatory countable time during any time other than in-season.

These rules are in place to protect the student-athlete from exploitation and to allow them to spend the necessary time to succeed in the classroom. Despite these restrictions, a 2015 NCAA survey of Division I student-athletes reported an average of 34 hours per week spent on athletics-related activities. Further, 67% of the survey participants indicated spending about as much time on their sport during the off-season as during the season (NCAA, 2015).

Given the time demands placed on student-athletes, it is not surprising that career development activities are often neglected (Navaro, 2015; Sailes & Harrison, 2008; Shurts & Shoffner, 2004; Petitpas & Champagne, 1988; Ogilvie & Howe, 1982). Important career-related activities, such as joining student clubs and organizations, engaging in volunteer work, or participating in an internship, are often out of reach for student-athletes as they juggle the time demands of their sport. Additionally, these time constraints mean that student-athletes find it difficult to attend career-related activities, such as career fairs, networking events, or company information sessions. The busy student-athlete will also find it nearly impossible to meet with a career counselor to engage in basic career preparation, such as developing a resume or learning networking skills. As a result of missing out on these career preparation activities in the service of their athletics-related time commitments, student-athletes may be at a considerable disadvantage compared to their nonathlete peers when entering the job market.

## Athletic Identity

To compete at the collegiate level, student-athletes have devoted much of their lives to the pursuit of athletics. This intense and often narrow focus on athletics generally comes at the expense of other interests and pursuits and can have an impact on identity development (Houle, Brewer, & Kluck, 2010). The demands of collegiate athletics often require the student-athlete to maintain a narrow focus on their sport to the exclusion of other aspects of life. At the extreme, student-athletes often experience identity foreclosure (Shurts & Shoffner, 2004; Nelson, 1983), as a large portion of personal identity is relegated to their student-athlete status. It is important to note that the majority of student-athletes do not necessarily believe they will participate in athletics forever. Rather, they simply place all of their focus on their current athletic participation. The student-athlete with high athletic identity may find it enormously difficult to contemplate a future existence as a nonathlete, particularly without having taken the necessary steps to prepare for a transition out of athletics.

The impact of a narrow or foreclosed identity on preparing for one's life after athletics generally occurs in two ways. First, the total focus on athletic identity prevents student-athletes from exploring and considering life options. The student-athlete is limited in the ability to experiment with the world around them especially as it relates to future career options. Because they are unable to entertain other possible identities, they may neglect to participate in activities that are important from a career development perspective. Research indicates that student-athletes engage in few, if any, activities related to exploring possible career paths (Petitpas & Champagne, 1988; Brewer, Van Raalte, & Linder, 1993; Beamon, 2012; Comeaux & Harrison, 2011). This can include formal career-related activities such as attending a networking event or career fair offered by the university career office, as well as informal activities such as talking with a professional in a field of interest or examining requirements for a particular career path. Whether formal or informal, when student-athletes fail to engage with these experiences, they miss out on valuable developmental opportunities that will help guide their journey from athlete to post-athletic opportunities.

The second challenge posed by a too narrow or a foreclosed identity occurs when student-athletes do not take advantage of the resources available to them for career development. Student-athletes consistently neglect to utilize career development assistance provided by their college or university (Martens & Cox, 2000; Smallman & Sowa, 1996; Murdock, Strear, Jenkins-Guarnieri, & Henderson, 2016). For some student-athletes, it is as if taking time for career development activities is not important because they are not focused on their future or ways in which career development would be of benefit to them. Basic career development skills such as resume construction, job search strategies, networking skills, and interview preparation are neglected because, in the tunnel-vision of collegiate athletics, the purpose and benefits of career development is not readily apparent.

## Academic Clustering

The NCAA mandates that student-athletes meet certain academic standards in order to maintain eligibility, including making measurable progress toward the degree at a passing grade point average. To facilitate this, some university administrators may engage in a process known as academic clustering (Fountain & Finley, 2011). In academic clustering, student-athletes are encouraged to select academic majors that are not overly rigorous so as not to threaten their academic eligibility. Furthermore, these majors are not examined for their relevance to students' future career paths but are instead selected only to help them maintain academic eligibility for sports. This entire process also has the potential to have a negative impact on the career preparation and career readiness of student-athletes. Some career paths require a specific major, while others do not. For example, a student-athlete who aspires toward a career as a nurse or an accountant would be well advised to declare a major in nursing or accounting. On the other hand, some career paths (e.g., sales) can be reached from a variety of different starting points. Counselors and academic advising professionals working with student-athletes must be knowledgeable about the educational requirements of certain careers in order to assist them in selecting potential majors.

## Best Practices in Career Counseling with Student-Athletes

### *Happenstance Learning Theory*

Given the career-related challenges facing student-athletes navigating toward the finish line of athletics participation, it is important for helping professionals to have a solid foundation and approach to career counseling. Many evidence-based models of career counseling for college students exist (Holland, 1985; Super, 1990; Savickas et al., 2009), and there is no uniform approach to the preparations for graduation and athletic retirement of student-athletes (Leonard & Schimmel, 2016). The happenstance learning theory (HLT) (Krumboltz, 2009) approach to career counseling represents one excellent model for working with student-athletes, both while they are students and as they transition away from athletics and into careers.

One of the primary goals of the happenstance learning theory is to prepare individuals to both seek out important experiences as well as to recognize and respond to unexpected experiences. Krumboltz (2009, p.135) stated: "...the HLT posits that human behavior is the product of countless numbers of learning experiences made available by both planned and unplanned situations in which individuals find themselves." In terms of career path, individuals' paths are comprised of factors over which they have control and others over which they do not, and both types of factors provide useful fodder for career exploration and preparation.

Krumboltz (2009) identified four fundamental propositions that make up the happenstance learning theory. First, "the goal of career counseling is to help clients learn to take actions to achieve more satisfying careers and personal lives—not to make a single career decision" (p. 141). Career counselors must help their clients develop the necessary skills to examine their experiences and take effective actions. Thus, career counselors should not define success as helping the client pick a single occupation but rather as helping them develop the ability to navigate life experiences and to take appropriate actions. The most challenging part of this proposition is to move beyond thinking and planning and into action.

Given the challenges that student-athletes face in career development and in making career decisions, this first proposition provides focused direction for the work of a career counselor. No longer is the goal for the student-athlete to simply pick a career. Rather, the goal is to help student-athletes explore the events, both planned and unplanned, that have lead them to that place in life and to examine the actions they took in response to these events. This exploration can occur in one-on-one meetings or in larger group settings. Due to time constraints, this work can occur in scheduled groups such as life skills training or academic advising meetings. This approach also can be helpful in dealing with the narrow or foreclosed identity that often hinders student-athletes. Because the focus is on building skills through the exploration of past situations, this approach can make excellent use of the student-athlete's athletic experiences. The student-athlete is not forced to imagine life without athletics, but instead can focus on the present to learn skills and concepts so that they can be applied later. For example, the helping professional might encourage the student-athlete to generate a list of skills they have developed through sport participation that could translate into job-related skills. Such a list might include time management skills, leadership qualities, and the ability to work on a team to name just a few.

The second proposition from the happenstance learning theory states that "career assessments are used to stimulate learning, not to match personal characteristics with occupational characteristics" (Krumboltz, 2009, p. 143). Again, the process here is not to find the answer, but rather to help the student-athlete engage in a process of self-exploration that leads to further action. An interest assessment, such as the Strong Interest Inventory, is a useful tool that can identify career areas for future exploration based upon interest similarities. Likewise, a personality assessment such as the Myers-Briggs Type Indicator (MBTI) may be used as a way to facilitate self-exploration and understanding of the role personality characteristics play in the processing of life experiences. Career assessments can be an important tool for work with student-athletes because they offer real data to help in the career development process. The time needed (20–30 minutes for the Strong Interest Inventory or MBTI) to take an assessment is not prohibitive, even with a busy schedule, and interpretation of results can occur in regularly scheduled career sessions, advising sessions, or group sessions.

The third proposition of the happenstance learning theory emphasizes the importance of the client engaging in exploratory actions to generate beneficial unplanned events (Krumboltz, 2009, p. 144). The word happenstance can seem as if it is a passive experience, but in actuality the key to this concept is in clients actively engaging with their environments. Krumboltz (2009) identified three key steps involved in this process:

1. Take actions that put you in situations to experience new and unplanned events.

2. Pay attention while engaging in activities so that you can recognize new opportunities.

3. Take action so that you can benefit from the unplanned event. (p. 144)

Engaging in exploratory activities is in many ways the cornerstone of the happenstance learning theory model, and it is this active process of getting involved that then leads to new knowledge and relationships that become critical to one's journey. The demands on a student-athlete's time are well-established and this would seem to be a big obstacle for this proposition. Despite the challenge of finding time, career counseling with student-athletes utilizing the happenstance learning theory approach can be highly effective even within limited time constraints. First, student-athletes often engage in a variety of activities that are well suited for this type of exploration. Some of these activities include community service projects with their team, networking events organized by life-skills programs, and informal exposure to alumni, athletic department staff, and university staff. Meeting the director of a local nonprofit while on a community service project or connecting with an alum who is successful in the business world can become important experiences that lead to future activities and experiences for the student-athlete. Counselors working with student-athletes should prepare them to take advantage of these existing opportunities as they arise.

Counselors also can serve as a guide for student-athletes to make valuable use of the precious free time that they get. For example, the student-athlete who joins a fashion marketing student club will likely have many more chances to create beneficial unplanned events than one who joins an online gaming student club.

Because these exploratory actions are not chosen stemming from a specific career match but are instead chosen to create unplanned events, the happenstance learning theory model is ideal for student-athletes who are not ready or able to consider other identity aspects beyond that of an athlete. For these student-athletes, the goal is to expose them to events and opportunities that are genuinely interesting to them, not to force the emergence of new identities.

The challenge of dealing with academic eligibility pressures and major selection are also handled well with the happenstance learning theory approach to career counseling. In the happenstance learning theory model, the student's major does not drive the important exploratory actions, but vice versa. By committing to the process of exploring one's unplanned or informally occurring experiences, the student-athlete will experience a multitude of unanticipated events that will then inform and influence their academic and subsequent career path. By learning to observe one's reactions during these experiences, student-athletes might discover career interests that are not strictly aligned with their current major, and may choose not to switch majors in order to stay eligible to compete. Instead, they may discover graduate programs leading to that career path that they can pursue following their retirement from sport. Many graduate programs do not require a specific undergraduate major for admission.

The final proposition in the happenstance learning theory maintains that career counseling is successful when the client accomplishes changes in the real world, not because of decisions or breakthroughs in the counseling session (Krumboltz,

2009). The counselor is encouraged to help the client plan actual activities that they will attempt before the next counseling session. Krumboltz (2009) emphasized two main points: (1) the assignment that the client should complete should not be called homework, but rather action steps, and (2) the client is asked to set a deadline for completion of the action steps and notify the counselor when they have completed them. An important consideration for the helping professional at this stage of the process is that failure to complete action steps is never blamed on the client. Rather, the decision not to complete the action steps is processed in the next session and potential roadblocks are identified and addressed.

For the student-athlete, the concept of action steps fits well with life involved in a competitive sport. Results are constantly measured in the weight room, in the classroom, and on the field or court. Athletics is all about taking action steps to improve and then to test that improvement in competition. This approach of the happenstance learning theory resonates well with student-athletes and enables counselors to help them in a way that is similar to other areas of their athletic and academic lives.

## Five Components of Career Counseling Using the Happenstance Learning Theory

The first component for counselors is to orient client expectations (Krumboltz, 2009). The goal at this step is to educate and prepare the client for the process of the happenstance learning theory. It is likely that busy student-athletes will enter this process seeking quick answers to their questions and the helping professional may need to encourage patience. Even though most people can remember a time when an unplanned event had a major impact on their life, basing a significant life decision around this can be unsettling for some. Helping the client understand the value of experiencing these unplanned events and to take actions in response to them is at the core of the happenstance learning theory approach.

The second component of the happenstance learning theory is to make the client's presenting concern the starting point for the process (Krumboltz, 2009). It is important to help clients identify what they want to change or improve and also to identify activities in their lives where they feel excited and experience joy. Although there typically is a concern or problem that underlies help seeking, the role of the counselor is to acknowledge this starting point and also to bring awareness of success to recollections of past experiences.

The third component of the happenstance learning theory is to help clients recall past experiences with unplanned events and connect those with the desired future actions (Krumboltz, 2009). Assisting clients to remember and retell stories of past unplanned events that resulted in a positive effect is imperative in the counseling process. This likely involves drilling down to the details of the past experience, including how it occurred, the response it elicited, and how it was helpful. For student-athletes, this will often involve the recollection of their lengthy involvement as a competitor in their sport.

The fourth component of the happenstance learning theory is to help "sensitize clients to recognize potential opportunities" (Krumboltz, 2009). This will involve speculating or brainstorming about possible types of events that the client would like to experience and then planning for the best response to that event. In addition to setting plans for responding to unplanned events, counselors can also assist clients in determining which actions will lead to an increase in the likelihood of experiencing beneficial unplanned events. Fortunately, student-athletes know that one key to athletic success is to take in feedback and to implement suggestions for improvement, e.g., coaching. Taking and implementing feedback is very translatable to this component of the happenstance learning theory.

The final component is helping clients "overcome blocks to action" (Krumboltz, 2009, p. 148). It is important to remember that the emphasis should be on the actions taken, not on the unplanned events. The happenstance learning theory model assumes that these unplanned events will help the client discover new approaches to career and life satisfaction. The counselor must focus on helping the client work through blocks to taking action so that the process can take place and the benefits can be reaped.

Applying each of these counseling elements to work with student-athletes involves several considerations. Athletes and coaches operate in a sphere in which preparation is crucial and leaving things to chance is not generally acceptable. However, athletes are also able to easily recall instances during competitions that could best be described as luck, so this is not a foreign concept—just not a preferred one. It may be beneficial to establish the existence of so many instances of unplanned events by using sport-related examples from the student-athlete's lived experience and exploring them to see how actions taken after they occurred had the most impact on the outcome of the situation.

The remaining four components present unique challenges for working with student-athletes as they often are in competition with the narrow self-identity many athletes hold. Multiple career counseling sessions might be difficult to schedule with student-athletes and furthermore, those that are solely focused on their athletic identity might find it hard to move into these exercises of future possibilities outside of athletics. The goal here has two parts. First, it is important to introduce these ideas and help student-athletes recall past unplanned events, as well as the actions they took in response to these and the positive outcomes that they experienced. Educating the student-athlete to these principles of the happenstance learning theory is imperative, even if the process of taking action and making career decisions is going to be delayed until their athletic career is over. Certainly, this is not the case with all student-athletes, but for many it is a focus on preparation, knowing that using the lessons and skills will be delayed.

Career counselors will also have the experience of working with student-athletes who are very aware and accepting of their athletic career timeline and will orient towards future career paths. For student-athletes in this category, the challenge will be to help them connect experiences both inside and outside of their athletic career that were unplanned and that later had a significant impact on their life. Because of the huge commitment to athletics that it often takes to become a college level athlete, these experiences might often be connected to athletics. It is important to utilize these experiences as well as search for experiences outside of their athletic experiences. The main emphasis here is to help the student-athlete recall unplanned events that have had an impact on their life, and to build on these and prepare the student-athlete to both recognize important unplanned activities in the future and learn the skills to take actions that will enable these unplanned events to have a significant impact on their future life.

## Conclusion

The career development process of student-athletes at the collegiate level can be a challenging and exciting experience for both the student-athlete and the counselor. Krumboltz's (2009) happenstance learning theory offers a powerful career counseling approach for working with student-athletes. Time constraints, athletic focused self-identity, and academic focus often pose unique hurdles to the career development process and the happenstance learning theory is well positioned to address them. The systematic exploration of unplanned events and positive action steps taken in response can be a powerful guide in career development. Student-athletes will benefit from the application of this theory due to the unique challenges and opportunities that they face in their college athletic careers and in their occupational careers.

## Discussion Questions

1. What were the biggest challenges Jan faced in making career decisions?

2. How would you have worked with Jan if she were your client?

3. How does happenstance learning theory apply to the career decisions facing Jan?

# References

Beamon, K. (2012). "I'm a baller": Athletic identity foreclosure among African-American former student-athletes. *Journal of African American Studies, 16*(2), 195–208.

Brewer, W. B., Van Raalte, J. L., & Linder, D. E. (1993). Athletic identity: Hercules' muscles or Achilles' heel? *International Journal of Sport Psychology, 29*, 17–26.

Comeaux, E., & Harrison, C. K. (2011). A conceptual model academic success for student-athletes. *Educational Researcher, 40*, 235–245.

Fountain, J. J., & Finley, P. S. (2011). Academic clustering: A longitudinal analysis of Division I football programs. *Journal of Issues in Intercollegiate Athletics, 4*, 23–41.

Holland, J. L. (1985). *Making vocational choices: A theory of careers.* Englewood Cliffs, NJ: Prentice Hall.

Houle, J. L. W., Brewer, B. W., & Kluck, A. S. (2010). Developmental trends in athletic identity: A two-part retrospective study. *Journal of Sport Behavior, 33*, 146–159.

Kennedy, S. R., & Dimick, K. M. (1987). Career maturity and professional sports expectations of college football and basketball players. *Journal of College Student Personnel, 28*, 293–297.

Krumboltz, J. D. (2009). The happenstance learning theory. *Journal of Career Assessment, 17*(2), 135–154.

Leonard, J. M., & Schimmel, C. J. (2016). Theory of work adjustment and student-athletes' transition out of sport. *Journal of Issues in Intercollegiate Athletics, 9*, 62–85.

Martens, M. P., & Cox, R. H. (2000). Career development in college varsity athletes. *Journal of College Student Development, 41*, 172–180.

Murdock, J. L., Strear, M. M., Jenkins-Guarnieri, M. A., & Henderson, A. C. (2016). Collegiate athletes and career identity. *Sport, Education and Society, 21*(3), 396–410.

Navaro, K. M. (2015). An examination of the alignment of student-athletes' undergraduate major choices and career field aspirations in life after sports. *Journal of College Student Development, 56*(4), 364–379.

National Collegiate Athletic Association. (2009). *Defining countable athletically related activities.* Retrieved from http://www.ncaa.org/sites/default/files/Charts.pdf

National Collegiate Athletic Association. (2015). *Time management: What division I student-athletes should expect.* Retrieved from http://www.ncaa.org/sites/default/files/StudentAthleteTimeManagement.pdf

Nelson, E. S. (1983). How the myth of the dumb jock becomes fact: A developmental view for counselors. *Counseling and Values, 27*, 176–185.

Ogilvie, B. C., & Howe, M. A. (1982). *Career crisis in sports.* Unpublished manuscript.

Petitpas, A. J., & Champagne, D. E. (1988). Developmental programming for intercollegiate athletes. *Journal of College Student Development, 29*, 454–460.

Sailes, G., & Harrison, L. (2008). Social issues of sports. In A. Leslie-Toogood & E. Gill (Eds.), *Advising student-athletes: Comprehensive approach to success* (pp. 13–21). Manhattan, KS: National Academic Advising Association.

Savickas, M. L., Nota, L., Rossier, J., Dauwalder, J. P., Duarte, M. E., Guichard, J., & van Vianen, A. E. M. (2009). Life designing: A paradigm for career construction in the 21st century. *Journal of Vocational Behavior, 75,* 239–250. doi:10.1016/j.jvb.2009.04.00

Shurts, W. M., & Shoffner, M. F. (2004). Providing career counseling for collegiate student-athletes: A learning theory approach. *Journal of Career Development, 31*(2), 97–109.

Smallman, E., & Sowa, C.J. (1996). Career maturity levels of male intercollegiate varsity athletes. *The Career Development Quarterly, 44,* 270–277.

Sowa, C. J., & Gressard, C. F. (1983). Athletic participation: Its relationship to student development. *Journal of College Student Personnel, 24,* 236–239.

Super, D. E. (1990). A life-span, life-space approach to career development. In D. Brown, & L. Brooks (Eds.), *Career choice and development: Applying contemporary theories to practice* (2nd ed. pp. 197–261). San Francisco, CA: Josey-Bass.

Tyrance, S. C., Harris, H. L., & Post, P. (2013). Predicting positive career planning attitudes among NCAA division I college student-athletes. *Journal of Clinical Sport Psychology, 7*(1), 22–40.

# 5

# Disordered Eating in College Student-Athletes

*Jennifer E. Carter*

## CASE STUDY: EMILY

Emily managed to hold off tears until after she left her college coach's office. In high school, her backstroke time had ranked in the top ten in the country, thus earning her a swimming scholarship at an elite university. As a first-year swimmer on her college team, she aspired to impress her coaches, but her coach had just told her that she needed to get fitter in order to have a successful college career. Her muscular body had only 21% body fat, but Emily knew what "fitter" meant—she needed to lose weight. She was already worried about balancing school, swimming, and friends, and now she had to add another item to her full agenda. She didn't even have time to cry about it.

Throughout the autumn, she skipped breakfast and delayed eating despite feeling tired and lightheaded during her two grueling practices each day. She avoided particular "bad" foods. Even though she lost a little weight, her coach still wasn't pleased by her lackluster effort at practices. Emily determined she needed to try harder, so she cut out lunch, as well. All she could think about was food, but she wouldn't allow herself to eat until dinner.

While studying for chemistry one night, she kept returning to the dorm vending machine and was horrified to realize she'd eaten five candy bars. "I'm never eating again," she vowed, but the next day her stomach growled all afternoon. After consuming a small dinner, Emily and her teammates attended a party at the swimming house, where she tossed down vodka mixed drinks. When an older teammate ordered food, Emily couldn't get enough and consumed almost an entire large pizza.

She returned to the dorm feeling tipsy, uncomfortably full, and disgusted with herself. After stumbling to the bathroom, she vomited. A sense of relief overtook her.

Less than a week later, she lost control while studying at night and consumed a loaf of bread and a jar of peanut butter. Terrified of gaining weight, she made herself throw up. By the end of November, she'd started binge eating and purging almost every night. She hated herself and felt scared of anyone finding out her revolting secret. Emily had developed bulimia nervosa.

In November, Emily's coaches noticed that she wasn't performing well in practice. Her assistant coach, Tricia, asked how she was doing. At first, Emily claimed she was fine, but Tricia shared her concerns about Emily appearing tired and irritable all the time, in contrast to her sunny disposition as a recruit. Emily confessed that she was extremely stressed and embarrassed that she couldn't lose weight despite hardly eating at all. Tricia referred her to the team dietitian, Sonja.

Emily's restricting became evident after she completed a food record for Sonja, but it wasn't until pointed questions from Sonja that Emily revealed the binge eating and purging. Sonja created a meal plan and referred Emily to the team physician and the department's sport psychologist, Brian.

Though Brian was not an eating disorder (ED) specialist, he had pursued extra training, and he consulted regularly with a specialist at the university's counseling center. Brian explained to Emily that student-athletes could be driven and dedicated, taking efforts to improve their sport performance to the extreme, and that she could apply that same goal-directed nature to her recovery.

Brian recommended she read *Life Without Ed*, and he taught her about vasopressin and rebound bloating—two body responses to dehydration after vomiting. Vasopressin, a hormone released after vomiting to restore fluid into the cells, creates a sense of euphoria. Rebound bloating occurs when the body retains fluid after vomiting, causing temporary weight gain. Both vasopressin and rebound bloating can make purging feel addictive, but knowing the water weight gain was temporary could help Emily tolerate her discomfort without turning to restriction.

Brian encouraged Emily to follow her meal plan, regardless of her hunger, since her hunger signals were not working correctly due to her eating disorder behaviors. He told Emily that she met criteria for the diagnoses of generalized anxiety disorder and bulimia nervosa.

"This is so much food!" Emily thought when she started her meal plan. But her coaches and team physician had told her that she needed to follow the treatment team's recommendations to keep swimming, so she forced herself to eat three meals and snacks each day. She ate lunch with Brian or Sonja during their sessions, and she asked teammates to eat dinner with her to distract and support her. Emily learned that food wasn't good or bad—all foods could fit into her meal plan in moderation. In a short period of time, she was surprised that she reduced her binge/purge behaviors to once a week.

In counseling, Emily realized that eating disorder and alcohol use behaviors had only increased her anxiety in the long term, and she started learning skills to manage her chronic worry more effectively. She practiced challenging dysfunctional thoughts ("I'll never get everything done" to "I always get the important stuff done; one thing at a time"). A binge trigger was Emily's irritation about her roommate's boyfriend sleeping in their small dorm room. After she learned assertive communication, she expressed her irritation directly and forged a compromise about her roommate's boyfriend's visits. Emily took to mindfulness skills like a barracuda in the water. She learned to notice and accept her anxious thoughts and feelings, growing to appreciate her sensitive nature that helped her care deeply about her teammates and her sport (Johnston, 2010). After only a few months of counseling, Emily stopped restricting, binge eating, and purging. She continued to struggle with food preoccupation and negative body image as her brain and body healed, but soon she had minimal anxiety around food.

To help prevent eating disorders in Emily's teammates, the dietitian and athletic trainer met with her head coach to encourage nutritional education for the team. The coach was concerned that weight gain by some of his swimmers had interfered with their performance. The dietitian explained that a small weight gain is common in college (Mihalopoulos, Auinger, & Klein, 2008), and in athletes that gain likely related to increased muscle mass from extensive strength training. Citing a position statement from the National Athletic Trainers Association (Turocy et al., 2011), the athletic trainer educated the coach about healthy body fat ranges for athletes. Asking athletes on the low end of the range, like Emily, to lose weight meant their accompanying muscle loss could slow them down in the water. The subsequent weekly nutrition education helped the team fuel their excellent performance.

Unfortunately, stories like Emily's are increasingly common in university athletic departments. Sport participation offers wonderful opportunities to become the best we can be, but sport culture can also foster eating disorders. Emily's story highlights a unique eating disorder risk factor in athletics: the pressure to be lean for athletic performance. With increasing pressure and psychopathology in university athletic departments, counselors working with college student-athletes need to understand eating disorders to be effective.

Eating disorders include psychiatric diagnoses of anorexia nervosa, bulimia nervosa, binge eating disorder, and other specified feeding and eating disorder (American Psychiatric Association, 2013). This chapter explores the following topics related to eating disorders in college student-athletes: (1) definitions and prevalence, (2) effects of sport on eating disorder risk, (3) prevention and policy, and (4) assessment and treatment.

## Eating Disorders: A Problem in College Athletics

Although a complete review of the diagnostic criteria for each disorder is beyond the scope of this chapter, brief summaries follow. Anorexia nervosa involves significantly low body weight, intense fear of weight gain, and body image distortion. Bulimia nervosa consists of episodes of binge-eating followed by purging (e.g., self-induced vomiting, use of laxatives, over-exercise) and self-evaluation unduly influenced by body shape and size. Binge eating disorder involves binge eating without compensatory behaviors. Other specified feeding or eating disorder consists of a wide range of anorexia nervosa and bulimia nervosa eating/body image problems, including atypical anorexia nervosa (with normal or above-average weight, which may be more common among muscular athletes) and purging without binge eating (American Psychiatric Association, 2013).

In the general population and in athletics, anorexia nervosa is the least common eating disorder, but the deadliest. Bulimia nervosa is more common than anorexia nervosa, and binge eating disorder is the most common (American Psychiatric Association, 2013). About nine out of ten individuals seeking treatment for anorexia nervosa and bulimia nervosa are female, whereas about six out of ten seeking treatment for binge eating disorder are female. Male culture (and the masculine culture of athletics) discourages help-seeking, so prevalence numbers for men are likely higher than those represented in treatment samples (Striegel-Moore et al., 2009).

Are athletes more at risk for eating disorders than nonathletes? It is true that sport participation can enhance self-esteem and emphasize the body's function instead of form (Wang & Veugelers, 2008), and a few studies have found decreased prevalence of eating disorders in athletes compared to nonathletes (Carter & Rudd, 2005; Wollenberg, Shriver, & Gates, 2015). Others have found comparable rates in athlete and nonathlete samples (Reinking & Alexander, 2005; Sanford-Martens et al., 2005).

However, sport participation involves increased pressure from coaches and teammates—as in the case of Emily (Thompson and Sherman, 2010), revealing uniforms (Greenleaf, Petrie, Carter, & Reel, 2009), voracious appetites (Cooper & Winter, 2017), and the reinforcement of personality factors that coincide with eating disorder risk, such as perfectionism and pain tolerance (Fulkerson, Keel, Leon, & Door, 1999). Many studies have indicated increased risk of eating disorders in athletes (Sundgot-Borgen & Torstveit, 2004; Thompson & Sherman, 2014).

Several studies, mostly on female college athletes, have found that prevalence rates are less than 3% for clinical eating disorders and 15–30% for subclinical problems (symptoms of eating disorder not meeting full criteria; Beals & Manore, 2002; Carter & Rudd, 2005; Johnson, Powers, & Dick, 1999). Greenleaf et al. (2009) found that female athletes were more likely to exhibit subclinical eating disorder symptoms than meet criteria for clinical eating disorders, but the subclinical symptoms still can lead to substantial health risks (Petrie, Greenleaf, Reel, & Carter, 2009).

It appears that the type of sport influences prevalence rates, with elite athletes from "lean" sports being more at risk for eating disorders than nonathletes (Smolak, Murnen, & Ruble, 2000; Thompson & Sherman, 2010). Lean sports emphasize thinness for performance (e.g., running, rowing) and/or aesthetics (e.g., gymnastics, diving, and synchronized swimming). Two meta-analyses found that high school and recreational athletes may experience more positive body image (Hausenblas & Downs, 2001) and fewer eating disorders (Smolak et al., 2000) than nonathletes, highlighting the benefits of sport participation, particularly for nonelite athletes.

## Effects of Sport on Eating Disorder Risk

To work effectively with student-athletes, helping professionals need to understand the unique culture of sport. Aspects of sport both increase eating disorder risk and protect against eating disorders.

### *Risk Factors in Sport*

Genetics and neurobiology play a role in eating disorder risk, and sociocultural factors also contribute. In particular, the culture of athletics may enable eating disorder symptoms. These cultural factors include beliefs about body type and leanness affecting sport performance, the "no-excuses", insider culture of athletics, pressures from coaches, revealing uniforms, athletic injuries and energy imbalance, and personality traits that overlap between high-achieving individuals and those with eating disorders.

**Drive for leanness**. There is a pervasive belief that athletes in each sport must possess a particular type of body to perform well. Most female athletes want to be leaner, whereas most male athletes strive for muscular physiques. However, this emphasis on one ideal ignores evidence that bodies of all types have been successful in sport. For example, there is a large variety of body types among major-league baseball pitchers.

Even a particular body composition is not the gold standard for athletic performance. One college swim coach measured swimmers' body composition over a period of twenty years and found that body fat percentages of national champion swimmers varied from 12–30% (Steen, personal communication, 2004)—quite a broad range. The National Athletic Trainers' Association recommends healthy body fat ranges for female athletes (20– 32%) and male athletes (10–22%) that are higher than many coaches perpetuate as the ideal (Turocy, et al., 2011).

**No excuses.** The "no excuses," insider culture of collegiate sport may have negative effects on mental health (Reardon, 2017; Rice et al., 2016). Despite the decrease of anxiety and depression associated with exercise, there is increased pressure to perform, as well as reluctance to seek help, resulting in either the failure to notice or to intervene when an athlete exhibits signs of distress (Roberts, Faull, & Tod, 2016). Athletics is an insider culture, in which coaches and athletes may not trust the assistance provided by "outsiders." In the absence of full-time mental health staff in the athletic department, it is important that administrators, medical staff, and coaches form relationships with university and community units (National Collegiate Athletic Association, 2014).

**Injury.** Athletic injury serves both as a risk factor and a maintaining factor for eating disorders. Student-athletes often feel distraught following injury, including increased anxiety and depression (Brewer, 2017; Covassin, Elbin, Beidler, Lafevor, & Kontos, 2017). Not only does injury add grief to individuals' lives, it also steals away a primary coping mechanism to manage that grief—exercise. Additionally, injured student-athletes might fear weight gain due to changes in their energy balance. Student-athletes may not know how to deal with the negative emotional states associated with injury other than turning to food restriction, binge-eating, and/or purging, thus leading to malnutrition.

Malnutrition, on the other hand, increases risk of injury, particularly stress fractures. Restricting food intake and/or engaging in compulsive exercise can lead to an energy imbalance, which then leads to deleterious health effects. In 2005, the International Olympic Committee issued a consensus statement about the female athlete triad (Drinkwater, Loucks, Sherman, Sundgot-Borgen, & Thompson, 2005). The triad consists of disordered eating, amenorrhea (lack of menstrual cycle for three months or more), and bone density loss/osteoporosis. When there is an energy imbalance, the body enters survival mode and shuts down nonessential operations (Thomas & Heymsfield, 2016). Reproduction is not essential for survival, and women may lose menses. The lower estrogen levels make it difficult for calcium to enter the bones, resulting in brittle bones and an increased risk of stress fractures.

The IOC later renamed the female athlete triad syndrome as relative energy deficiency in sport (Mountjoy et al., 2014), to acknowledge that energy imbalance affects multiple body systems in women and men. These systems include metabolic rate, immunity, protein synthesis, and cardiovascular health. For example, heart rates below 50 beats per minute may indicate a survival emergency, rather than fitness, in athletes who are in a state of energy imbalance.

**Personality.** Another risk factor in athletics is personality traits that overlap between high-achieving athletes and individuals with disordered eating, such as perfectionism, over-compliance, excessive discipline, and high tolerance for pain (Hausenblas & Carron, 1999). Additionally, driven athletes are more at risk to use performance-enhancing substances, such as steroids and nutritional supplements (Pope, Phillips, & Olivardia, 2000).

Female athletes and male athletes have different personality risk factors for eating disorders (Galli, Petrie, Greenleaf, Reel, & Carter, 2014; Petrie, Greenleaf, Reel, & Carter, 2007). Perfectionism and appearance orientation appear to be risk factors for female athletes only, and male-specific risk factors may include drive for muscularity (Galli, Petrie, Reel, Greenleaf, & Carter, 2015).

## Protective Factors in Sport

Although risk factors abound in athletics, sport participation also presents opportunities to improve body image and nutritional health. A growing body of evidence shows that exercise has positive effects on mental health (Babyak et al., 2000; Kvam, Kleppe, Nordhus, & Hovland, 2016; Wegner et al., 2014). Specifically, athletic participation has been shown to increase self-esteem (Spence, McGannon, & Poon, 2005). Also, achievement in sport provides an avenue to improve body image. Large, muscular athletes often struggle with negative body image when comparing themselves to underweight models in the media, yet their size and muscularity can help them perform well in sport. When Shaquille O'Neal learned his body mass index of 31.6 labeled him as obese, he was quoted as saying, "I've read that same formula, but as an athlete, I'm classified as phenomenal" (as cited in Associated Press, 2005). Finally, many athletes seek nutritional information and make subsequent dietary changes to fuel their bodies for performance. Student-athletes may have access to more nutritional resources (e.g., sport dietitians, athletic trainers, and team physicians) than nonathletes.

## Complicating Sport Factors

In addition to risk and protective factors, sport-related factors that affect eating disorder risk include contextual body image, varying nutritional needs, exercise balance, and retirement from sport.

**Context.** Student-athletes face competing body image demands from the popular culture and sport environment. For female student-athletes, the media emphasizes a thin build, whereas athletics tends to reward a muscular build, and female athletes may fear that weight training will make them too bulky to be accepted in daily life outside of athletics. Dutch researchers named this phenomenon "contextual body image," finding that student-athletes have two body images in the contexts of sport and daily life. The struggle to maintain a positive body image in both sport and daily life can contribute to eating disorder risk (Bruin, Oudejans, Bakker, & Woertman, 2011).

Male student-athletes experience unique body image pressures, in which many men wish to gain muscularity (McCreary & Sasse, 2000; Pope et al., 2000), although some men focus more on leanness. These pressures put men at risk for unbalanced exercise, steroid and supplement use, and body dissatisfaction.

**Caloric needs.** It is difficult to recognize binge-eating in an athletic population with such high caloric needs. The *Diagnostic and Statistical Manual of Mental Disorders* (*DSM–5*) defines binge-eating as consuming a significantly larger amount of food than most would consume in one sitting, combined with a sense of lack of control (American Psychiatric Association, 2013). Some student-athletes need to consume over 5,000 calories per day, but, if the consumption feels under their control (e.g., that they can easily stop), they are not binge eating.

**Exercise balance.** It is also difficult to recognize unbalanced exercise in a population that views twice-a-day practices or three-hour workouts as the norm, but student-athletes may be more at risk for the purging behavior of compulsive or unbalanced exercise. Exercising in addition to scheduled practices is one indication of unbalanced exercise. For example, a lacrosse player may exercise for two hours at the student recreation center in the morning, and then attend her two-hour team practice in the afternoon. Not surprisingly, her teammates and coaches might reward such "dedication" without realizing the additional exercise could be an eating disorder symptom (Powers & Thompson, 2008).

One reason athletes are more at risk for unbalanced exercise is that we applaud athletes who run the extra mile—believing the further effort is a sign of grit rather than an eating disorder symptom. If a student-athlete runs through leg pain, fails to take a day off, or secretly pumps out endless push-ups and sit-ups before bed, then she has lost control over her exercise (Stenseng, Haugen, Torstveit, & Høigaard, 2014). Powers and Thompson (2008) recommended assessing functional impairment and the quality of exercise to identify unbalanced exercise. For example, has exercise interfered with daily activities like school, work, or relationships? If motivations for exercise include punishment, gaining permission to eat, and/or burning calories, an eating disorder mindset may be present. More balanced motivations include health maintenance, training for a sport, stress reduction, fun, and mind-body connection.

**Retirement from sport.** Student-athletes accustomed to eating large quantities may struggle with nutrition upon retirement. Athletes from weight-cycling sports (e.g., wrestling) experience increased risk of obesity after sport (Nieman, 2007). Retirement may also affect body image. To address continued body dissatisfaction after sport, counselors can educate student-athletes about expected body changes occurring with reduced training loads, and encourage expanding identity beyond athletics (Papathomas, Petrie, & Plateau, 2018).

## Prevention and Policy

With the multitude of mental health issues facing college student-athletes, how can athletic departments prevent eating disorders? How do athletic organizations help student-athletes who are afraid that admitting a problem will interfere with their sport participation? How can large athletic departments facilitate communication among the multiple units involved in helping student-athletes? One potential answer to these questions is a sound policy regarding disordered eating for the athletic department. Key aspects of an eating disorder policy include sections on prevention/education, identification of eating disorders, intervention approaches, weight/body composition goals, treatment, and return-to-play (The Department of Athletics, 2010).

### Prevention

Thompson and Sherman (2010) outlined several guidelines for preventing eating disorders in athletes. They recommended that athletic department staff emphasize health and performance (e.g., being strong and fit) instead of weight and avoiding comments about weight and appearance. Thompson and Sherman (2010) also encouraged athletic organizations to offer nutritional education, eliminate group weigh-ins, treat athletes individually, and monitor attempts by athletes to modify their weight.

Coaches can have a large impact on preventing eating disorders when they send clear messages about healthy body image and behaviors (Sherman & Thompson, 2008). Counselors can encourage coaches to emphasize function instead of form regarding athletes' bodies. For example, if an athlete complains that her thighs are too big, coaches can tell her, "your strong legs allow you to stay balanced and solid on defense." If an athlete complains that his chest is not big enough, coaches might say, "you demonstrate a lot of speed and flexibility in your position." Helping professionals should encourage coaches to emphasize the athlete rather than the athlete's body (providing feedback such as "you need to work harder" and "I love the way you encourage your teammates"). Coaches should be clear about the acceptability of weight-management strategies (e.g., "It is not healthy to fast. Fasting will lead to binge-eating, and both behaviors will harm your performance and health.").

Prevention efforts work best when they are more interactive than didactic, targeting at-risk populations (Bar, Cassin, & Dionne, 2015). Voelker and Petrie (2017) created one such evidence-based program, Bodies in Motion, to support positive body image in female college student-athletes. Bodies in Motion combines the applied concepts of cognitive dissonance and mindful self-compassion. In a study of the program's effectiveness, the intervention group reported significantly lower internalization of the thin ideal and fewer body shape concerns, as well as greater body appreciation, confidence, happiness, pride, self-compassion, and mindfulness than did the wait-list control group.

## Weight/Body Composition Goals

Because sport culture often emphasizes winning at all costs and views weight/body composition changes as essential for winning, athletes and coaches may set unrealistic weight and body composition goals. Eating disorder policies can discourage coaches from setting arbitrary goals for their athletes, particularly group goals for individuals with varying needs and risk factors. It is not uncommon for coaches to have their own body image and nutrition struggles, and it is rare for them to have sound nutritional, medical, and psychological training. Therefore, the medical staff should be responsible for consulting with athletes about weight changes—not the coaches. Manore and Thompson (2000) mentioned the following factors to consider in defining an ideal body weight or composition: one that is individualized, relatively easily maintained, and associated with optimal health, nutrition, and performance.

## Identification

Policies often include *DSM–5* criteria for eating disorders as well as common signs in athletes. It is a challenge for coaches to identify eating problems, especially if they lack awareness or feel partly to blame. The illogical nature of eating disorders makes it difficult for teammates and parents to approach and help student-athletes (Thompson, 2014).

## Approaching a Student-Athlete

Teammates, family, and coaches are often bewildered about how to help student-athletes suffering from eating disorders. Thompson and Sherman (2010) recommended that we consider the eating disorder as an injury that requires evaluation and treatment before continuing on with sport participation. The first step involves a gentle, private discussion: "I'm concerned that you skip team meals and look wiped out. I want you to meet with the [counselor, dietitian, and/or physician] to assess what's going on. I'll check back with you in a week to see if you've made the appointment(s)." There may be reactions of denial or even hostility.

## Return to Play

The treatment team typically consists of counselor, dietitian, athletic trainer, and team physician. Because of the protective factors presented by sports, continued athletic participation can help student-athletes recover from eating disorders. However, if health becomes endangered, team physicians may need to withhold athletic participation. It is important to be specific, in writing, about expectations and guidelines for return to play.

## Assessment and Treatment

Athletic culture discourages vulnerability and help-seeking behavior, making accurate assessment a challenge (Reardon, 2017). Eating disorder specialists know which questions to ask to avoid colluding with potential denial. In addition to a thorough mental health assessment, including anxiety disorders that commonly co-occur (Kaye, Bulik, Thornton, Barbarich, & Masters, 2004), helping professionals should assess height and weight, food intake over the past 24 hours, restricting (including food rules, avoidance of food, fasting), overeating, binge eating and purging (frequency and severity), physical health, and thinking/feeling about food, weight, and shape (Fairburn, Cooper, & O'Connor, 2008).

Because eating disorders have multiple causes, treatment needs to be multidisciplinary, involving counselors, dietitians, and medical staff. Compulsive behaviors such as restricting, binge eating, and purging often serve a purpose: to avoid or numb negative emotion. Therefore, counseling teaches athletes more effective coping skills so that they no longer need eating disorder behaviors. Early treatment encourages student-athletes to follow the meal plan they create with the dietitian. Athletes benefit from support to face the anxiety created by proper nutrition. Once the brain becomes more nourished, counselors teach coping skills like cognitive reconstruction, mindfulness, and emotion regulation.

Several treatments have shown effectiveness in the general population, including cognitive-behavioral therapy (Mitchell, Agras, & Wonderlich, 2007), dialectical-behavioral therapy (DBT; Linehan, 2015), family-based therapy (Wilson, Grilo, & Vitousek, 2007), and interpersonal therapy (Fairburn, 2005). These empirically validated treatments can also be effective for student-athletes when delivered by counselors with training in sport science. According to an expert in the area of treating athletes with eating disorders, "treatment professionals working with student-athletes need experience and expertise in treating eating disorders and athletes, but more importantly need to understand and appreciate the importance of sport in the life of a serious student-athlete" (Thompson, 2014). To suggest right away that athletes need to quit their sport to heal from their eating disorder may result in a loss of credibility for the mental health professional.

## Perfectionism

Perfectionism is a personality trait that overlaps between high-achieving athletes and those at risk for eating disorders. Many student-athletes in either of these categories (or both) believe that relaxing their impossibly high standards will make them soft and lazy, but the opposite is true. Setting more realistic goals and encouraging oneself often improves performance. Brown (2010) distinguished healthy striving from perfectionism. Healthy striving—what student-athletes engage in daily—is internally focused and about being the best one can be. Perfectionism, on the other hand, is worry about what others will think. To challenge perfectionism in athletes, interpersonal therapy can be helpful. An interpersonal approach might involve examining where the critical perfectionism originated in the family, comparing the past versus current usefulness of perfectionism, and practicing new ways of relating.

Student-athletes learn how to cope with success and failure through the ups and downs of athletic competition. However, perfectionistic athletes often feel crushed following an athletic defeat. It can be difficult to motivate individuals with eating disorders in treatment, and one early goal for student-athletes might be learning how to bounce back from failure more quickly as a means of improving athletic performance. Student-athletes who feel frightened about giving up their eating disorders may buy into this treatment focus more easily because of the intense emotional pain they feel when falling short of their goals.

## Other Treatments

More recent treatments include incorporating neurobiology and mindfulness skills. If a student-athlete's low weight causes injuries, why does she not just eat more? Neurobiological research shows promise for explaining vexing eating disorder symptoms. Kaye, Fudge, and Paulus (2009) reported that individuals with anorexia nervosa have higher levels of serotonin receptor activity that cause them to feel agitated. Because the body synthesizes serotonin from food, when individuals with anorexia nervosa restrict their food intake, their brain serotonin activity decreases, and they feel a sense of calm. However, their bodies obviously do not function well without food. When they try to eat, serotonin receptor activity again skyrockets, leading to distress. There are other neurobiological abnormalities in anorexia nervosa like impaired insula functioning that makes it difficult for individuals to know when they are hungry or full (Hill, 2012).

A cornerstone of dialectical-behavioral therapy, mindfulness is an increasingly popular intervention in sport psychology (Baltzell, Caraballo, Chipman, & Hayden, 2014; Gardner & Moore, 2012; Kaufman, Glass, & Pineau, 2018). Not only do mindfulness skills show promise for improving sport performance, but also for decreasing eating disorder symptoms. Binge eating is mindless eating, and teaching student-athletes to eat mindfully without the distractions of TV or computer can prevent binges. Mindful eating involves awareness of the five senses (Albers, 2012)—for example, savoring a brownie by smelling the chocolate, tasting the sweetness, and slowly chewing each bite. Mindful meditation is also helpful for managing elevated anxiety common in eating disorders (Wehrenberg & Prinz, 2007).

Improving self-compassion skills by learning to talk to ourselves as we would to a friend is a promising direction in treatment (Neff, 2015). One mindfulness skill from dialectical-behavioral therapy that relates to self-compassion is the nonjudgmental skill—noticing facts instead of evaluating. Athletes can practice nonjudgment by noting facts about the situation. If they judge themselves by thinking, "I'm fat," they can list facts such as, "I'm uncomfortable in my body"; "I'm wearing the same clothing size today as yesterday"; and "Muscle weighs more than fat."

What about pharmacotherapy? Antidepressants such as Selective Serotonin Re-uptake Inhibitors (SSRIs) have been used at higher doses with some effectiveness to treat binge eating and purging (Mitchell et al., 2007). Student-athletes are often wary of taking medications for fear of decreased athletic performance, but one study found no such effects for SSRI medications (Parise, Bosman, Boecker, Barry, & Tarnopolsky, 2001). Atypical antipsychotic medications also have been found to be effective in assisting in keeping anxiety and obsessive thoughts at manageable levels during the re-feeding process (Kaye et al., 2003). The best medication for eating disorders, however, is food.

## Conclusion

It is important for helping professionals who work in intercollegiate athletics to be well versed in the identification, prevention, assessment, and treatment of eating disorders in athletes. These disorders can be frightening and confusing, but recovery offers student-athletes the opportunity for awesome healthy striving.

Effectively addressing eating disorders among athletes includes appreciating the unique aspects of the sports culture, including demands for leanness and muscularity, and the importance of educating teammates and coaches. Athletic organizations can benefit from implementing policies outlining identification, treatment, and return-to-play issues. Although it is unrealistic to expect a quick resolution of disordered behaviors, especially if they have endured for years, it is encouraging and rewarding to assist student-athletes in recovery from eating disorders.

## Discussion Questions

1. How does Emily's case study demonstrate the co-occurrence of other mental health disorders with eating disorders?

2. Discuss the importance of the multidisciplinary team approach in treating eating disorders in student-athletes.

3. What are three nutrition or health myths that may increase eating disorder risk in athletics, and how would you challenge these myths?

## References

Albers, S. (2012). *Eating mindfully: How to end mindless eating and enjoy a balanced relationship with food.* Oakland, CA: New Harbinger Publications.

American Psychiatric Association. (2013). *Diagnostic and statistical manual for mental disorders* (5th ed.). Washington, DC: Author.

Associated Press. (2005, March 8). Athlete study exposes flaw of BMI obesity measure. *Fox News.* Retrieved from http://foxnews.com/story/2005/03/08/athlete-study-exposes-flaw-bmi-obesity-measure.html

Babyak, M., Blumenthal, J. A., Herman, S., Khatri, P., Doraiswamy, M., Moore, K., Craighead, W. E., Baldewicz, T. T., & Krishnan, K. R. (2000). Exercise treatment for major depression: Maintenance of therapeutic benefit at 10 months. *Psychosomatic Medicine, 62*(5), 633–638.

Baltzell, A., Caraballo, N., Chipman, K., & Hayden, L. (2014). A qualitative study of the mindfulness meditation training for sport: Division I female soccer players' experience. *Journal of Clinical Sport Psychology, 8*(3), 221–244. doi:10.1123/jcsp.2014-0030

Bar, R. J., Cassin, S. E., & Dionne, M. M. (2015). Eating disorder prevention initiatives for athletes: A review. *European Journal of Sport Science, 16*(3), 325–335. doi:10.1080/1 7461391.2015.1013995

Beals, K. A., & Manore, M. M. (2002). Disorders of the female athlete triad among collegiate student-athletes. *International Journal of Sport Nutrition and Exercise Metabolism, 12,* 281–293.

Brewer, B. W. (2017). Psychological responses to sport injury. In B. W. Brewer & C. J. Redmond (Eds.), *Psychology of Sport Injury*. Champaign, IL: Human Kinetics, 59–77. doi:10.1002/9781118270011

Brown, B. (2010). *The gifts of imperfection: Let go of who you think you're supposed to be and embrace who you are.* Center City, MN: Hazelden.

Bruin, A. P., Oudejans, R. R., Bakker, F. C., & Woertman, L. (2011). Contextual body image and athletes disordered eating: The contribution of athletic body image to disordered eating in high performance women athletes. *European Eating Disorders Review, 19*(3), 201–215. doi:10.1002/erv.1112

Carter, J. E., & Rudd, N. A. (2005). Disordered eating assessment in college student-athletes. *Women in Sport & Physical Activity Journal, 14,* 62–71.

Cooper, H., & Winter, S. (2017). Exploring the conceptualization and persistence of disordered eating in swimmers. *Journal of Clinical Sport Psychology, 11,* 222–239. https:// doi.org/10.1123/jcsp.2016-0038

Covassin, T., Elbin, R. J., Beidler, E., Lafevor, M., & Kontos, A. P. (2017). A review of psychological issues that may be associated with a sport-related concussion in youth and collegiate athletes. *Sport, Exercise & Performance Psychology, 6*(3), 220–229. doi:10.1037/spy0000105

The Department of Athletics at The Ohio State University. (2010). *Department of Athletics Policies.* Retreieved from http://grfx.cstv.com/photos/schools/osu/genrel/auto_pdf/ 2010-11/misc_non_event/sa-handbook5.pdf

Drinkwater, B., Loucks, A., Sherman, R., Sundgot-Borgen, J., & Thompson, R. (2005). IOC Consensus Statement on the Female Athlete Triad. *The International Olymic Committee.* http://www.olympic.org/Documents/Reports/EN/en_report_917.pdf

Fairburn, C. G. (2005). Interpersonal psychotherapy for eating disorders. In C. G. Fairburn & K. D. Brownell (Eds.), *Eating disorders and obesity* (pp. 320–324). New York: The Guilford Press.

Fairburn, C. G., Cooper, Z., & O'Connor, M. (2008). Eating disorder examination (Edition 16.0D). In C. G. Fairburn (Ed.), *Cognitive behavior therapy and eating disorders* (pp. 265–308). New York: The Guilford Press.

Fulkerson, J. A., Keel, P. K., Leon, G. R., & Dorr, T. (1999). Eating-disordered behaviors and personality characteristics of high school athletes and nonathletes. *International Journal of Eating Disorders, 26*(1), 73–79. doi:10.1002/ (sici)1098-108x(199907)26:1<73::aid-eat9>3.0.co;2-f

Galli, N., Petrie, T. A., Greenleaf, C., Reel, J. J., & Carter, J. E. (2014). Personality and psychological correlates of eating disorder symptoms among male collegiate athletes. *Eating Behaviors, 15*(4), 615–618. doi:10.1016/j.eatbeh.2014.08.007

Galli, N., Petrie, T., Reel, J. J., Greenleaf, C., & Carter, J. E. (2015). Psychosocial predictors of drive for muscularity in male collegiate athletes. *Body Image, 14*, 62–66. doi:10.1016/j.bodyim.2015.03.009

Gardner, F. L., & Moore, Z. E. (2012). Mindfulness and acceptance models in sport psychology: A decade of basic and applied scientific advancements. *Canadian Psychology, 53*(4), 309–318. doi:10.1037/a0030220

Greenleaf, C., Petrie, T. A., Carter, J., & Reel, J. J. (2009). Female collegiate athletes: Prevalence of eating disorders and disordered eating behaviors. *Journal of American College Health, 57*(5), 489–496. doi:10.3200/JACH.57.5.489-496

Hausenblas, H., & Carron, A. (1999). Eating disorder indices and athletes: An integration. *Journal of Sport and Exercise Psychology, 21*, 230–258.

Hausenblas, H., & Downs, D. (2001). Comparison of body image between athletes and non-athletes: A meta-analytic review. *Journal of Applied Sport Psychology, 13*(3), 323–339.

Hill, L. (2012). ED in the head. In S. Atlan (Ed.), *Family Eating Disorders Manual* (pp. 47–80). Worthington, OH: The Center for Balanced Living.

Johnson, C., Powers, P. S., & Dick, R. (1999). Athletes and eating disorders: The National Collegiate Athletic Association study. *International Journal of Eating Disorders, 26*, 179–188.

Johnston, A. (2010). *Eating in the light of the moon.* Carlsbad, CA: Gurze.

Kaufman, K. A., Glass, C. R., & Pineau, T. R. (2018). *Mindful Sport Performance Enhancement.* Washington, DC: American Psychological Association.

Kaye, W. H., Barbarich, N. C., Putnam, K., Gendall, K. A., Fernstrom, J., Fernstrom, M., McConaha, C .W., & Kishore, A. (2003). Anxiolytic effects of acute tryptophan depletion in Anorexia Nervosa. *International Journal of Eating Disorders, 33*, 257–267.

Kaye, W., Bulik, C., Thornton, L., Barbarich, N., & Masters, K. (2004). Comorbidities of anxiety disorders with anorexia nervosa and bulimia nervosa. *American Journal of Psychiatry, 161*, 2215–2221.

Kaye, W., Fudge, J. L., & Paulus, M. (2009). New insights into symptoms and neurocircuit function of anorexia nervosa. *Nature Reviews Neuroscience, 10*, 573–584.

Kvam, S., Kleppe, C. L., Nordhus, I. H., & Hovland, A. (2016). Exercise as a treatment for depression: A meta-analysis. *Journal of Affective Disorders, 202*, 67–86. doi:10.1016/j.jad.2016.03.063

Linehan, M. (2015). *DBT skills training handouts and worksheets.* New York: Guilford.

Manore, M., & Thompson, J. (2000). *Sport nutrition for health and performance.* Champaign, IL: Human Kinetics.

McCreary, D. R., & Sasse, D. K. (2000). An exploration of the drive for muscularity in adolescent boys and girls. *Journal of American College Health, 48*, 297–304.

Mihalopoulos, N. L., Auinger, P., & Klein, J. D. (2008). The freshman 15: Is it real? *Journal of American College Health, 56*(5), 531–534. doi:10.3200/jach.56.5.531-534

Mitchell, J. E., Agras, S., & Wonderlich, S. (2007). Treatment of bulimia nervosa: Where are we and where are we going? *International Journal of Eating Disorders, 40*, 95–101.

Mountjoy, M., Sundgot-Borgen, J., Burke, L., Carter, S., Constantini, N., Lebrun, C., & Lungqvist, A. (2014). The IOC consensus statement: Beyond the female athlete triad—Relative energy deficiency in sport (RED-S). *British Journal of Sports Medicine, 48*, 491–497. doi:10.1136/bjsports-2014-093502

National Collegiate Athletic Association. (2014). *Mind, body, and sport: Understanding and supporting student-athlete mental wellness.* Indianapolis, IN: Author.

Neff, K. (2015). *Self-compassion: the proven power of being kind to yourself.* New York, NY: William Morrow.

Nieman, D. (2007). Weight cycling of athletes and subsequent weight gain in middleage. *Yearbook of Sports Medicine, 2007*, 227–229. doi:10.1016/s0162-0908(08)70183-1

Papathomas, A., Petrie, T. A., & Plateau, C. R. (2018). Changes in body image perceptions upon leaving elite sport: The retired female athlete paradox. *Sport, Exercise, and Performance Psychology, 7*(1), 30–45. doi:10.1037/spy0000111

Parise, G., Bosman, M. J., Boecker, D. R., Barry, M. J., & Tarnopolsky, M. A. (2001). Selective serotonin reuptake inhibitors: Their effect on high-intensity exercise performance. *Archives of Physical Medicine and Rehabilitation, 82*(7), 867–871. doi:10.1053/apmr.2001.23275

Petrie, T., Greenleaf, C., Reel, J., & Carter, J. E. (2007). Psychosocial correlates of disordered eating among male collegiate athletes. *Journal of Clinical Sport Psychology, 1*, 340–357.

Petrie, T., Greenleaf, C., Reel, J., & Carter, J. E. (2009). An examination of psychosocial correlates of disordered eating among female collegiate athletes. *Research Quarterly for Exercise & Sport, 80*(3), 621–632. doi:10.5641/027013609x13088500159886

Pope, H. G., Phillips, K. A., & Olivardia, R. (2000). *The Adonis complex: The secret crisis of male body obsession.* New York: The Free Press.

Powers, P., & Thompson, R. A. (2008). *The exercise balance.* Carlsbad, CA: Gurze.

Reardon, C. L. (2017). Psychiatric comorbidities in sports. *Neurologic Clinics, 35*(3), 537–548.

Reinking, M. F., & Alexander, L. E. (2005). Prevalence of disordered-eating behaviors in undergraduate female collegiate athletes and nonathletes. *Journal of Athletic Training, 40*(1), 47–51.

Rice, S. M., Purcell, R., De Silva, S., Mawren, D., McGorry, P. D., & Parker, A. G. (2016). The mental health of elite athletes: A narrative systematic review. *Sports Medicine, 46*, 1333–1353. doi: 10.1007/s40279-016-0492-2

Roberts, C. M., Faull, A. L., & Tod, D. (2016). Blurred lines: Performance enhancement, common mental disorders and referral in the U.K. athletic population. *Frontiers in Psychology, 7*, 1067. doi: 10.3389/fpsyg.2016.01067

Sanford-Martens, T., Davidson, M., Yakushko, O., Martens, M., Hinton, P., & Beck, N. (2005). Clinical and subclinical eating disorders: An examination of female athletes. *Journal of Applied Sport Psychology, 17*(1), 79–86.

Sherman, R. T., & Thompson, R. A. (2008). Managing the female athlete triad. *NCAA Coaches Handbook.* Retrieved from www.ncaa.org

Smolak, L., Murnen, S. K., & Ruble, A. E. (2000). Female athletes and eating problems: A meta-analysis. *International Journal of Eating Disorders, 27*, 371–380.

Spence, J. C., McGannon, K. R., & Poon, P. (2005). The effect of exercise on global self-esteem. *Journal of Sport & Exercise Psychology, 27*(3), 311–334.

Stenseng, F., Haugen, T., Torstveit, M. K., & Høigaard, R. (2015). When it's "All About the Bike"—Intrapersonal conflict in light of passion for cycling and exercise dependence. *Sport, Exercise, and Performance Psychology, 4*(2), 127–139. doi:10.1037/spy0000028

Striegel-Moore, R. H., Rosselli, F., Perrin, N., Debar, L., Wilson, G. T., May, A., & Kraemer, H. C. (2009). Gender difference in the prevalence of eating disorder symptoms. *International Journal of Eating Disorders, 42*(5), 471–474. doi:10.1002/eat.20625

Sundgot-Bergen, J., & Torstveit, M. K. (2004). Prevalence of eating disorders in elite athletes is higher than in the general population. *Clinical Journal of Sports Medicine, 14*(1), 25–32.

Thomas, D. M., & Heymsfield, S. B. (2016). Exercise: Is more always better? *Current Biology, 26*, R102–R124. http://dx.doi.org/10.1016/j.cub.2015.12.031

Thompson, R. (2014). Eating disorders. In *Mind, body, and sport: Understanding and supporting student-athlete mental wellness*. Indianapolis, IN: National Collegiate Athletic Association, 25–28.

Thompson, R. A., & Sherman, R. (2010). *Eating disorders in sport*. New York: Routledge.

Thompson, R. A., & Sherman, R. (2014). Reflections on athletes and eating disorders. *Psychology of Sport and Exercise, 15*, 729–734. doi:10.1016/j.psychsport.2014.06.005

Turocy, P. S., DePalma, B. F., Horswill, C. A., Laquale, K. M., Martin, T. J., Perry, A. C., & Utter, A. C. (2011). NATA position statement: Safe weight loss and maintenance practices in sport and exercise. *Journal of Athletic Training, 46*(3), 322–336.

Voelker, D. K., & Petrie, T. A. (2017). Bodies in motion: An evaluation of a program to support positive body image in female collegiate athletes. *NCAA Innovations in Research and Practice Grant Program*. Retrieved from http://www.ncaa.org/sites/default/files/2017RES_NCAAGrant-FinalReportExtension-VoelkerPetrie-FINAL_20171106.pdf

Wang, F., & Veugelers, P. J. (2008). Self-esteem and cognitive development in the era of the childhood obesity epidemic. *Obesity Reviews, 9*, 615–623. doi:10.1111/j.1467-789X.2008.00507.x

Wegner, M., Helmich, I., Machado, S., Nardi, A. E., Arias-Carrion, O., & Budde, H. (2014). Effects of exercise on anxiety and depression disorders: Review of meta-analyses and neurobiological mechanisms. *CNS & Neurobiological Disorders, 13*, 1002–1014.

Wehrenberg, M., & Prinz, S. (2007). *The anxious brain: The neurobiological basis of anxiety disorders and how to effectively treat them*. New York: W. W. Norton & Co.

Wilson, G. T., Grilo, C. M., & Vitousek, K. M. (2007). Psychological treatment of eating disorders. *American Psychologist, 62*(3), 199–216.

Wollenberg, G., Shriver, L.H., & Gates, G. E. (2015). Comparison of disordered eating symptoms and emotion regulation difficulties between female college athletes and non-athletes. *Eating Behaviors, 18*, 1–6.

# 6

# Clinical Depression and College Student-Athletes

*Sam Maniar and John P. Sullivan*

## CASE STUDY: MARTIN

Martin is a 21-year-old junior student-athlete at Eastern State University, a Division II powerhouse in men's soccer. Martin began playing soccer at the age of seven and was the captain of his high school team. Soccer had always been a source of pleasure for Martin, and he was thrilled to be recruited to play at Eastern State. At the end of last season, Martin saw considerable playing time and was considered to be a lock to crack the starting line-up this year. During the off-season, Martin maintained a strict training regimen and spent extra time watching game film in an effort to begin the new season at the top of his game.

During preseason, Martin noticed that he was sharing the scrimmage time in the starting rotation with Paul, a first-year team member. He told himself that the competition would make him a better player, but he couldn't help wondering if maybe all of his hard work might not pay off after all. As the season began, Martin found himself feeling increasingly down, not just during soccer practice, but during other times of the day also. He noticed having trouble concentrating, and his grades began to suffer as a result. It seemed that the harder he tried to "snap out of it," the darker his moods became. He sometimes snapped at Page, his girlfriend, for no apparent reason and began to make excuses to avoid social situations. Although he felt tired most of the time, Martin was only sleeping about 4-5 hours per night, often-times waking up at 2:30 a.m. and lying in bed tossing and turning until his alarm went off at 6 a.m. for morning practice.

This was not the first time that Martin had experienced an episode like this. Once before, during his senior year in high school, Martin went through a period of six weeks feeling similarly down. That time hadn't been as bad as this time around, and he had been able to feel better on his own without any sort of intervention.

A few games into the season, Martin's performance on the field was miserable. It became clear that not only would he lose his starting spot, but he would see limited playing time. His poor performance had not gone unnoticed by his coach who pulled him from a game and at practice the next day asked Martin what had gotten into him. Martin was at a loss for words, but inside he was feeling empty and hopeless. That night in his dorm room Martin found himself thinking about death and wondered if maybe that would be the only way to end his pain. When he started to think about ways to kill himself, Martin became frightened but was worried that if he told someone, he would lose the little playing time he was getting.

The next day, Martin missed treatment for his ankle with his athletic trainer, Bill. Bill pulled Martin aside and expressed concern for him. He shared some behavioral observations and suggested Martin meet with Dr. Eckert, the psychologist used by the athletic department.

Martin stated that he was fine, but Bill was persistent—again sharing the changes in behavior he had observed. He also shared some anonymous stories about how Dr. Eckert had helped other student-athletes improve their mood and their athletic performance. He also shared that Dr. Eckert was not permitted to tell anyone about their sessions, so Martin did not have to worry about the coach taking playing time away. Bill even offered to schedule the appointment for Martin and accompany him to the first session.

After overcoming the initial awkwardness of sharing his thoughts and feelings with Dr. Eckert, Martin was surprised by how relieved he felt to talk about his dark thoughts and his worries of never feeling better. Together, Dr. Eckert and Martin labeled Martin's experience as depression and devised a plan that included improved self-care, regular counseling sessions, and an evaluation by a psychiatrist to consider whether anti-depressant would be helpful.

> With Bill's help, Martin eventually shared his diagnosis of depression with his coach and was surprised at the coach's reassurance that his spot on the team was not in jeopardy. Dr. Eckert taught Martin how to recognize self-defeating thoughts and how to treat himself with self-compassion.

The case above is relatively common example of how depression, and the reluctance to seek help, can be manifested among student-athletes. If depression is gone untreated or unnoticed, it can lead to serious impairment and even suicide. Unfortunately, it seems as though student-athlete suicides are becoming too common in the world of sports, such as with Kyle Ambrogi (see Drehs, 2006a, 2006b), Madison Holleran (see Fagan, 2017), and Tyler Hilinski (see Hille, 2018). Our society is becoming more aware that student-athletes, even those who are highly successful, are not immune to depression. Moreover, student-athletes may not exhibit some of the telltale signs of depression that nonathletes might. For these reasons, depression is a key area to address for providers who care for this population.

Depression is a bio-psycho-social-spiritual condition characterized primarily by the core symptoms of sadness and/or irritability. At any given time, approximately 6–13% of college students suffer from depressive conditions, depending upon school setting, race, gender, income, and other factors. White students are more likely to be diagnosed with depression than Black students, and women are diagnosed with depression at approximately twice the rate of men (Jonas, Brody, Roper, & Narrow, 2003; Riolo, Nguyen, Greden, & King, 2005; Williams et al., 2007). Specific to college athletes, a recent examination of American College Health Association (ACHA) surveys indicated 21% of male student-athletes and 28% of female student-athletes reported feeling depressed over the prior 12 months (National Collegiate Athletic Association [NCAA], 2014).

Understanding the prevalence of health or disease is complicated, which often leads to errors in understanding true population trends and influences. The incidence of mental illness has been underestimated within both the total population and the sporting realm (e.g., athletes, coaches, and support personnel). A recent examination of population trends has revealed that 80% of people will develop a diagnosable mental health disorder at some point in their lives (Schaefer et al., 2017). Given these findings, one can infer that diagnosable mental health disorders occur at higher rates than previously estimated and suggests that the protective factors of sport may be overestimated. On the basis of current evidence, student-athletes are not immune to mental health disorders and they seem to have a comparable prevalence to the general population. Athletes' risk for mental health disorders further increases when training loads are not dosed properly—when they are overtrained, experience abusive coaching, become injured, approach retirement, experience performance difficulty, are faced with a personal life stressor(s), or are managing a combination of these issues (Beable, Fulcher, Lee, & Hamilton, 2017; Rice et al., 2016; Sherwin, 2017; Uphill, Sly, & Swain, 2016).

Many individuals with depressive diagnoses think about, attempt, or complete suicide (Sommers-Flanagan & Sommers-Flanagan, 2015). A large-scale survey revealed that over 28% of college students with significant depressive symptoms reported having suicidal thoughts within a four-week period (Garlow, Purselle, & Heninger, 2007). Additionally, although males are only half as likely to be diagnosed with a depressive disorder as females, they are about four times more likely to complete suicide (Sommers-Flanagan & Sommers-Flanagan, 2015). Depression and suicide among student-athletes also has received increased attention from the NCAA (NCAA, 2007, 2014) and media (Drehs, 2006a, 2006b; Fagan, 2017; Flanagan, 2014; Hille, 2018). Therefore, the monitoring and treatment of depression among college students, including college student-athletes, is essential (Etzel, Watson, Visek, & Maniar, 2006; Maniar, Chamberlain, & Moore, 2005; NCAA, 2014; Rao & Hong, 2016; Sommers-Flanagan & Sommers-Flanagan, 1995, 2007; Trojian, 2016).

Although most depressive symptoms can be resolved with treatment, the majority of college students with mental health problems apparently do not seek professional help, for a variety of reasons, including stigmatization (Eisenberg, Golberstein, & Gollust, 2007). This is also true for student-athletes, who may resist appearing weak or may be discouraged from seeking help by the values and practices of the athletic culture (Etzel et al., 2006; Maniar, Curry, Sommers-Flanagan, & Walsh, 2001). This chapter provides information about clinical depression and its manifestation among student-athletes. Information is presented about depression screening, assessment, and referral guidelines for professionals who work with student-athletes.

## The Faces of Clinical Depression

The fifth edition of the American Psychiatric Association's *Diagnostic and Statistical Manual of Mental Disorders* (*DSM-5*) lists eight categories of depressive disorders, including (1) disruptive mood regulation disorder, (2) major depressive disorder, (3) persistent depressive disorder (dysthymia), (4) premenstrual dysphoric disorder, (5) substance/medication-induced depressive disorder, (6) depressive disorder due to another medical condition, (7) other unspecified depressive disorder, and (8) unspecified depressive disorder. Disturbances of mood also are found elsewhere in the *DSM-5*. Bipolar disorder is characterized by the presence of both depressive and manic (or hypomanic) episodes. Adjustment disorder with depressed mood is characterized by depressive symptoms that emerge in response to an identifiable stressor. This chapter primarily focuses on three common depression-related diagnostic categories: (1) major depressive disorder, (2) persistent depressive disorder (dysthymia), and (3) adjustment disorder with depressed mood. For the purposes of this chapter, student-athletes are identified as having clinical depression if they meet the diagnostic criteria for any of the above disorders (American Psychiatric Association, 2013).

## Depression Among College Student-Athletes

Relatively little research has been conducted on the incidence of depression among student-athletes, but a recent increase in suicides and suicidality has prompted athletic departments and university administrators to pay considerably more attention to depression in this population (Etzel et al., 2006; Maniar et al., 2005; NCAA, 2006, 2014). Although the findings are inconsistent, research suggests that student-athletes experience depressive symptoms and disorders at similar or higher rates than nonathlete students (Maniar & Carter, 2003; Storch, Storch, Killainy, & Roberti, 2005). By one report, one in four student-athletes have experienced depressive symptoms in the past 12 months (NCAA, 2014). Moreover, as with nonathletes, research indicates that student-athletes underutilize mental health services (Barnard, 2016; Eisenberg et al., 2007; Lopez et al., 2013; Moreland et al., 2017; Pinkerton et al., 1989; Schinke et al., 2017).

Depression is a critical issue to address among student-athletes since it can negatively affect athletic performance, as well as academic performance, injury healing, and overall personal well-being. However, the relationship between sport and depression is confusing and seemingly contradictory at times.

One set of research studies indicates that participation in athletics may decrease the likelihood of depression. For example, numerous studies have shown the salutary effects of exercise on mood (see Tkachuk & Martin, 1999). Originally, Franz and Hamilton (1905) conducted the first known empirical study of the effects of exercise on depression, concluding that exercise "retarded" depression—and their findings have stood the test of time. Additionally, given the high demands associated with intercollegiate sport participation, it seems intuitive that individuals with severe psychopathology might be "weeded out" of athletics by the time they reach college. Morgan (1985) stated, "success in sport is inversely correlated with psychopathology" (p. 71). Consequently, it might be assumed that collegiate student-athletes are at less risk for depression than nonathletes.

However, other research indicates that student-athletes are equally (or more) at-risk for depression compared to their nonathlete peers. Storch et al. (2005)

reported that both male and female student-athletes and nonathletes suffered from similar rates of clinical depression. Moreover, Maniar and Carter (2003) reported that, among college students presenting for counseling services, student-athletes were diagnosed with major depressive disorder equally as often as nonathletes. In fact, it has been suggested that student-athletes may be more at-risk for depression than nonathletes because of the increased demands they face (e.g., practice time, travel, physical stress, and balancing academics with sport).

Overall, as observed by Storch et al. (2005), it is important to "underscore the need for early detection and intervention" of mental health issues among student-athletes (p. 94). The incidence of depression among student-athletes, combined with student-athletes' traditional tendency to under-utilize mental health services, makes them an at-risk population (Barnard, 2016; Eisenberg et al., 2007; Lopez et al., 2013; Moreland et al., 2017; Pinkerton et al., 1989; Schinke et al., 2017).

## Unique Causes and Symptoms of Depression Among Athletes

Modern formulations of clinical depression include biological, psychological, social/cultural, and spiritual components (Corveleyn, Luyten, Blatt, & Lens-Gielis, 2005). From the biological perspective, depression is hypothesized as being influenced by various neurotransmitter deficiencies (e.g., serotonin), genetic abnormalities, hormonal imbalances, general inflammation, and other physiological phenomena (Walsh, 2009). From the psychological perspective, cognitive factors, including persistent negative thoughts about oneself, the world, and the future, are seen as a primary cause of depression (Beck & Alford, 2009). Similarly, social isolation, destructive relationship patterns, unemployment and poverty, and an absence of purpose or meaning in life are viewed as social, cultural, and spiritual contributors to depressive conditions (Walsh, 2009). Overall, it is clear that clinical depression is precipitated and maintained by a wide range of contributing factors (Wittenborn et al., 2016). Additionally, the particular depressive symptoms displayed by individuals are typically related to specific cultural and situational factors. Unique contributing factors and symptom patterns among college student-athletes are summarized below.

## Athletic Culture

Although glorified by some, student-athletes' lives have been described as over-protected (Despres, Brady, and McGowan, 2011), socially depleted and isolated (Bowen & Levin, 2005), and rigidly structured (Despres et al., 2011). Moreover, some student-athletes may internalize negative evaluations or identities of society

(Balague, 1999; Engstrom & Sedlacek, 1991), and others may not have adequate academic preparation to succeed in college (Comeaux & Harrison, 2011). Furthermore, many student-athletes experience stress related to the demands of juggling multiple responsibilities and balancing realistic life expectations with idealistic goals (Smallman, Sowa, & Young, 1991). Finally, although the athletic culture is highly supportive of excellence in performance, it is typically much less supportive when athletes suffer from emotional problems. Former Pittsburgh Steelers Quarterback Terry Bradshaw described the athletic culture's response to clinical depression: "We're supposed to be big, tough guys. 'You have depression? Shoot, that's not depression. That's weakness.' That's how the thinking goes" (Wertheim, 2003, p. 76). These attributes of the athletic culture most likely exacerbate depressive problems among athletes (Schinke et al., 2017).

## Physical Demands

Collegiate student-athletes must function in a demanding environment, comparable to a workplace term called an extreme job. Extreme jobs are characterized by work demands exceeding the typical 40-hour work week along with challenging work flow, responsibilities/demands, and a significant amount of time spent traveling away from one's home environment (Hewlett & Luce, 2006). These demands negatively affect overall well-being and the ability to perform their primary roles as both student and athlete.

In addition, student-athletes' competitive seasons may entail frequent travel, varied sleep environments, time zone changes, and disruptive schedules, all of which lead to sleep difficulties ranging from minor to severe degrees of disturbance. For collegiate athletes, sleep disturbance has been identified as part of a cycle of inadequate recovery, leading to chronic overload of the central nervous system (Fullagar et al., 2015; Gaultney, 2010; Gayles & Hu, 2009; Kulics, Kornspan, & Kretovics, 2015; Mah, Mah, Kezirian, & Dement, 2011; Sargent, Lastella, Halson, & Roach, 2014; Taylor, Vatthauer, Bramoweth, Ruggero, & Roane, 2013).

In addition to sleep disturbance, other physical and psychological demands that may contribute to the development of depression include year-round training, frequent overtraining, disruptions in social connectedness, and chances of injury or physical set-backs. These stressors all negatively impact the functioning of the central nervous system (CNS) and autonomic nervous system (ANS).

## Injury

Athletic injuries may contribute to depressive symptoms in several ways. An injury may be perceived as a threat to one's athletic identity (Brewer, 1994; Brewer,

Van Raalte, & Linder, 1991, 1993; Kolt, 2004; Petitipas & Danish, 1995), and if the threat is not addressed, it may lead to depression. It has been estimated that 5–24% of injured athletes experience clinically significant emotional distress (Brewer & Petrie, 2002), and the most at-risk period may be in the first month following an injury (Appaneal, Levine, Perna, & Roh, 2009; Newcomer, Perna, Maniar, Roh, & Stilger, 1999). Athletes who have the hardest time coping with an injury usually are deeply immersed in their athletic identity to the exclusion of other aspects of the self. This is referred to as a foreclosed identity (Miller, 2003).

In addition, some injury conditions contribute more directly to depression. For example, in a recent study, college athletes with mild traumatic brain injury (i.e., concussion) exhibited a significant increase in depression, confusion, and mood disturbances (Mainwaring et al., 2014). Helping professionals working with concussed student-athletes should be attuned to the possibility of accompanying depressive symptoms.

## Retirement

Similar to injury, athletic retirement can threaten an athlete's identity and contribute to depressive symptoms (Baillie & Danish, 1992; Grove, Lavallee, Gordon, & Harvey, 1998; Lavallee & Andersen, 2000). Many student-athletes report disappointment and confusion about what they will do with their lives at the end of their athletic career (Brewer, Van Raalte, & Linder, 1993). Interestingly, for some the opposite may also be the case. It is likely that some athletes experience stress relief when the pressures of competing end, particularly if they continue to engage in regular physical activity. Wyshak (2001) reported that athletic activity was negatively correlated with self-reported physician-diagnosed depression in a sample of female post-collegiate athletes. Additional research indicates that the athlete's perception of control regarding retirement may impact their adjustment to life after sport (Stambulova et al., 2009; Stambulova, 2016).

Retirement from sport, particularly when accompanied by significant reductions in physical activity, also can impact individuals' neurochemistry due to negative effects on the gut-brain axis. Exercise, when dosed properly, increases both protective and neurological resilience factors related to neurochemistry and neuroplasticity (Watson et al., 2015). These protective factors are related to mood and, more importantly, to neuro-stimulation as a means to both enhance growth and vasodilation within the central nervous system (CNS), enteric nervous system (ENS), and the autonomic nervous system (ANS) (Cryan & Dinan, 2012; Mattson & Wan, 2008; Palma, Collins, Bercik, & Verdu, 2014). Notably, there are few prevention and transition programs in place for collegiate athletes to address the psychobiological changes that are a part of transition or retirement.

## Performance-Related Stress and Coping

Student-athletes report stress related to elite performance expectations (Birky, 2007; Maniar & Carter, 2003). This performance-related stress is a well-known contributor to alcohol abuse, drug abuse, eating disorders, and other destructive behavior patterns (Miller, 2003). As Timothy Neal, former assistant athletics director for sports medicine at Syracuse University stated, "One in every four to five young adults has mental health issues, but what is unique about the student-athlete is they have stressors and expectations of them unlike the other students that could either trigger a psychological concern or exacerbate an existing mental health issue" (Noren, 2014). When athletes are placed in the spotlight and faced with high performance expectations, it is not unusual for them to begin using destructive coping strategies (e.g., excessive alcohol consumption). Chronic use of destructive coping strategies may, in turn, increase depressive symptoms.

## Athlete-Specific Depressive Symptoms

Because of the fight-through-pain and never-show-weakness culture of athletics, some athletes may not be comfortable talking openly about their depressive symptoms (Wertheim, 2003). For similar reasons, athletes may not even be aware of their depressive symptoms until the symptoms become quite severe. Consequently, it is crucial for coaches and professionals who work with student-athletes to be aware of some of the subtle signs of depression. These signs may include, but are not limited to: missed rehabilitation appointments, vague or specific physical complaints, reduced quickness or psychomotor speed, lack of responsiveness to training and performance opportunities, withdrawal from social interactions, increased alcohol or drug use, and repeated expression of dissatisfaction or unhappiness. Although symptoms from the preceding list are not always indicative of clinical depression, awareness of these potential signs is nonetheless important. The importance of early identification cannot be underestimated, yet the nature of sport environments is such that athletes are often encouraged to 'tough it out' and ignore signs of degrading health. It can be said that we live in a somewhat Hollywood-inspired cultural ethos that is focused on false narratives of toughness, grit, and invulnerability. This can disguise student-athletes' emotional struggles, as they may buy into this false way of being (Owusu-Sekyere & Gervis, 2016; Caddick & Ryall, 2012; Credé, Tynan, & Harms, 2016; Stamatis, Robinson, & Morgan, 2017; Sullivan, 2017).

In addition to the documented psychological consequences of adhering to these cultural norms, there are potential physiological consequences of ignoring mental and bodily sensations. Recent research has suggested that the suppression of neurological signaling reduces neuronal resilience within the enteric nervous system

(ENS), also known as the gut-brain axis. This in turn leads to gastrointestinal inflammation, thought to be related to reduced well-being and emotional dysregulation (Clark & Mach, 2016; Daskalakis et al., 2016; Horn, Charney, & Feder, 2016; Sinha, Lacadie, Constable, & Seo, 2016).

Student-athletes are required to perform in two environments—academic and athletic—and the prevailing narrative of required toughness is counterproductive in both realms because it supposes that health and the ability to perform are not connected. The emphasis on toughness over common sense characterizes the human organism in ways that do not stand up to the established norms in neuropsychology, neurophysiology, and neuroscience (Caddick & Ryall, 2012; Crust, 2008; Gerber et al., 2013; Owusu-Sekyere & Gervis, 2016).

Helping professionals need to be aware of the potential consequences of overtraining on student-athletes' psychological health. Prescribing stress or a workload (physical, cognitive, or emotional) beyond athletes' coping capacity may lead to insufficient recovery, and eventually to states of neurophysiologic dysregulation. Teaching athletes to ignore signs and symptoms or their own natural biofeedback/neurofeedback may result in a lack of resiliency or poor choice points rather than the development of healthy coping strategies.

## Assessment of Clinical Depression

The assessment of psychological disorders requires specialized training and supervised experience, ideally by licensed mental health professionals (e.g., psychologists, psychiatrists, social workers, professional counselors, and marriage and family therapists). Many mental health professionals are able to make an accurate diagnosis of depressive disorders via an interview or symptom checklist from the *DSM-5*; however, some clinicians prefer to supplement interviews with formalized assessment measures. Formal assessment measures augment clinicians' observations with objective data. Further, student-athletes may answer assessment items more honestly than clinicians' verbal inquiries (Grayson & Cooper, 2006).

Many assessment measures for depression are self-report (i.e., the client fills out a symptom checklist based on their own recollection of their symptoms), while others are structured-interview templates (with scoring) for the clinician to follow. Examples of widely-used self-report depression instruments are the Beck Depression Inventory-II (BDI-II; Beck, Steer, & Brown, 1996) and the Center for Epidemiological Studies Depression (CES-D) Scale (Radloff, 1977). The Hamilton Depression Rating Scale (Hamilton, 1960) is a commonly used structured interview assessment. It should be noted that a thorough assessment of depression should also include asking questions about suicidality (NCAA, 2006).

## Treatment of Student-Athlete Clients with Depression

Student-athletes with depression and other mental health problems present a particular challenge to coaches, trainers, and athletic programs, yet it is a challenge worth meeting. The following recommendations are offered to help athletic programs and personnel develop a system that is sensitive and responsive to student-athletes with clinical depression.

### Develop Procedures and Systems that Encourage Genuine Self-Disclosure

Athletic programs should develop procedures and systems that encourage self-disclosure—even when such disclosure includes depressive content that might traditionally be viewed as signs of weakness. These procedures could include (1) instituting regular check-ins by specific personnel on how student-athletes are doing off the field, (2) displaying posters articulating messages that help-seeking is a sign of strength, and (3) holding small-group open forums where student-athletes have an opportunity to articulate their concerns to administrators and/or helping professionals. Overall, it is crucial for collegiate athletic programs to fight the stigma that prevent athletes from talking about and seeking help for their mental health concerns.

### Identify Referral Sources in Advance

It is impossible to know in advance when a student-athlete will need mental health services. Consequently, as advocated by the NCAA (2006, 2007, 2014), athletic programs should proactively identify referral sources for athletes struggling with depression. Referral sources may include, but are not limited to: (1) athletic department academic support services; (2) athletic department sports medicine or counseling services; (3) university health and counseling services; (4) counseling or medical services offered through university graduate programs or medical schools; and (5) local community resources.

It is often very difficult to get athletes to follow through on contacting referral sources. To address this issue, it is wise for athletic program staff to establish positive working relationships in advance with university counseling center and/or medical personnel. Ideally, these professionals (or professionals-in-training) will have previous experience working directly with student-athletes. This is important because athletes often view their problems as unique and may devalue assistance from individuals without understanding of the competitive athletic experience. Ideally, the identified helping professionals will have familiarity and working relationships with other members of the sports medicine team.

## *Screen and Monitor for Depressive Symptoms*

Screening and monitoring for depressive symptoms is not necessarily the responsibility of athletic program personnel. Any screening should be conducted by appropriately credentialed mental health professionals affiliated with the athletics department. As recommended by the NCAA Depression Guidelines (2014), one potential time to screen athletes for depression is during pre-participation exams using self-report instruments, such as the PHQ-9 (Kroenke, Spitzer, & Williams, 2001), CES-D Scale (Radloff, 1977), or the BDI-II (Beck et al., 1996). Nevertheless, research reports suggest that the practice of mental health screening for collegiate athletes is infrequent, inconsistent, and highly variable (Kroshus, 2016).

Because athletic personnel may have more contact with athletes than anyone else, it is desirable for all athletic personnel to have general awareness of the signs and symptoms of depression. Specific diagnostic criteria can be found in the *DSM-5* (American Psychiatric Association, 2013), however, in general, helping professionals screening for depression should look for disturbances in sleep, appetite, energy, mood, interest, social engagement, and any mention of suicidal thoughts or plans. In addition, there are also warning signs of depression unique to student-athletes. These include, but are not limited to (1) social withdrawal; (2) recurrent headaches or other body aches and pains; (3) missing classes, practices, or rehabilitation appointments; (4) increased irritability; and (5) increased negativity (e.g., complaints and criticisms).

## *Screen and Monitor for Suicide Warning Signs*

Although suicide is a rare event, it is very important is for athletic personnel to be apprised of two of the most pernicious of all suicide myths: (1) suicidal people do not usually talk about suicide in advance (in fact, they usually do and this is an important warning sign); and (2) one should never ask about suicide because it might plant the idea of suicide into a depressed person's mind (in fact, asking about suicide is the right thing to do).

Recent thinking around suicide risk factors posits that checklists and risk factors are unhelpful in understanding suicidal risk (Sommers-Flanagan, 2018). Even suicidal ideation has been shown to be a poor predictor of suicide (Linehan, 1993). Instead, Sommers-Flanagan (2018) recommends that helpers seek to understand clients within the context of the following eight pre-suicide dimensions: unbearable psychological/emotional distress, problem-solving impairment, agitation or arousal, thwarted belongingness and perceived burdensomeness, hopelessness, suicide desensitization, suicide plan or intent, and lethal means. It is imperative for athletic personnel to be educated about (and consequently, ask about) potential suicide dimensions. When athletic personnel are concerned about moderate to severe depression with or without suicidality, a timely referral to a qualified mental health professional is imperative.

## Treatment of Clinical Depression

Fortunately, depression is amenable to treatment, particularly when appropriately and promptly diagnosed. The preponderance of outcome studies suggest that counseling/psychotherapy aimed at symptom reduction can be highly effective, particularly for mild depression and/or during a first episode. Additionally, supplementing counseling with antidepressant medication has been found to "jumpstart" recovery for some individuals. For this reason, the sports medicine team should ideally include medical professionals with detailed knowledge about prescribing these medications, including dosages, side-effects, and contraindications. Frequent communication between members of the treatment team, including active participation from the student-athlete, is considered best-practice in the treatment of depression.

## Recent Advances in Assessment and Treatment

The introduction of data analytics and player tracking in sport has introduced the possibility for a more ecological, real-time, comprehensive approach to assessments and interventions for student-athletes struggling with depression. Systematic ecological momentary assessment (EMA) and ecological momentary intervention (EMI) are technologies used to track fluctuations in experiences and prompt behavioral responses within the context of daily life. Most commonly delivered via smartphone, EMA and EMI have the potential to provide simple, cost-effective, and user-led treatment for student-athletes. This augmented assessment, prevention, and treatment is a new chapter in the field of psychology/sport psychology in which student-athletes' mental health can be monitored and treated in real-time.

In addition to data regarding student-athletes' mood, recent advances in technology also enable data collection regarding heart rate, heart rate variability, respiration, energy expenditure, and measures of distance travelled and intensity. Used in combination, these data can provide a comprehensive picture of athletes' training load and recovery, both key factors in the neurophysiological aspects of depression. Thus, it is possible for helping professionals to use technology to develop personalized interventions, hopefully resulting in more effective prevention, assessment, and treatment (Doré, Silvers, & Ochsner, 2016).

There are ethical and legal considerations to address before adopting technology-based interventions and they include, but are not limited to the following:

- Is there any chance of harm?

- Has validation research been conducted on the technology itself (e.g., construct, signal, laboratory, and ecological validation)?

- Who will be handling the data?

- How are the data protected?

- Who has the competency to interpret the data?

- How will the data be used? (Halson, Peake, & Sullivan, 2016)

## Conclusion

Organizations like the NCAA have recognized the significance of mental health issues in the lives of student-athletes (NCAA, 2014). The severity and range of presenting concerns of student-athlete clients is extensive, likely reflecting a mental health crisis that exists on campus today (Benton, Robertson, Tseng, Newton, & Benton, 2003; Fagan, 2017; Kadison & DiGeronimo, 2004).

Clinical depression has many faces and is a potentially serious condition that affects college students in general and student-athletes in particular. Although it is a great challenge for athletic programs and personnel to remain vigilant for depressive signs and symptoms in their athletes and to treat them with sensitivity and emotional support, it is crucial for helping professionals to work together to meet this important challenge today and in the years to come.

## Discussion Questions

1. What are some of the barriers that prevented Martin from seeking help sooner? How can mental health professionals working with student-athletes contribute to breaking down those barriers?

2. In what ways were Martin's depression symptoms similar to those of nonathletes? In what ways were they unique?

3. Why is it important for the treatment of depression to involve a multidisciplinary team approach?

## References

American Psychiatric Association. (2013). *Diagnostic and statistical manual of mental disorders* (5th ed.). Arlington, VA: American Psychiatric Association

Appaneal, R. N., Levine, B. R., Perna, F. M., & Roh, J. (2009). Measuring postinjury depression among male and female competitive athletes. *Journal of Sport & Exercise Psychology, 31*, 60–76.

Baillie, P. H. F., & Danish, S. J. (1992). Understanding the career transitions of athletes. *The Sport Psychologist, 6*, 77–98.

Balague, G. (1999). Understanding identity, value, and meaning when working with elite athletes. *The Sport Psychologist, 13*, 89–98.

Barnard, J. D. (2016). Student-athletes' perceptions of mental illness and attitudes toward help-seeking. *Journal of College Student Psychotherapy*, 30, 161–175.

Basso, J. C., & Suzuki, W. A. (2017). The effects of acute exercise on mood, cognition, neurophysiology, and neurochemical pathways: A review. *Brain Plasticity, 2*, 127–152.

Beable, S., Fulcher, M., Hamilton, B., & Chun-Lee, A. (2017). SHARPSports mental health awareness research project: Prevalence and risk factors of depressive symptoms and life stress in elite athletes. *Journal of Science and Medicine in Sport, 20*, 1047–1052.

Beck, A. T., & Alford, B. A. (2009). *Depression: Causes and treatment* (2nd ed.). University of Pennsylvania Press.

Beck, A. T., Steer, R. A., & Brown, G. K. (1996). *Manual for the Beck Depression Inventory II*. San Antonio, TX: The Psychological Corporation.

Benton, S. A., Robertson, J. M., Tseng, W., Newton, F. B., & Benton, S. L. (2003). Changes in counseling center client problems across 13 years. *Professional Psychology: Research and Practice, 34*(1), 66–72.

Birky, I. (2007). Counseling student athletes: Sport psychology as a specialization. In J. A. Lipincott & R. A. Lipincott (Eds.), *Special populations in college counseling: A handbook for mental health professionals* (pp. 21–35). Alexandria, VA: American Counseling Association.

Bowen, W. G., & Levin, S. A. (2005). *Reclaiming the game: College sports and educational values*. Princeton University Press.

Brewer, B. W. (1994). Review and critique of models of psychological adjustment to athletic injury. *Journal of Applied Sport Psychology, 6*, 87–100.

Brewer, B. W., & Petrie, T. A. (2002). Psychopathology in sport and exercise. In J. L. Van Raalte & B. W. Brewer (Eds.), *Exploring sport and exercise psychology* (2nd ed.) (pp. 307–324). Washington, DC: American Psychological Association.

Brewer, B. W., Van Raalte, J. L., & Linder, D. E. (1991). Role of the sport psychologist in treating injured athletes: A survey of sports medicine providers. *Journal of Applied Sport Psychology, 3*, 183–190.

Brewer, B. W., Van Raalte, J. L., & Linder, D. E. (1993). Athletic identity: Hercules' muscles or Achilles' heel. *International Journal of Sport Psychology, 24*, 237–254.

Caddick, N., & Ryall, E. (2012). The social construction of 'mental toughness'–A fascistoid ideology?. *Journal of the Philosophy of Sport, 39*(1), 137–154.

Clark, A., & Mach, N. (2016). Exercise-induced stress behavior, gut-microbiota-brain axis and diet: a systematic review for athletes. *Journal of the International Society of Sports Nutrition, 1* (13), 1–21.

Comeaux, E., & Harrison, K. C. (2011). A conceptual model of academic success for student-athletes. *Educational Researcher, 40,* 235–245.

Corveleyn, J., Luyten, P., Blatt, S. J., & Lens-Gielis, H. (2005). *Theory and treatment of depression: Towards a dynamic interactionism model.* New York: Lawrence Erlbaum.

Credé, M., Tynan, M. C., & Harms, P. D. (2017). Much ado about grit: A meta-analytic synthesis of the grit literature. *Journal of Personality and Social Psychology, 1*(13), 1–21.

Crust, L. (2008). A review and conceptual re-examination of mental toughness: Implications for future researchers. *Personality and Individual Differences, 45,* 576–583.

Cryan, J. F., & Dinan, T. G. (2012). Mind-altering microorganisms: The impact of the gut microbiota on brain and behaviour. *Nature Reviews Neuroscience, 13,* 701–712.

Daskalakis, N. P., Cohen, H., Nievergelt, C. M., Baker, D. G., Buxbaum, J. D., Russo, S. J., & Yehuda, R. (2016). New translational perspectives for blood-based biomarkers of PTSD: From glucocorticoid to immune mediators of stress susceptibility. *Experimental Neurology, 284,* 133–140.

Despres, J., Brady, F., & McGowan, A. S. (2011). Understanding the culture of the student-athlete: Implications for college counselors. *Journal of Humanistic Counseling, 47,* 200–211.

Drehs, W. (2006a). Tragic turn. *ESPN.com.* Retrieved November 27, 2017 from http://sports.espn.go.com/espn/eticket/story?page=ambrogi

Drehs, W. (2006b). An inexplicable loss. *ESPN.com.* Retrieved November 27, 2017 from http://sports.espn.go.com/espn/eticket/story?page=ambrogi&num=2

Doré, B.P., Silvers, J.A., & Ochsner, K.N. (2016). Towards a personalized science of emotion regulation. *Social and Personality Psychology Compass, 10,* 171–187.

Eisenberg, D., Golberstein, E., & Gollust, S. E. (2007). Help-seeking and access to mental health care in a university student population. *Medical Care, 45,* 594–601.

Engstrom, C. M., & Sedlacek, W. E. (1991). A study of prejudice toward university student-athletes. *Journal of Counseling and Development, 70,* 189–193.

Etzel, E. F., Watson, J. C., Visek, A. J., & Maniar, S. D. (2006). Understanding and promoting college student-athlete health: Essential issues for student affairs professionals. *National Association of Student Personnel Administrators Journal, 43,* 518–546.

Fagan, K. (2017). *What made Maddy run: The secret struggles and tragic death of an All-American teen.* New York: Little, Brown, & Co.

Flanagan, L. (2014). When college athletes face depression. *The Atlantic.* Retrieved December 8, 2017 from https://www.theatlantic.com/education/archive/2014/03/when-college-athletes-face-depression/284484/

Franz, S. I., & Hamilton, G. V. (1905). The effects of exercise upon the retardation in conditions of depression. *American Journal of Insanity, 62,* 239–256.

Fullagar, H. H., Skorski, S., Duffield, R., Hammes, D., Coutts, A. J., & Meyer, T. (2015). Sleep and athletic performance: The effects of sleep loss on exercise performance, and physiological and cognitive responses to exercise. *Sports Medicine, 45,* 161–186.

Garlow, S. J., Purselle, D. C., & Heninger, M. (2007). Cocaine and alcohol use preceding suicide in African American and white adolescents. *Journal of Psychiatric Research, 41,* 53–56.

Gaultney, J. F. (2010). The prevalence of sleep disorders in college students: Impact on academic performance. *Journal of American College Health, 59,* 91–97.

Gayles, J. G., & Hu, S. (2009). The influence of student engagement and sport participation on college outcomes among Division I student athletes. *The Journal of Higher Education, 80,* 315–333.

Gerber, M., Kalak, N., Lemola, S., Clough, P. J., Perry, J. L., Pühse, U., Elliot, C., Holsboer-Trachsler, E., & Brand, S. (2013). Are adolescents with high mental toughness levels more resilient against stress? *Stress and Health, 29,* 164–171.

Grayson, P. A., & Cooper, S. (2006). Depression and anxiety. In P. A. Grayson & P. W. Meilman (Eds.), *College mental health practice* (pp. 113–134). New York: Routledge.

Grove, J. R., Lavallee, D., Gordon, S., & Harvey, J. H. (1998). Account-making: A model for understanding and resolving distressful reactions to retirement from sport. *The Sport Psychologist, 12,* 52–67.

Halson, S. L., Peake, J. M., & Sullivan, J. P. (2016). Wearable technology for athletes: Information overload and pseudoscience?.

Hamilton, M. (1960). A rating scale for depression. *Journal of Neurology, Neurosurgery & Psychiatry, 23,* 56–62.

Hewlett, S. A., & Luce, C. B. (2006). Extreme jobs: The dangerous allure of the 70-hour workweek. *Harvard Business Review, 84*(12), 49–59.

Hille, B. (2018, January 27). Tyler Hilinski suicide: Details emerge from Washington State QB's death. *Sporting News.* Retrieved April 26, 2018 from http://www.sportingnews.com/ncaa-football/news/tyler-hilinski-suicide-details-rifle-teammates-luke-falk-tribute-washington-state-qb/10i5euchrtor61rcuc7qk17ae6.

Horn, S. R., Charney, D. S., & Feder, A. (2016). Understanding resilience: New approaches for preventing and treating PTSD. *Experimental Neurology, 284,* 119–132.

Jonas, B. S., Brody, D., Roper, M., & Narrow, W. E. (2003). Prevalence of mood disorders in a national sample of young American adults. *Social Psychiatry and Psychiatric Epidemiology, 38,* 618–624.

Kadison, R., & DiGeronimo, T. F. (2004). *College of the overwhelmed: The campus mental health crisis and what to do about it.* San Francisco: Jossey-Bass.

Kolt, G. (2004). Injury from sport, exercise, and physical activity. In G. S. Kolt & M. B. Andersen (Eds.), *Psychology in the physical and manual therapies* (pp. 247–267). Edinburgh, UK: Churchill Livingstone.

Kroenke, K., Spitzer, R. L., & Williams, J. B. (2001). The PHQ-9. *Journal of General Internal Medicine, 16,* 606–613.

Kroshus, E. (2016). Variability in institutional screening practices relates to collegiate student-athlete mental health. *Journal of Athletic Training, 51*(5), 389-397.

Kulics, J. M., Kornspan, A. S., & Kretovics, M. (2015). An analysis of the academic behaviors and beliefs of Division I student-athletes: The impact of the increased percentage toward degree requirements. *College Student Journal, 49*(1), 1–12.

Lanning, W. (1982). The privileged few: Special counseling needs of athletes. *Journal of Sport Psychology, 4,* 19–23.

Lavallee, D., & Andersen, M. B. (2000). Leaving sport: Easing career transitions. In M. B. Andersen (Ed.), *Doing sport psychology* (pp. 249–260). Champaign, IL: Human Kinetics.

Linehan, M. (1993). *Cognitive behavioral therapy of borderline personality disorder.* New York, NY: Guilford Press.

Lopez, R. L., & Levy, J. J. (2013). Student athletes' perceived barriers to and preferences for seeking counseling. *Journal of College Counseling, 16*(1), 19–31.

Mah, C. D., Mah, K. E., Kezirian, E. J., & Dement, W. C. (2011). The effects of sleep extension on the athletic performance of collegiate basketball players. *Sleep, 34*, 943–950.

Mainwaring, L. M., Bisschop, S. M., Green, R. E. A., Antoniazzi, M., Comper, P., Kristman, V., Provvidenza, C., & Richards, D. W. (2004). Emotional reaction of varsity athletes to sport-related concussion. *Journal of Sport and Exercise Psychology, 26*, 119–135.

Maniar, S. D., & Carter, J. (2003, October). Characteristics of university student-athletes seeking sport psychology services: Part I. In S. D. Maniar (Chair), *Getting creative with university-based sport psychology services: Typical issues in an atypical field.* Symposium presented at the 17th annual meeting of the Association for the Advancement of Applied Sport Psychology, Philadelphia, PA.

Maniar, S. D., Chamberlain, R., & Moore, N. (2005, November 7). Suicide risk is real for student-athletes. *NCAA News, 42*(23), 4, 20.

Maniar, S. D., Curry, L. A., Sommers-Flanagan, J., & Walsh, J. A. (2001). Student-athlete preferences in seeking help when confronted with sport performance problems. *The Sport Psychologist, 15*, 205–223.

Mattson, M. P., & Wan, R. (2008). Neurotrophic factors in autonomic nervous system plasticity and dysfunction. *Neuromolecular Medicine, 10*, 157–168.

Miller, P. S. (2003). The role experimentation of intercollegiate student athletes. *The Sport Psychologist, 17*, 196–219.

Morgan, W. P. (1985). Selected psychological factors limiting performance: A mental health model. In D. J. Clark & H. M. Eckert (Eds.), *Limits of human performance* (pp. 70–80). Champaign, IL: Human Kinetics.

Moreland, J. J., Coxe, K. A., & Yang, J. (2017). Collegiate athletes' mental health services utilization: A systematic review of conceptualizations, operationalizations, facilitators, and barriers. *Journal of Sport and Health Science, 7*, 58–69.

National Collegiate Athletic Association. (2006). Guideline 2o: Depression: Interventions for collegiate athletics. In *2006-07 NCAA Sports Medicine Handbook* (pp. 64–68). Indianapolis: Author.

National Collegiate Athletic Association. (2007). *Managing student-athletes' mental health issues.* Retrieved July 25, 2007 from: http://www.ncaa.org/library/sports_sciences/mental_health/2007_managing_mental_health.pdf

National Collegiate Athletic Association. (2014). *Mind, body, and sport: Understanding and supporting student-athlete mental wellness.* Indianapolis: NCAA.

Newcomer, R., Perna, F., Maniar, S., Roh, J., & Stilger, V. (1999, September). Depressive symptomotology distinguishing injured from noninjured athletes. In F. Perna (Chair), *Pre-injury screening and post-injury assessment: Interactions between sport psychologists and the sports medicine team*. Symposium conducted at the 13th annual meeting of the Association for the Advancement of Applied Sport Psychology, Banff, Alberta, Canada.

Noren, N. (2014). Taking notice of the hidden injury. *ESPN.com*. Retrieved November 27, 2017 from http://www.espn.com/espn/otl/story/_/id/10335925/awareness-better-treatment-college-athletes-mental-health-begins-take-shape

Owusu-Sekyere, F., & Gervis, M. (2016). In the pursuit of mental toughness. *International Journal of Coaching Science, 10*(1), 3–23.

Palma, G., Collins, S. M., Bercik, P., & Verdu, E. F. (2014). The microbiota–gut–brain axis in gastrointestinal disorders: Stressed bugs, stressed brain or both? *The Journal of Physiology, 592*, 2989–2997.

Petitipas, A., & Danish, S. J. (1995). Caring for injured athletes. In S. M. Murphy (Ed.), *Sport psychology interventions* (pp. 255–281). Champaign, IL: Human Kinetics.

Pinkerton, R. S., Hinz, L. D., & Barrow, J. C. (1989). The college student-athlete: Psychological considerations and interventions. *Journal of American College Health, 37*, 218–226.

Radloff, L. S. (1977). The CES-D Scale: A self-report depression scale for research in the general population. *Applied Psychological Measurement, 1*, 385–401.

Rao, A. L., & Hong, E. S. (2016). Understanding depression and suicide in college athletes: Emerging concepts and future directions. *British Journal of Sports Medicine, 50*(3). doi:10.1136/bjsports-2015-095658

Rice, S. M., Purcell, R., De Silva, S., Mawren, D., McGorry, P. D., & Parker, A. G. (2016). The mental health of elite athletes: A narrative systematic review. *Sports Medicine, 46*, 1333–1353.

Riolo, S. A., Nguyen, T. A., Greden, J. F., & King, C. A. (2005). Prevalence of depression by race/ethnicity: Findings from the National Health and Nutrition Examination Survey III. *American Journal of Public Health, 95*, 998–1000.

Sargent, C., Lastella, M., Halson, S. L., & Roach, G. D. (2014). The impact of training schedules on the sleep and fatigue of elite athletes. *Chronobiology International, 31*, 1160–1168.

Schaefer, J. D., Caspi, A., Belsky, D. W., Harrington, H., Houts, R., Horwood, L. J., Hussong, A., Ramrakha, S., Poulton, R., & Moffitt, T. E. (2017). Enduring mental health: Prevalence and prediction. *Journal of Abnormal Psychology, 126*, 212–224.

Schinke, R. J., Stambulova, N. B., Si, G., & Moore, Z. (2017, April). International society of sport psychology position stand: Athletes' mental health, performance, and development. *International Journal of Sport and Exercise Psychology*, 1–18.

Sherwin, I. (2017). Commentary: From mental health to mental wealth in athletes: Looking back and moving forward. *Frontiers in Psychology, 8*, 693.

Sinha, R., Lacadie, C. M., Constable, R. T., & Seo, D. (2016). Dynamic neural activity during stress signals resilient coping. *Proceedings of the National Academy of Sciences, 113*, 8837–8842.

Smallman, E., Sowa, C. J., & Young, B. D. (1991). Ethnic and gender differences in student athletes' responses to stressful life events. *Journal of College Student Development, 32,* 230–235.

Sommers-Flanagan, J. (2018, Winter). Conversations about suicide: Strategies for detecting and assessing suicide risk. *Journal of Health Service Psychology, 44,* 33–45.

Sommers-Flanagan, J., & Sommers-Flanagan, R. (1995). Intake interviewing with suicidal patients: A systematic approach. *Professional Psychology: Research and Practice, 30,* 1–7.

Sommers-Flanagan, J., & Sommers-Flanagan, R. (2007). *Tough kids, cool counseling: User-friendly approaches to working with challenging youth* (2nd ed.). Washington, DC: American Counseling Association.

Sommers-Flanagan, J., & Sommers-Flanagan, R. (2015). *Clinical interviewing* (5th ed.). New York: Wiley.

Stamatis, A., Robinson, E. L., & Morgan, G. B. (2017) Mental toughness in strength and conditioning training: Is it really necessary? Perspectives of elite NCAA strength and conditioning coaches. *International Journal of Exercise Science: Conference Proceedings, 2*(9), 56.

Stambulova, N. B. (2016). Theoretical developments in career transition research: Contributions of European sport psychology. In M. Raab, P. Wylleman, R. Seiler, A. Elbe, & A. Hatzigeorhiadis (Eds.), Sport and exercise psychology research: From theory to practice (pp. 251–268). Amerstam: Academic Press.

Stambulova, N., Alfermann, D., Statler, T., & Côté, J. E. A. N. (2009). ISSP position stand: Career development and transitions of athletes. *International Journal of Sport and Exercise Psychology, 7,* 395–412.

Storch, E. A., Storch, J. B., Killainy, E. M., & Roberti, J. W. (2005). Self-reported psychopathology in athletes: A comparison of intercollegiate student-athletes and non-athletes. *Journal of Sport Behavior, 28,* 86–97.

Sullivan, J. (2017). Resilience and sport: Neurophysiology and readiness, rather than mental toughness and grit. Medium. Retrieved October 2, 2017 from https://medium.com/@jps_98483/resilience-and-sport-neurophysiology-and-readiness-rather-than-mental-toughness-and-grit-ade89938283a

Taylor, D. J., Vatthauer, K. E., Bramoweth, A. D., Ruggero, C., & Roane, B. (2013). The role of sleep in predicting college academic performance: Is it a unique predictor? *Behavioral Sleep Medicine, 11,* 159–172.

Tkachuk, G. A., & Martin, G. L. (1999). Exercise therapy for patients with psychiatric disorders: Research and clinical implications. *Professional Psychology: Research and Practice, 30,* 275–282.

Trojian, T. (2016). Depression is under-recognised in the sport setting: Time for primary care sports medicine to be proactive and screen widely for depression symptoms. *British Journal of Sports Medicine, 50*(3), 137–139.

Uphill, M., Sly, D., & Swain, J. (2016). From mental health to mental wealth in athletes: Looking back and moving forward. *Frontiers in Psychology, 7,* 935.

Walsh, L. (2009). *Depression care across the lifespan.* West Sussex, UK: Wiley-Blackwell.

Watson, N., Ji, X., Yasuhara, T., Date, I., Kaneko, Y., Tajiri, N., & Borlongan, C. V. (2015). No pain, no gain: Lack of exercise obstructs neurogenesis. *Cell Transplantation, 24,* 591–597.

Wertheim, L. J. (2003, September 8). Prisoners of depression. *Sports Illustrated,* 71–79.

Williams, D. R., Gonzalez, H. M., Neighbors, H. Nesse, R., Abelson, J. M., Sweetman, J., & Jackson, J. S. (2007). Prevalence and distribution of major depressive disorder in African Americans, Caribbean blacks, and non-Hispanic whites: Results from the National Survey of American Life. *Archives of General Psychiatry, 64,* 305–315.

Wittenborn, A. K., Rahmandad, H., Rick, J., & Hosseinichimeh, N. (2016). Depression as a systemic syndrome: Mapping the feedback loops of major depressive disorder. *Psychological Medicine, 46,* 551–562.

Wyshak, G. (2001). Women's college physical activity and self-reports of physician-diagnosed depression and of current symptoms of psychiatric distress. *Journal of Women's Health & Gender-Based Medicine, 10,* 363–370.

# 7

# Trauma and College Student-Athletes

*Mitch Abrams and Michelle Bartlett*

## CASE STUDY: JOHNNY

Twenty-year-old linebacker Johnny was heavily recruited out of high school, even though he had been rumored to have a substance abuse problem. During his junior year in high school, a drug screen tested positive for cocaine and marijuana, resulting in temporary suspensions from both school and the football team. He came back to play an outstanding senior season and was offered scholarships to three of his top five college choices.

His freshman year at Blank University was positive, but uneventful. He seemed to adjust to the team nicely—he socialized with teammates and received high grades from the coaching staff about his potential. He partied some, but there were no red flags to indicate he was struggling until he was found unconscious at a party and brought to the emergency room with alcohol poisoning. Following his discharge from the hospital, Johnny's coaches told him that going to counseling was a condition of his staying on the team.

On his intake forms, Johnny reported difficulties sleeping and endorsed occasional rumination about sex. During the initial interview, Johnny told his counselor, Dr. Jones, that he was only there because he was forced to go—that he would attend, but that no one could make him talk. He denied ever being on medication, but he admitted to drinking alcohol in varying amounts through his life and said that he dabbled with other drugs. He denied any personal or family history of mental or medical illness or treatment. He also denied any family substance abuse.

During the next session Dr. Jones asked a very simple question about his drinking alcohol. "There are tons of college students, and student-athletes, for that matter, who drink, but they're not here. For you, and only you, why? Why do you drink?" Johnny quickly replied, "To not dream." A single tear appeared and rolled down his left cheek, and Johnny stated, "I don't want to talk about it. It's nothing." Johnny and Dr. Jones sat in silence for several minutes and Johnny stood up and said, "I gotta go. See you next time."

Johnny came to the next session with a relieved look on his face. "I'm ready. I'm ready to talk, but you can't tell anyone, okay?" Dr. Jones reminded Johnny of the confidentiality of the counseling relationship. Johnny then started talking.

"I don't like to sleep. That's when I have the bad dreams about the old stuff. So I have used Adderall and cocaine and caffeine to stay up. People thought I was using them to amp up and improve my play, but it was never that. It was to stay up, to not fall asleep, to keep the nightmares away. The problem was that I could stay up for days on whatever I was using, and it only wound up hurting me. So, I cut back on them and turned to alcohol. I would always drink enough to knock me out, because when I fell asleep drunk, the nightmares wouldn't be there, or at least I wouldn't wake up from them in the middle of the night. And I wouldn't remember them the next day, so all of the stuff you heard about my drugs and alcohol, it was all to get away from the dreams."

"Johnny, why did this happen now?"

Johnny then filled in all of the blanks. "Two weeks ago, after practice, in the showers, one of the guys called me a fag and smacked my ass," Johnny explained, "and it took me right back. Right back to when I was six." Johnny then reported that from the ages of six until he was nine, his uncle, who also coached his youth football team, sexually abused him—usually in the shower. Uncle Tim—known in town as Coach—would watch Johnny after school several times per week. Johnny said he never told anyone because he was embarrassed and was afraid that people would think he was gay. Johnny explained that he started having nightmares when he was eight years old and was confused that they did not go away when the abuse stopped.

At age 17, Johnny's first sexual experience with his girlfriend precipitated his first panic attack. In addition to the panic attacks and nightmares, Johnny also became depressed and confused. These symptoms worsened in frequency and severity, except when he was on the football field. Johnny's athletic prowess brought him fleeting feelings of powerfulness and invincibility and he struggled with feeling strangely indebted to Uncle Tim. One weekend, Johnny discovered that he was able to get temporary relief when he drank enough alcohol.

After this disclosure, Johnny and Dr. Jones embarked on their work together to help Johnny process these events and to develop more adaptive coping strategies.

---

Trauma can be defined as the result of having a deeply distressing or disturbing experience from events typically outside of the range of normal human experience (Black & Grant, 2014). According to Freud (as cited in Dalenberg, Straus, & Carlson, 2017), trauma confronts individuals with an acute or overwhelming threat (James & Gilliland, 2012) that exceeds their ability to cope (Dalenberg, Straus, & Carlson, 2017). In sport-related research, trauma has been defined more softly as "a memorable challenge that was perceived to disrupt a performer's development" (Savage, Collins, & Cruickshank, 2017, p. 102). In counseling, if a person can effectively assimilate their traumatic experience into conscious awareness and organize it as a past event (versus a current one), functionality can return. If trauma is not effectively processed, it can re-emerge as a current stressor, debilitating normal functioning (James & Gilliland, 2012). As we discuss throughout this chapter, trauma can take several forms with different presentations, and there are added factors in the athletic world that can complicate or hide traumatic symptomology that may prevent the student-athlete from seeking counseling and/or receiving trauma-informed care.

It is important to appreciate that helping professionals who work with student-athletes must possess a thorough understanding of trauma. This chapter will explore traumatic events that evoke stress in most people in most circumstances (Dalenberg et al., 2017) and present a critical review of historical approaches, including difficulties that have rendered those programs inadequate. Finally, the chapter will discuss evidence-based comprehensive treatment approaches, including those approaches most suitable for student-athletes.

## PTSD and Trauma

Post-traumatic stress disorder (PTSD) is a complex and serious psychological condition that results from exposure to one or more traumatic events. The lifetime rate of PTSD in the American civilian population is about 7–8% (National Center for PTSD, 2016a). Symptoms must exceed at least four weeks in duration and include flashbacks or the reliving of a traumatic event, avoidance of associations with the event (e.g., people, places, things), emotion numbing or lability, and increased activation of the central nervous system (Foa, Keane, & Friedman, 2000). Acute Stress Disorder is the pre-PTSD diagnosis, whereby symptoms are similar but have not met a duration of four weeks. PTSD can severely decrease quality of life, can lower the ability to function, and can lead to significant disability. PTSD may also be accompanied by other comorbidities (e.g., substance abuse, suicidality, and eating disorders), requiring clinical sensitivity and skills by the helping professional.

The National Center for PTSD (2016a) reports that 60% of men and 50% of women will experience trauma at some point in their lives. Despite its widespread nature, it is critical to understand that trauma is a very personal experience. Similar to harassment, an outsider does not have the authority to say "that is not a traumatic event" because they do not experience it as such. For student-athletes, a traumatic event may be an injury, a missed selection, transition out of sport, or even a poor performance (Savage et al., 2017). In fact, when a large group of people are exposed to the same potentially traumatic event, some will develop traditional PTSD symptoms, some will develop nonPTSD symptoms (e.g., anxiety or depression), some will develop symptoms that do not require treatment, and some will develop no symptoms at all. A person's age, history of psychiatric illness, baseline coping abilities, and proximity to the stressor are all factors that can affect the development of PTSD (Black & Grant, 2014).

In addition to the categorization of psychological responses to trauma, the traumatic experiences themselves fall into two categories with differing associated characteristics and consequences.

## Type 1 Trauma

Type 1 trauma follows a single event and often results from being in an accident, being the victim of a crime, or witnessing a natural disaster. It is often the precursor to what is now coined simple PTSD. Simple PTSD, as outlined by the *Diagnostic Statistical Manual—Fifth Edition* (*DSM-5*; American Psychiatric Association, 2013), manifests itself with symptoms meeting a constellation of specific criteria related to (1) the exposure to the traumatic event, (2) the re-experiencing of the event, (3) the avoidance of trauma-related stimuli, (4) symptomatic thoughts and/or feelings, and (5) arousal/reactivity difficulties. The diagnostic criteria also specify duration (a period of at least one month), functional impairment, and the elimination of medication, substance use, or illness as a causal factor.

## Type 2 Trauma

Type 2 trauma, however, is the result of long-term exposure to traumatic events, such as ongoing sexual abuse, parental neglect and/or abuse, being a prisoner of war, or some prolonged period of trauma. Judith Herman (1992) first coined the term complex PTSD and noted the following symptom clusters:

- *Emotional regulation.* May include persistent sadness, suicidal thoughts, explosive anger, or inhibited anger.

- *Consciousness.* Includes forgetting traumatic events, reliving traumatic events, or having episodes in which one feels detached from one's mental processes or body (dissociation).

- *Self-perception.* May include helplessness, shame, guilt, stigma, and a sense of being completely different from other human beings.

- *Distorted perceptions of the perpetrator.* Examples include attributing total power to the perpetrator, becoming preoccupied with the relationship to the perpetrator, or preoccupied with revenge.

- *Relations with others.* Examples include isolation, distrust, or a repeated search for a rescuer.

- *One's system of meanings.* May include a loss of sustaining faith or a sense of hopelessness and despair.

Complex PTSD may resemble other diagnostic manifestations, including borderline personality disorder (BPD). Both complex PTSD and BPD involve affective dysregulation, social impairment, and potential difficulties with cognitive processing. However, there are significant distinctions between these diagnoses. For example, complex PTSD requires the presence of a precipitating traumatic event, while BPD does not. A BPD diagnosis requires the fear of abandonment, while complex PTSD does not. Although both disorders may involve self-injurious behavior, BPD also frequently is accompanied by impulsivity (Cloitre, Garvert, Weiss, Carlson, & Bryant, 2014). It is important to note that for some individuals, PTSD and BPD may be comorbid diagnoses.

Finally, there are times when events would seem to fit neatly into the Type 1 trauma experience (e.g., the World Trade Center attack of September 11th), but then the recurring media bombardment leads to chronic, traumatizing exposure over time. As such, there are circumstances that don't neatly fit into the dichotomous Type 1 versus Type 2 categories.

## Physiology of Trauma

A substantial body of literature exists delineating the neurobiological features of the stress response. When an individual is exposed to a stressful event, there are neuroendocrine, neurochemical, and neuroanatomical effects on the body. For example, there is a post-trauma spike in cortisol (a stress hormone) that interferes with the functioning of the hippocampus (a brain structure; Bremner, 2006). The hippocampus is responsible for encoding of memories, so when it does not function normally, the individual stores what happened as "sensory packets" rather than a narrative memory—a story that explains the meaning of what happened. This is why the trauma survivor may remember a particular smell or a particular sound that coincided with the event, but may struggle with telling the story as to what happened chronologically. It is important to note that there are individual differences in how one responds and how the body handles the accompanying stress. Similarly, trauma-associated changes to the body's regulation of certain neurotransmitters may result in a decreased ability to regulate the sympathetic nervous system (e.g., the fight or flight response; Sherin & Nemeroff, 2011).

A detailed exploration of the physiology of trauma is beyond the scope of this chapter, but helping professionals working in this area need to have a basic understanding of these issues in order to provide psychoeducation to student-athletes struggling with the aftermath of trauma.

## Phases of Recovery

In working with a student-athlete who has experienced a traumatic event, helping professionals must conduct a thorough assessment, including a gauge of where the individual is in relation to the trauma's aftermath. Brende and Parson (1985) outlined five stages of recovery from PTSD:

1. *The emergency or outcry phase.* This phase is marked by extreme autonomous nervous system arousal and activation (i.e., "fight or flight" response). The client may be plagued by intrusive thoughts about the event, why it happened, and the projected consequences. Feelings of fear and loss of control dominate.

2. *The emotional numbing and denial phase.* In an effort to regain functionality, the client will submerge memories of the event into the subconscious and try to "forget" about it in order to protect their well-being. Temporary reduction of anxiety is possible but eradication attempts are futile. Many clients remain in this phase indefinitely without treatment.

3. *The intrusive-repetitive phase.* The thoughts that were submerged into the subconscious in the previous phase manifest with symptomology of mood swings,

irritability, nightmares, and exacerbated startle responses. Other suboptimal defensive mechanisms may be utilized to attempt to re-numb against the trauma, such as substance abuse and/or behavioral addictions. The stage can be so overpowering that the client is either motivated to seek help or outside intervention is mandated.

4. *The reflective-transition phase.* The victim is now a survivor who has come to grips with the trauma and becomes forward looking rather than backward looking.

5. *The integration phase.* The survivor successfully integrates the experience with all past experiences where the trauma is solely a past event. Stability of life is restored.

## Treatment

Trauma-informed treatment can aim to reduce symptoms of psychological dysfunction and PTSD (either one symptom cluster or several), and also can emphasize the capacity to enrich the therapeutic process or functional improvement with less emphasis on symptom reduction (Foa et al., 2000). Treatment of PTSD typically focuses on three principle components: (1) processing the traumatic event, its meaning, and consequences, and coming to terms with it; (2) managing the physiological and biological presentation of the stress response; and (3) reestablishing supportive social relationships and overall life functioning (James & Gilliland, 2012).

Research efficacy on the treatment of PTSD and trauma-related issues began in the 1980s with the induction of the disorder into the American Psychiatric Association's *DSM-III* (Foa et al., 2000). In 2017, the American Psychological Association published the Clinical Practice Guideline for the Treatment of Post-traumatic Stress Disorder (PTSD) in Adults. The report's authors conducted a meta-analysis on PTSD outcome research studies to draw conclusions regarding best practices. The published report focused on symptom reduction and reduction of adverse events as the benchmarks for successful treatment. The report's recommendations included strong evidence to support the use of (1) cognitive behavioral therapy, (2) cognitive processing therapy, (3) cognitive therapy, and (4) prolonged exposure therapy. The report also offered conditional support (and recommended additional confirmatory outcome research) for the use of (1) brief eclectic psychotherapy, (2) eye movement desensitization and reprocessing (EMDR), and (3) narrative exposure therapy (American Psychological Association, 2017).

After a comprehensive assessment via structured or semi-structured interviews and empirically derived measures (see Dalenberg et al., 2017) determining the presence of PTSD, the general treatment protocol is as follows (Foa et al., 2000):

1. The helping professional should first establish a therapeutic alliance with special consideration given to trust and safety issues.

2. The helping professional should ascertain that the patient is not actively in danger.

3. The client should be educated on PTSD and trauma-related symptomology.

4. Symptoms presentation should be dimensionalized over time.

5. Comorbid conditions should be assessed/ruled-out.

6. The helping professional should assess and establish the utility of the client's social support as therapeutic relationships.

7. Helping professionals should consider the client's readiness for treatment (see phases of recovery) when embarking on treatment modalities.

While there are numerous treatment modalities for trauma victims, the selection below has been provided specifically with the population of student-athletes in mind. There have not been any athlete-specific approaches developed for either prevention of PTSD or the treatment of trauma-related symptoms. It is important to note that helping professionals seeking to develop a specialization in providing treatment to trauma survivors should take care to undergo the appropriate level of training and supervision. The failure to do so would be considered an ethical violation.

## Critical Incident Stress Debriefing (CISD)

Prevention is more parsimonious than treatment, so helping professionals have sought to prevent the development of PTSD after exposure to a traumatic event with varying efficacy. The Jeffrey Mitchell model of critical incident stress debriefing (CISD) was used to meet with first responders shortly after they witnessed a traumatic event and facilitated them sharing their memories as a group to develop a group narrative (Mitchell, 1983). It was believed that by doing so, this typically single-session intervention would prevent PTSD symptom genesis by promoting emotional processing through the ventilation and regularization of reactions (Bisson, McFarlane, & Rose, 2000). Initially, it was seen as a momentous success, but subsequent research showed mixed results—some people improved and did not develop PTSD, but some developed even worse symptoms than predicted. Examination led to the conclusion that debriefing prior to helping the individual tend to their needs (i.e., Maslow's Hierarchy of Needs) only contributed to their stress. Now debriefing is not seen as a treatment itself but may be useful for screening, education, and support.

## Psychological First Aid

With the equivocal effectiveness of critical incident stress debriefing (CISD), a newer approach was developed in an attempt to prevent the emergence of PTSD. Psychological First Aid (PFA) was developed by the National Center for Post-Traumatic Stress Disorder (NC-PTSD), a section of the United States Department of Veterans Affairs, in 2006. It utilizes the following core actions: contact and engagement, safety and comfort, stabilization, information gathering, current needs and concerns, practical assistance, connection with social supports, information on coping, and linkage with collaborative services (National Child Traumatic Stress Network, 2006). PFA addresses many of the problems found in CISD.* It is not compulsory and can be done in multiple sessions while greater links are offered for those who need more services. It deals with practical issues that are often more pressing and create stress. It also improves self-efficacy by letting people cope their own way.

## Exposure Therapies

It is the improper encoding of the traumatic memories that leads to the reliving symptom sequelae of PTSD. Trauma survivors will often relive and/or re-enact the traumatic event until they gain mastery over it. This is why exposure therapies, specifically prolonged exposure (PE) therapy, developed by Edna Foa, are so effective for trauma survivors (American Psychological Association, 2017; Foa, Hembree, & Rothbaum, 2007; Rothbaum, Meadows, Resick, & Foy, 2000). In exposure therapies, the goal is for the client to achieve the desensitization to the traumatic stimulus via continual presentation of the fear-evoking stimuli (James & Gilliland, 2012).

Traditional desensitization treatment is done in conjunction with relaxation training where specific stress-reduction skills (e.g., deep breathing, passive/progressive muscle relaxation) are deployed to counteract the activation that previously came with exposure to the traumatic stimulus. In exposure therapy, the individual relives/retells the traumatic event from beginning to end, despite it being very upsetting, and, by doing so, gets through the whole story, develops a narrative, and the symptom sequelae subsequently fall. This is an example of imaginal flooding, where exposure to the actual stimulus would not be possible (Corey, 2016). It is recommended that the client develop relaxation skills before embarking on exposure therapies.

However, many individuals develop the other symptoms of PTSD without the reliving symptomology. This is because these individuals were psychologically

---

* For the *Psychological First Aid: Field Operations Guide*, see National Center for PTSD, 2016b.

traumatized by the event and they react in all of the other ways, but they did not experience the physiological hippocampal dysfunction. When there is the presence of hippocampal dysfunction, exposure therapies appear to be the most effective. When reliving is not the main symptom presentation, or in cases where memories have been at least partially encoded, other modalities—such as cognitive processing therapy—can be beneficial.

## Cognitive Processing Therapy

Cognitive processing therapy (CPT) was designed as a therapeutic intervention specifically for sexual assault survivors (Rothbaum et al., 2000), but modified versions have been used in the treatment of PTSD with other populations, including combat veterans (Forbes et al., 2012; Resick, Monson, & Chard, 2007). CPT postulates that the memory of the trauma is retained within a cognitive structure that contains a stimulus, response, and a meaning element that serves as a mechanism to remove the individual from danger. However, because the individual is no longer in actual danger, that structure is maladaptive to current life function. In the example of a student-athlete who was sexually assaulted, the stimulus may be the smell of alcohol, the response may be an increase in heart rate, and the meaning element would be to escape and avert danger. In other words, trauma-related information enters into the conscious mind (e.g., flashbacks). CPT aims to change the maladaptive meaning to something adaptive (Foa & Kozak, 1986). Other goals of CPT include processing and reducing problematic emotions associated with the traumatic event and working towards realistic and adaptive beliefs about the event. This is accomplished via cognitive therapy techniques (e.g., Ellis' Rational Emotive Behavioral Therapy and Beck's Cognitive Therapy), such as disputing irrational beliefs and defeating cognitive distortions held about the traumatic event.

## Eye Movement Desensitization and Reprocessing

Eye movement desensitization and reprocessing (EMDR) is a behavioral therapy that has garnered much attention in the treatment of trauma and PTSD since the mid-1990s. Developed by Francine Shapiro, EMDR combines eye movement with other bilateral movement in conjunction with cognitive reprocessing and restructuring to treat traumatic stress.* EMDR consists of eight linear phases:

---

* A brief overview of EDMR has been provided, but it is recommended that helping professionals seek formal education and clinical training in EMDR before use with clients. For a more comprehensive review, see Shapiro and Maxfield, 2002.

1. *History and treatment planning.* It is essential that clients be evaluated on their ability to handle what may be a challenging treatment. Here, specific targets to be reprocessed are determined (trauma-associated memories and present anxiety-inducing situations) and needed skills and behaviors are developed.

2. *Preparation phase.* Here the therapeutic alliance is established. Creation of a safe space and trust in the counselor-client relationship is crucial for success in future stages. The client is also educated on the EMDR process and effects.

3. *Assessment.* The client is required to maintain awareness in one or more of the following: the image of the traumatic memory, the negative perceptions/emotions associated with it, and the associated physiological (anxiety) response. The task is then to find a more positive or adaptive cognition that would decrease the associated anxiety. Rating scales to rate discomfort (0 = no anxiety, 10 = highest anxiety possible) and cognitions (1 = cognition is completely untrue, 7 = cognition is completely true) are used. Clients then generate new positive statements that reflect how they desire to feel (positive).

4. *Desensitization.* As the client may have difficulty accepting the new cognitions and emotions that they feel in themselves, this stage incorporates eye movement to lessen the intensity of the negativity associated with the negative cognition. The client is asked to imagine the traumatic memory and its associated noxious cognitions and emotions while the counselor's finger is moved rhythmically back and forth across the field of vision 12–14 times for one set (called a *saccade*) (James & Gilliland, 2006). After each set, the clients are asked to "erase" the image and its associations and subsequently rate their discomfort again. This is continued until discomfort is rated at a 1.

5. *Installation.* Installation of a new, positive image and cognitions is the goal of this phase. In conjunction with saccades, the client imagines the new image until the cognition is rated as a 7 (the cognition is completely true).

6. *Body scan.* In this phase, the client looks for residual somatic anxiety. If some is found, processing in conjunction with saccades is completed again. This may help to uncover new areas of unprocessed material to process toward a full treatment.

7. *Closure.* When images and cognitions fully cease, the client is debriefed on the process. A recommendation is made to journal if any new images arise for use during future processing.

8. *Reevaluation.* At the start of each session, the client is asked to reprocess previous targets, and any intrusions evident in the journaling are examined. Several behavioral processes are used, such as reconceptualization of goals, further desensitization, and the continuance of cognitive restructuring and self-monitoring (Corey, 2016).

Critical analysis has led to controversy over whether or not EMDR is effective as a treatment for PTSD, and if it is effective, the mechanism of action is questionable. A critical review of the literature suggests that there does appear to be effectiveness present, though not with the empirical support of Prolonged Exposure. Some factors that likely contribute to EMDR's effectiveness are the following:

- EMDR is a form of exposure therapy and exposure therapies help PTSD.

- There is less vicarious traumatization of the helping professionals that do not hear the traumatic events in graphic detail. This reduces the risk of burnout, and in turn, assists helping professionals to remain upbeat and optimistic.

- There is a "magical" component to the EMDR tools—whether waiving a wand, following a finger, or listening to alternating tapping. This suggestive power can also contribute to the client's perception of relief in placebo-like fashion.

Ultimately, the research on the mechanism of action—lateralization (whether or not the alternating visual [or listening] fields)—actually assists in ameliorating PTSD symptoms has mixed results, so the findings from additional research efforts are needed.

## Trauma-Sensitive Yoga

Trauma-sensitive or trauma-informed yoga (TSY) is the use of the practice of hatha yoga as a complimentary mindfulness-based intervention in the treatment of PTSD. It was created by Emerson, Sharma, Chaudhry, and Turner (2009) at the Trauma Center Yoga Program in Brookline, MA. It specifically utilizes a safe environment, recognition of choice, and the development of the ability to be action-oriented in the treatment of trauma. For work with a student-athlete in a college environment, TSY would not be something that the helping professional would be directly engaged in with the client as a treatment (unless they are registered with the Yoga Alliance and certified by the Trauma Center Yoga Program). However, it is important to be aware of the potential of yoga as an additive treatment for trauma so that an appropriate referral may be made. This may be a particularly appealing treatment for student-athletes in conjunction with their familiarity with physical activity and heightened kinesthetic intelligence.

TSY may be particularly helpful for those for whom trauma is "remembered" in the body. West, Liang, and Spinazzola (2017) highlight the following benefits of yoga with regard to the symptoms of PTSD:

- focused breathing as promoting increased emotional regulation and sympathetic nervous system function;

- meditative components to decrease anxiety and depression;

- movement and stretching to decrease muscular tension and pain; and

- resulting biochemical changes from practice decrease stress, dysfunctional coping, and avoidance while increasing personal growth and self-confidence.

## Treatment Barriers and Considerations

A counselor working with victims of trauma must be aware of these related, yet crucial, points. First, individuals can develop depression, anxiety, anger, or other problems related to a traumatic event without the development of traditional PTSD symptomology. A trauma survivor may develop a perception that the world is a dangerous place; a world that they cannot control. Sometimes, student-athletes respond to this by seeking to control whatever elements of their lives they can. This can manifest itself as an eating disorder or even burnout, as the individual may use exercise and training as a way to escape from painful memories or emotions and/or to gain protection from future harm. A question the authors will often ask a trauma survivor using exercise to feel better is, "are you running away from something or towards something?" The answers have varied, but the metaphor often plays out that early in treatment they are running away from the trauma, and, as they improve, they are running toward their new selves.

Second, there is nothing about being an athlete that makes the individual immune to the impact of trauma. Student-athletes experience eating disorders, substance abuse, and social anxiety at levels similar to those of their peers (Gill, 2008; Wahto, Swift, & Whipple, 2016; Wolanin, Hong, Marks, Ranchoo, & Gross, 2016). Student-athletes may even be at greater risk because there are factors in the athlete culture that decrease the reporting of symptoms and seeking mental health assistance (Wahto et al., 2016; Watson, 2005). For example, there is a self-stigma and public stigma that seeking psychological help is a sign of weakness (Wahto et al., 2016). Rather than identifying how one feels and becoming stronger around it, there is the myth that showing emotions is "being weak". Of course, this belies the idea that real strength comes from addressing one's shortcomings. Nonetheless, student-athletes often hide their emotions and experiences for fear of being judged poorly by coaches, teammates, and fans, and have less positive attitudes toward help-seeking behavior than their nonathlete peers (Watson, 2005). This is not conducive to seeking counseling when needed. Given these issues, it is recommended that treatment for student-athletes dealing with trauma be primarily provided in an individual setting versus a group therapy setting.

There are many other variables that may preclude student-athletes from getting the help that they need. Often, with sexual abuse, the perpetrator may threaten that either no one will believe the victim if they try to report what occurred or that they will be harmed if they report. Thus, the victim is ambivalent to come forward. Further, because shame is often experienced in relation to trauma, there is a compounding effect that can make student-athletes who have been traumatized even more susceptible to suffering without assistance.

Among undergraduate students, 23.1% of females and 5.4% of males are raped or sexually assaulted through physical force, violence, or incapacitation (Cantor et al., 2015). The incidence rate of sexual assaults on college campuses has stayed fairly unchanged over the past two decades (Fedina, Holmes, & Backes, 2016). Conley et al. (2017) emphasized that sexual assault is the most common form of violence on college campuses, but only about 12% of sexual assaults are actually reported (Coray, 2016). In women, the most frequent traumatic event is a physical assault (Black & Grant, 2014) and PTSD rates are twice as high for woman than for men (10.4% vs. 5%) over the course of a lifetime (Foa et al., 2000). There have been many documented cases in which prominent coaches and/or athletic staff were sexually abusing the athletes under their authority, and student-athletes are victims, as well (e.g., Dr. Larry Nassar at US Gymnastics and affiliated with Michigan State Athletics). Greater attention needs to be paid to these circumstances and, slowly, needed changes are evolving in the manner in which these events are handled.

Interestingly, while teachers and health professionals are mandated reporters for child abuse, many coaches currently do not have this demand; nor do they consistently receive standard education about identification of abuse and what they should do to assist athletes. It is recommended that coaches be strongly encouraged to undergo training in these matters and that coaches be included under the umbrella of mandated reporters.

Another factor that should be considered regarding student-athlete vulnerability is the common assumption that athletes, because they are physically healthy, must be psychologically healthy as well. We should presume the risk of abuse is ubiquitous and counselors and coaches should have an ever-watching eye out for hints of trauma that merit further exploration and referral to treatment. This is true in consideration of general mental health for the student-athlete. Especially in revenue-producing college athletics, there is a risk that athletes are seen less humanistically, and more as the vehicle to bring in more money. Unfortunately, this has led to a history of coaches and athletic department staff looking the other way when student-athletes evidenced apparent psychological or behavioral difficulties. This is collectively short-sighted because student-athletes who receive the appropriate support and treatment, are far more likely to perform better in sport and in life. This is particularly true for trauma survivors (Savage et al., 2017).

There is also research that points to student-athletes having more difficulties with substance abuse than one might expect (National Colligate Athletic Association, 2014). Athletic life may lead to alcohol or drug abuse for many reasons, including for performance enhancement, to self-treat untreated mental illness, and to cope with stressors, such as pressure to perform, injuries, pain, and retirement from sport (Reardon & Credo, 2014). Therefore, athletes who are struggling with substance abuse problems should be screened for the possibility that they may be self-medicating trauma-related symptomology. If the helping professional does not have sufficient expertise to provide this assessment, a referral should be made to a sport psychologist with enough training and experience with clinical issues, substance abuse, and trauma to make such a determination. Following this procedure can ensure appropriate treatment planning for the student-athlete.

In many ways, issues of assessment and treatment of trauma go beyond the scope of this chapter because they require specialized training beyond the general preparation of graduate school. It is strongly recommended that when a student-athlete is the victim of an episode of violence, or is thought to have experienced trauma of any sort, a professional with experience and training with working with these issues should be enlisted. Ideally, this professional also should have knowledge and expertise of collegiate student-athletes.

## Discussion Questions

1. Based on the above criteria, how would you categorize Johnny's trauma experiences? What additional information would you need to make this determination?

2. In what ways did Dr. Jones facilitate a therapeutic alliance with Johnny? What education would you provide to Johnny to help him better understand his experience?

3. In Johnny's case, how would Dr. Jones use an intervention like Cognitive Processing Therapy? What maladaptive meaning from Johnny's traumatic history would need to be addressed? How would Dr. Jones ascertain whether Johnny has maladaptive or irrational beliefs about his experiences?

4. Based on the topics covered in this chapter, how would you estimate Johnny's prognosis? What care should be taken to ensure that Johnny gets the help he needs to recover?

## References

American Psychiatric Association. (2013). *Diagnostic and statistical manual of mental health disorders* (5th ed.). Washington, DC.

American Psychological Association. (2017). Clinical practice guideline for the treatment of posttraumatic stress disorder (PTSD) in adults. *American Psychological Association Guideline Development Panel for the Treatment of PTSD in Adults.* Retrieved from http://www.apa.org/ptsd-guideline/ptsd.pdf

Bisson, J. I., McFarlane, A. C., & Rose, S. (2000). Psychological debriefing. In E. B. Foa, T. M. Keane, & M. J. Freidman (Eds.), *Effective treatments for PTSD* (pp. 39–59). New York: Guilford Press.

Black, D. W., & Grant, J. E. (2014). Trauma- and stressor-related disorders. In D. W. Black & J. E. Grant (Eds). *DSM-5 guidebook: The essential companion to the diagnostic and statistical manual of mental disorders, fifth edition* (pp. 169–190). Washington, DC: American Psychological Association.

Bremner, J. D. (2006). Traumatic stress: Effects on the brain. *Dialogues in Clinical Neuroscience, 8*(4), 445–461.

Brende, J. O., & Parsons E. R. (1985). *Vietnam veterans: The road to recovery.* New York: Plenum Press.

Cantor, D., Fisher, B., Chibnall, S., Bruce, C., Townsend, R., Thomas, G., & Hyunshik, L. (2015). Report on the the AAU campus climate survey on sexual assault and sexual misconduct. *Westat.* Retrieved from http://www.upenn.edu/ir/surveys/AAU/Report%20and%20Tables%20on%20AAU%20Campus%20Climate%20Survey.pdf

Conley, A. H., Overstreet, C. M., Hawn, S. E., Kendler, K. S., Dick, D. M., & Amstadter, A. B. (2017). Prevalance and predictors of sexual assault among a college sample. *Journal of American College Health, 65*(1), 41–49.

Coray, E. (2016). Victim protection or revictimization: Should college disciplinary boards handle sexual assault claims? *Boston College Journal of Law & Social Justice, 36,* 59–90.

Cloitre, M., Garvert, D. W., Weiss, B., Carlson, E. B., & Bryant, R. A. (2014). Distinguishing PTSD, complex PTSD, and borderine personality disorder: A latent class analysis. *European Journal of Psychotraumatology, 5*(1). http://doi.org/10.3402/ejpt.v5.25097

Corey, G. (2016). *Theory and practice of counseling and psychotherapy* (6th ed). Belmont, CA: Wadsworth.

Dalenberg, C. J, Straus, E., & Carlson, E. B. (2017). Defining trauma. In S. N. Gold (Ed.), *APA Handbook of Trauma Psychology, Vol 1, Foundations in Knowledge,* (pp. 15–31), Washington, DC: American Psychological Association.

Emerson, D., Sharma, R., Chaudhry, S., & Turner, J. (2009). Trauma-sensitive yoga: Principles, practice, and research. *International Journal of Yoga Therapy, 19*(1), 123–128.

Fedina, L., Holmes, J. L., & Backes, B. L. (2016). Campus sexual assault: A systematic review of prevalence research from 2000–2015. *Trauma, Violence, & Abuse, 19*(1), 76–93.

Foa, E. B., & Kozak, M. J. (1986). Emotional processing of fear: exposure to corrective information. *Psychological Bulletin, 99*(1), 20.

Foa, E. B., Keane, T. M., & Friedman, M. J. (2000). Guidelines for treatment of PTSD. *Journal of traumatic stress, 13*(4), 539–588.

Foa, E. B., Hembree, E. A., & Rothbaum, B. O. (2007). *Prolonged exposure therapy for PTSD*. New York: Oxford University.

Forbes, D., Lloyd, D., Nixon, R. D., Elliott, P., Varker, T., Perry, D., Bryant, R. A., & Creamer, M. (2012). A multisite randomized controlled effectiveness trial of cognitive processing therapy for military-related posttraumatic stress disorder. *Journal of Anxiety Disorders, 26*, 442–452.

Gill, E. L. (2008). Mental health in college athletics: Its time for social work to get in the game. *Social Work, 53*(1), 85–88.

Herman, J. L. (1992). *Trauma and recovery*. New York: BasicBooks.

James, R., & Gilliland, B. (2012). *Crisis intervention strategies*. Nelson Education.

Mitchell, J. T. (1983). When disaster strikes: The critical incident stress debriefing process. *Journal of Emergency Medical Services, 8*(1), 36–39.

National Center for PTSD. (2016a). *PTSD for the public: How common is PTSD?* Retrieved from https://www.ptsd.va.gov/public/ptsd-overview/basics/how-common-is-ptsd.asp

National Center for PTSD. (2016b). *Psychological first aid: Field operations guide*. Retrieved from https://www.ptsd.va.gov/professional/materials/manuals/psych-first-aid.asp

National Child Traumatic Stress Network. (2006). *Psychological first aid field operations guide* (2nd ed.). Retrieved from https://www.nctsn.org/resources/psychological-first-aid-pfa-field-operations-guide-2nd-edition

National Collegiate Athletic Association. (2014). *NCAA student-athlete substance abuse use study: Executive summary August 2014*. Retrieved from http://www.ncaa.org/about/resources/research/ncaa-student-athlete-substance-use-study-executive-summary-august-2014

Reardon, C. L., & Credo, S. (2014). Drug abuse in athletes. *Substance Abuse and Rehabilitation, 5*, 95–105.

Resick, P. A., Monson, C. M., & Chard, K. M. (2007). *Cognitive processing therapy: Veteran/military version*. Washington, DC: U.S. Department of Veterans Affairs.

Rothbaum, B. O., Meadows, E. A., Resick, P., & Foy, D. W. (2000). Cognitive–behavioral therapy. In E. B. Foa, T. M. Keane, & M. J. Friedman (Eds.), *Effective treatments for PTSD: Practice guidelines from the International Society for Traumatic Stress Studies* (pp. 320–325). New York: Guilford Press.

Savage, J., Collins, D., & Cruickshank, A. (2017). Exploring traumas in the development of talent: What are they, what do they do, and what do they require? *Journal of Applied Sport Psychology, 29*(1), 101–117.

Shapiro, F., & Maxfield, L. (2002). Eye movement desensitization and reprocessing (EMDR): Information processing in the treatment of trauma. *Journal of Clinical Psychology, 58*(8), 933–948.

Sherin, J. E., & Nemeroff, C. B. (2011). Post-traumatic stress disorder: The neurobiological impact of psychological trauma. *Dialogues in Clinical Neuroscience, 13*(3), 263–278.

Wahto, R. S., Swift, J. K., & Whipple, J. L. (2016). The role of stigma and referral source in predicting college student-athletes' attitudes toward psychological help-seeking. *Journal of Clinical Sport Psychology, 10*(2), 85–98.

Watson, J. C. (2005). College student-athletes' attitudes toward help-seeking behavior and expectations of counseling services. *Journal of College Student Development, 46*(4), 442–449. http://doi.org/10.1353/csd.2005.0044

West, J., Liang, B., & Spinazzola, J. (2017). Trauma sensitive yoga as a complementary treatment for posttraumatic stress disorder: A qualitative descriptive analysis. *International Journal of Stress Management, 24*(2), 173.

Wolanin, A., Hong, E., Marks, D., Panchoo, K., and Gross, M. (2016). Prevalence of clinically elevated depressive symptoms in college athletes and differences by gender and sport. *British Journal of Sports Med. 50*, 167–171. *doi: 10.1136/bjsports-2015-095756*

# 8

# Concussion and Collegiate Student-Athletes

*Daniel Charek, Brandon Gillie, Natalie Sandel, and Anthony P. Kontos*

## CASE STUDY: ARTHUR

In 2016, Arthur, a 23-year-old collegiate male lacrosse player, sustained a concussion during a lacrosse game in his junior season. The athlete was tripped and fell to the ground, hitting the back of his head against the turf. He immediately experienced bilateral tinnitus, blurred vision, headache, and intense dizziness (rated as 7 on a scale of 1–10), but continued to play for the remainder of the game. Following the game, he reported his symptoms to a certified athletic trainer and was advised to remain out of all physical activity for one week. Over the following week, Arthur reported that his symptoms persisted, and he endured significantly increased headache with visual-based activities including reading, schoolwork, and computer use. Within two weeks, he exhibited minimal symptom improvement and, as a result, he was referred to a specialty care center comprised of neuropsychologists, physical therapists, and primary care sports medicine practitioners for multimodal assessment, treatment, and rehabilitation of his concussion.

At the initial appointment, 25 days post-injury, a clinical interview was conducted to obtain details of Arthur's mechanism of injury, acute and current symptoms, and biopsychosocial history, including a family medical history and premorbid risk factors. Arthur reported experiencing daily, frontally localized headache that was typically between 5–6 out of 10 and worsened visual activities. He also reported significant fatigue (rated 8 out of 10), light sensitivity, concentration difficulties, difficulty falling and staying asleep, as well as depression, including passive thoughts of suicidal ideation for which he sought mental health treatment. He did not report any degree of pre-injury risk factors and had no history of concussion. At this appointment, he completed neurocognitive testing (ImPACT), which revealed slowed processing speed and reduced visual memory in comparison to his pre-injury baseline. Arthur underwent vestibular therapy evaluation that revealed convergence and accommodative insufficiencies; an exertion therapy evaluation revealed no symptom provocation with physical exertion. He was instructed on the importance of utilizing behavioral regulation strategies to help manage his symptoms, including the need to be more socially active in order to reduce depression. The athlete was also encouraged to complete daily vergence and accommodative exercises designed to correct his degree of oculomotor dysfunction.

Arthur returned two weeks later for re-evaluation and reported significant improvement in all of his symptoms. At that time, his only remaining symptoms were intermittent, mild headache (3 out of 10), light sensitivity, and sadness. He had engaged in noncontact practice activities without symptom provocation and continued to attend counseling sessions for treatment of depression, though he denied experiencing any additional suicidal ideation. He attributed much of his recovery to the following factors: resuming physical activity, engaging in oculomotor exercises, and being more social. His progress was supported by neurocognitive testing that revealed significantly improved scores, though he had yet to return to his pre-injury level of performance. Additionally, his near point of convergence and accommodation were improved, yet both remained outside normal limits. He was advised to continue with all treatment recommendations and return for re-evaluation when asymptomatic.

Arthur returned one week later and stated that he was asymptomatic with rest and physical activity. He produced neurocognitive test scores that were entirely consistent with his pre-injury baseline. He no longer exhibited oculomotor dysfunction and was able to complete an exertion evaluation without any symptom provocation. As a result, he was determined to be fully recovered and was granted clearance to return to unrestricted athletic activities exactly 45 days after his injury.

Sports-related concussion is being increasingly recognized as a public health concern that involves a wide variety of specialties, including athletic training, physical therapy, primary care sports medicine, and psychology. Understanding key aspects of sports-related concussion—including its diagnosis, pathophysiological and behavioral conceptualizations, risk factors and predictors of poor outcome, and assessment and treatment approaches—is essential for sport psychologists and other healthcare professionals who may be tasked with providing services to athletes who have sustained a concussion. The importance of this issue is highlighted by the fact that an estimated 300,000 sports-related concussions occur annually, with many potential injuries going undiagnosed as symptoms are not reported or not recognized (Marar, McIlvain, Fields, & Comstock, 2012; McCrea, Hammeke, Olsen, Leo, & Guskiewicz, 2004).

The number of nationally reported sports-related concussions within specific sports is increasing, though it is unclear whether this is attributable to increased identification or frequency of concussions (Zuckerman et al., 2015). In terms of sport-specific risk, data from the NCAA Injury Surveillance program indicated that men's football had the largest annual number of reported sports-related concussions, followed by women's soccer, and women's basketball; however, men's wrestling evidenced the highest concussion rate (10.92 concussions per 10,000 athletic exposures) among college sports (Zuckerman et al., 2015). Although it is important to be aware of such sport-specific trends, a sports-related concussion can occur through a variety of different mechanisms and activities that occur during athletic participation.

## Sports-Related Concussion: Signs, Symptoms, and Impairment

Sports-related concussion is a form of mild traumatic brain injury induced by biomechanical forces that may be caused by a direct blow to the head, face, neck, or elsewhere on the body with an impulsive force transmitted to the head that transiently disrupts neurological functioning and results in a range of clinical signs and symptoms (McCrory et al., 2017). In most cases, the acute signs and symptoms of sports-related concussion are most appropriately conceptualized as resulting from a disturbance in neurobiological functioning, as opposed to a structural injury (e.g., skull fracture, intracranial bleed), in which a disruptive neurometabolic cascade occurs that includes intracellular fluctuations in ion concentrations, hyperglycolysis, changes in axon permeability, and altered neurotransmission, among other processes, and lasts approximately 7–10 days in animal models (Barkhoudarian, Hovda, & Giza, 2016; Giza & Hovda, 2014). It is thought that these physiological perturbations underlie the clinical characteristics of concussion. Perhaps the most diagnostic signs of sports-related concussion include acute markers of injury such as loss of consciousness, posttraumatic amnesia, disorientation, and confusion. However, a common misconception is that these markers must be present to diagnose concussion, when in actuality, the majority of sports-related concussions occur without loss of consciousness or other frank neurological signs (McCrory et al., 2017).

Sports-related concussion is a heterogeneous injury that can produce a diverse array of symptoms. Common symptoms may include headache, dizziness, loss of balance, fatigue, nausea, visual disturbance, mental fogginess, cognitive difficulties, increased emotionality, and sleep dysregulation. These symptoms typically manifest immediately after injury and can generally be classified into the following categories: physical, cognitive, emotional, and sleep domains (Kontos, Elbin et al., 2012; Merritt, Rabinowitz, & Arnett, 2015). Within the first week of injury, most concussed individuals demonstrate a similar cognitive-fatigue-migraine presentation with symptoms from several different clinical domains occurring in combination (Kontos, Elbin et al., 2012). However, changes in symptom presentation may occur overtime as concussed individuals begin to engage in physical and cognitive activities, and progress from acute to later phases of injury (Duhaime et al., 2012). Given the complex and evolving nature of concussion symptoms, clinicians and researchers have proposed conceptual models in order to better understand and treat sports-related concussion. Indeed, some conceptualize concussion symptoms and impairments in terms of distinct clinical profiles that warrant targeted and individualized treatments (Collins, Kontos, Reynolds, Murawski, & Fu, 2014; Ellis, Leddy, & Willer, 2015). In general, these models provide a framework for evaluating factors, including vestibular dysfunction, ocular-motor impairment, anxiety/mood difficulties, and other areas of dysfunction that are thought to underlie many of the commonly reported symptoms of concussion.

The Consensus Statement on Concussion in Sport (McCrory et al., 2017) define recovery as including a return to normal activities, including school, work, and sport, resolution of concussion symptoms, and a return to clinically normal balance and cognitive functioning. However, determining whether an athlete is fully recovered from a sports-related concussion is complicated by several factors, including the fact that concussion symptoms are frequently present among noninjured individuals (McCrory et al., 2017), as well as an inability to fully assess whether neurobiological recovery has occurred alongside clinical recovery (Vagnozzi et al., 2010). Nonetheless, several studies have investigated the issue of recovery from a sports-related concussion and found that the majority of athletes, in some cases upwards of 90% of individuals, recover from the acute effects of concussion within 7 to 14 days (McCrea et al., 2003; Belanger & Vanderploeg, 2005; Williams, Puetz, Giza, & Broglio, 2015). However, as clinical assessment of sports-related concussion has become more refined and comprehensive, recent research has shown that recovery across multiple domains of functioning may take as long as three to four weeks, on average (Henry, Elbin, Collins, Marchetti, & Kontos, 2016). Overall, it is becoming increasingly recognized that recovery from concussion is a complex issue that is multifaceted and influenced by pre-injury and concurrent factors at the time of injury.

Although a vast majority of athletes do eventually experience complete recovery from concussion, a subset of individuals demonstrate a protracted recovery that can take several months or even years. Post-concussion syndrome refers to the persistence of concussion symptoms beyond a three-month period, a significant decline from a previous (i.e., pre-injury) level of functioning, and significant impairment in social or occupational functioning. Estimates of the prevalence of post-concussion syndrome vary, however, some studies indicate that among young athletes, post-concussion syndrome may develop following sports-related concussion in 1.5% to 15% of cases (Makdissi, Cantu, Johnston, McCrory, & Meeuwisse, 2013; Meehan, d'Hemecourt, & Comstock, 2010). One of the most notable aspects of post-concussion syndrome is its association with mental health disorders. Several studies have found that adults and adolescents who sustain a mild traumatic brain injury and who exhibit a prolonged course of symptoms, are at greater risk of a new onset of anxiety disorders, including posttraumatic stress disorder, panic disorder, social phobia, and agoraphobia (Moore, Terryberry-Spohr, & Hope, 2006; Whelan-Goodinson, Ponsford, Johnston, & Grant, 2009; Massagli et al., 2004), as well as mood disorders such as depression (Bryant et al., 2010; Tsai et al., 2014.) Given that persistent sports-related concussions can have a debilitating effect on health-related quality of life and overall functionality (Russell et al., 2017), preventing the development of post-concussion syndrome should be among the primary goals of clinicians who evaluate and manage sports-related concussions.

## Risk Factors for Sustaining Concussion and Prolonged Recovery

The literature on risk factors associated with the incidence of and recovery from sport-related concussion among collegiate student-athletes continues to expand as our understanding of the nature of sports-related concussions, assessment tools for evaluation, and treatment methods evolve. Risk factors that render athletes more vulnerable to sustaining a sports-related concussion are considered primary risk factors, while secondary risk factors are those that may predispose athletes to a complicated or prolonged recovery from the injury. Initial research on such risk factors has largely focused on basic demographic characteristics (e.g., age, sex) to identify athlete populations that may be at an increased risk of injury. However, a growing trend in the literature is the exploration of a biopsychosocial model towards sports-related concussion, in which aspects of an athlete's medical history (e.g., history of migraine or mental health disorder) or acute symptom presentation are taken into consideration when prognosticating recovery time. This section summarizes the extant literature on risk factors that have been identified in collegiate athlete populations.

## Primary Risk Factors

**Age.** Several studies exploring age as a potential risk factor in sports-related concussion have compared samples of high school and collegiate athletes. In terms of incidence, the role of age in modifying susceptibility to the injury remains an area of debate. Some studies indicate that collegiate athletes have higher rates of sports-related concussion per athletic exposure relative to high school athletes (Gessel, Fields, Collins, Dick, & Comstock, 2007; Abrahams, McFie, Patricios, Posthumus, & September, 2013), while other studies have found that younger, amateur athletes are more susceptible to the injury (Guskiewicz, Weaver, Padua, & Garrett, 2000; Shankar, Fields, Collins, Dick, & Comstock, 2007). A systematic review on age as a risk factor found that more studies indicate greater risk of sports-related concussion in collegiate athletes, but given contrasting findings across studies it remains debated on whether age plays a role in the incidence (Abrahams et al., 2013).

The role of age in terms of recovery time from concussion has also been investigated between high school and collegiate athletes. A recent meta-analysis (Williams et al., 2015) found that collegiate athletes tend to recover more quickly from concussion relative to younger athletes, and high school athletes demonstrate more variable recovery times. Studies have consistently demonstrated that collegiate athletes appear to recover faster both in terms of subjective symptom reporting (Corwin et al., 2014) and performance on objective measures (Field, Collins, Lovell, & Maroon, 2003; Covassin, Elbin, Harris, Parker, & Kontos, 2012.) Several potential theories have been proposed to explain longer recovery times in youth. Potential explanations include collegiate athletes being more physically gifted and less injury prone based on self-selection, underreporting of symptoms among collegiate athletes, and the immature brain being more susceptible to the neurometabolic crisis that ensues after concussion (Field et al., 2003; Williams et al., 2015).

**Sex.** Investigating differences in sports-related concussion risk among male and female athletes is confounded by differences in sport and the style of play between the sexes. Types of sports played, game rules, equipment worn, and level of physicality are often different between males and females and may modify risk of sustaining a sports-related concussion (Lincoln et al., 2011). When males and females are compared in gender-neutral sports (e.g., soccer, basketball), females demonstrate a 1.5 to 3 times higher risk of incidence of sports-related concussion relative to their male counterparts (Covassin, Schatz, & Swanik, 2007; Abrahams et al., 2013). Female sex also appears to be a risk factor for a complicated recovery from concussion. Female athletes consistently display more symptoms after injury and perform more poorly on neurocognitive testing (Chiang Colvin et al., 2009; Broshek et al., 2005; Dougan, Horswill, & Geffen, 2014), but further research is warranted to determine if female athletes take longer to recover from concussion relative to males (Henry et al., 2016; Sandel, Schatz, Goldberg, & Lazar, 2017). Theories for underlying mechanisms contributing to differences in males' versus females' response to concussion may be attributable to differences in neuroanatomy, sex hormones, cerebral blood flow, rates of glucose metabolism, head-neck stabilization, and/or sociocultural influences in symptom reporting.

**Competitive play.** Research on the incidence of sports-related concussion per athletic exposure (AE) indicates that collegiate athletes are more likely to sustain a concussion during a game versus practice (Guskiewicz et al., 2000; Shankar et al., 2007; Hootman, Dick, & Agel, 2007). Hootman et al. (2007) reported that the incidence rate of sports-related concussion in games was 12.8 per 1000 AEs, while it was 4.0 per 1000 AEs in practices. It is speculated that the more aggressive playing style in games may result in more high impact collisions and thus raise the risk of sports-related concussion (Abrahams et al., 2013).

**History of prior concussions.** Collegiate athletes with a prior history of concussion consistently demonstrate an increased risk of sustaining a future sports-related concussion (Abrahams et al., 2013). There appears to be a dose-response relationship between the number of prior concussions reported by an athlete and the likelihood of sustaining a subsequent injury (Guskiewicz et al., 2003; Teel, Marshall, Shankar, McCrea, & Guskiewicz, 2017). For instance, athletes with a history of three or more concussions demonstrate a 3-fold risk of sustaining a concussion relative to athletes without a history of concussion (Guskiewicz et al., 2003; Teel et al., 2017). Athletes with a history of multiple prior concussions also appear to take longer to recover from a newly sustained injury (Guskiewicz et al., 2003; Corwin et al., 2014). It is worth noting that the evaluation of an athlete with a history of multiple prior sports-related concussions requires extensive questioning to elucidate the nature of prior injuries. Specifically, understanding the timing between injuries, force of impact, athletes' medical and psychosocial history, assessment tools utilized to evaluate injuries, and prior treatments may be important for delineating the basis of recurrent concussion.

## Secondary Risk Factors

Emerging research suggests that athletes may have a pre-injury vulnerability to concussion based on risk factors in their medical history. Pre-injury risk factors that have been identified as potentially complicating recovery from concussion, include a history of a neurodevelopmental disorder (e.g., learning disability, attention disorder), a mental health disorder (e.g., anxiety, depression), and headache/migraine. There is also indication that experiencing specific symptoms immediately after sustaining a sports-related concussion may also be helpful for prognosticating recovery time. Further research is warranted to determine if certain pre-injury conditions are associated with immediate symptom presentation and clinical trajectories, as perhaps, athletes with pre-injury vulnerabilities may be predisposed to develop certain constellations of symptoms and deficits.

## Constitutional Risk Factors

**Headache/migraine history.** Emerging research indicates that athletes with a personal or family history of headaches or migraines may be at an increased vulnerability for sustaining a sports-related concussion and a prolonged recovery from the injury. Athletes diagnosed with migraine by a healthcare professional were 2.36 times more likely to report prior concussions (Gordon, Dooley, & Wood, 2006). Studies among youth and collegiate athletes similarly indicate that athletes with preseason headaches are more likely to experience sports-related concussions than those without a history of headaches (Schneider, Meeuwisse, Kang, Schneider, & Emery, 2013; Register-Mihalik, Guskiewicz, Mann, & Shields, 2007). Given that about 24% of NCAA Division-I athletes report a personal history of migraine and 12% report tension headaches, headache history may represent a significant risk factor for sports-related concussion in collegiate athlete populations (Seifert et al., 2017). There appears to be an association between sports-related concussion and a history of headache, however, it remains unclear if headache predisposes athletes to sports-related concussion or if athletes become more vulnerable to headaches post-injury (Eckner, Seifert, Pescovitz, Zeiger, & Kutcher, 2017).

**History of mental health disorder.** Research consistently demonstrates that athletes with a pre-injury history of a mental health disorder are at an increased risk of a complicated recovery from concussion, (Ponsford et al., 2012; Carroll et al., 2004). Although mild, transient emotional changes are common after sports-related concussion (Mainwaring, Hutchison, Bisschop, Comper, & Richards, 2010; Kontos, Elbin et al., 2012), a prior diagnosis of a mental health condition puts athletes with sports-related concussion at an increased risk of worsening of their emotional sequelae and onset of a novel mental health condition (McCauley et al. 2013). When athletes with a pre-injury mental health condition are evaluated at three months post-injury, the mental disorder serves as a better predictor of ongoing impairment than the sports-related concussion itself (McCauley et al., 2013). In addition to psychiatric diagnoses, there are other psychosocial factors that may contribute to a prolonged recovery time. Identified psychosocial factors include an avoidant coping style (Carroll, Cassidy, & Côté, 2006), poor capacity for emotional regulation (McCauley et al., 2013), environmental stress (Hou et al., 2012; Van Veldhoven et al., 2011), and interpersonal dynamics (Covassin et al., 2014; Olsson et al., 2013). It is speculated that the neurobiological effects of concussion on emotional circuitry in the brain (Chen, Johnston, Petrides, & Ptito, 2008) may predispose athletes to emotional changes that are less common in other sports injuries (Covassin et al., 2014).

**History of learning disability/ADHD.** Athletes with a history of a neurodevelopmental condition (i.e., learning disability [LD], ADHD) have a significantly greater lifetime history of concussion (Iverson et al., 2016; Alosco, Fedor, & Gunstad, 2014). Specifically, collegiate athletes with an LD or ADHD are at a nearly three-fold greater risk of having more than two prior concussions relative to control athletes (Mucha et al., 2014). Similarly, 14% of NCAA Division I athletes without ADHD report having a prior concussion, while greater than 50% of athletes with ADHD report at least one prior concussion (Alosco et al., 2014). Although these studies suggest that athletes with LD or ADHD are more likely to report prior concussions, it remains unclear if these athletes are more at risk of sustaining a concussion and/or demonstrate a different course of recovery from the injury (Iverson et al., 2016). Further research on the role of LD and ADHD as potential risk factors for increasing susceptibility to concussion (Iverson et al., 2016; Brehaut, Miller, Raina, & McGrail, 2003) or a complicated recovery from the injury (Iverson et al., 2017; Miller et al., 2016) is inconsistent and requires further study.

## Acute Presentation Post-Injury

Prognosticating the severity of a sports-related concussion in the acute phase of injury can be difficult given that traditional neurological grading scales are unreliable for classifying this injury (Lovell, Collins, Iverson, Johnston, & Bradley, 2004). The term severity in the sports-related concussion literature often equates with determining the length of time an athlete requires to achieve full recovery. Studies on predictors of recovery in the early phase of sports-related concussion suggest that an elevated symptom burden (Meehan, Mannix, Stracciolini, Elbin, & Collins, 2013; Meehan, Mannix, Monuteaux, Stein, & Bachur, 2014; Lau, Collins, & Lovell, 2012), positive findings on vestibular screening tools (Mucha et al., 2014; Anzalone et al., 2016), and notable decline on neurocognitive testing (Lau, Collins, & Lovell, 2011; 2012) may be good prognosticators of recovery time. There is a growing body of research investigating the potential long-term effects of sports-related concussion using advanced neuroimaging, but these tools require further validation before being deployed for clinical use (Eierud et al., 2014).

## *Acute Markers of Head Injury*

Traditional markers of head injury utilized to classify the severity of traumatic brain injury (TBI) include the presence/absence of certain neurological signs (e.g., loss of consciousness [LOC], posttraumatic amnesia [PTA], disorientation, or confusion) and score on the Glasgow Coma Scale (GCS). However, mild TBIs, such as sports-related concussion, yield a GCS score of 13–15, indicating adequate motor, verbal, and eye responses, and are not always accompanied by acute markers of head injury (Collins et al., 2003). Studies comparing sports-related concussion athletes who experienced a brief LOC to those without a LOC indicate that these groups did not differ in their initial report of symptoms, performance on sideline assessments, nor length of recovery time (Teel et al., 2017; Collins et al., 2003; Erlanger et al., 2003). Some studies do indicate however, that the presence of brief PTA immediately after concussion is predictive of symptom severity, worsened neurocognitive deficits, and a longer recovery time (Guskiewicz et al., 2003; Teel et al., 2017; Collins et al., 2003; Erlanger et al., 2003), but this finding is inconsistent in the literature (Meehan et al., 2013; Meehan et al., 2014). It appears that traditional markers of head injury are not reliable predictors of severity of concussion, and other signs or symptoms may be better prognosticators for estimating recovery time (Collins et al., 2003; Meehan et al., 2013; Lau, Kontos, Collins, Mucha, & Lovell, 2011).

## Symptoms

When acute markers (e.g., LOC, PTA) and reported symptoms (e.g., headache, nausea) at the time of injury are considered, self-report of dizziness is the best predictor of prolonged recovery in high school male athletes. Football players reporting on-field dizziness at the time of injury appear at a six-fold greater risk of protracted recovery from concussion (Lau, Kontos et al., 2011).

The experience of post-traumatic dizziness is thought to be due to a central disturbance of the vestibular system. As such, a positive finding on screening tools of vestibular disturbance similarly are predictive of a prolonged recovery from concussion (Mucha et al., 2014; Anzalone et al., 2016). Headache is the most commonly reported symptom immediately after concussion (Meehan et al., 2010). Headaches that occur after a head injury and are accompanied by nausea and light and/or noise sensitivity are termed post-traumatic migraine (PTM). Comparison of groups of high school athletes with PTM, headache alone, and no headache, indicates that sports-related concussion athletes who demonstrate acute PTM exhibit worsened neurocognitive performance, higher levels of symptoms, and prolonged recovery times (Kontos et al., 2013; Mihalik et al., 2013). Kontos et al. (2013) found that high school athletes with PTM were 7.3 times more likely to have a prolonged recovery relative to athletes without a headache, and 2.6 times more likely to have a prolonged recovery relative to athletes endorsing headache alone. Further research is warranted to evaluate whether the association between PTM and prolonged recovery can be extrapolated to collegiate populations.

# Assessment

## Sideline Assessment

The initial goal of concussion assessment is to identify and accurately diagnose athletes with a suspected concussion so that they may be removed from play. The neurometabolic cascade following concussion (Giza & Hovda, 2014) may render the brain particularly susceptible to additional head injuries (Guskiewicz et al., 2003) or even catastrophic consequences (e.g., Second Impact Syndrome; Schnadower, Vazquez, Lee, Dayan, & Roskind, 2007; Bruce et al., 1981), and continued play following concussion is associated with poorer recovery outcomes (Elbin et al., 2016). To assist in expeditious and accurate sideline diagnosis, standardized sideline assessment tools have been developed. The most commonly used sideline tool is the Sport Concussion Assessment Tool–5 (SCAT-5), which can be used in athletes 13 and older (a child version also exists for use with children aged 5 through 12). This tool includes evaluation of symptoms, cognitive functioning, balance, neck integrity, and coordination. Clinically relevant metrics for this measure, such as sensitivity and normative data, have been published in the literature (Yengo-Kahn et al., 2016; Chin, Nelson, Barr, McCrory, & McCrea, 2016).

## Multimodal Clinical Assessment

Although sideline assessments can be useful in initially diagnosing concussions, evidence suggests these measures are insensitive to identifying deficits in balance beyond 3–5 days and mental status beyond 48 hours, and therefore are of limited utility in reaching return-to-play (RTP) decisions (McCrea et al., 2003). Because concussion is a heterogeneous injury associated with a myriad of physical, cognitive, and emotional symptoms, a multimodal assessment approach offers a nuanced understanding of the injury, allowing for specification of specific clinical trajectories or symptom profiles. Research suggests a multimodal or multifaceted test battery is more sensitive than any standalone measure in identifying concussion (Broglio, Macciocchi, & Ferrara, 2007; Resch et al., 2016; Register-Mihalik et al., 2013) and multimodal batteries have demonstrated good utility in predicting recovery duration (Sufrinko, Marchetti, Cohen, Elbin, Re, & Kontos, in press). Further, different domains of deficit may recover at different rates, and certain impairments can evolve or worsen in the days following injury (Duhaime et al., 2012), highlighting the importance of evaluating multiple relevant domains in a serial fashion when reaching RTP decisions. Domains targeted by a multimodal concussion assessment battery may include subjective symptoms, neurocognitive performance, vestibular function, postural stability, ocular-motor function, physical exertion tolerance, and psychological functioning.

**Symptom inventories.** Several standardized self-report measures of symptom severity have been developed, which often include a broad range of concussion symptoms, allowing for efficient sampling of the athlete's presenting complaints. Among the most commonly utilized self-report concussion symptom inventories is the Post-Concussion Symptom Scale, a 22-item self-report inventory, utilizing a 7-point Likert scale of symptom severity (Lovell et al., 2006), which has been shown to have 4-factor structure including cognitive-fatigue-migraine, affective, somatic, and sleep symptoms (Kontos, Elbin et al., 2012).

**Neurocognitive assessment.** Neurocognitive testing is a cornerstone of sports-related concussion management (McCrory et al., 2013) and has been shown to be sensitive to deficits acutely (e.g., <24 hours following injury) and may detect deficits even after an athlete reports being symptom free (Iverson, Brooks, Lovell, & Collins, 2006; McClincy, Lovell, Pardini, Collins, & Spore, 2006; Lovell et al., 2007). Such assessments may take paper and pencil (P&P) form, utilizing traditional neuro-psychology measures, such as the Hopkins Verbal Learning Test or Trail Making Test. Beginning in the 1990s, the development of computerized neurocognitive testing (CNT) introduced an efficient alternative for measuring the neurocognitive sequelae of concussion. As many as 68.5% of certified athletic trainers working in secondary school settings reported utilizing CNTs (Williams, Welch, Weber, Parsons, & Valovich McLeod, 2014), as does the NFL, NBA, NHL, and MLB (the NHL utilizes a combined P&P and CNT approach) (Webbe & Zimmer, 2015). Of the available CNT measures, The Immediate Post-Concussion Assessment and Cognitive Test (ImPACT), which is the only FDA-approved test, is the most exten-sively utilized and researched (Broglio et al., 2007; Schatz, Pardini, Lovell, Collins, & Podell, 2006; Schatz & Sandel, 2013).

**Vestibular and ocular-motor functioning.** The vestibular system is a sensorimo-tor processing pathway linking inner ear sensory organs with central processing areas. Vestibular input is utilized in coordinating gaze stabilizing eye movements (vestibulo-ocular reflex; VOR) and maintaining balance (vestibulo-spinal reflex; VSR) (Goldberg et al., 2012). Dysfunction to this system is common secondary to concussion (Naguib et al., 2012; Hoffer, Gottshall, Moore, Balough, & Wester, 2004), with 43% of athletes reporting balance disruption and 50% reporting dizzi-ness in the acute stages of injury (Lovell et al., 2004). Ocular-motor dysfunction, or problems with coordinated eye movements, occur in roughly 33% to 65% of sports-related concussions (Capó-Aponte, Urosevich, Temme, Tarbett, & Sanghera, 2012;

Scheiman et al., 2003; Ciuffreda et al., 2007). Traditionally, balance testing served as a proxy for assessment of overall vestibular dysfunction, with the Balance Error Scoring System (BESS) representing one of the most commonly utilized assessment techniques, however, limited changes in BESS performance have been reported outside of the very acute stage of injury, limiting its clinical utility (McCrea et al., 2013; Bressel, Yonker, Kras, & Heath, 2007; McCrea et al., 2005). To more directly screen for both vestibular and ocular-motor sequelae of sports-related concussion, the Vestibular/Ocular-Motor Screening Assessment (VOMS) was developed, which briefly screens five domains, including smooth pursuits, saccadic eye movements, near point of convergence, vestibulo-ocular reflex (VOR), and visual motion sensitivity (VMS) (Mucha et al., 2014). Clinicians assess for symptom exacerbation during each phase of screening, attend to relevant behavioral information (e.g., hypometric saccades), and measure near point of convergence (NPC) across three trials. The VOMS is an internally consistent measure with an acceptable false positive rate and sensitivity for identifying athletes with concussions (Mucha et al., 2014; Kontos, Sufrinko, Elbin, Puskar, & Collins, 2016).

**Exertion testing.** Assessment of athletes' response to exertion may be a useful tool in determining when to return injured athletes to exercise and sports activities. Consensus statements recommend completion of a graduated exertion protocol before returning to play (RTP), progressing from no activity to full contact practice (McCrory et al., 2013). The Buffalo Concussion Treadmill Test (BCTT) is a modified version of the cardiac Balke protocol and assesses perceived exertional output and symptom provocation during straight-line cardiovascular activity (Leddy & Willer, 2013). Given the nature of the vestibulo-ocular reflex (Goldberg et al., 2012), assessment of response to dynamic exercise may be useful in reaching RTP decisions, as this is particularly relevant with athletes given most sport-related activity is dynamic in nature.

**Psychological assessment.** Assessment of an athletes' psychological health is another key assessment domain, as many athletes experience mood-related sequelae, especially those experiencing prolonged recovery (McCrory et al., 2013; Kontos, Covassin, Elbin, & Parker, 2012). Even subclinical affective responses may interfere with the athlete's response to treatment (Kontos, Deitrick, & Reynolds, 2016). Assessment of psychological functioning is an ongoing and multifaceted process that may benefit from inclusion of standardized assessment measures. Self-report inventories, such as the Beck Anxiety Inventory, measure state or acute emotional functioning and are useful in detecting affective symptoms emerging secondary to concussion. Other self-report measures, such as the Minnesota Multiphasic Personality Inventory-II Revised Factor, assess more trait-like psychological constructs. While these measures are not commonly utilized in concussion management, they may be useful in cases of prolonged recovery with prominent psychological features.

## Treatment

### *Prescribed Cognitive and Physical Rest*

Physical and cognitive rest has historically stood as the cornerstone of concussion management (McCrory et al., 2013). The rationale for this approach is largely conceptual in nature, with it being suggested that nonessential activity further depletes the body of glycogen and oxygen, potentially exacerbating the patho-physiological energy crisis that occurs when a concussive injury is sustained (Broglio, Collins, Williams, Mucha, & Kontos, 2015). Further, physical and cognitive activity often provoke concussion symptoms, increasing patient burden (Giza, Griesbach, & Hovda, 2005; Griesbach, Hovda, Molteni, Wu, & Gomez-Pinilla, 2004). Despite this conceptual foundation, empirical justification for a rest-based approach is equivocal. In fact, research suggests prolonged periods of rest may actually have detrimental effects in some cases (Gibson, Nigrovic, O'Brien, & Meehan, 2013; Brown et al., 2014). A randomized controlled trial found that athletes prescribed one to two days of rest, followed by a moderated return to activity, reported fewer symptoms and faster symptom resolution compared to those prescribed five days of strict rest (Thomas et al., 2015), and retrospective studies have found that athletes reporting low levels of physical and cognitive activity within the first month of injury had poorer neurocognitive and symptom-related outcomes relative to athletes who reported moderate activity (Majerske et al, 2008). Strict rest may pose negative mood-related consequences due to being withheld from enjoyable activities and adaptive outlets, as well as deconditioning and academic difficulties (Karlin, 2011; DiFazio, Silverberg, Kirkwood, Bernier, & Iverson, 2016). Athletes withheld from sports for three or more weeks evidence higher rates of depression relative to noninjured athletes (Manuel et al., 2002).

### *Active Behavioral Regulation Strategies*

An alternative to a rest-based approach is prescription of a regulated daily schedule, including maintenance of a consistent sleep-wake cycle, adequate hydration, regular meal consumption, stress management, and regular noncontact light intensity exercise (Womble & Collins, 2016), as dysregulation in these behaviors increases symptomatology (Choe & Blume, 2016; Kacperski, Hung, & Blume, 2016). The conceptual foundation for these recommendations borrows from the migraine literature, which shares a common pathophysiology with concussion (Choe & Blume, 2016). These behavioral management strategies serve as the foundation of clinical management, with clinicians then creating targeted treatment plans and making appropriate referrals based on the presentation of the athlete.

## Vestibular Rehabilitation

Concussions may be associated with a variety of vestibular system difficulties, including Benign Paroxysmal Positional Vertigo (BPPV; brief dizziness caused by crystals dislodged from the otolith organs moving within the semicircular canals of the inner ear), VOR impairment (problems with vision stabilizing eye movements), VMS (sensitivity to stimuli due to problems integrating visual and vestibular input), balance impairment, exertion-induced dizziness, and cervicogenic dizziness (Naguib et al., 2012; Hoffer et al., 2004; Lovell et al., 2004; Kontos, Deitrick, Collins, & Mucha, 2017). The efficacy of vestibular rehabilitation for treatment of these conditions is well established in nonconcussion specific populations (Hillier & McDonnell, 2011; Pavlou, 2010; Pavlou, Bronstein, & Davies, 2013), and preliminary evidence for the use of vestibular rehabilitation in the treatment of sports-related concussion is promising (Hoffer et al., 2004; Gottshall & Hoffer, 2010; Gottshall, 2011; Alsalaheen et al., 2010; Schneider et al., 2014).

## Ocular-Motor Rehabilitation/Vision Therapy

Although ocular-motor (i.e., vision) abnormalities are relatively common secondary to concussion (Capó-Aponte et al., 2012; Kontos, Elbin et al., 2012; Gallaway, Scheiman, & Mitchell, 2017), there is limited research investigating the efficacy of vision-based rehabilitation strategies in treating sports-related concussion. Studies on the utility of vision therapies in concussion populations have provided preliminary evidence for the effectiveness of targeted ocular-motor therapies including vergence, versional, and accommodative exercises (Gallaway et al., 2017; Ciuffreda et al., 2008; Thiagarajan & Ciuffreda, 2014; Thiagarajan, Ciuffreda, Capó-Aponte, Ludlam, & Kapoor, 2014).

## Psychological Interventions

Anxiety and mood-related issues may occur as a direct result of concussion or as an adjustment response to the recovery process. These symptoms can interfere with an athlete's ability to engage in active rehabilitation programs (McCrory et al., 2013; Kontos, Covassin et al., 2012; Kontos, Dietrick et al., 2016.) One advantage of the behavioral regulation strategies introduced above is the athlete remains regulated and active, combating conditioned avoidance and social isolation (Kontos, Dietrick et al., 2016). In some cases, more intensive interventions may be necessary to address mood-related difficulties. Cognitive Behavioral Therapy (CBT) is a form of psychotherapy incorporating behavioral activation strategies and cognitive restructuring of maladaptive thought patterns. This treatment has promising evidence in treating post-concussive syndrome (Al Sayegh, Sandford, & Carson, 2010).

In cases of insomnia, Cognitive Behavioral Therapy for Insomnia (CBT-I) has been found efficacious with a variety of clinical populations, although only a single case report investigates this treatment with traumatic brain injury patients, reporting promising results (Ouellet & Morin, 2007.)

## *Pharmacological Intervention*

Pharmacological intervention for concussion symptoms, particularly with athletes experiencing protracted recovery, has been reported by as many as 89% of clinicians (Kinnaman, Mannix, Comstock, & Meehan, 2013). A frequent target of pharmacological intervention is anxiety and/or depression, which may involve prescription of tricyclic antidepressants (e.g., amitriptyline), selective serotonin reuptake inhibitors (SSRI; e.g., sertraline), or selective norepinephrine reuptake inhibitors (SNRI; e.g., venlafaxine) (Kinnaman et al., 2013; Broglio et al., 2015). Post-traumatic migraine symptoms are also sometimes addressed pharmacologically utilizing anticonvulsants (e.g., topiramate), beta-blockers (e.g., propranolol), triptans (e.g., Imitrex), and tricyclic antidepressants (e.g., amitriptyline) (Bell, Kraus, & Zasler, 1999). Athletes with pronounced symptoms of fatigue and cognitive concerns are sometimes treated via a neurostimulant. Amantadine is most commonly prescribed, and preliminary evidence suggests it may be effective for treating cognitive symptoms (Reddy, Collins, Lovell, & Kontos, 2013). Sleep disruption secondary to concussion is also sometimes treated via melatonin in combination with sleep hygiene strategies (Petraglia, Maroon, & Bailes, 2012; Meehan, 2011).

## Future Directions

Clinicians and researchers face a number of challenges and opportunities in terms of understanding recovery and management of sports-related concussion. As it stands, clinicians primarily use clinical judgment and expert opinion to guide decisions on how and when to best reintroduce cognitive and physical activities to promote recovery. However, as clinicians adopt a more active management style as suggested by the Consensus Statement on Concussion in Sport (McCrory et al, 2017), the need for evidence-based guidelines on how to do so in a safe and effective manner will be critical. Randomized controlled trials (RCTs) that compare the effectiveness of active vs. rest-based approaches on recovery from concussion will help to accomplish this goal. Thomas and colleagues (2015) used an RCT design to show that strict cognitive rest for five days post-injury led to worsened symptoms and delayed recovery as compared with 1–2 days cognitive rest followed by gradual return to normal cognitive activity. Others have shown that an active rehabilitation approach that included moderated physical activity was associated with a quicker recovery in terms of self-reported symptoms compared to a less active control group

(Chan et al., 2017). Despite these initial findings, additional information is needed to inform clinical decision-making. Several additional studies have sought to examine the effects of physical rest vs. early re-introduction of physical activity through controlled trials, (Ledoux et al., 2017; Reed et al., 2015) though the results of these studies have yet to be published.

Perhaps the most controversial issue surrounding sports-related concussion is its connection to possible long-term effects, including the development of chronic traumatic encephalopathy—a progressive, neurological disorder thought to be associated with repetitive head impact. In a recent systematic review, Manley et al. (2017) concluded that multiple concussions appear to be associated with the development of later-life cognitive impairment and mental health problems in some retired athletes. However, it was also noted that causes of these problems are multifactorial and that as of yet, no clear causal relationship between repetitive head impact exposure, concussions, and long-term brain health exists (Manley et al., 2017). Although the potential long-term effects of concussion have received a high degree of media attention, it is important to keep in mind that these issues remain poorly understood and require further study. Thus, clinicians should address the potential risks associated with long-term sport participation and repetitive head injury with concussed athletes while also taking care to not make claims that go beyond what is currently supported by a growing body of empirical research.

## Discussion Questions

1. Which of the risk factors mentioned above were present in the case of Arthur?

2. Consider the case of Arthur. What are the advantages of using a multimodal assessment strategy for this student-athlete versus relying only on a sideline assessment?

3. What strategies mentioned above were included in Arthur's treatment plan?

4. What is the importance of communication between the members of his treatment team, particularly as it pertains to the decision regarding his return to play?

## References

Abrahams, S., McFie, S., Patricios, J., Posthumus, M., & September, A. V. (2013). Risk factors for sports concussion: An evidence-based systematic review. *British Journal of Sports Medicine, 48*(2), 91–97.

Al Sayegh, A., Sandford, D., & Carson, A. J. (2010). Psychological approaches to treatment of postconcussion syndrome: A systematic review. *Journal of Neurology, Neurosurgery, and Psychiatry, 81*(10), 1128–1134. doi:10.1136/jnnp.2008.170092

Alosco, M. L., Fedor, A. F., & Gunstad, J. (2014). Attention deficit hyperactivity disorder as a risk factor for concussions in NCAA division-I athletes. *Brain injury, 28*(4), 472–474.

Alsalaheen, B. A., Mucha, A., Morris, L. O., Whitney, S. L., Furman, J. M., Camiolo-Reddy, C. E., Collins, M. W., Lovell, M. R., & Sparto, P. J. (2010). Vestibular rehabilitation for dizziness and balance disorders after concussion. *Journal of Neurologic Physical Therapy, 34*(2), 87–93. doi:10.1097/NPT.0b013e3181dde568

Anzalone, A. J., Blueitt, D., Case, T., McGuffin, T., Pollard, K., Garrison, J. C., Jones, M. T., Pavur, R., Turner, S., & Oliver, J. M. (2016). A positive vestibular/ocular motor screening (VOMS) is associated with increased recovery time after sports-related concussion in youth and adolescent athletes. *The American Journal of Sports Medicine, 45*(2), 474–479.

Barkhoudarian, G., Hovda, D. A., & Giza, C. C. (2016). The molecular pathophysiology of concussive brain injury–an update. *Physical Medicine and Rehabilitation Clinics, 27*(2), 373–393.

Belanger, H. G., & Vanderploeg, R. D. (2005). The neuropsychological impact of sports-related concussion: A meta-analysis. *Journal of the International Neuropsychological Society, 11*(4), 345–357.

Bell, K. R., Kraus, E. E., & Zasler, N. D. (1999). Medical management of posttraumatic headaches: Pharmacological and physical treatment. *The Journal of Head Trauma Rehabilitation, 14*(1), 34–48.

Brehaut, J. C., Miller, A., Raina, P., & McGrail, K. M. (2003). Childhood behavior disorders and injuries among children and youth: A population-based study. *Pediatrics, 111*(2), 262–269.

Bressel, E., Yonker, J. C., Kras, J., & Heath, E. M. (2007). Comparison of static and dynamic balance in female collegiate soccer, basketball, and gymnastics athletes. *Journal Of Athletic Training, 42*(1), 42–46.

Broglio, S. P., Collins, M. W., Williams, R. M., Mucha, A., & Kontos, A. P. (2015). Current and emerging rehabilitation for concussion: A review of the evidence. *Clinics in Sports Medicine, 34*(2), 213–231. doi:10.1016/j.csm.2014.12.005

Broglio, S. P., Macciocchi, S. N., & Ferrara, M. S. (2007). Sensitivity of the concussion assessment battery. *Neurosurgery, 60*(6), 1050–1057.

Broshek, D. K., Kaushik, T., Freeman, J. R., Erlanger, D., Webbe, F., & Barth, J. T. (2005). Sex differences in outcome following sports-related concussion. *Journal of Neurosurgery, 102*(5), 856–863.

Brown, N. J., Mannix, R. C., O'Brien, M. J., Gostine, D., Collins, M. W., & Meehan, III, W. P. (2014). Effect of cognitive activity level on duration of post-concussion symptoms. *Pediatrics, 133*(2), e299–e304. doi:10.1542/peds.2013-2125

Bruce, D. A., Alavi, A., Bilaniuk, L., Dolinskas, C., Obrist, W., & Uzzell, B. (1981). Diffuse cerebral swelling following head injuries in children: The syndrome of "malignant brain edema". *Journal Of Neurosurgery, 54*(2), 170–178.

Bryant, R. A., O'donnell, M. L., Creamer, M., McFarlane, A. C., Clark, C. R., & Silove, D. (2010). The psychiatric sequelae of traumatic injury. *American Journal of Psychiatry, 167*(3), 312–320.

Capó-Aponte, J. E., Urosevich, T. G., Temme, L. A., Tarbett, A. K., & Sanghera, N. K. (2012). Visual dysfunctions and symptoms during the subacute stage of blast-induced mild traumatic brain injury. *Military Medicine, 177*(7), 804–813.

Carroll, L. J., Cassidy, J. D., & Côté, P. (2006). The role of pain coping strategies in prognosis after whiplash injury: passive coping predicts slowed recovery. *Pain, 124*(1), 18–26.

Carroll, L., Cassidy, J. D., Peloso, P., Borg, J., Von Holst, H., Holm, L., Paniak, C., & Pépin, M. (2004). Prognosis for mild traumatic brain injury: Results of the WHO collaborating centre task force on mild traumatic brain injury. *Journal of Rehabilitation Medicine, 36*(0), 84–105.

Chan, C., Iverson, G. L., Purtzki, J., Wong, K., Kwan, V., Gagnon, I., & Silverberg, N. D. (2017). Safety of active rehabilitation for persistent symptoms after pediatric sport-related concussion: A randomized controlled trial. *Archives of Physical Medicine and Rehabilitation, 99*(2), 242–249. doi:10.1016/j.apmr.2017.09.108

Chen, J. K., Johnston, K. M., Petrides, M., & Ptito, A. (2008). Neural substrates of symptoms of depression following concussion in male athletes with persisting postconcussion symptoms. *Archives of General Psychiatry, 65*(1), 81–89.

Chiang Colvin, A., Mullen, J., Lovell, M. R., Vereeke West, R., Collins, M. W., & Groh, M. (2009). The role of concussion history and gender in recovery from soccer-related concussion. *The American Journal of Sports Medicine, 37*(9), 1699–1704.

Chin, E. Y., Nelson, L. D., Barr, W. B., McCrory, P., & McCrea, M. A. (2016). Reliability and validity of the Sport Concussion Assessment Tool–3 (SCAT3) in high school and collegiate athletes. *The American Journal of Sports Medicine, 44*(9), 2276–2285.

Choe, M. C., & Blume, H. K. (2016). Pediatric Posttraumatic Headache: A Review. *Journal Of Child Neurology, 31*(1), 76–85. doi:10.1177/0883073814568152

Ciuffreda, K. J., Kapoor, N., Rutner, D., Suchoff, I. B., Han, M. E., & Craig, S. (2007). Occurrence of oculomotor dysfunctions in acquired brain injury: A retrospective analysis. *Optometry-Journal of the American Optometric Association, 78*(4), 155–161.

Ciuffreda, K. J., Rutner, D., Kapoor, N., Suchoff, I. B., Craig, S., & Han, M. E. (2008). Vision therapy for oculomotor dysfunctions in acquired brain injury: A retrospective analysis. *Optometry-Journal of American Optometric Association, 79*(1), 18–22.

Collins, M. W., Iverson, G. L., Lovell, M. R., McKeag, D. B., Norwig, J., & Maroon, J. (2003). On-field predictors of neuropsychological and symptom deficit following sports-related concussion. *Clinical Journal of Sport Medicine, 13*(4), 222–229.

Collins, M. W., Kontos, A. P., Reynolds, E., Murawski, C. D., & Fu, F. H. (2014). A comprehensive, targeted approach to the clinical care of athletes following sport-related concussion. *Knee Surgery, Sports Traumatology, Arthroscopy, 22*(2), 235–246.

Corwin, D. J., Zonfrillo, M. R., Master, C. L., Arbogast, K. B., Grady, M. F., Robinson, R. L., Goodman, A. M., & Wiebe, D. J. (2014). Characteristics of prolonged concussion recovery in a pediatric subspecialty referral population. *The Journal of Pediatrics, 165*(6), 1207–1215.

Covassin, T., Crutcher, B., Bleecker, A., Heiden, E. O., Dailey, A., & Yang, J. (2014). Postinjury anxiety and social support among collegiate athletes: A comparison between orthopaedic injuries and concussions. *Journal of Athletic Training, 49*(4), 462–468.

Covassin, T., Elbin, R. J., Harris, W., Parker, T., & Kontos, A. (2012). The role of age and sex in symptoms, neurocognitive performance, and postural stability in athletes after concussion. *The American Journal of Sports Medicine, 40*(6), 1303–1312.

Covassin, T., Schatz, P., & Swanik, C. B. (2007). Sex differences in neuropsychological function and post-concussion symptoms of concussed collegiate athletes. *Neurosurgery, 61*(2), 345–351.

DiFazio, M., Silverberg, N. D., Kirkwood, M. W., Bernier, R., & Iverson, G. L. (2016). Prolonged activity restriction after concussion: Are we worsening outcomes?. *Clinical Pediatrics, 55*(5), 443–451. doi:10.1177/0009922815589914

Dougan, B. K., Horswill, M. S., & Geffen, G. M. (2014). Athletes' age, sex, and years of education moderate the acute neuropsychological impact of sports-related concussion: A meta-analysis. *Journal of the International Neuropsychological Society, 20*(1), 64–80.

Duhaime, A. C., Beckwith, J. G., Maerlender, A. C., McAllister, T. W., Crisco, J. J., Duma, S. M., Brolinson, P/ G., Rpwson, S., Flashman, Laura A., Chu, J. J., & Greenwald, R. M. (2012). Spectrum of acute clinical characteristics of diagnosed concussions in college athletes wearing instrumented helmets. *Journal of Neurosurgery, 117*(6), 1092–1099.

Eckner, J. T., Seifert, T., Pescovitz, A., Zeiger, M., & Kutcher, J. S. (2017). Is migraine headache associated with concussion in athletes? A case-control study. *Clinical Journal of Sport Medicine, 27*(3), 266–270.

Eierud, C., Craddock, R. C., Fletcher, S., Aulakh, M., King-Casas, B., Kuehl, D., & LaConte, S. M. (2014). Neuroimaging after mild traumatic brain injury: Review and meta-analysis. *NeuroImage: Clinical, 4*, 283–294.

Elbin, R. J., Sufrinko, A., Schatz, P., French, J., Henry, L., Burkhart, S., Collins, M. W., & Kontos, A. P. (2016). Removal from play after concussion and recovery time. *Pediatrics, 138*(3). doi:10.1542/peds.2016-0910

Ellis, M. J., Leddy, J. J., & Willer, B. (2015). Physiological, vestibulo-ocular and cervicogenic post-concussion disorders: An evidence-based classification system with directions for treatment. *Brain Injury, 29*(2), 238–248.

Erlanger, D., Kaushik, T., Cantu, R., Barth, J. T., Broshek, D. K., Freeman, J. R., & Webbe, F. M. (2003). Symptom-based assessment of the severity of a concussion. *Journal of Neurosurgery, 98*(3), 477–484.

Field, M., Collins, M. W., Lovell, M. R., & Maroon, J. (2003). Does age play a role in recovery from sports-related concussion? A comparison of high school and collegiate athletes. *The Journal of Pediatrics, 142*(5), 546–553.

Gallaway, M., Scheiman, M., & Mitchell, G. L. (2017). Vision therapy for post-concussion vision disorders. *Optometry And Vision Science: Official Publication Of The American Academy Of Optometry, 94*(1), 68–73. doi:10.1097/OPX.0000000000000935

Gessel, L. M., Fields, S. K., Collins, C. L., Dick, R. W., & Comstock, R. D. (2007). Concussions among United States high school and collegiate athletes. *Journal of Athletic Training, 42*(4), 495.

Gibson, S., Nigrovic, L. E., O'Brien, M., & Meehan, III, W. P. (2013). The effect of recommending cognitive rest on recovery from sport-related concussion. *Brain Injury, 27*(7–8), 839–842. doi:10.3109/02699052.2013.775494

Giza, C. C., Griesbach, G. S., & Hovda, D. A. (2005). Experience-dependent behavioral plasticity is disturbed following traumatic injury to the immature brain. *Behavioural Brain Research, 157*(1), 11–22.

Giza, C. C., & Hovda, D. A. (2014). The new neurometabolic cascade of concussion. *Neurosurgery, 75*(4), S24–S33.

Goldberg, J. M., Wilson, V. J., Cullen, K. E., Angelaki, D. E., Broussard, D. M., Buttner-Ennever, J., Fukushima, K., & Minor, L. B. (2012). *The vestibular system: A sixth sense.* Oxford University Press. doi:10.1093/acprof:oso/9780195167085.001.0001

Gordon, K. E., Dooley, J. M., & Wood, E. P. (2006). Is migraine a risk factor for the development of concussion?. *British Journal of Sports Medicine, 40*(2), 184–185.

Gottshall, K. (2011). Vestibular rehabilitation after mild traumatic brain injury with vestibular pathology. *Neurorehabilitation, 29*(2), 167–171. doi:10.3233/NRE-2011-0691

Gottshall, K. R., & Hoffer, M. E. (2010). Tracking recovery of vestibular function in individuals with blast-induced head trauma using vestibular-visual-cognitive interaction tests. *Journal of Neurologic Physical Therapy: JNPT, 34*(2), 94–97. doi:10.1097/NPT.0b013e3181dead12

Griesbach, G. S., Hovda, D. A., Molteni, R., Wu, A., & Gomez-Pinilla, F. (2004). Voluntary exercise following traumatic brain injury: Brain-derived neurotrophic factors upregulattion and recovery of function. *Neuroscience, 125*(1), 129–139.

Guskiewicz, K. M., McCrea, M., Marshall, S. W., Cantu, R. C., Randolph, C., Barr, W., Onate, J. A., & Kelly, J. P. (2003). Cumulative effects associated with recurrent concussion in collegiate football players: The NCAA concussion study. *Jama, 290*(19), 2549–2555.

Guskiewicz, K. M., Weaver, N. L., Padua, D. A., & Garrett, W. E. (2000). Epidemiology of concussion in collegiate and high school football players. *The American Journal of Sports Medicine, 28*(5), 643–650.

Henry, L. C., Elbin, R. J., Collins, M. W., Marchetti, G., & Kontos, A. P. (2016). Examining recovery trajectories after sport-related concussion with a multimodal clinical assessment approach. *Neurosurgery, 78*(2), 232–241.

Hillier, S. L., & McDonnell, M. (2011). Vestibular rehabilitation for unilateral peripheral vestibular dysfunction. *The Cochrane Database of Systematic Reviews,* (2), CD005397. doi:10.1002/14651858.CD005397.pub3

Hoffer, M. E., Gottshall, K. R., Moore, R., Balough, B. J., & Wester, D. (2004). Characterizing and treating dizziness after mild head trauma. *Otology & Neurotology: Official Publication of the American Otological Society, American Neurotology Society [and] European Academy of Otology and Neurotology, 25*(2), 135–138.

Hootman, J. M., Dick, R., & Agel, J. (2007). Epidemiology of collegiate injuries for 15 sports: Summary and recommendations for injury prevention initiatives. *Journal of Athletic Training, 42*(2), 311.

Hou, R., Moss-Morris, R., Peveler, R., Mogg, K., Bradley, B. P., & Belli, A. (2012). When a minor head injury results in enduring symptoms: A prospective investigation of risk factors for postconcussional syndrome after mild traumatic brain injury. *Journal of Neurology, Neurosurgery, & Psychiatry, 83*(2), 217–223.

Iverson, G., Brooks, B., Lovell, M., & Collins, M. (2006). No cumulative effects for one or two previous concussions. *British Journal of Sports Medicine,* (1), 72–75.

Iverson, G. L., Wojtowicz, M., Brooks, B. L., Maxwell, B. A., Atkins, J. E., Zafonte, R., & Berkner, P. D. (2016). High school athletes with ADHD and learning difficulties have a greater lifetime concussion history. *Journal of Attention Disorders.* doi:1087054716657410

Iverson, G. L., Gardner, A. J., Terry, D. P., Ponsford, J. L., Sills, A. K., Broshek, D. K., & Solomon, G. S. (2017). Predictors of clinical recovery from concussion: A systematic review. *British Journal of Sports Medicine, 51*(12), 941–948.

Kacperski, J., Hung, R., & Blume, H. K. (2016). Pediatric Posttraumatic Headache. *Seminars in Pediatric Neurology, 23*(1), 27–34. doi:10.1016/j.spen.2015.08.005

Karlin, A. M. (2011). Concussion in the pediatric and adolescent population: "Different population, different concerns". *PM & R: The Journal of Injury, Function, and Rehabilitation, 3*(10), S369–S379. doi:10.1016/j.pmrj.2011.07.015

Kinnaman, K. A., Mannix, R. C., Comstock, R. D., & Meehan, W. E. (2013). Management strategies and medication use for treating paediatric patients with concussions. *Acta Paediatrica (Oslo, Norway: 1992), 102*(9), e424–e428. doi:10.1111/apa.12315

Kontos, A. P., Covassin, T., Elbin, R., & Parker, T. (2012). Depression and neurocognitive performance after concussion among male and female high school and collegiate athletes. *Archives of Physical Medicine & Rehabilitation, 93*(10), 1751–1756.

Kontos, A. P., Deitrick, J. M., Collins, M. W., & Mucha, A. (2017). Review of vestibular and oculomotor screening and concussion rehabilitation. *Journal of Athletic Training, 52*(3), 256–261. doi:10.4085/1062-6050-51.11.05

Kontos, A. P., Deitrick, J. M., & Reynolds, E. (2016). Mental health implications and consequences following sport-related concussion. *British Journal of Sports Medicine, 50*(3), 139–140. doi.org/10.1136/bjsports-2015-095564

Kontos, A. P., Elbin, R. J., Lau, B., Simensky, S., Freund, B., French, J., & Collins, M. W. (2013). Posttraumatic migraine as a predictor of recovery and cognitive impairment after sport-related concussion. *The American Journal of Sports Medicine, 41*(7), 1497–1504.

Kontos, A. P., Elbin, R. J., Schatz, P., Covassin, T., Henry, L., Pardini, J., & Collins, M. W. (2012). A revised factor structure for the post-concussion symptom scale: baseline and postconcussion factors. *The American Journal of Sports Medicine, 40*(10), 2375–2384.

Kontos, A. P., Sufrinko, A., Elbin, R. J., Puskar, A., & Collins, M. W. (2016). Reliability and associated risk factors for performance on the vestibular/ocular motor screening (VOMS) tool in healthy collegiate athletes. *The American Journal of Sports Medicine, 44*(6), 1400–1406.

Lau, B. C., Collins, M. W., & Lovell, M. R. (2011). Sensitivity and specificity of subacute computerized neurocognitive testing and symptom evaluation in predicting outcomes after sports-related concussion. *The American Journal of Sports Medicine, 39*(6), 1209–1216.

Lau, B. C., Collins, M. W., & Lovell, M. R. (2012). Cutoff scores in neurocognitive testing and symptom clusters that predict protracted recovery from concussions in high school athletes. *Neurosurgery, 70*(2), 371–379.

Lau, B. C., Kontos, A. P., Collins, M. W., Mucha, A., & Lovell, M. R. (2011). Which on-field signs/symptoms predict protracted recovery from sport-related concussion among high school football players?. *The American Journal Of Sports Medicine, 39*(11), 2311–2318. doi:10.1177/0363546511410655

Leddy, J. J., & Willer, B. (2013). Use of graded exercise testing in concussion and return-to-activity management. *Current Sports Medicine Reports, 12*(6), 370–376. doi:10.1249/JSR.0000000000000008

Ledoux, A., Barrowman, N. J., Boutis, K., Davis, A., Reid, S., Sangha, G., Farion, K., Belanger, K., Tremblay, M., DeMatteo, C., Reed, N., &. Zemek, R. (2017). Multicentre, randomised clinical trial of paediatric concussion assessment of rest and exertion (PedCARE): A study to determine when to resume physical activities following concussion in children. *British Journal Of Sports Medicine.* doi:10.1136/bjsports-2017-097981

Lincoln, A. E., Caswell, S. V., Almquist, J. L., Dunn, R. E., Norris, J. B., & Hinton, R. Y. (2011). Trends in concussion incidence in high school sports: A prospective 11-year study. *The American Journal of Sports Medicine, 39*(5), 958–963.

Lovell, M. R., Collins, M. W., Iverson, G. L., Johnston, K. M., & Bradley, J. P. (2004). Grade 1 or "ding" concussions in high school athletes. *The American Journal of Sports Medicine, 32*(1), 47-54.

Lovell, M. R., Iverson, G. L., Collins, M. W., Podell, K., Johnston, K. M., Pardini, D., & … Maroon, J. C. (2006). Measurement of symptoms following sports-related concussion: Reliability and normative data for the post-concussion scale. *Applied Neuropsychology, 13*(3), 166–174.

Lovell, M., Pardini, J., Welling, J., Collins, M., Bakal, J., Lazar, N., & … Becker, J. (2007). Functional brain abnormalities are related to clinical recovery and time to return-to-play in athletes. *Neurosurgery, 200761*(2), 352–359.

Mainwaring, L. M., Hutchison, M., Bisschop, S. M., Comper, P., & Richards, D. W. (2010). Emotional response to sport concussion compared to ACL injury. *Brain Injury, 24*(4), 589–597.

Majerske, C. W., Mihalik, J. P., Ren, D., Collins, M. W., Reddy, C. C., Lovell, M. R., & Wagner, A. K. (2008). Concussion in sports: Postconcussive activity levels, symptoms, and neurocognitive performance. *Journal Of Athletic Training, 43*(3), 265–274. doi:10.4085/1062-6050-43.3.265

Makdissi, M., Cantu, R. C., Johnston, K. M., McCrory, P., & Meeuwisse, W. H. (2013). The difficult concussion patient: What is the best approach to investigation and management of persistent (> 10 days) postconcussive symptoms?. *British Journal of Sports Medicine, 47*(5), 308–313.

Manley, G., Gardner, A. J., Schneider, K. J., Guskiewicz, K. M., Bailes, J., Cantu, R. C., & … Iverson, G. L. (2017). A systematic review of potential long-term effects of sport-related concussion. *British Journal of Sports Medicine, 51*(12), 969–977. doi:10.1136/bjsports-2017-097791

Manuel, J. C., Shilt, J. S., Curl, W. W., Smith, J. A., Durant, R. H., Lester, L., & Sinal, S. H. (2002). Coping with sports injuries: An examination of the adolescent athlete. *The Journal Of Adolescent Health: Official Publication Of The Society For Adolescent Medicine, 31*(5), 391–393.

Marar, M., McIlvain, N. M., Fields, S. K., & Comstock, R. D. (2012). Epidemiology of concussions among United States high school athletes in 20 sports. *The American Journal of Sports Medicine, 40*(4), 747–755.

Massagli, T. L., Fann, J. R., Burington, B. E., Jaffe, K. M., Katon, W. J., & Thompson, R. S. (2004). Psychiatric illness after mild traumatic brain injury in children. *Archives of Physical Medicine and Rehabilitation, 85*(9), 1428–1434.

McCauley, S. R., Wilde, E. A., Miller, E. R., Frisby, M. L., Garza, H. M., Varghese, R., ... & McCarthy, J. J. (2013). Preinjury resilience and mood as predictors of early outcome following mild traumatic brain injury. *Journal of Neurotrauma, 30*(8), 642–652.

McClincy, M. P., Lovell, M. R., Pardini, J., Collins, M. W., & Spore, M. K. (2006). Recovery from sports concussion in high school and collegiate athletes. *Brain Injury, 20*(1), 33–39.

McCrea, M., Barr, W. B., Guskiewicz, K., Randolph, C., Marshall, S. W., Cantu, R., & ... Kelly, J. P. (2005). Standard regression-based methods for measuring recovery after sport-related concussion. *Journal Of The International Neuropsychological Society, 11*(1), 58–69.

McCrea, M., Guskiewicz, K. M., Marshall, S. W., Barr, W., Randolph, C., Cantu, R. C., ... & Kelly, J. P. (2003). Acute effects and recovery time following concussion in collegiate football players: The NCAA Concussion Study. *Jama, 290*(19), 2556–2563.

McCrea, M., Guskiewicz, K., Randolph, C., Barr, W. B., Hammeke, T. A., Marshall, S. W., & ... Kelly, J. P. (2013). Incidence, clinical course, and predictors of prolonged recovery time following sport-related concussion in high school and college athletes. *Journal of The International Neuropsychological Society, 19*(1), 22–33. doi:10.1017/S1355617712000872

McCrea, M., Hammeke, T., Olsen, G., Leo, P., & Guskiewicz, K. (2004). Unreported concussion in high school football players: Implications for prevention. *Clinical Journal of Sport Medicine, 14*(1), 13–17.

McCrory, P., Meeuwisse, W., Aubry, M., Cantu, B., Dvorak, J., Echemendia, R., & Turner, M. (2013). Consensus statement on concussion in sport: The 4th International Conference on Concussion in Sport held in Zurich, November 2012. *Journal of Science and Medicine in Sport, 16,* 178–189.

McCrory, P., Meeuwisse, W., Dvorak, J., Aubry, M., Bailes, J., Broglio, S., & ... Vos, P. E. (2017). Consensus statement on concussion in sport-the 5th international conference on concussion in sport held in Berlin, October 2016. *British Journal of Sports Medicine,* (11). 838.

Meehan III, W. P. (2011). Medical therapies for concussion. *Clinics in Sports Medicine, 30*(1), 115. doi:10.1016/j.csm.2010.08.003

Meehan III, W. P., d'Hemecourt, P., & Comstock, R. D. (2010). High school concussions in the 2008-2009 academic year: Mechanism, symptoms, and management. *The American Journal of Sports Medicine, 38*(12), 2405–2409.

Meehan, W. P., Mannix, R., Monuteaux, M. C., Stein, C. J., & Bachur, R. G. (2014). Early symptom burden predicts recovery after sport-related concussion. *Neurology, 83*(24), 2204–2210.

Meehan, W. P., Mannix, R. C., Stracciolini, A., Elbin, R. J., & Collins, M. W. (2013). Symptom severity predicts prolonged recovery after sport-related concussion, but age and amnesia do not. *The Journal of Pediatrics, 163*(3), 721–725.

Meehan III, W. P., Zhang, J., Mannix, R., & Whalen, M. J. (2012). Increasing recovery time between injuries improves cognitive outcome after repetitive mild concussive brain injuries in mice. *Neurosurgery, 71*(4), 885–891.

Merritt, V. C., Rabinowitz, A. R., & Arnett, P. A. (2015). Injury-related predictors of symptom severity following sports-related concussion. *Journal of Clinical and Experimental Neuropsychology, 37*(3), 265–275.

Mihalik, J. P., Register-Mihalik, J., Kerr, Z. Y., Marshall, S. W., McCrea, M. C., & Guśkiewicz, K. M. (2013). Recovery of posttraumatic migraine characteristics in patients after mild traumatic brain injury. *The American Journal of Sports Medicine, 41*(7), 1490–1496.

Miller, J. H., Gill, C., Kuhn, E. N., Rocque, B. G., Menendez, J. Y., O'Neill, J. A., … & Ferguson, D. (2016). Predictors of delayed recovery following pediatric sports-related concussion: A case-control study. *Journal of Neurosurgery: Pediatrics, 17*(4), 491–496.

Moore, E. L., Terryberry-Spohr, L., & Hope, D. A. (2006). Mild traumatic brain injury and anxiety sequelae: A review of the literature. *Brain Injury, 20*(2), 117–132.

Mucha, A., Collins, M. W., Elbin, R. J., Furman, J. M., Troutman-Enseki, C., DeWolf, R. M., … & Kontos, A. P. (2014). A brief vestibular/ocular motor screening (VOMS) assessment to evaluate concussions: Preliminary findings. *The American Journal of Sports Medicine, 42*(10), 2479-2486.

Naguib, M. B., Madian, Y., Refaat, M., Mohsen, O., El Tabakh, M., & Abo-Setta, A. (2012). Characterisation and objective monitoring of balance disorders following head trauma, using videonystagmography. *The Journal Of Laryngology and Otology, 126*(1), 26–33. doi:10.1017/S002221511100291X

Olsson, K. A., Lloyd, O. T., LeBrocque, R. M., McKinlay, L., Anderson, V. A., & Kenardy, J. A. (2013). Predictors of child post-concussion symptoms at 6 and 18 months following mild traumatic brain injury. *Brain Injury, 27*(2), 145–157.

Ouellet, M., & Morin, C. M. (2007). Efficacy of cognitive-behavioral therapy for insomnia associated with traumatic brain injury: a single-case experimental design. *Archives of Physical Medicine and Rehabilitation, 88*(12), 1581–1592.

Pavlou, M. (2010). The use of optokinetic stimulation in vestibular rehabilitation. *Journal Of Neurologic Physical Therapy, 34*(2), 105–110. doi:10.1097/NPT.0b013e3181dde6bf

Pavlou, M., Bronstein, A. M., & Davies, R. A. (2013). Randomized trial of supervised versus unsupervised optokinetic exercise in persons with peripheral vestibular disorders. *Neurorehabilitation And Neural Repair, (3)*, 208.

Petraglia, A. L., Maroon, J. C., & Bailes, J. E. (2012). From the field of play to the field of combat: A review of the pharmacological management of concussion. *Neurosurgery, 70*(6), 1520–1533. doi:10.1227/NEU.0b013e31824cebe8

Ponsford, J., Cameron, P., Fitzgerald, M., Grant, M., Mikocka-Walus, A., & Schönberger, M. (2012). Predictors of postconcussive symptoms 3 months after mild traumatic brain injury. *Neuropsychology, 26*(3), 304–313.

Reddy, C. C., Collins, M., Lovell, M., & Kontos, A. P. (2013). Efficacy of amantadine treatment on symptoms and neurocognitive performance among adolescents following sports-related concussion. *The Journal of Head Trauma Rehabilitation*, (4), 260.

Reed, N., Greenspoon, D., Iverson, G. L., DeMatteo, C., Fait, P., Gauvin-Lepage, J., & ... Gagnon, I. J. (2015). Management of persistent postconcussion symptoms in youth: A randomised control trial protocol. *BMJ Open*, *5*(7), e008468. doi:10.1136/bmjopen-2015-008468

Register-Mihalik, J., Guskiewicz, K. M., Mann, J. D., & Shields, E. W. (2007). The effects of headache on clinical measures of neurocognitive function. *Clinical Journal of Sport Medicine*, *17*(4), 282–288.

Register-Mihalik, J. K., Guskiewicz, K. M., Mihalik, J. P., Schmidt, J. D., Kerr, Z. Y., & McCrea, M. A. (2013). Reliable change, sensitivity, and specificity of a multidimensional concussion assessment battery: Implications for caution in clinical practice. *The Journal Of Head Trauma Rehabilitation*, *28*(4), 274–283. doi:10.1097/HTR.0b013e3182585d37

Resch, J. E., Brown, C. N., Schmidt, J., Macciocchi, S. N., Blueitt, D., Cullum, C. M., & Ferrara, M. S. (2016). The sensitivity and specificity of clinical measures of sport concussion: Three tests are better than one. *BMJ Open Sport & Exercise Medicine*, *2*(1), e000012.

Russell, K., Selci, E., Chu, S., Fineblit, S., Ritchie, L., & Ellis, M. J. (2017). Longitudinal assessment of health-related quality of life following adolescent aports-related concussion. *Journal of Neurotrauma*, *34*(13), 2147–2153

Sandel, N. K., Schatz, P., Goldberg, K. B., & Lazar, M. (2017). Sex-based differences in cognitive deficits and symptom reporting among acutely concussed adolescent lacrosse and soccer players. *The American Journal of Sports Medicine*, *45*(4), 937–944.

Schatz, P., Pardini, J. E., Lovell, M. R., Collins, M. W., & Podell, K. (2006). Sensitivity and specificity of the ImPACT Test Battery for concussion in athletes. *Archives Of Clinical Neuropsychology: The Official Journal of The National Academy of Neuropsychologists*, *21*(1), 91–99.

Schatz, P., & Sandel, N. (2013). Sensitivity and specificity of the online version of ImPACT in high school and collegiate athletes. *The American Journal of Sports Medicine*, *41*(2), 321–326. doi:10.1177/0363546512466038

Scheiman, M., Gallaway, M., Frantz, K. A., Peters, R. J., Hatch, S., Cuff, M., & Mitchell, G. L. (2003). Nearpoint of convergence: Test procedure, target selection, and normative data. *Optometry and Vision Science: Official Publication of the American Academy of Optometry*, *80*(3), 214–225.

Schnadower, D., Vazquez, H., Lee, J., Dayan, P., & Roskind, C. G. (2007). Controversies in the evaluation and management of minor blunt head trauma in children. *Current Opinion in Pediatrics*, *19*(3), 258–264.

Schneider, K. J., Meeuwisse, W. H., Kang, J., Schneider, G. M., & Emery, C. A. (2013). Preseason reports of neck pain, dizziness, and headache as risk factors for concussion in male youth ice hockey players. *Clinical Journal of Sport Medicine*, *23*(4), 267–272.

Schneider, K. J., Meeuwisse, W. H., Nettel-Aguirre, A., Barlow, K., Boyd, L., Kang, J., & Emery, C. A. (2014). Cervicovestibular rehabilitation in sport-related concussion: A randomised controlled trial. *British Journal of Sports Medicine, 48*(17), 1294–1298. doi:10.1136/bjsports-2013-093267

Seifert, T., Sufrinko, A., Cowan, R., Scott Black, W., Watson, D., Edwards, B., ... & Kontos, A. P. (2017). Comprehensive headache experience in collegiate student athletes: An initial report from the NCAA headache task force. *Headache: The Journal of Head and Face Pain, 57*(6), 877–886.

Shankar, P. R., Fields, S. K., Collins, C. L., Dick, R. W., & Comstock, R. D. (2007). Epidemiology of high school and collegiate football injuries in the United States, 2005–2006. *The American Journal of Sports Medicine, 35*(8), 1295–1303.

Sufrinko, A. M., Marchetti, G. F., Cohen, P. E., Elbin, R., Re, V., & Kontos, A. P. (in press). Using acute performance on a comprehensive neurocognitive, vestibular, and ocular motor assessment battery to predict recovery duration after sport-related concussions. *The American Journal of Sports Medicine,* (5), 1187.

Teel, E. F., Marshall, S. W., Shankar, V., McCrea, M., & Guskiewicz, K. M. (2017). Predicting recovery patterns after sport-related concussion. *Journal of Athletic Training, 52*(3), 288–298.

Thiagarajan, P., & Ciuffreda, K. (2014). Versional eye tracking in mild traumatic brain injury (mTBI): Effects of oculomotor training (OMT). *Brain Injury, 2014*28(7), 930–943.

Thiagarajan, P., Ciuffreda, K., Capó-Aponte, J., Ludlam, D., & Kapoor, N. (2014). Oculomotor neurorehabilitation for reading in mild traumatic brain injury (mTBI): An integrative approach. *Neurorehabilitation, 2014*34(1), 129–146.

Thomas, D. G., Apps, J. N., Hoffmann, R. G., McCrea, M., & Hammeke, T. (2015). Benefits of strict rest after acute concussion: A randomized controlled trial. *Pediatrics, 135*(2), 213–223. doi:10.1542/peds.2014-0966

Tsai, M. C., Tsai, K. J., Wang, H. K., Sung, P. S., Wu, M. H., Hung, K. W., & Lin, S. H. (2014). Mood disorders after traumatic brain injury in adolescents and young adults: A nationwide population-based cohort study. *The Journal of Pediatrics, 164*(1), 136–141.

Vagnozzi, R., Signoretti, S., Cristofori, L., Alessandrini, F., Floris, R., Isgrò, E., ... & Del Bolgia, F. (2010). Assessment of metabolic brain damage and recovery following mild traumatic brain injury: A multicentre, proton magnetic resonance spectroscopic study in concussed patients. *Brain, 133*(11), 3232–3242.

Van Veldhoven, L. M., Sander, A. M., Struchen, M. A., Sherer, M., Clark, A. N., Hudnall, G. E., & Hannay, H. J. (2011). Predictive ability of preinjury stressful life events and Post-traumatic stress symptoms for outcomes following mild traumatic brain injury: analysis in a prospective emergency room sample. *Journal of Neurology, Neurosurgery & Psychiatry, 82*, 782–787.

Webbe, F. M., & Zimmer, A. (2015). History of neuropsychological study of sport-related concussion. *Brain Injury, 29*(2), 129–138. doi:10.3109/02699052.2014.937746

Whelan-Goodinson, R., Ponsford, J., Johnston, L., & Grant, F. (2009). Psychiatric disorders following traumatic brain injury: Their nature and frequency. *The Journal of Head Trauma Rehabilitation, 24*(5), 324–332.

Williams, R. M., Welch, C. E., Weber, M. L., Parsons, J. T., & Valovich McLeod, T. C. (2014). Athletic trainers' management practices and referral patterns for adolescent athletes after sport-related concussion. *Sports Health, 6*(5), 434–439. doi:10.1177/1941738114545612

Williams, R. M., Puetz, T. W., Giza, C. C., & Broglio, S. P. (2015). Concussion recovery time among high school and collegiate athletes: A systematic review and meta-analysis. *Sports Medicine, 45*(6), 893–903.

Womble, M. N., & Collins, M. W. (2016). Concussions in American Football. *American Journal Of Orthopedics (Belle Mead, N.J.), 45*(6), 352–356.

Yengo-Kahn, A. M., Hale, A. T., Zalneraitis, B. H., Zuckerman, S. L., Sills, A. K., & Solomon, G. S. (2016). The sport concussion assessment tool: A systematic review. *Neurosurgical Focus, 40*(4), E6.

Zuckerman, S. L., Kerr, Z. Y., Yengo-Kahn, A., Wasserman, E., Covassin, T., & Solomon, G. S. (2015). Epidemiology of sports-related concussion in NCAA athletes from 2009–2010 to 2013–2014: Incidence, recurrence, and mechanisms. *The American Journal of Sports Medicine, 43*(11), 2654–2662.

# 9

# Substance Abuse in College Student-Athletes

*Michael B. Johnson*

## CASE STUDY: JIM

Jim is a 21-year-old, single, White, male swimmer from a large city located over 500 miles from his college campus. Jim twice failed a random drug test administered by his athletic department. He had engaged in substance abuse counseling since his first drug test failure due to marijuana use. His drug test results identified elevated levels of THC in his system after both the first and second test. It appears that his initial substance abuse counseling was ineffective at eliciting behavioral change. Jim lives by himself in an apartment within a mile of campus and has a 3.95 GPA in a business major. He reportedly is not taking any prescribed medications and has no history of legal trouble. Jim has one sibling (a brother two years younger) who is in his first year at a different university. Jim's parents are married and live together. His mother is a middle school teacher, and his father works in a blue collar field. Jim reported no social problems with teammates or friends, and his coach identifies Jim as a "great guy." He reported no history of trauma, psychological issues, or medical history other than shoulder pain that kept him from training for a week during his junior year in high school. After discussing and signing the informed consent form and reviewing the limits of confidentiality, Jim self-identified as a copious smoker of marijuana. Jim identified his presenting problem as being suspended from competition for the next two meets due to failing the institution's drug test.

Jim's counseling incorporated motivational interviewing (MI) and the transtheoretical model (TTM) principles. Jim's work in session focused on how to develop his ability to pass his next drug test so that he could reach his goal of competing for his team. Carefully woven into this goal was a nonconfrontational and accepting discussion of any possible negative effects related to his marijuana use. Any behavior that impeded achieving Jim's goals was discussed in session, and this discussion was handled in a supportive and empathic manner. As his counseling unfolded Jim began to share other details that presented a clearer picture of why Jim used marijuana. For example, Jim could only fly commercially while under the influence of marijuana—he otherwise experienced fecal incontinence due to anxiety. As Jim's and his counselor's shared understanding of his physiological reactions to anxiety became clearer, Jim was identifying a number of symptoms of agoraphobia. Jim reported smoking heavily for a number of years as his only effective coping strategy.

During his initial sessions, Jim also identified that his social supports included his head coach and the team physician, but not his parents. Therefore, after extensive discussions in session, Jim agreed to include the coach and the physician in his counseling in a consultative role. Jim was experiencing a mental health challenge that indicated long-term therapy, but his strong desire to regain his eligibility to compete suggested the necessity of a short-term approach.

Jim's treatment plan included engaging the support of others while continuing weekly talk therapy designed to move him along the transtheoretical model stages. The team physician prescribed medication that would allow Jim to travel via air. The coach learned how to enhance his supportive role while incorporating patience and realistic optimism. Meanwhile, Jim continued to adhere to the team rules that included refraining from the use of banned substances.

The course of treatment was not uniformly smooth. On several occasions, Jim was very uncomfortable (e.g., physical distress) and had to miss a few classes and practices. Jim may have been suffering from substance withdrawal, but while doing so he also found himself in a consistently emotionally and physically supportive environment. Jim was able to pass his subsequent follow-up drug test and return to competition.

---

Substance abuse by student-athletes is a complex topic with multiple causes, contributing factors, and sequelae. Since substance abuse can result in death, counselors working with student-athletes must develop expertise on this topic. This chapter begins by exploring the prevalence of student-athlete substance abuse, followed by the consequences and underlying causes of abusing substances. Evidence-based practices regarding substance abuse treatment also are presented. Finally, the chapter concludes with a case study to illustrate the previous sections' constructs and treatment approaches.

Although this chapter's title includes "substance abuse," the topic herein is conceptualized via the fifth edition of the *Diagnostic and Statistical Manual for Mental Health Disorders* (*DSM–5*; American Psychiatric Association, 2013). The *DSM–5* does not include the term "abuse." Instead, the *DSM–5* identifies substance use disorder and substance-induced disorders (i.e., substance intoxication and substance withdrawal). The *DSM–5* (American Psychiatric Association, 2013, p. 481) includes 10 separate classes of substances: alcohol, caffeine, cannabis, hallucinogens, inhalants, opioids, sedatives-hypnotics-anxiolytics, stimulants, tobacco, and other (or unknown) substances. Of these, only caffeine use cannot receive a diagnosis of use disorder. Additionally, tobacco use cannot receive a diagnosis of substance intoxication, and neither use of inhalants nor hallucinogens can receive a diagnosis of substance withdrawal.

The use of one or more of these 10 substances can be, but is not necessarily, identified as a disorder. By definition, diagnosing a person as having a mental health disorder can occur only if the user neglects their normal and productive activity due to the use of a substance(s). The *DSM–5* (American Psychiatric Association, 2013) defines a mental disorder as

> *a syndrome characterized by clinically significant disturbance in an individual's cognition, emotion regulation, or behavior that reflects a dysfunction in the psychological, biological, or developmental processes... usually associated with significant distress or disability in social, occupational, or other important activities. (p. 20)*

It is important to note that there is a difference between a mental health disorder and a legal issue. For example, although consuming an alcoholic beverage in the United States when one is 19 years of age is illegal (i.e., part of a socially constructed system of laws and rules), this act does not constitute a mental health disorder. However, if an individual of any age experiences significant disturbances or distress cognitively, emotionally, or behaviorally in social, occupational, or other important activities due to the consumption of alcohol, then an alcohol use disorder is present. Therefore, the purpose of this chapter is not to evaluate the legality of substance use, but to focus on mental health and counseling issues related to substance abuse by student-athletes.

## Prevalence of Substance Abuse

A number of resources identify the prevalence of substance use by college students and student-athletes. Some information is from scientific journals (i.e., peer-reviewed outlets), while other data is available from national governing bodies (e.g., NCAA). Although the NCAA publications do not have the scientific rigor of a peer-reviewed journal, they provide insights into student-athlete substance use demographics for the following: alcohol, tobacco, marijuana, cocaine, amphetamines, adrenergics, and pain medications.

### Alcohol

Alcohol has had a long history as the most commonly used substance. A 2014 report identified that 81% of student-athletes acknowledged alcohol use, which represented a decrease from the same self-report study of four years prior (National Colligate Athletic Association [NCAA], 2014). There does not appear to be a statistically significant difference between gender groups in overall alcohol use. However, when binge drinking (i.e., more than three drinks for women and more than four drinks for men over a two-hour time span) (United States Department of Agriculture, 2015) is explored, a gap between genders is evident (44% of men compared with 33% of women). Moreover, once 10 or more drinks in a single sitting is analyzed, men's prevalence rates (18%) are six times higher than women's. Other survey data (Schulenberg et al., 2017) identified very similar percentages of alcohol use among all college students (i.e., 78.9% in 2016). No empirical work was uncovered in the literature that deviated with any significance from these data.

The NCAA (2014) analyzed reported alcohol use among student-athletes, including categorization by sport and race. Among men's sports, ice hockey players had the highest prevalence rate (97%), while lacrosse players had the highest prevalence rate among women's sports (95%). At the low end of the alcohol use spectrum were men's basketball and women's track (both 72%). Regarding race, White student-athletes had a higher rate of alcohol consumption (85%) than their Black counterparts (64%).

Comparisons of drinking prevalence among various college student groups also exist. Intramural college athletes binge drink more than club athletes, who imbibe more than intercollegiate student-athletes, with nonathletes consuming the least (Barry, Howell, Riplinger, & Piazza-Gardner, 2015). Additionally, Greek-lettered social groups consume alcohol at rates higher than that of student-athletes (Meilman, Leichliter, & Presley, 1999; Turrisi, Mallett, Mastroleo, & Larimer, 2006).

## Tobacco and Marijuana

Tobacco and marijuana use by student-athletes is evident according to the NCAA's most recent data (2014). Cigarettes (overall 10%; 13% males, 6% females) and marijuana (overall 22%; 25% males, 17% females) are used by some student-athletes. Regarding differences among sports, the highest rate for cigarette use was lacrosse (25% men, 17% women). For marijuana, the highest usage rates occurred in lacrosse for men (46%) and ice hockey for women (25%). Although these rates are troubling, student-athlete tobacco and marijuana use rates are considerably lower when compared with those of the general college student population (Lisha & Sussman, 2010). Schulenberg et al. (2017) identified an overall student cigarette smoking rate of 18.7% (vs. 10%) and marijuana smoking rate of 39.3% (vs. 22%).

## Stimulants and Performance Enhancing Drugs (PEDs)

The category of stimulants consists of a variety of substances (e.g., cocaine, amphetamine, Ritalin, and Adderall). According to the NCAA (2014), 2% of student-athletes reportedly used cocaine, and 9% used Adderall or Ritalin sans prescription. The highest rates of amphetamine use occur in wrestling (13%) for men and lacrosse (8%) for women, with an overall reported use rate of 5%. In the general college population, 4.0% reported cocaine use, and 9.8% of college students reported using amphetamines (Schulenberg et al., 2017).

Anabolic steroids and ephedrine are considered performance enhancing substances (PEDs). The reported rates of anabolic steroid and ephedrine use are less than 1.0% for student-athletes (NCAA, 2014). Shulenberg et al. (2017) identified very similar steroid use rates among college students as a whole, but did not report use rates of ephedrine.

## Pain Management Medication

Some student-athletes who have undergone surgical procedures are prescribed pain medications to aid recovery. Briefly, pain medications included in the NCAA (2014) data were Vicodin, OxyContin, and Percocet, and the student-athlete reported use rate without a prescription was 5.8%. The college student data compiled by Schulenberg et al. (2017) included only OxyContin (1.9%) and Vicodin (1.6%), therefore a determination regarding a between-groups comparison is difficult to make. However, drugs with the addictive potential of pain management medications (Martell et al., 2007) warrant great attention.

In summary, there is considerable between- and among-group variation in reported substance use rates. The type of substance, sport, gender, and ethnicity each play a predictive role in prevalence rates. As stated earlier, use alone does not dictate a problem; consequences of use do.

## Consequences of Substance Use

Student-athletes' possible experiences following substance use vary and can include negative health consequences, legal difficulties, suspension or removal from sport due to a positive drug-test (Wilfert, 2017), or even death (Darke, Kaye, & Duflou, 2006; Hingson, Heeren, Winter, & Wechsler, 2005).

It is well documented that excessive alcohol use can negatively impact the quality of one's life. The NCAA (2014) identified that 63% of student-athletes reported an alcohol-related hangover at least once within the last calendar year. Over half (51%) acknowledged becoming nauseous or vomiting. Additionally, 30% of student-athletes described memory loss or having engaged in actions that they later regretted. However, only 6% were willing to affirm feeling they had a drinking problem. The likely negative consequences of alcohol use that are especially pertinent to student-athletes include dehydration, hampered muscle recovery, and increased injury rates (El-Sayed, Omar, & Lin, 2000; Gutgesell & Canterbury, 1999; Shirreffs & Maughan, 1997). These intrapersonal quality of life issues can be exacerbated by environmental and social experiences.

Almost one in 10 (10%) student-athletes acknowledged alcohol-related legal (e.g., police, college authorities) issues (NCAA, 2014). Moreover, the same report (NCAA, 2014) reflected that while student-athletes were under the influence, 7% had damaged property, 23% indicated having gotten into at least one argument/fight, and 14% specified driving, although only 1% had been arrested for DUI. Others have affirmed these social consequences as well (O'Brien et al., 2012). O'Brien et al. (2012) reported their finding that athletes made unwanted sexual advances while intoxicated (similar to nonathletes' rates) and reported incidents of having been sexually assaulted (lower than nonathletes' rates). Alcohol-related risk-taking behaviors are well-documented (Perkins, 2002), one result of which can be death (Hingson et al., 2005).

The inappropriate use of substances such as Adderall, cocaine, and steroids can lead to negative feelings, physiological responses, social discord, property damage, and death (Darke et al., 2006; Varga, 2012). Individuals dependent on opioids experience elevated levels of physical discomfort (e.g., headache, nausea) and conflict with others (Hartwell, Back, McRae-Clark, Shaftman, & Brady, 2012). Additionally, there is a high correlation between substance abuse and mental health disorders (Bizzari et al., 2007; Brady & Sinha, 2005). It is likely that some substance abuse represents attempts at self-medication to deal with anxiety and/or distress, including posttraumatic stress disorder (PTSD). Substance abuse also is associated with higher rates of suicide attempts (Leeies, Pagura, Sareen, & Bolton, 2010).

In the case of performance enhancing drugs (PEDs), steroid use promotes acne, liver dysfunction, reduced testicular size and baldness in men, and masculinization in women (Wadler & Hainline, 1989), yet despite these consequences, some continue to use PEDs and other related substances. It is remarkable that having knowledge of PEDs's effects has not been found to deter their use (Wanjek, Rosendahl, Strauss, & Gabriel, 2007), a finding also true of marijuana and cocaine use (Licciardone, 2003). Miller and Rollnick (2002) stated, "It is the hallmark of addictive behaviors that they persist despite what seems overwhelming evidence of their destructiveness. . . We are not always sensible creatures" (p. 4). Clearly, awareness of negative consequences is not a sufficient deterrent for some student-athletes. Therefore, the underlying reasons for substance use and abuse warrant exploration.

## Reasons for Substance Use

When a substance-related problem is identified, answering the question, "Why?" becomes important information that is useful in developing and implementing effective treatment. Research exploring the reasons and motivations for substance use has identified a number of factors including the systems within which these factors function. Many of these factors interact with one another.

## *Genetics and Personality Traits*

Two individuals can abuse the same substance for very different reasons. A constellation of factors may be involved in student-athletes' substance use. Cloninger (1987) provided a succinct conceptualization of this: Type I/A abusers are coping with distress and/or anxiety (low in novelty seeking; high in harm avoidance and reward dependence), while Type II/B abusers seek excitement and stimulation (high in novelty seeking; low in harm avoidance and reward dependence). Johnson, Sacks, and Edmonds (2010) extended this model by incorporating a Type III/C user—one who is predisposed to competitiveness. Competitive individuals exhibit elevated levels of novelty seeking and reward dependence, while also being low in harm avoidance. Competitiveness as a contributing factor to substance abuse has found support in the literature as strongly linked with alcohol consumption, but not with alcohol related problems (Serrao, Martens, Marin, & Rocha, 2008).

Genetics and traits (e.g., impulsivity, sensation-seeking, negative emotionality, emotional dysregulation, and personality disorder symptoms) have been correlated with substance use among college students (Dennhardt & Murphy, 2013). Trait urgency, general coping motives, and positive reinforcement motives have shown to be related to alcohol-related problems such as passing out, embarrassing oneself, missed classes, and regretted sexual situations (Martens, Pedersen, Smith, Steward, & O'Brien, 2011). Buckman, Yusko, White, & Pandina (2009) identified a strong relationship in male athletes between the sensation-seeking personality trait and their use of PEDs and other problem-related substances (e.g., cocaine, psychedelics). Leeies et al. (2010) also identified that mental health disorders (i.e., dysthymia, borderline personality disorder), which can have a genetic etiology, have a strong correlation with substance use. This is congruent with the mounting evidence of neurobiological similarities among those who have disorders such as depression, ADHD, and substance use disorder (Brady & Sinha, 2005). Research studies also have identified that being White and having elevated sensation-seeking tendencies correlated with past-year marijuana use (Buckman, Yusko, Farris, White, & Pandina, 2011). These lines of evidence support the contention that there likely is a genetic-environment interaction involved with student-athlete substance use.

## Environmental and Situational Factors

Environmental factors correlated with substance use in student-athletes. For example, individual sport athletes used alcohol at greater rates than team sport athletes (Martens, Watson, & Beck, 2006; Taylor, Ward, & Hardin, 2017). Individual sport athletes' motivators may include (1) the internally positive reinforcement feelings derived from drinking and (2) the desire to conform with one's social group. Research (Massengale, Ma, Rulison, Milroy, & Wyrick, 2017; Perkins & Craig, 2012) has not only provided support for the social group motivator hypothesis, but also identified that student-athletes' perceptions, rather than objective facts of others' drinking behaviors, strongly predicted their drinking habits, which also correlated with marijuana use (Buckman et al., 2011). Additionally, men appeared to be motivated to drink based on social or positive intrapersonal reinforcement experiences (Taylor et al., 2017). Women, on the other hand, tended to be more sensitive to substances' positive social reinforcement effects than males (Bizzari et al., 2007). This gender-based difference in motivations suggests that men and women may respond differently to similar substance abuse interventions.

A potentially powerful concept involved with substance abuse is positive social reinforcement. Marijuana dependence can result from subjectively identified elevated levels of pleasant emotions (e.g., happy, relaxed, content) and enjoyable times with others (e.g., celebrations) (Hartwell et al., 2012). College students generally have a perception that alcohol consumption provides a higher level of positive reinforcement than do alternative environmental stimuli (Joyner et al., 2016). In addition to potential positive reinforcement principles, abusing substances can be analogous to a powerful negative punishment, that is, a possible decrease in unpleasant emotional experiences. Trauma is an example of an experience associated with highly unpleasant emotions. Posttraumatic stress disorder has been shown to have a strong relationship with substance abuse for the purpose of coping with the resultant negative emotions (Leeies et al., 2010). Read, Ouimette, White, Colder, and Farrow (2011) reported that 66% of college students experienced trauma exposure (e.g., unwanted sex, physical violence) and 9% met the criteria for PTSD, with gender (women) and (low) socioeconomic status (SES) positively correlated with trauma severity. Therefore, if an athletic department's student-athlete population is approximately 50% female, and if a number of the males are from a low SES background, then the quantity of student-athletes with PTSD associated emotional symptoms is likely to be significant. Concordantly, the chances of substance abuse by that department's student-athletes are high. In a related manner, some student-athletes may consume prescription pain medications due to coping with an injury and eventually develop an addiction (O'Connell & Manschreck, 2012). To further complicate the etiology of substance abuse, the age of many student-athletes places them in a developmental stage in which the subjectively perceived rewards from substance-induced stimulation outweigh the related risks (Johnson, 2012). Clearly, there are a number of potential culprits involved in the etiology of substance abuse, and these factors likely are influenced further by systemic or contextual influences.

## Systemic Conceptualization

Environmental factors (e.g., social norms, culture, SES), genetics, personality, developmental experiences, epigenesis, and so on, interact in complex ways. Such interactions among these influences can result in decisions by an athlete to either use a substance(s) or to abstain. Models exist that aid our understanding of why a student-athlete might use PEDs, for example, and one model emphasizes the complexity of such a system (Johnson, 2011; Johnson, 2012). Student-athletes uniquely operate within their systems. Counselors working with student-athletes must work to understand these systemic factors in order to design and provide effective treatment related to substance use and abuse for their clients.

## Treating Substance Abuse in Student-Athletes

Prevention, treatment, and crisis intervention efforts are part and parcel of a collection of mental healthcare initiatives. Prevention is preferred. However, this section of the chapter focuses primarily on treatment. Identifying the reason(s) that a particular individual likely is using will guide the practitioner in their choice of treatment. Effective treatments are grounded in sound theory and empirical evidence, with the most effective treatments embracing the idiosyncratic nature of each person, including their states, traits, and an appreciation of their environment (Dennhardt & Murphy, 2013).

Specific interventions based on the transtheoretical model (Prochaska & DiClemente, 1986) and motivational interviewing (MI; Miller & Rollnick, 2002) continue to accumulate evidence of their efficaciousness. White et al. (2006) compared two brief substance abuse prevention interventions for college students mandated for treatment (e.g., the student had been caught drinking in their dorm room): (1) a motivational interviewing intervention and (2) a written feedback intervention. At the three-month follow up, there were no between-group differences in the major factors of interest (e.g., substance use, negative consequences of use). However, at 15 months, White, Mun, Pugh, and Morgan (2007) identified that the motivational interviewing group showed lower levels of alcohol-related problems and that those who received this personal (i.e., more costly) intervention were more successful at decreasing future alcohol use, likely resulting in cost savings in the long run. Of likely importance, however, is the finding that both treatment groups experienced a decrease in their substance use and related problems compared to baseline measurements (White et al., 2007).

Introspective therapeutic MI-type interventions, designed to increase self-monitoring and awareness, also seem to be promising approaches to substance abuse treatment. In a study outside the US, McCambridge and Strang (2004) uncovered a reduction in London vocational college students' illicit drug use via a single-session motivational interviewing intervention. Implementing a campus-wide alcohol and drug abuse prevention program (Miller, Toscova, Miller, & Sanchez, 2000) that focused on willingness to change (i.e., a transtheoretical model principle) resulted in decreased risky behaviors (e.g., riding with a driver who has used a substance) and marijuana use, particularly when compared to a control group. Even though there was no statistically significant change in alcohol use for those in the treatment group, when comparing alcohol consumption in the treatment group to the control group, Miller et al.'s (2000) study evidenced an increase in alcohol use in the control group over time, but there was no such trend in the treatment group. Fischer et al. (2013) used a brief motivational interviewing treatment (e.g., short, concise, information, awareness, or motivational sessions) for a group of college students and results showed reduced marijuana use as well as a reduction in some risky behaviors (e.g., driving under the influence).

In-person treatments are not the only effective methods. Online programs have also yielded promising results. Lee, Neighbors, Kilmer, and Larimer (2010) tested the effectiveness of a web-based intervention that emphasized personalized feedback. Although this study did not identify an overall intervention effect, it appeared that the web-based program was promising for college students (1) whose family possessed a history of drug use and (2) who had advanced beyond transtheoretical model's precontemplation stage. Another study that utilized a web-based methodology (Doumas, Haustveit, & Coll, 2010) identified that high-risk student-athlete participants experienced significant reductions in heavy drinking, while the participants' perceptions of others' drinking levels mediated the intervention's effects. Web-based programs tailored to these specific populations show promise.

Including an understanding of a student-athlete's socially constructed worldview of themselves and others is clinically necessary for effective motivational interviewing and transtheoretical model interventions to be effective. For example, one specific factor influencing student-athletes' alcohol consumption is their consistent overestimation of their peers' consumption (Perkins & Craig, 2012). To test a way to ameliorate this misperception, Wyrick, Milroy, Reifsteck, Day, and Kelly (2016) used myPlaybook, an online curriculum designed to promote health and well-being in first-year student-athletes (NCAA Sport Science Institute, n.d.). Results indicated that after the program, student-athletes reported greater intentions to use harm prevention strategies and had developed a more accurate assessment of their peers' alcohol consumption. In another study that attempted to improve college students' perceptions of peer substance use, Labrie, Hummer, Huchting, and Neighbors (2009) implemented a group intervention. This study involved participants privately identifying their substance use frequency and quantity. Their responses were shared in the aggregate with all participants. This process impacted participants' perceived norms and prosocial behavior as evidenced by a one-month and two-month follow up that identified improvements in participants' behaviors, attitudes, and negative alcohol-related consequences. Other studies have reported similar results for social norms programming for student-athletes (Perkins & Craig, 2006). An early study on this topic by Williams, Hadden, and Marcavage (1983) provided additional evidence supporting the benefits of understanding clients' social contexts. These researchers implemented an effective assertiveness training program for nonassertive college students aimed at reducing participants' drug use.

Related studies addressing binge drinking and drug use among college students identified reductions in use when implementing a brief motivational enhancement intervention called the Brief Alcohol Screen and Intervention in College Students program (BASICS; Amaro et al., 2010). The BASICS program involves two meetings lasting less than one hour each. The first meeting culls participants' substance use behaviors and provides self-monitoring cards to fill out between the two sessions. In the second session, the participants' cards are evaluated, resulting in their reception of individualized feedback. A brief personalized motivational interviewing intervention grounded in BASIC's principles specifically designed for student-athletes positively affected participants' alcohol use, negative consequences of alcohol abuse, protective behavioral strategies, and helped student-athletes accurately perceive their peers' usage (Cimini et al., 2015). At the six-month follow up, those who received personalized feedback (i.e., a motivational interviewing principle) had lower average peak blood alcohol levels (Martens, Kilmer, Beck, & Zamboanga, 2010). When results from just the heavy drinkers, rather than the full set of participants, were analyzed, personalized interventions were superior to the education only treatment group and were shown to be effective at achieving positive behavioral change. Grossbard et al.'s (2010) study incorporated first year college students who had been high school athletes. This research identified a treatment effect when using a combination of parental involvement and BASICS, but no effect for using either of the two by themselves, but even then only for some substances. Other researchers argue that including coaches in a treatment system would be effective (Nolt, Sachs, & Brenner, 2013).

Intervention programs can be challenging when the goal is to decrease substance use. Research supports the effectiveness of introspective protective behavioral strategies (e.g., setting a drink limit number, avoiding drinking games, using a designated driver) (Martens et al., 2005; Weaver, Martens, & Smith, 2012) as correlated with fewer alcohol-related negative consequences (Benton et al., 2004; Delva et al., 2004). Behavioral, motivational interviewing, and transtheoretical model strategies involve action on the part of the student-athlete. There are also more passive, educational programs, to be described in the next section.

## Educational Programs

Empirical support for the effectiveness of anti-drinking educational programs is lacking. Marcello, Danish, and Stolberg (1989) studied the effectiveness of a program for student-athletes that consisted of education, skill training for prevention, and skills to deal with peer pressure. Their results identified no statistical differences between treatment and control groups. It appears that when student-athletes solely learn what to do without internally embracing the behavior and increasing their motivation to change, that intervention is likely doomed to failure. In short, teaching alone is ineffective. Looby, De Young, and Earleywine (2013) reached a similar conclusion when unsuccessfully attempting to modify stimulant use based on an educational program.

## Drug Testing

A final area worth discussing is the effectiveness of drug testing as part of a substance abuse prevention program. The NCAA, international sport governing bodies, professional sports leagues, as well as a number of high school jurisdictions, all incorporate drug testing programs. At the high school level there is evidence that random drug tests do not reduce high school students' substance misuse (Sznitman

& Romer, 2014). Additionally, testing for this population is invasive and expensive (Bahrke, 2015). In the workplace, drug testing appears to result in decreased disclosure of employee substance use (Carpenter, 2007). However, Carpenter (2007) also identified that frequent testing and severe penalties reduce substance use. A review of the pertinent literature uncovered no scientific sources supporting a decrease in substance use due to NCAA drug testing. Moreover, there is strong evidence suggesting that implementing a punitive paradigm via a set of rigid rules is not clinically indicated (Johnson et al., 2010; Wyrick, Rulison, Fearnow-Kenney, Milroy, & Collins, 2014). That said, one upside to a drug testing program is it can help identify student-athletes in need of substance abuse counseling who are reticent to self-disclose.

## Conclusion

Interventions based on motivational interviewing and/or transtheoretical model principles appear to have strong support in the literature and, as such, are recommended for those working with student-athletes who abuse substances. In motivational interviewing based programs, the clinician should aim to (1) be empathic through reflective listening, (2) help the client raise awareness of any discrepancy between their goals and their current behavior, (3) aid client confidence and self-efficacy, (4) work through client resistance rather than oppose it directly, and (5) avoid disagreement and confrontation (Miller & Rollnick, 2002). Clinicians encountering these issues should work to embrace principles grounded in the transtheoretical model, such as identifying the client's stage of readiness for change and being aware of the different techniques that affect positive change at each stage (Prochaska & DiClemente, 1986).

This chapter presented a brief overview of the prevalence of substance abuse among student-athletes, as well as the effects some experience due to abusing substances. It can seem counterintuitive that an individual would behave in a manner that hinders their future success, so research was shared that identifies why student-athletes may abuse substances, as well as an overview of effective treatment approaches. Due to the idiosyncratic nature of every student-athlete, it appears that an equity-based individual treatment plan is warranted, and such a plan must be flexible. Motivational interviewing and transtheoretical model principles are recommended within treatment when possible.

## Discussion Questions

1. What are some of the factors underlying Jim's marijuana use?

2. What were the positive and negative impact of drug testing in Jim's case?

3. What are the longer-term treatment goals you would work toward if Jim were your client?

# References


Amaro, H., Reed, E., Rowe, E., Picci, J., Mantella, P., & Prado, G. (2010). Brief screening and intervention for alcohol and drug use in a college student health clinic: Feasibility, implementation, and outcomes. *Journal of American College Health, 58*(4), 357–364.

American Psychiatric Association. (2013). *Diagnostic and statistical manual of mental health disorders* (5th ed.). Washington, DC: Author.

Bahrke, M. S. (2015). Drug testing US student-athletes for performance-enhancing substance misuse: A flowed process. *Substance Use & Misuse, 50,* 1144–1147.

Barry, A. E., Howell, S. M., Riplinger, A., & Piazza-Gardner, A. K. (2015). Alcohol use among college athletes: Do intercollegiate, club, or intramural student athletes drink differently? *Substance Use & Misuse, 50,* 302–307. doi:10.3109/10826084.2014.977398

Benton, S. L., Schmidt, J. L., Newton, F. B., Shin, K., Benton, S. A., & Newton, D. W. (2004). College student protective strategies and drinking consequences. *Journal of Studies on Alcohol and Drugs, 65,* 115–121.

Bizzarri, J. V., Rucci, P., Sbrana, A., Gonnelli, C., Massei, G. J., Ravani, L., Girelli, M., Dell'osso, L., & Cassano G. B. (2007). Reasons for substance use and vulnerability factors in patients with substance use disorder and anxiety or mood disorders. *Addictive Behaviors, 32,* 384–391.

Brady, K. T., & Sinha, R. (2005). Co-occurring mental and substance use disorders: The neurobiological effect of chronic stress. *American Journal of Psychiatry, 162,* 1483–1493.

Buckman, J. F., Yusko, D. A., Farris, S. G., White, H. R., & Pandina, R. J. (2011). Risk of marijuana use in male and female college student athletes and nonathletes. *Journal of Student Alcohol and Drugs, 72,* 586–591.

Buckman, J. F., Yusko, D. A., White, H. R., & Pandina, R. J. (2009). Risk profile of male college athletes who use performance-enhancing substances. *Journal of Student Alcohol and Drugs, 70,* 919–923.

Carpenter, C. C. (2007). Workplace drug testing and worker drug use. *Health Services Research, 42*(2), 795–810.

Cimini, M. D., Monserrat, J. M., Sokolowski, K. L., Dewitt-Parker, J. Y., Rivero, E. M., & McElroy, L. A. (2015). Reducing high-risk drinking among student-athletes: The effects of a targeted athlete-specific brief intervention. *Journal of American College Health, 63*(6), 343–352.

Cloninger, C. R. (1987). Neurogenetic adaptive mechanisms in alcoholism. *Science, 236,* 410–416.

Darke, S., Kaye, S., & Duflou, J. (2006). Comparative cardiac pathology among deaths due to cocaine toxicity, opioid toxicity and non-drug-related causes. *Addiction, 101*(12), 1771–1777.

Delva, J., Smith, M. P., Howell, R. L., Harrison, D. F., Wilke, D., & Jackson, D. L. (2004). A study of the relationship between protective behaviors and drinking consequences among undergraduate college students. *Journal of American College Health, 53*, 19–27.

Dennhardt, A. A., & Murphy, J. G. (2013). Prevention and treatment of college student drug use: A review of the literature. *Addictive Behaviors, 38*, 2607–2618.

Doumas, D. M., Haustveit, T., & Coll, K. M. (2010). Reducing heaving drinking among first year intercollegiate athletes: A randomized controlled trial of web-based normative feedback. *Journal of Applied Sport Psychology, 22*, 247–261.

El-Sayed, M., & Omar, A., & Lin, X. (2000). Post-exercise alcohol ingestion perturbs blood homeostasis during recovery. *Thrombosis Research, 99*, 523–530.

Fischer, B., Dawe, M., McGuire, F., Shuper, P. A., Capler, R., Bilsker, D., Jones, W., Taylor, B., Rudzinski, K., & Rehm, J. (2013). Feasibility and impact of brief interventions for frequent cannabis users in Canada. *Journal of Substance Abuse Treatment, 44*(1), 132–138.

Grossbard, J. R., Mastroleo, N. R., Kilmer, J. R., Lee, C. M., Turrisi, R., Larimer, M. E., & Ray, A. (2010). Substance use patterns among first-year college students: Secondary effects of a combined alcohol intervention. *Journal of Substance Abuse Treatment, 39*(4), 384-390.

Gutgesell, M., & Canterbury, R. (1999). Alcohol usage in sport and exercise. *Addiction Biology, 4*, 373–383. doi:10.1080/13556219971353

Hartwell, K. J., Back, S. E., McRae-Clark, A. L., Shaftman, S. R., & Brady, K. T. (2012). Motives for using: A comparison of prescription opioid, marijuana and cocaine dependent individuals. *Addictive Behaviors, 37*, 373–378. doi:10.1016/j.addbeh.2011.11014

Hingson, R. W., Heeren, T., Winter, M., & Wechsler, H. (2005). Magnitude of alcohol-related mortality and morbidity among U.S. college students ages 18–24: Changes from 1998–2001. *Annual Review of Public Health, 26*, 259–279.

Johnson, M. B. (2011). A systemic model of doping behavior. *American Journal of Psychology, 124*(2), 151–162.

Johnson, M. B. (2012). A systemic social-cognitive perspective on doping. *Psychology of Sport and Exercise, 13*, 317–323.

Johnson, M. B., Sacks, D. N., & Edmonds, W. A. (2010). Counseling athletes who use performance-enhancing drugs: A new conceptual framework linked to clinical practice. *Journal of Social, Behavioral, and Health Sciences, 4*(1), 1–29.

Joyner, K. J., Pickover, A. M., Soltis, K. E., Dennhardt, A. A., Martens, M. P., & Murphy, J. G. (2016). Deficits in access to reward are associated with college student alcohol use disorder. *Alcoholism: Clinical and Experimental Research, 40*(12), 2685–2691.

Labrie, J. W., Hummer, J. F., Huchting, K. K., & Neighbors, C. (2009). A brief live interactive normative group intervention using wireless keypads to reduce drinking and alcohol consequences in college student athletes. *Drug and Alcohol Review, 28*, 40–47.

Lee, C. M., Neighbors, C., Kilmer, J. R., & Larimer, M. E. (2010). A brief, web-based personalized feedback selective intervention for college student marijuana use: A randomized clinical trial. *Psychology of Addictive Behaviors, 24*(2), 265–273.

Leeies, M., Pagura, J., Sareen, J., & Bolton, J. M. (2010). The use of alcohol and drugs to self-medicate symptoms of posttraumatic stress disorder. *Depression and Anxiety, 27*, 731–736.

Licciardone, J. (2003). Outcomes of a federally funded program for alcohol and other drug prevention in higher education. *The American Journal of Drug and Alcohol Abuse, 29*(4), 803–827. doi:10.1081/ADA-120026262

Lisha, N. E., & Sussman, S. (2010). Relationship of high school and college sport participation with alcohol, tobacco, and illicit drug us: A review. *Addiction Behavior, 35*(5), 399–407.

Looby, A., De Young, K. P., & Earleywine, M. (2013). Challenging expectancies to prevent nonmedical prescription stimulant use: A randomized, controlled trial. *Drug and Alcohol Dependence, 132*, 362–368. doi:10.1016/j.drugalcdep.2013.03.003

Marcello, R. J., Danish, S. J., & Stolberg, A. L. (1989). An evaluation of strategies developed to prevent substance abuse among student-athletes. *The Sport Psychologist, 3*(3), 196–211.

Martell, B. A., O'Connor, P. G., Kerns, R. D., Becker, W. C., Morales, K. H., Kosten, T. R., & Fiellin, D. A. (2007). Systematic review: Opioid treatment for chronic back pain: Prevalence, efficacy, and association with addiction. *Annals of Internal Medicine, 146*, 116–127.

Martens, M. P., Ferrier, A. G., Sheehy, M. J., Corbett, K., Anderson, D. A., & Simmons, A. (2005). Development of the protective behavioral strategies survey. *Journal of Studies on Alcohol and Drugs, 66*, 698–705.

Martens, M. P., Kilmer, J. R., Beck, N. C., & Zamboanga, B. L. (2010). The efficacy of a targeted personalized drinking feedback intervention among intercollegiate athletes: A randomized controlled trial. *Psychology of Addictive Behaviors, 24*(4), 660–669.

Martens, M. P., Pedersen, E. R., Smith, A. E., Stewart, S. H., & O'Brien, K. (2011). Predictors of alcohol-related outcomes in college athletes: The roles of trait urgency and drinking motives. *Addictive Behaviors, 36*, 456–464. doi:10.1016/j.addbeh.2010.12.025

Martens, M. P., Watson, J. C., & Beck N. C. (2006). Sport-type differences alcohol use among intercollegiate athletes. *Journal of Applied Sport Psychology, 18*, 136–150.

Massengale, K. E. C., Ma, A., Rulison, K. L., Milroy, J. J., & Wyrick, D. L. (2017). Perceived norms of alcohol use among first-year college student-athletes' different types of friends. *Journal of American College Health, 65*(1), 32–40.

McCambridge, J., & Strang, J. (2004). The efficacy of single-session motivational interviewing in reducing drug consumption and perceptions of drug-related risk and harm among young people: Results from a multi-site cluster randomized trial. *Addiction, 99*, 39–52.

Meilman, P. W., Leichliter, J. S., & Presley, C. A. (1999). Greeks and athletes: Who drinks more? *College Health, 47*, 187–190.

Miller, W. R., & Rollnick, S. (2002). *Motivational interviewing: Preparing people for change* (2nd ed.). New York, NY: Guilford.

Miller, W. R., Toscova, R. T., Miller, J. H., & Sanchez, V. (2000). A theory-based motivational approach for reduction alcohol/drug problems in college. *Health Education & Behavior, 27*(6), 744–759.

National Colliegate Athletic Association. (2014). *NCAA national study of substance use habits of college student-athletes.* Indianapolis, IN: Author.

NCAA Sport Science Institute. (n.d.). myPlaybook: The freshman experience. *NCAA.* Retrieved from http://www.ncaa.org/sport-science-institute/myplaybook-freshman-experience

Nolt, K. L., Sachs, M. L., & Brenner, J. W. (2013). The effects of collegiate head coaches' knowledge and attitudes toward alcohol consumption by student-athletes. *Journal of Multidisciplinary Research, 5*(3), 7–16.

O'Brien, K. S., Kolt, G. S., Martens, M. P., Ruffman, T., Miller, P. G., & Lynott, D. (2012). Alcohol-related aggression and antisocial behaviour in sportspeople/athletes. *Journal of Science and Medicine in Sport, 15,* 292–297.

O'Connell, S., & Manschreck, T. C. (2012). Playing through the pain: Psychiatric risks among athletes. *Current Psychology, 11*(7), 16–20.

Perkins, H. W. (2002). Surveying the damage: A review of research on consequences of alcohol misuse in college populations. *Journal of Studies on Alcohol, (Suppl. 14),* 91–100.

Perkins, H. W., & Craig, D. W. (2006). A successful social norms campaign to reduce alcohol misuse among college student-athletes. *Journal of Studies on Alcohol and Drugs, 67*(6), 880–889.

Perkins, H. W., & Craig, D. W. (2012). Student-athletes' misperceptions of male and female peer drinking norms: A multi-site investigation of the "Reign of Error." *Journal of College Student Development, 53*(3), 367–382.

Prochaska, J. O., & DiClemente, C. C. (1986). Toward a comprehensive model of change. In: Miller, W. R. & Heather, N. (Eds). *Treating addictive behaviors: Processes of change.* New York, NY: Plenum Press.

Read, J. P., Ouimette, P., White, J., Colder, C., & Farrow, S. (2011). Rates of DSM-IV-TR trauma exposure and posttraumatic stress disorder among newly matriculated college students. *Psychological Trauma, 3*(2), 148–156. doi: 10.1037/a0021260

Schulenberg, J. E., Johnston, L. D., O'Malley, P. M., Bachman, J. G., Miech, R. A. & Patrick, M. E. (2017). *Monitoring the future national survey results on drug use, 1975–2016: Volume II, college students and adults ages 19–55.* Ann Arbor, MI: Institute for Social Research, University of Michigan.

Serrao, H. F., Martens, M. P., Martin, J. L., & Rocha, T. L. (2008). Competitiveness and alcohol use among recreational and elite collegiate athletes. *Journal of Clinical Sport Psychology, 2,* 205–215.

Shirreffs, S. M., & Maughan, R. J. (1997). Restoration of fluid balnceafter exercise-induced dehydration: Effects of alcohol consumption. *Journal of Applied Physiology, 83,* 1152–1158.

Sznitman, S. R., & Romer, D. (2014). Student drug testing and positive school climates: Testing the relation between two school characteristics and drug use behavior in a longitudinal study. *Journal of Studies on Alcohol and Drugs, 75*(1), 65–73.

Taylor, E. A., Ward, R. M., & Hardin, R. (2017). Examination of drinking habits and motives of collegiate student-athletes. *Journal of Applied Sport Management, 9*(1), 56–77.

Turrisi, R., Mallett, K. A., Mastroleo, N. R., & Larimer, M. E. (2006). Heavy drinking in college students: Who is at risk and what is being done about it? *The Journal of General Psychology, 133,* 401–420.

United States Department of Agriculture. (2015). *Dietary guidelines for Americans* (8th ed.). Washington, DC: Author.

Varga, M. D. (2012). Adderall abuse on college campuses: A comprehensive literature review. *Journal of Evidence-Based Social Work, 9*(3), 293–313.

Wadler, G. I., & Hainline, B. (1989). *Drugs and the athlete.* Philadelphia, PA: Davis.

Wanjek, B., Rosendahl, J., Strauss, B., & Garbriel, H. H. (2007). Doping, drugs and drug abuse among adolescents in the State of Thuringia (Germany): Prevalence, knowledge and attitudes. *Behavioral Sciences, 28,* 346–353. doi:10.1055/s-2006-924353

Weaver, C. C., Martens, M. P., & Smith, A. E. (2012). Do protective behavioral strategies moderate the relationship between negative urgency and alcohol-related outcomes among intercollegiate athletes? *Journal of Studies on Alcohol and Drugs, 73*(3), 498–503.

White, H. R., Morgan, T. J., Pugh, L. A., Celinska, K., Labouvie, E. W., & Pandina, R. J. (2006). Evaluating two brief substance-use interventions for mandated college students. *Journal of Studies on Alcohol, 67*(2), 309–317. doi:10.15288/jsa.2006.67.309

White, H. R., Mun, E. Y., Pugh, L., & Morgan, T. J. (2007). Long-term effects of brief substance use interventions for mandated college students: Sleeper effects of an in-person personal feedback intervention. *Alcoholism: Clinical and Experimental Research, 31*(8), 1380–1391.

Wilfert, M. (Ed.) (2017). *NCAA drug-testing program: 2017-18.* Indianapolis, IN: NCAA Sport Science Institute.

Williams J. H., Hadden C., & Marcavage E. (1983). Experimental study of assertion training as a drug-prevention strategy for use with college students. *Journal of College Student Personnel, 24,* 201–206.

Wyrick, D. L., Milroy, J. J., Reifsteck, E. J., Day, T., & Kelly, S. E. (2016). The effects of a web-based alcohol prevention program on social norms, expectancies, and intentions to prevent harm among college student-athletes. *The Sport Psychologist, 30,* 113–122.

Wyrick, D. L., Rulison, K. L., Fearnow-Kenney, M., Milroy, J. J., & Collins, L. M. (2014). Moving beyond the treatment package approach to developing behavioral interventions: Addressing questions that arose during an application of the Multiphase Optimization Strategy (MOST). *Translational Behavioral Medicine, 4,* 252–259. doi:10.1007/s13142-013-0247-7

# 10

# Counseling Student-Athletes with Physical Injuries and/or Cognitive Disabilities

*Leigh Skvarla and Jessica Dale Bartley*

## CASE STUDY: MARTY

Marty is a 20-year-old, marketing student at a D1 university. A left-handed pitcher who made headlines during his high school career, Marty was recruited to play baseball and is well known across campus, given that his hometown is less than an hour away. At the middle of last season, Marty—now a junior—began to experience a lot of shoulder pain, and the pain did not go away with treatment; the athletic trainer had recommended massage, ice, heat, rest, and over the counter pain medication. During an important game against a long-time rival, Marty recalled hearing some sort of popping and feeling a deep pain in his shoulder but told himself to ignore it so that he could lead the team to victory.

Ultimately, four weeks after the game, Marty went to the hospital, where an intern suspected that he either had a rotator cuff injury or a tear in his labrum (also called a SLAP tear). A consult with a surgeon confirmed that Marty would indeed need surgery to repair a torn supraspinatus tendon. At his intake session, he explains that he will be in the sling for up to eight weeks. He states that his Internet-based research indicates that he could be pain-free in just a few weeks, but potentially not healed for up to 12 months. "What am I going to do?" he asks. "This sport is my life. It's what people know me for. It's how I met my best friends, how I'm helping my folks not have to pay for tuition. Plus, I'm not the best with academics. My ADHD sometimes gets in the way."

In his first session, Marty spends a lot of time talking about how this injury must have been coming, as he put in many hours after regular practices and games to work on his technique and his upper-body strength. And yet, he says he's angry that this happened: "I've never taken a steroid, never drank during the season, and never did stupid stuff on random Friday nights. I played by all the rules. I respected the game. And here's what it's given me, just before my senior season." Marty reports finding it difficult to get out of bed most mornings, and his grades have fallen since mid-semester. He expresses his ADHD has been well managed so far at college, but his organizational skills and ability to pay attention seem to be deteriorating this semester. He and his girlfriend got into a big fight last week and he is not sure if they are going to break up or not. He says his Mom has called him a few times on the phone, but his Dad (who is actively serving in the Navy) has not called since the surgery.

Helping professionals who work in the college environment need to be aware of the many visible and invisible disabilities and differences among students. These disabilities and differences come in various forms, including but not limited to temporary and permanent injuries, learning challenges, and mental health concerns. This chapter provides an overview of physical injury and its potential impact on student-athletes' mentality and well-being, and then discusses the implications for student-athletes with cognitive disabilities, including learning disorders, attention-deficit hyperactivity disorder, and mood disorders. In particular, this chapter focuses on providing the helping professional with an overview of issues these student-athletes may be facing and describes the role of the counselor in supporting them.

## Defining Injury

Currently, the NCAA uses three criteria to define a physical injury to a student-athlete: (1) the injury occurs within the training or competition environment, (2) the injury requires an athletic trainer or physician's attention or treatment, and (3) the injury restricts or prevents the athlete from participating in at least one subsequent day's activities. Based on this definition, an athlete who rolls an ankle while walking to class and then ices it before practice is not considered injured. However, an athlete who rolls an ankle during warm-up, has it treated by the trainer on site, and decides to rest for the remainder of the week is considered injured. It should be noted that this chapter focuses on injuries sustained anywhere on the body, with the exception of concussions.*

## Defining Disability

According to the Americans with Disabilities Act of 1990, an individual with a disability is a person who has a physical or mental impairment that substantially limits one or more major life activities. In this chapter, when using the term "disability," we refer to a cognitive difference that the student-athlete has in comparison to their peer group. Unlike physical injury, where the student-athlete can typically be seen limping or wearing a cast, cognitive differences are generally not visible to the eye. As such, they are sometimes referred to as hidden disabilities (also known as invisible disabilities), which are "disabilities that are not immediately apparent" (U.S. Department of Education, 1995). This can include mood disorders—discussed elsewhere in this book—and neurodevelopmental disorders such as specific learning disorders/disabilities (LD) and attention-deficit/hyperactivity disorders (ADHD). In 2011, it was estimated that over 8% of men and women in the United States reported work limitations due to a hidden disability (Nazarov & Lee, 2012). Given that this statistic is likely an underestimation, it is critical that helping professionals be prepared to recognize and support student-athletes with these disabilities.

## Injury in the Athletic Culture

College student-athletes are often viewed as some of the fittest, healthiest, most active people on campus. However, the risk of injury is inherent in sports participation, and injuries can sideline athletes from their typical training and competition routines. For instance, one might expect that at some point a gymnast will not land properly on a four-inch wide wooden beam, or that a football player will fall awkwardly after making contact with an opposing linebacker. Over the course of an athlete's career, there is a strong likelihood that he or she will sustain at least one significant injury. Between the competition years 2009–2010 and 2013–2014, it is estimated that over one million injuries occurred in the college sports environment (Kerr et al., 2015). This is by no means a small number, and statistics like this indicate that injury is an experience that many student-athletes will bring to a coach, athletic trainer, faculty advisor, academic counselor, or counseling/wellness center professional.

---

* For more on concussions, see Chapter 8.

While student-athletes may be cognitively aware of their susceptibility to injury, this awareness may be influenced by the larger sports culture and the social norms of athletics departments and/or teams. Phrases like "no pain, no gain" and "push through it" can often be heard on the field, court, or ice, or worn proudly on the backs of training t-shirts. The message behind these words can be a challenge when working to help student-athletes express their feelings and acknowledge the extent of their limitations. Indeed, a high pain tolerance is typically required of athletes and this tolerance is sometimes rewarded with verbal praise, nonverbal feedback, and/or in the form of "promotions," including more playing time or leadership roles. Previous research has suggested that, in some ways, playing through pain and injury is a behavior to be respected (Nixon, 1994). The student-athletes who are willing to sacrifice their safety and/or their bodies are frequently hailed as heroic and strong, both in the stands and in the news cycle.

These kinds of sociocultural norms may be particularly apparent in sports where physical displays of assertiveness, violence, and masculinity are desirable. Football, rugby, wrestling, and ice hockey, among others, are a few examples. Some student-athletes may view injury as a "masculinizing" experience, and one that reinforces their physical and mental fortitude (Young, White, & McTeer, 1994). However, helping professionals should be mindful that these sociocultural messages about sacrificing oneself for the team, the score, or the legacy are not solely placed on men. Female athletes are also susceptible to these socially-driven messages surrounding toughness and playing through pain (Weinberg, Vernau, & Horn, 2013).

Researchers have collectively referred to student-athletes' (over)adherence to these kinds of expectations or ideals as (over)conformity to the sport ethic (Hughes & Coakley, 1991). The sport ethic essentially encapsulates the idea that those who meet and exceed the physical and psychological demands of sport will be revered amongst their team and its fan base. This can be seen, too, in the commentary of live-action announcers and television broadcasters, who frequently applaud a hard hit or "gutsy" play, followed by the athlete's quick rebound.

There is also a widely understood, but rarely discussed, difference between being "hurt" and being "injured." In the former case, the athlete is expected to shake off the pain and return to the field, court, or ice as soon as possible—sometimes as early as the next snap in football or the next throw-in in soccer. In the latter case, an athlete who is injured is understood to be in a significant amount of pain or discomfort, and rest and treatment can be explained and normalized by the need for medical assistance from an athletic trainer or team physician.

NCAA Division I, II, and III athletic departments usually have a lead trainer and/or assistants readily available during all practices and competitions, as well as daytime, walk-in availability for those competitors who need additional treatment or rehabilitation support. As such, athletic trainers often serve as a point of contact for injury-related concerns and may be one of the primary people through which mental health and sport psychology referrals are made (Andersen & Tod, 2006; Neal et al., 2013; Sherman, Thompson, Dehass, & Wilfert, 2005).

Surrendering to pain or injury, or asking for help, can be difficult for student-athletes, as these actions could be interpreted as weak or not "mentally strong." The stigma surrounding pain, injury, and any help-seeking behavior is important for helping professionals to recognize and address with the athletes that they serve (Sudano, Collins, & Miles, 2017). Student-athletes may be hesitant to express help-seeking behaviors due to the aforementioned cultural norms, as well as a myriad of individual factors. These factors might include a perceived lack of time, denial of the issue, fear of the unknown, financial constraints, uncertainty about treatment effectiveness, little knowledge about mental health services, and concerns about confidentiality, among others (Gulliver, Griffiths, & Christensen, 2012). When expressed, help-seeking behaviors in the athletic environment may include changes in performance; absenteeism; social withdrawal or isolation; excessive emotion and/or lack thereof; self-harm; substance use/abuse; unexplained weight gain or loss; problems concentrating, focusing, or remembering; fighting or difficulty with authority figures; increased negative self-talk; irritability and/or agitation; reports of stomach aches and headaches; and unresolved injuries.

## Response to Injury

Every student-athlete responds differently to injury. This should not come as a surprise, given that each person's experience is colored by a variety of physiological, cognitive, social, and cultural factors. Helping professionals are encouraged to think about the injury response as a kaleidoscope—where one small turn of the object results in a new, complex interplay of shapes, colors, and patterns. As such, there is no single, predictable reaction that can allow for helping professionals to follow a set protocol or sequence of interventions (Putukian, 2014). Nevertheless, counselors and other helping professionals are strongly encouraged to use academic-based literature, peer consultation, and best practices in their field to address each athlete's response to their unique set of circumstances.

Much of the peer-reviewed literature on sport injury offers concrete suggestions to helping professionals based on models and theories of grief, loss, and adjustment/transition. While grief and loss may be more traditionally associated with death and dying, these emotions are also a natural response to injury, particularly if the injury means that the athlete will have to detach from their typical routines and peer group, or if they will no longer be able to participate in their sport. The following bullet-points provide a basic summary of several models and approaches that have been used to conceptualize student-athletes' response to injury:

- There are five stages of grief or loss that may be applicable to understanding a student-athlete's response to injury. Theses stages are (1) denial, (2) anger, (3) bargaining, (4) depression, and (5) acceptance (Kubler-Ross, 1969).

- The interaction between pre-injury factors (i.e., personality, life stress, coping resources, and interventions), personal factors, and situational factors can assist helping professionals in explaining behavioral and emotional responses to injury and the subsequent rehabilitation process (Wiese-Bjornstal, Smith, Shaffer, & Morrey, 1998).

- The reaction to a loss such as an injury can be understood through the following emotions and transitions: (1) shock, (2) realization, (3) mourning, (4) acknowledgment, and (5) coping or reformulation (Kerr, 1961; Tunick, Clement, & Etzel, 2009).

- A person's ability to manage stress may decrease, along with their self-esteem, during times of loss and grieving. Loss could mean the loss of a person, but also the loss of a particular social role. The three biologically-driven stages proposed in this approach are (1) shock and disbelief, (2) despondency and depression, and (3) recovery (Averill, 1968).

- Initially, from a bereavement perspective, one model suggests that there are three stages or transitions for those who have experienced a loss: (1) shock, including disbelief and hope; (2) coping, including attempts to problem-solve given the new reality; and (3) adaptation, including feelings and behaviors related to resolution (Evans & Hardy, 1995; Karl, 1987).

As is evident in the above list, a phase or stage approach is quite common in the research literature. While these phases or stages are presented conceptually in a linear fashion, it should be noted that some athletes will work through these stages in a different order, experience them all at once, and/or return to earlier stages depending on situational circumstances, such as a setback in treatment or a change in social support.

During the initial shock and subsequent processing of the injury experience, helping professionals should be mindful of the context in which student-athletes typically practice and compete. From an ecological theory perspective (Bronfenbrenner, 1979), the systemic messages sent and received include expectations and ideals about mental toughness, and specific definitions of health and success. For instance, an athlete may look at a win as a concrete outcome, such as a score or ranking. A helping professional can introduce the athlete to a more gray approach, as opposed to falling into a pattern of all-or-nothing thinking. This could help with confronting and reframing statements, such as "I'm hurt, therefore I'm useless" or "I'm either totally healthy or I'm not at all." The helping professional can also assist the athlete in identifying other cognitive traps and self-fulfilling prophecies.

Dealing with uncertainty is another issue of concern for some injured student-athletes. While performance is often defined in concrete terms (e.g., percentages, points), the process and demands of recovery and rehabilitation may not be so certain. At times, student-athletes may need to cope with a change in prognosis, uncertain timelines, unexpected or prolonged side effects of surgery or medication, and the inherent challenges that come with allowing the mind and body to heal from injury.

Furthermore, for athletes who have defined themselves by what they "do," the injury process can be particularly difficult. The concept of athletic identity may be important to discuss in a counseling, or similar, setting (Brewer, Van Raalte, & Linder, 1993). Student-athletes may be asking themselves questions about who they are and what they should do during the recovery period. For instance, a 21-year-old athlete who has participated in track and field since fifth grade has likely developed friendships that are rooted in her sport and gone for near-daily runs for a decade. Her accomplishments may have been acknowledged in newspapers, yearbooks, or local TV features. Now, she may feel a lack of self-concept, direction, and future aspirations.

In some cases, athletes who are in the process of returning to training and competition may experience hesitations when getting back on the field, court, or ice. These hesitations are often referred to as re-injury anxiety, in which athletes who are eager to get back to their sport find themselves feeling nervous about injuring themselves again, or worried about their bodies not being ready for full competition (Podlog, Dimmock, & Miller, 2011). "What if this happens again? Is this a safe sport? I lost playing time, so am I actually ready to be back?" It is important that the counselor validate these concerns, as they are reasonable, given the student-athlete's injury in the first place.

In contrast to re-injury anxiety, some athletes may yearn to continue despite the medical necessity of ceasing participation. Not returning to sport means different things to different student-athletes (Stoltenburg, Kamphoff, & Bremer, 2011), and once again the metaphor of a kaleidoscope may assist helping professionals in conceptualizing their approach. For some student-athletes, depression may be the primary emotional experience, and so helping professionals will need to determine the proper level and intensity of care as the student-athlete deals with a mental health diagnosis. Still, for other student-athletes, feelings of relief may become prominent. Perhaps now that they do not have to get up every morning to train, they can focus on their goal of becoming a nurse, writer, teacher, or engineer.

For student-athletes who are on an athletic scholarship, obtaining all relevant information about financial status may help to clarify the athlete's mental picture of the future. Sometimes the athlete may choose to find a new role to perform within their sport (e.g., volunteer coach, equipment manager). Additionally, some may be inspired by their injury experience, and set their sights on helping others who may have similar experiences later on (e.g., study to become an athletic trainer, physician, sport psychologist, or coach).

## Social Impact

Developmentally, college is a time when many students leave their homes or home-towns and begin to make meaningful connections with their peers on a daily basis. Students live, study, take classes, and eat with their peers. For student-athletes, this also means training, traveling, and competing with members of their peer group. Therefore, the social impact has the potential to be quite strong for athletes who have received diagnoses and prognoses of longer than a few weeks' time. Changes in a student-athlete's injury status may mean that they no longer attend practice, and instead report to the athletic training room for treatment. Without the daily socialization that they typically get during work-outs, injured athletes may begin to socially withdraw, and find themselves feeling alone.

Unfortunately, in some instances isolation can lead to or exacerbate negative coping strategies, such as over- or under-eating, substance use/abuse, irregular sleeping patterns, rumination surrounding self-doubt or guilt, and harmful behaviors towards oneself or others. Additionally, without the typical supports in place, student-athletes may find that their academic performance suffers, or that they struggle to find motivation to attend class or ask for help. Athletes who are far away from home and/or struggling financially may be at particularly high risk for mental health and academic performance concerns.

Ideally, during this time, student-athletes should receive peer support as well as athletic department and university support. At a time when attachment could feel like it is at an all-time low (Bowlby, 1961; Evans & Hardy, 1995), student-athletes can benefit from perceiving their support system as "in it" with them, even if these persons have not had the same experience and therefore "don't get it." Support can come in many forms, from catching a car ride to campus with a teammate, to getting assistance with making an appointment at the counseling center.

## Normal versus Abnormal Responses

Most athletes will adjust to the injury process and navigate their way through it without significant changes in their mental health and overall well-being. However, some athletes will struggle with the initial shock, followed by grief, loss, and/or issues related to identity and purpose. Naturally, how important this loss/injury is to them may be a strong determinant of how they cope and then adjust to the realities of their injury (Evans & Hardy, 1995).

Counselors and other helping professionals should be mindful of any significant or sudden changes in the student-athlete's behavior, academic performance, and personality. If such changes are noted, helping professionals can encourage the student-athlete to consider additional or higher levels of care to address any new or ongoing mental health concerns that may arise as a result of the injury experience. It is possible that the athlete could find themselves in legal trouble or begin using illegal or unhealthy substances; in other cases, the behaviors may not be so pronounced. Therefore, counselors and other helping professionals should document their interactions with each injured student-athlete in a timely manner, and reflect on changes in the athlete's appearance, emotional tone/affect, communication patterns, self-reported thoughts, and any other information that is appropriate and ethical to note.

Although athletic trainers are not expected to diagnose mental health disorders, and counselors are not expected to know everything about range of motion, it is imperative that all treatment team members be transparent with the athlete about concerns they may have, and provide emotional and informational support in helping the student-athlete connect to the people and the services that they need.

## The Sports Medicine Team

Student-athletes across Divisions I, II, and III form a variety of relationships during training and competition. Of course, they spend time with their teammates, coaches, and athletic trainers. However, injured athletes may also get to know other members of the support and medical staff, such as team physicians, sport psychology consultants, and/or outside specialists, such as orthopedic surgeons and physical therapists.

Members of the sports medicine team have the ability to provide the student-athlete with concrete, specific information about their injury, including but not limited to their diagnosis, planned course of treatment, and prognosis. This information can be very valuable to the student-athlete, who may find a sense of comfort in knowing what is happening physiologically. Also, knowing what is coming next can help reduce feelings of uncertainty, especially for those athletes who have never experienced injury before. Additionally, by having a conversation with the student-athlete about their injury, team physicians and athletic trainers can invite and normalize further discussion of the athlete's injury experience and help to prepare them mentally for the rehabilitation and/or return to play process ahead.

Given the myriad of body types, skill sets, and personalities involved in athletics, it is perhaps not surprising that student-athletes will have different expectations about the injury rehabilitation process, and how their athletic trainers and sports medicine team personnel will interact with them (Arvinen-Barrow et al., 2016). As a general guideline, while the athlete is in treatment and recovery, the sports medicine team should continue to provide helpful information about the athlete's progress and to build or maintain their motivation. In addition, these helping professionals can serve as supports for the athlete's mental health. First and foremost, medical staff can avoid using all-or-nothing or judgmental language, such as "Yikes, your swelling should have gone down days ago. That's not good!" Statements like these can be difficult for student-athletes to hear, who in most cases are depending upon their providers to help them through their recovery through information-based and emotional support.

Medical providers should also avoid making promises to the athlete that they cannot guarantee. For instance, saying "you'll be back by next season" prior to seeing how the athlete responds to a surgical procedure or the first few weeks of rehabilitation can create a false sense of optimism that is not realistic given the athlete's injury. Physicians and trainers are encouraged to provide encouragement, and when appropriate, time ranges or estimates for recovery, while acknowledging potential setbacks for which they and the athlete can prepare.

Finally, sports medicine team members can help to communicate the student-athlete's needs to the coaching staff and make recommendations about the environment in which they recover. In most cases, student-athletes will benefit from remaining connected to their teammates and coaches. This will look different depending on several factors (e.g., treatment schedule, time of season, accessibility of facilities), however, it is likely that attending a film session or pre-competition meal will not hurt the team and can benefit the student-athlete's well-being.

## Role of the Counselor or Other Helping Professional

Counselors have the ability to positively support the student-athlete's injury recovery or, when need be, their transition out of sport. In some cases, the athlete may come to counseling of their own choosing, and other times they may do so as a result of a referral. In all cases, counselors are in a unique position to be at least somewhat removed from the sport culture and possess certain skills and ethical sensitivity that can empower the student-athlete to make sense of their current injury status and explore their next steps.

Basic counseling skills such as active listening, summarizing, paraphrasing, reflection of feeling, and reflection of meaning can be very impactful for a student-athlete who is recovering from injury. Whether it be an injury that will only take a few weeks to heal, or an injury that has ended one's competitive career, having someone listen to and affirm the emotions, met and unmet goals, and future plans can be useful. It is likely that the athlete has some knowledge of the specifics of their injury—the location of the fracture, the normality of swelling or bruising, the results of the x-ray. Nevertheless, the athlete may be struggling with questions that a WebMD search cannot answer: "How did this happen?" "Why is God punishing me?" "Would this have happened if I trained more?" "Was I not focused enough?" Counselors are encouraged to be mindful of student-athletes' beliefs surrounding the injury incident. It is not uncommon for athletes to look for reasons to explain their injury. Helping athletes identify their cognitive appraisal of the injury experience can lead to further insights.

Additionally, the therapeutic approach can have a positive impact on a student-athlete's recovery. Building a trusting relationship with a helping professional is one of the most important aspects of client development and behavior change (Martin, Garske, & Davis, 2000; Semaia, 2014). With rapport building comes an unbiased or outsider perspective and unconditional positive regard. Particularly for athletes who have defined themselves by their sports participation, meeting a counselor who sees the person behind the athlete can be helpful. Furthermore, counselors who can introduce student-athletes to the concepts of social support and resourcing are able to set up the student-athlete for success with general life skills, such as communication, self-awareness, relaxation, and stress management. Moreover, student-athletes may find it comforting to know that what they choose to share is considered private and confidential, with very few exceptions.

Like other sports medicine professionals, counselors should avoid making promises about the athlete's prognosis, especially without proper supporting information. Instead, counselors are encouraged to direct athletes' attention to what they can control, such as attitude, adherence to the rehabilitation process, and expression of positive help-seeking behaviors. Counselors can also provide psychoeducation to athletes on the grief and loss processes and empower the athlete to take ownership of their personal narrative by setting realistic goals, building motivation, and finding sources of social support. In some cases, athletes may sign a release form to allow the counselor to consult with other sports medicine team members, so that continuity of care is upheld.

Should issues surrounding re-injury anxiety surface, a helping professional can empower the student-athlete to appropriately respond to and reframe their concerns. For instance, athletes can remind themselves that: (1) they were fully cleared by the medical staff, (2) injury is an inherent part of their participation and was a risk even before they were injured, and (3) their support team will be continually monitoring them as they re-engage with the team to train and compete. For cases where return to play is less certain, therapeutic approaches that involve mindfulness can assist the student-athlete in their acceptance of uncertainty and identify ways that they can behave during this time that are consistent with their values and sense of purpose.

Overall, counselors and other helping professionals are responsible for supporting student-athletes' decision-making surrounding their injury experience, and fostering the confidence and competencies to manage emotions, build supports, and identify the necessary steps to return to play or explore new courses of action. There are several interventions that counselors can use when working with injured student-athletes. Counselors and other helping professionals are encouraged to engage in case consultation and/or supervision to determine the best course of treatment for each client, based on the information provided by the athlete and any relevant third parties. A brief summary of theoretical orientations, counseling approaches, and interventions to consider are listed here:

**Social support and resourcing.** Counselors can assist athletes in identifying who can provide tangible support (e.g., car rides, financial support, ice/heat/medication supervision, note-taking assistance in class); emotional support (e.g., hearing out feelings and concerns); and informational support (e.g., details of diagnosis and prognosis). Previous research has indicated that athletes' perceptions of social support are a strong component of successful injury recovery (e.g., Clement & Shannon, 2011).

**Psychoeducation.** Counselors can help student-athletes to understand the relationship between stress and injury (Smith, Ptacek, & Patterson, 2000; Williams & Andersen, 1998) and ways that they can increase their motivation for rehabilitation adherence, among other topics. This intervention may also extend to other members of the student-athlete's family of origin or sports team, if deemed appropriate by the counselor and the client.

**Mental skills training.** Counselors who have the competencies to integrate sport psychology interventions into their practice can introduce injured athletes to strategies such as relaxation, imagery, and goal setting. Within these strategies are a plethora of resources for athletes to use during their recovery process, as well as their everyday activities. Skills such as deep breathing, progressive muscle relaxation, and body scans can help the athlete to gain a sense of control over their nervous system and remain calm during stressful times (e.g., test-taking, dating, public speaking). Additionally, counselors can guide student-athletes through healing imagery scripts and help them develop imagery routines to cope with pain and discomfort. Imagery training can also be used for motivational purposes (e.g., return to play) and coping purposes (e.g., Kabat-Zinn's Mountain Meditation). Lastly, goal-setting can be introduced by both counselors and the medical team (including athletic trainers; Wayda, Armenth-Brothers, & Boyce, 1998). Helping athletes to set short- and long-term goals can help them to gain a sense of autonomy and competence during rehabilitation and/or to plan next steps if they are not returning to their sport.

**Cognitive behavioral therapy.** Counselors can help student-athletes identify and address cognitive traps, such as forecasting, mind reading, and overgeneralizing (Greenberg, Reiner, & Meiran, 2012). By empowering them to increase their awareness of these kinds of thought patterns, student-athletes can then work to reframe, refute, or change their thoughts surrounding the injury experience. In some cases, assigning homework or providing the athlete with a workbook may help to make their progress tangible (e.g., number of pages completed, measured improvement towards treatment goals).

**Acceptance and commitment therapy.** Counselors can use acceptance and mindfulness strategies with commitment and behavior-change strategies to increase student-athletes' psychological flexibility. Rather than working to help athletes eliminate or avoid thoughts or feelings, this approach can help them understand how to remain in the present moment and move toward a life of value. For example, injury may provide a much-needed break from sport or performance domains and gives the student-athlete the opportunity to focus on the mental side of the game.

**Trauma-focused cognitive behavioral therapy.** If student-athletes' injury and/or surgery experiences were perceived to be traumatic, addressing their negative beliefs surrounding the most disturbing parts of the event, and how they can reduce the intensity of their responses, may be helpful. This approach first involves psychoeducation about trauma and the brain's normal response to abnormal events. Counselors need to remain up-to-date with the literature on psychosomatic responses to injury and other traumatic events (Marich, 2014; van der Kolk, 2014). While not present in most cases, it is possible for a physical injury to trigger or heighten an emotional trauma that the student-athlete has (un)consciously chosen not to address.

**Identity development focus.** Counselors can implement activity-based discussions to help the athlete to identify the other parts of their identity (i.e., other than being an athlete). For instance, a SWOT analysis might encourage the athlete to identify their personal Strengths, areas for improvement (Weaknesses), Opportunities in the near future, and any Threats to those opportunities that the athlete can work to overcome (Cumming, 2015). Additionally, counselors can encourage student-athletes to create personality profiles that address all of the roles that they occupy (e.g., daughter/son, friend, partner, student), and support curiosity about career aspirations by using materials like the Occupational Outlook Handbook or the campus career center. In fact, talking about student-athletes' goals beyond college sports, regardless of injury status, can be an important part of their personal and academic development (Semaia, 2014).

## Final Thoughts on Injury

Injuries happen. They happen to most student-athletes at some point during their careers, either prior to their arrival to campus or while they are representing their institutions in collegiate competition. Student-athlete responses are as unique as the individuals themselves. However, helping professionals can rely on academic research, peer consultation, and their own training and competencies to assist their clients as they navigate this experience. It is important to remember that most student-athletes will adaptively cope with their injuries and decide to return to play or to find new opportunities. For those who struggle to cope and find themselves in need of higher levels of care, helping professionals can make a positive difference by encouraging social support, self-awareness, and small steps towards recovery and life goals.

## NCAA Guidelines for Disabilities

According to the National Collegiate Athletic Association (NCAA, 2015), participation by student-athletes with disabilities is encouraged in intercollegiate athletics "to the full extent of their interests and abilities." The association further states, "an NCAA member institution will have the right to seek, on behalf of any student-athlete with a disability participating on the member's team, a reasonable modification or accommodation of a playing rule, provided that the modification or accommodation would not (1) compromise the safety of, or increase the risk of injury to, any other student-athlete; (2) change an essential element that would fundamentally alter the nature of the game; or (3) provide the student-athlete an unfair advantage over the other competitors."

### *NCAA Modifications and Accommodations for Disability*

For a student-athlete with a disability to receive a reasonable modification or accommodation of a playing rule, member institutions must complete a waiver process with the NCAA. It is important to note that helping professionals can often provide valuable information about a student-athlete in this waiver process. Since many helping professionals have consistent contact with student-athletes, they might be able to provide important insight into existing disabilities as well as previously undiagnosed disabilities and how academics, athletics, and/or general well-being of a student-athlete have been impacted by these disabilities. Due to stigma, many student-athletes might not be willing to self-identify disabilities and might need support from providers to help understand their disability and the modifications and/or accommodations that might be possible.

### *NCAA Waivers and the Waiver Process*

Many student-athletes struggle with their disabilities in various contexts in the college experience (e.g., academics, athletics, general well-being). The NCAA has created an explicit waiver process in Divisions I, II, and III for an education-impacting disability (EID) to support student-athletes in the classroom (Ridpath, 2014). The

NCAA defines an EID for student-athletes as "a current impairment that has a substantial educational impact on a student's academic performance and requires accommodation." An EID can be filed for a student-athlete for any of the following disorders: LD, ADHD, mental health disorders, medical conditions, hearing impairments, or autism spectrum disorders.

While mood disorders are addressed elsewhere in the book, the most common mental health disorders, including mood disorders, considered EID are major depressive disorder, generalized anxiety disorder, social anxiety disorder/social phobia, adjustment disorder, obsessive/compulsive disorder, oppositional defiant disorder, alcohol use disorders, post traumatic stress disorder, panic disorder, and bipolar disorder. To document an EID with the NCAA Eligibility Center,* a student-athlete must submit documentation supporting the diagnosis.

## Diagnosis and Treatment of Learning Disorders/Disabilities and Attention-Deficit Hyperactivity Disorder

Since mood disorders and other mental health concerns are addressed elsewhere in the book, we focus primarily on how helping professionals can aid in the diagnosis and treatment of LD and ADHD for the remainder of this chapter. Often LD and ADHD have been diagnosed by a family physician or by a mental health professional without appropriate documentation, but there are specific assessment batteries that need to be completed by trained professionals for the disability to be filed with the NCAA—especially if the student-athlete is intending to ask for modification or accommodations. For LD and ADHD, an assessment battery is likely to include a diagnostic interview, aptitude tests, achievement tests, cognitive and information processing tests, and rating scales (Bender, 1993; Bender, 2007).

While formal diagnosis of ADHD requires an assessment battery by a licensed psychologist, and specific learning disabilities/disorders require documentation from licensed psychologists and/or medical professionals, any helping professional (e.g., coaches, athletic trainers, academic advisors) working with student-athletes should be aware of the signs. According to the National Institute of Child Health and Human Development (2016), common signs that a person may have learning disorders/disabilities include difficulty with reading and/or writing; problems with math skills; difficulty remembering; problems paying attention; trouble following directions; poor coordination; difficulty with concepts related to time; and problems staying organized. A student-athlete with a learning disorder/disability also may exhibit one or more of the following: impetuous behavior; inappropriate responses in school

---

* For the most up-to-date documentation, helping professionals should consult the NCAA website at http://www.ncaa.org.

or social situations; difficulty staying on task (easily distracted); difficulty finding the right way to say something; inconsistent school performance; immature way of speaking; difficulty listening well; problems dealing with new things in life; and problems understanding words or concepts. In the *Diagnostic and Statistical Manual of Mental Disorders*, 5th edition (*DSM-5*; American Psychiatric Association, 2013), the standard classification manual utilized by mental health professionals in the United States, Attention-Deficit Hyperactivity Disorder (ADHD) has been further divided into categories of inattention, hyperactivity, and impulsivity. With inattention, a student-athlete might procrastinate, not complete tasks like homework or chores, or frequently move from one uncompleted activity to another (Barkley, 2014). He or she may also be disorganized; lack focus; have a hard time paying attention to details and a tendency to make careless mistakes; have work that might be messy and seem careless; have trouble staying on topic while talking, not listening to others, and not following social rules; be forgetful about daily activities (for example, missing appointments, forgetting to bring lunch); and be easily distracted by things like trivial noises or events that are usually ignored by others. A student-athlete with hyperactivity may fidget and squirm when seated; get up frequently to walk or run around; exhibit restlessness; have trouble playing quietly or doing quiet hobbies; always be "on the go;" and talk excessively. A student-athlete with impulsivity may be impatient; have a hard time waiting to talk or react; have a hard time waiting for their turn; blurt out answers before someone finishes asking them a question; frequently interrupt or intrude on others; and start conversations at inappropriate times.

After the NCAA has accepted an education-impacting disability (EID) waiver from a member institution on behalf of a student-athlete, the NCAA will work closely with the member institution's disability office to determine reasonable accommodations and/or modifications specific to the student-athlete. Some of the modifications and accommodations can include, but are not limited to: extended time on assignments and/or exams, exam proctoring, exam relocation, classroom relocation, alternate formats of printed materials, audio descriptions, note-taking services, captioning services, document conversion, prepared materials before class, recording device use, and assistive technology (Vickers, 2010). The NCAA can also work with medical professionals when prescription medications will be considered. This consultation may include informing which medications are listed on the banned substances list, namely stimulants.

## Implications/Suggestions for Counselors and Other Helping Professionals

The role of counselors and other helping professionals working with student-athletes with disabilities can vary greatly. Although some student-athletes come to college with knowledge of their disabilities, other student-athletes might discover their disability for the first time with the support of their counselor or helping professional. Helping professionals might assist student-athletes to communicate their disability to coaches, teammates, and academic advisors or to manage the modifications and accommodations related to the NCAA waiver process. The role of the counselor and the helping professional can be incredibly important in ensuring student-athletes' success.

## Conclusion

As the prevalence of LD, ADHD, and mental health concerns continue to rise, it is important for counselors and other helping professionals to not only understand how to diagnose and treat disabilities, but also understand the nuances to supporting student-athletes on and off the field. The ways to support student-athletes are always evolving, but simply being there to listen can potentially have the greatest impact.

## Discussion Questions

1. How might the larger sports culture influence Marty's decision to ignore or suppress his physical pain in order to help his team achieve success against a strong opponent?

2. What is the potential impact of Marty's injury on his self-concept, particularly his identity as an athlete? What campus resources might be useful in providing Marty with greater support?

3. Why might it be important for the counselor working with Marty to help him express his feelings of grief and loss associated with his injury? How would the counselor assist Marty in either returning to play or coping with the end of his baseball career?

## References

American Psychiatric Association. (2013). *Diagnostic and statistical manual of mental disorders* (5th ed.). Arlington, VA: American Psychiatric Publishing.

Andersen, M., & Tod, D. (2006). When to refer athletes for counseling and psychotherapy. In J. Williams (Ed.), *Applied sport psychology: Personal growth to peak performance* (pp. 483–504). Champaign, IL: Human Kinetics.

Arvinen-Barrow, M., Clement, D., Hamson-Utley, J. J., Kamphoff, C., Zakrajzek, R., Lee, S-M., ... Martin, S. (2016). Athletes' expectations about sport injury rehabilitation: A cross-cultural study. *Journal of Sport Rehabilitation, 24*(4), 338–347.

Averill, J. A. (1968). Grief: Its nature and significance. *Psychological Bulletin, 70,* 721–748.

Barkley, R. A. (2014). *Attention deficit hyperactivity disorder: A handbook for diagnosis and treatment* (4th edition). New York: Guilford Press.

Bender, W. N. (Eds.) (1993). *Learning disabilities: Best practices for professionals.* Boston: Andover Medical Publishers.

Bender, W. N. (2007). *Learning disabilities: Characteristics, identification, and teaching strategies* (6th edition). Boston: Pearson.

Bowlby, J. (1961). Process of mourning. *International Journal of Psychoanalysis, 42,* 315–340.

Brewer, B. W., Van Raalte, J. L., & Linder, D. E. (1993). Athletic identity: Hercules' muscles or Achilles heel? *International Journal of Sport Psychology, 24*(2), 237–254.

Bronfenbrenner, U. (1979). *The ecology of human development.* Cambridge, MA: Harvard University Press.

Clement, D., & Shannon, V. (2011). Injured athletes' perceptions about social support. *Journal of Sport Rehabilitation, 20*(4), 457–470.

Cumming, J. (2015, April). *A sport psychologist's guide for helping athletes develop better self-awareness.* Retrieved from https://jennifercumming.com/2015/04/10/a-sport-psychologists-guide-for-helping-athletes-develop-better-self-awareness/

Evans, L., & Hardy, L. (1995). Sport injury and grief responses: A review. *Journal of Sport & Exercise Psychology, 17*(3), 227–245.

Greenberg, J., Reiner, K., & Meiran, N. (2012). "Mind the trap": Mindfulness practice reduces cognitive rigidity. *Plos ONE, 7*(5), 1–8. doi:10.1371/journal.pone.0036206

Gulliver, A., Griffiths, K. M., & Christensen, H. (2012). Barriers and facilitators to mental health help-seeking for young elite athletes: A qualitative study. *BMC Psychiatry, 12*(1), 157. https://doi.org/10.1186/1471-244X-12-157

Hughes, R., & Coakley, J. (1991). Positive deviance among athletes: The implications of overconformity to the sport ethic. *Sociology of Sport Journal, 8*(4), 307–325.

Karl, G.T. (1987). Janforum: A new look at grief. *Journal of Advanced Nursing, 12,* 641–645.

Kerr, N. (1961). Understanding the process of adjustment to disability. *Journal of Rehabilitation, 27*(6), 16–18.

Kerr, Z. Y., Marshall, S. W., Dompier, T. P., Corlette, J., Klossner, D. A., & Gilchrist, J. (2015, December). College sports-related injuries: United States, 2009–10 through 2013–14 academic years. *Morbidity and Mortality Weekly Report (MMWR), 64*(48), 1330–1336. Retrieved from https://www.cdc.gov/mmwr/preview/mmwrhtml/mm6448a2.htm

Kubler-Ross, E. (1969). *On death and dying.* London: Tavistock.

Marich, J. (2014). *Trauma made simple: Competencies in assessment, treatment and working with survivors.* Eau Claire, WI: PESI Publishing & Media, PESI Inc.

Martin, D. J., Garske, J. P., & Davis, M. K. (2000). Relation of the therapeutic alliance with outcome and other variables: A meta-analytic review. *Journal of Consulting and Clinical Psychology, 68*(3), 438–450.

National Collegiate Athletic Association. (2015). *Student-athletes with disabilities.* Retrieved from http://www.ncaa.org/about/resources/inclusion/student-athletes-disabilities

National Institute of Child Health and Human Development. (2016). *What are the indicators of learning disabilities?* Retrieved from https://www.nichd.nih.gov/health/topics/learning/conditioninfo/pages/symptoms.aspx

Nazarov, Z., & Lee, C. G. (2012). *Disability statistics from the current population survey (CPS)*. Ithaca, NY: Cornell University Rehabilitation Research and Training Center on Disability Demographics and Statistics (StatsRRTC). Retrieved from www.disabilitystatistics.org

Neal, T. L., Diamond, A. B., Goldman, S., Klossner, D., Morse, E. D., Pajak, D. E., … Welzant, V. (2013). Inter-association recommendations for developing a plan to recognize and refer student-athletes with psychological concerns at the collegiate level: An executive summary of a consensus statement. *Journal of Athletic Training, 48*(5), 716–720.

Nixon, H. (1994). Coaches' views of risk, pain, and injury in sport, with specific reference to gender differences. *Sociology of Sport Journal, 11*, 79–87.

Podlog, L., Dimmock, J. & Miller, J. (2011). A review of return to sport concerns following injury rehabilitation: Practitioner strategies for enhancing recovery outcomes. *Physical Therapy in Sport, 12*, 36–42.

Putukian, M. (2014). Mind, body, and sport. Understanding and supporting student-athlete mental wellness. In Gary T. Brown (Ed.). *Mind, body and sport: Understanding and supporting student-athlete mental wellness* (pp. 61–64). Indianapolis: National Collegiate Athletic Association. Retrieved from http://www.ncaapublications.com/productdownloads/MindBodySport.pdf

Ridpath, M. (2014). Education-impacting disabilities and the NCAA waiver process. In Gary T. Brown (Ed.) *Mind, body, and sport: Understanding and supporting student-athlete mental-wellness* (57–59). Indianapolis, IN: National Collegiate Athletic Association.

Semaia, P., (2014). Supporting student-athletes in transition. In Gary T. Brown (Ed.). *Mind, Body and Sport: Understanding and Supporting Student-Athlete Mental Wellness* (pp. 69–71). Indianapolis, IN: National Collegiate Athletic Association.

Sherman, R. T., Thompson, R. A., Dehass, D., & Wilfert, M. (2005). NCAA coaches survey: The role of the coach in identifying and managing athletes with disordered eating. *The Journal of Treatment & Prevention, 13*(5), 447–466.

Smith, R. E., Ptacek, J. T., & Patterson, E. (2000). Moderator effects of cognitive and somatic trait anxiety on the relation between life stress and physical injuries. *Anxiety, Stress, & Coping: An International Journal, 13*(3), 269–288.

Stoltenburg, A. L., Kamphoff, C. S., & Bremer, L. K. (2011). Transitioning out of sport: The psychosocial effects of collegiate athletes' career-ending injuries. *Athletic Insight, 11*(2), 1–11.

Sudano, L. E., Collins, G., & Miles, C. M. (2017). Reducing barriers to mental health care for student-athletes: An integrated care model. *Families, Systems, & Health, 35*(1), 77–84.

Tunick, R., Clement, D., & Etzel, E. F. (2009). Counseling injured and disabled student-athletes: A guide for understanding and intervention. In E. F. Etzel (Ed.) *Counseling and psychological services for college student-athletes* (pp. 403–450). Morgantown, WV: Fitness Information Technology.

U.S. Department of Education (1995). *The Civil Rights of Students with Hidden Disabilities Under Section 504 of the Rehabilitation Act of 1973*. Retrieved from https://www2.ed.gov/about/offices/list/ocr/docs/hq5269.html

van der Kolk, B. (2014). *The body keeps the score: Brain, mind, and body in the healing of trauma*. New York, NY: Penguin Books.

Vickers, M. Z. (2010, March). Accommodating college students with learning disabilities: ADD, ADHD, and dyslexia. *Pope Center Series on Higher Education*. Retrieved from https://www.jamesgmartin.center/acrobat/vickers-mar2010.pdf

Wayda, V., Armenth-Brothers, F., & Boyce, B. A. (1998). Goal setting: A key to injury rehabilitation. *Athletic Therapy Today*, 21–25.

Weinberg, R., Vernau, D., & Horn, T. (2013). Playing through pain and injury: Psychosocial considerations. *Journal of Clinical Sport Psychology, 7*, 41–59.

Wiese-Bjornstal, D. M., Smith, A. M., Shaffer, S. M., & Morrey, M. A. (1998). An integrated model of response to sport injury: Psychological and sociological dynamics. *Journal of Applied Sport Psychology, 10*(1), 46–69.

Williams, J. M., & Andersen, M. D. (1998). Psychosocial antecedents of sport injury: Review and critique of the stress and injury model. *Journal of Applied Sport Psychology, 10*(1), 5–25.

Young, K., White, P., & McTeer, W. (1994). Body talk: Male athletes reflect on sport, injury, and pain. *Sociology of Sport Journal, 11*, 175–194.

# 11

# Gender Issues in Counseling Student-Athletes

*Meredith Deal and Mary Jo Loughran*

## CASE STUDY: LOU

Lou is a tennis player who attends Central U on a 50% athletic scholarship. A junior, Lou is majoring in communications and has a cumulative GPA of 3.0/4.0. On the tennis team, Lou holds the second singles position with a cumulative three-year record of 57 wins—21 losses and was the runner-up for the past two years in the conference championship. As a teenager, Lou had aspirations to play tennis professionally, but was told by a coach at a tennis camp that this was a longshot and encouraged college-level play as a better option, citing Lou's hot-and-cold temperment as the chief reason for this recommendation. Lou was recruited by several competetive programs and chose Central U because of its impressive tennis facilities and the reputation of the head coach (Devin), who had won the NCAA singles championship as a college player 20 years previously. Karen is the team's athletic trainer and has recently become concerned about Lou's inconsistent play and anger issues on the court. Lou's doubles partner has requested a partner change and Coach Devin has threatened to take Lou's scholarship away after a recent on-court outburst following a questionable call. Karen referred Lou to a counselor for counseling.

During the first meeting with Lou, the counselor established rapport and gathered relevant family, educational, medical, and social history. Lou's developmental history is unremarkable, there was no reported trauma history, and suicidal and homicidal ideation were denied. Lou expressed an interest in working with the counselor to develop better on- and off-court stress management strategies, to explore ways to ease longstanding parental pressures around tennis, and to resolve some career indecision issues. The counselor agreed to meet weekly for four weeks and to assess the progress at that time.

In the case study above, "Lou" could be a nickname for Louis (man) or Louise (woman). Did you assume that "Lou" was a man or a woman? This chapter illustrates that, depending upon your answers to this question, you may have arrived at different conclusions about the underlying issues and path forward in working with this student-athlete.

The most frequent question people ask upon hearing of a new baby's birth is, "is it a boy or a girl?" This question is often asked even before an inquiry regarding the infant's and/or mother's health, suggesting the central role that gender plays as an organizing principle in people's worlds. Gender is, of course, a salient part of the student-athlete's world, as well. It dictates whom they compete with and against, how they interact with one another, how they interact with their coaches, and in some instances how they are sometimes treated by others. Gender is also integral to the counseling process, influencing how problems are presented, how they are managed and treated, and, even at times, what diagnoses are applied. This chapter explores these issues to create a lens for helping professionals to manage the complexity of the gender dynamic in college sports and in the psychological treatment of student-athletes.

While sex is defined as the assignment at birth of being either male or female, gender is a socially constructed phenomenon in which individuals experience themselves in relation to the attributes typically associated with being male or female. For this chapter, we consider a binary view of male and female genders, in part due to the structure and organization of collegiate athletics.* Here we consider the student-athlete's gender, as well as the counselor's gender, and its influence on the therapeutic process. We also explore frequently encountered issues specific to male and female student-athletes.

Presently, at the societal level, gender is a hot button issue across many groups and settings. The #metoo movement has swept across the US and the globe to protest sexual harassment of women in the workplace. A companion movement, #TimesUp, expanded #metoo's mission of publicizing accusations of harassment into enlisting women and allies to advocate for meaningful change in the ways women are treated at work and beyond. Both movements began in the entertainment industry and have since expanded into journalism, politics, and many other walks of life, including sport.

---

* See Chapter 12 for a more thorough discussion of nonbinary gender identity, sexuality, and sexual orientation issues in collegiate athletics.

Gender cannot be separated from the discussion of sports and athletics. Indeed, even the very sports themselves have long been categorized as "masculine," "feminine," or "gender-neutral." According to one study (Koivula, 2001), the sports designated as masculine shared the perceived characteristics of being violent or risky, requiring speed, strength, and endurance, and engendering team spirit (e.g., football or wrestling). The same study described feminine sports as characterized by aesthetics (e.g., figure skating or gymnastics) or having the purpose of shaping the body or weight management (e.g., aerobics; Koivula, 2001). It stands to reason that if sports are perceived with a gender role assignment, so too must be the participants of those sports. Males who compete in gymnastics and females who compete in ice hockey run the risk of breaching stereotypical gender norms, with repercussions that include changes in the ways the student-athlete is perceived by both self and others. Hardin & Greer (2009) termed this persistence in old gender-related stereotypes the "stagnation of gender typing in sports."

## Gender Issues in Counseling

Likewise, gender has also long been considered an important and influential factor in the helping relationship from both the client's and the counselor's perspective. The body of counseling outcome research devoted to gender matching between counselors and their clients indicates that while there is some evidence suggesting a positive correlation between gender similarity and favorable counseling outcomes, an even more salient predictive variable is multicultural competence, including sensitivity to gender-related issues (Tao, Owen, Pace, & Imel, 2015). In their study of a large sample of university counseling center clients, Owen, Wong, and Rodolfa (2009) confirmed the relationship between the ability to facilitate desired therapeutic outcomes with male or female clients, aka, gender competence, and client improvement in well-being. This finding underscores the necessity for helping professionals to develop gender-related self-awareness, knowledge, and skills in order to work effectively with female and male student-athletes. In recent years, the American Psychological Association (APA) has developed several sets of guidelines for working with different client populations, including one for women and girls (APA, 2017), and one for boys and men (APA, 2018).

The first step toward achieving gender competence involves counselors' exploration of their gender-based biases and stereotypes (APA, 2017; 2018; Mahalik, Good, Tager, Levant, & Mackowiak, 2012). The literature highlights the importance of counselors paying attention to their own experiences of gender socialization, including the development and maintenance of gender role stereotypes. Further, counselors must become aware of how personal experiences intersect with the societally dictated gender roles, within the broader, dominant culture (APA,

2017; Mahalik et al., 2012). Counselors should be attuned to how these constructs influence the student-athletes' experiences of challenges, as well as their therapeutic responses to these challenges (Mahalik et al., 2012). It is beneficial, and frankly an ethical necessity, for counselors to engage in reflection toward increased self-awareness of their own gender-related preconceptions and issues. This includes an exploration of their own gender identities and their understanding and awareness of males, masculinity, females, and femininity, particularly during adolescence and early adulthood (Mahalik et al., 2012).

The potential consequences of leaving biases unexplored or unresolved are costly to the counseling relationship and/or the student-athlete's well-being. For example, a counselor who endorses the stereotypical norms of femininity may be predisposed to view their muscular, sweatclothes-adorned, make-up free female student-athlete client with a more negative diagnostic lens than they would if she presented with a more traditionally feminine appearance. The same counselor may ascribe more severe pathology to a male student-athlete who weeps while sharing their history than to one who remains stoic (Wong, Steinfeldt, LaFollette, & Tsao, 2011).

Mahalik et al. (2012) and the *Guidelines for Psychological Practice with Women and Girls* (APA, 2017) urged counselors to be mindful of the predisposition and prevalence rates of certain diagnoses by gender. This is a twofold consideration. First, females tend to receive more frequent diagnoses of depression (Salk, Hyde, & Abramson, 2017), anxiety disorders (Asher, Asnaani, & Aderka, 2017) and disordered eating (Sidor, Baba, Marton-Vasarhelyi, & Chereches, 2015), while males are diagnosed with more substance use disorders (Sallaup, Vaaler, Iversen, & Guzey, 2016). However, focusing too heavily on the gender trends may result in, for example, ignoring signs of substance abuse in women or depression in men. With this caution in mind, we next explore the issues pertinent to female and male student-athlete clients in greater detail.

## *Counseling Women Collegiate Athletes*

There is a preponderance of literature describing the physical and psychological benefits of sports participation for girls and women (Parsons & Betz, 2001). Even in the face of experiencing gender-based prejudice, discrimination, and challenges throughout their lifetimes, women and girls have shown to be quite resilient and able to manage and overcome these challenges. Simply stated, females cope differently than males, not worse. While males tend to rely on task-oriented coping, females turn to their social networks (Beasley, Thompson, & Davidson, 2003). It is important for counselors to recognize the strengths of women, but also to cultivate those resources further by using strengths-based approaches (APA, 2017).

The *Guidelines for Psychological Practice with Women and Girls* (APA, 2017) identified intersecting identities as an area of strength for women. For female student-athletes, this idea can be applied to the intersecting identities that will include student *and* athlete, as well as race, ethnicity, gender, gender identity, sexual orientation, and relational identities, such as daughter, roommate, sister, and dating partner. Counselors should recognize both the student and athlete identities in their female clients and highlight the value that being a student-athlete has added to their life experiences, while at the same time being receptive to the struggles that they may have as a result of their participation in sports. Strengths-based interventions identify and utilize clients' resources throughout the entire therapeutic process. Areas of strength and resilience for women may be personal, relational, educational, spiritual, cultural, and vocational (APA, 2017).

Intersecting identities can, however, be a double-edged sword. Often, assuming multiple roles is accompanied by numerous, sometimes competing, demands on time, energy, and psychological coping resources. McGuire, Ingram, Sachs, & Tierney (2017) conducted a study illustrating this concept in their tracking of depressive symptoms in male and female student-athletes over the course of a semester. During peak times of both the academic semester and the competitive seasons, female student-athletes reported significantly higher depressive symptoms than their male counterparts, leading the authors to conclude that women struggled more with achieving balance between the competing demands of study and sport.

Another obvious role conflict is the one that can occur between "female" and "athlete." Counselors need to be aware of the multiple, and often contradictory, messages that they receive about what it means to be female (APA, 2017). This may be relevant for female student-athletes, particularly when there is incongruence between the specific sport and societal expectations regarding femininity. A female with talent and passion for rugby, ice hockey, lacrosse, etc. may receive overt and covert messages from parents, peers, and society at large that playing her sport violates widely accepted gender norms and renders her "unfeminine" or even "masculine." From a counseling perspective, it is important to help female clients to identify the source and ascribed meanings of these conflicting messages. This exploration process creates and ensures "identity safety" by allowing athletes to explore and process their own likes and dislikes in relation to societal proscriptions and prescriptions (APA, 2017; 2018).

Counselors working with female student-athletes must work to avoid several landmines hidden in the therapeutic process. For example, overemphasizing individuality and autonomy while neglecting the relational nature of female behaviors can be problematic (APA, 2017). For the female student-athlete, relationships with her coaches and teammates may be a source of strength or, conversely, stress, both of which may significantly impact performance. Women are far more socially oriented than men and, in sports especially, many student-athletes will be coming from strong team environments where relationships and peer interactions are likely highly valued and, perhaps, crucial to the success of the student-athletes. Participation in an "individual" sport does not negate the relational quality of female behavior. Another landmine identified in the *Guidelines for Psychological Practice with Women and Girls* (APA, 2017) includes the helping professional's failure to maintain a holistic view of mental health, ignoring contextual influences, upholding masculine stereotypical lenses when defining positive mental health, and overemphasizing or misrepresenting aspects of common female experiences.

## Counseling Issues Specific to Women

Counselors working with female student-athletes will undoubtedly encounter issues related to body image, exploitive relationships, and homonegativity. Athleticism is typically defined by muscularity, physical strength, and power, all of which are directly associated with traditional conceptions of masculinity (Koivula, 2001). "Female athletes often participate in sport using standards of traditional male athleticism, yet at the same time attempt to manage societal expectations of conforming to traditional femininity" (Steinfeldt, Zakrajsek, Carter, & Steinfeldt, 2011, p. 401). As a result, the simple act of participating in sports goes against the traditional socially accepted and dictated roles for women. Participation alone, especially outside of the narrow window of sports deemed appropriate for girls and women, can create gender conflict that is problematic for the student-athlete. Participation in sports that are not traditionally feminine leave women having to make a choice, to be an athlete or to be a girl (Etzel, 2009). As with their male counterparts, gender conflicts can be detrimental to a female student-athlete's mental health and, consequently, her performance.

Koivula (2001) argued that the female body has been objectified by society, with the sole purpose of pleasing others. Participation in sports can challenge this perception and instill in women a sense of power and autonomy over one's own body. Despite this, collegiate athletics exists within a larger, male-centered culture, which makes it difficult to ignore the ongoing messages about what the female body should do, look like, feel like, etc. This dissonance can create struggles for female athletes. For example, female student-athletes typically score lower than male student-athletes on self-worth measures, particularly related to accepting one's physical appearance (Rangeon, Gilbert, & Bruner, 2012). Counselors working with female student-athletes should be sensitive to body image concerns and their impact on the student-athletes' self-esteem and overall well-being.

As with their nonathlete counterparts, female student-athletes may fall victim to exploitive relationships consisting of sexual violence, sexual victimization, sexual harassment, and abuse not only from their male peers, but also from their coaches and administrative staff. In some cases, the power dynamic typically found in the coach-athlete relationship may be conducive to sexual exploitation and harassment of athletes (Bringer, Brackenridge, & Johnston, 2002). Although approximately 50% of the athletes in one study acknowledged being subjected to sexual comments, only one-third of those participants reported them as such, instead making justifications that such behaviors are "just part of the game" (Bringer, Brackenridge, & Johnston, 2002). Counselors working with student-athletes must be prepared to ask questions about and to hear the accounts of their clients' experiences of exploitation and abuse.

Sexuality and sexual orientation are issues that may arise for the female student-athlete in counseling. Despite changing societal attitudes toward LGBTQ individuals, the athletic culture still contains a fair amount of homonegativity. It is common for female athletes to be labeled as lesbians, often leveled as an insult toward women who defy the cultural stereotypes for femininity.

## Counseling Men Collegiate Athletes

Successful counseling of male student-athletes requires similar considerations and best practices as those pertaining to their female counterparts. APA (2018) and Mahalik et al. (2012) identified several areas where men and boys experience gender strain that may lead to both physical and mental health challenges. For example, deviation from or failure to meet masculine gender norms, incongruent self-concepts based on gender stereotypes, and gender-based devaluation of self or others are among the root causes that may bring a male student-athlete into counseling. Ultimately, physical and mental health difficulties may arise when individual experiences of being male do not align with societal prescriptions. O'Neill (2008) described this as gender role conflict. At the root of gender role conflict are the fear of femininity and the embracing of narrow, culturally defined norms for male behavior. Together, these constraints manifest in four patterns for men: (1) success, power, and competition issues; (2) restrictive emotionality, (3) restrictive affectionate behavior between men, and (4) conflicts between work and family relations (O'Neill, 2008). The athletic culture represents a prime example of an environment that may cultivate gender role conflict, particularly if there is an explicit endorsement of stereotypical masculine norms coupled with a devaluation of feminine ones. Male student-athletes may struggle with gender role conflict when they are heavily steeped in their athletic identity, particularly if they are without any counterbalancing aspects of identity.

More recently, Vandello and Bosson (2013) proposed a theory of precarious manhood—suggesting that men encounter the expectation that they must continuously demonstrate their manhood or risk being viewed as weak or ineffectual. The result is increased anxiety, which they deal with by engaging in risky or aggressive behavior, particularly in situations in which they feel threatened by gender-related expectations. In this context, the male student-athlete may perceive the need to continuously demonstrate his masculinity to coaches, teammates, and fans by engaging in overly aggressive play or by taking unnecessary physical risks on the court or field.

The research literature supports the finding that males tend to have more severe and immediate treatment needs due to their delayed entrance into therapy (APA, 2018). The socialization surrounding emotional expression prevents men from seeking help, not only for mental health concerns but for physical health concerns as well, because of the societal expectation for men to be self-reliant and to minimize their problems (APA, 2017). Mahalik et al. (2012) posited that once men enter treatment, they often experience gender bias or microaggressions from counselors that may hamper treatment outcomes and further perpetuate the pattern of help-seeking avoidance. Additionally, men tend to receive externalizing disorder diagnoses more frequently than internalizing disorder diagnoses (APA, 2015). These issues, in combination with societal stigma surrounding psychological help-seeking, serve as barriers for men to coming forward with their struggles and from receiving prompt, adequate treatment.

The barriers to help-seeking are similar for both male and female student-athletes. However, the additional gender socialization and norms for men regarding emotional expression and perceptions of weakness may act to amplify the already powerful barriers facing student-athletes. All student-athletes must confront both internal barriers (personal attributes) and external barriers (situational pressures; Watson, 2006), in order to ask for psychological help. These include stigma, both public and self (Wahto, Swift, & Whipple, 2016), time, resource availability, as well as uncertainty surrounding the counselor's ability to relate to and understand the athletic experience (Watson, 2006; López & Levy, 2013; Brown, 2014). While the literature suggests that issues of stigma may be lower than in the past (Watson, 2006), it is still pertinent for student-athletes. Student-athletes must manage and navigate the dichotomous public misconceptions of being highly pampered and also superhuman, both of which often prevent students from seeking the necessary assistance for whatever challenges they are facing (Watson, 2006). Furthermore, fear of diagnoses, fear of scrutiny or repercussions from their teammates and coaching staff (Wahto, Swift, & Whipple, 2016), and fear of recognition in the counseling center (López & Levy, 2013), among many other factors, deter student-athletes.

This combination of barriers may result in many male student-athletes being left without the help they need.

A broad look at the concept of masculinity makes it clear why it is at the root of so many challenges for men. While several masculinities exist to account for various intersecting identities, traditional ideals of masculinity are often unattainable because of their basis in white, upper-class, able-bodied, and privileged individuals (APA, 2018). Similar to the recommendations for interventions with women, it is important for counselors to invite and facilitate exploration of dissonance in self-concepts and to create personal definitions of masculinity while also gaining an understanding of societal influences (APA, 2018).

The *Guidelines for Psychological Practice with Men and Boys* (APA, 2018) stipulates similar recommendations for the integration of client identities as that of the *Guidelines for Psychological Practice with Women and Girls* (APA, 2017). Gender identity development begins at birth and is a lifelong process influenced by individual experiences, the expectations of those around us, and the ever changing societal proscriptions and prescriptions. The male identity is an important one to consider because, in society at large, it is typically accompanied by privilege and power. The combination of male and student-athlete identities at the college level often comes with certain privileges and social power, and even reverence from others within and outside of the college community.

The privilege and power experienced by men renders them vulnerable to adopting misogynist or sexist attitudes, particularly among those who endorse stricter male gender roles. The result may be men exhibiting greater aggression and violence across settings and relationships, toward both men and women, when traditional male gender roles are threatened or challenged (APA, 2018). The *Guidelines for Psychological Practice with Men and Boys* (2018) recommend that counselors adopt pedagogical approaches that specifically highlight the negative consequences of sexism and are directly related to their own personal relationships.

In general, men and women approach interpersonal relationships differently. As previously mentioned, women place heavy emphasis on their relationships and social support systems. Contrarily, men may struggle to develop and maintain interpersonal relationships with both genders, in part due to their socialization that discourages intimacy in relationships and encourages self-reliance and independence (APA, 2018). Nonsexual intimate interpersonal relationships between and among men are important to men's health and well-being. Counselors must be attuned to the different language used to describe such relationships, such as, "my main man," "he's got my back," etc. Programming that promotes male-to-male bonding, gender empathy, and communication can work to improve both male-to-male and male-to-female relationships (APA, 2018).

Historically, men have been neglectful of their health from both a preventative and a reactive standpoint. Men are less likely to utilize preventative health care and are often unwilling to consult both medical and mental health care providers (APA, 2018). Further, men engage in more risk taking behaviors than women (Zamboanga, Horton, Leitkowski, & Wang, 2006; APA, 2018) There is evidence to suggest, however, that when maintenance of good health is integral to job performance, men are more likely to take the initiative to seek treatment (APA, 2018). It stands to reason, therefore, that male student-athletes may be prompted to seek mental health treatment if they are able to see the link between addressing psychological concerns and improved job (e.g., athletic) performance.

A body of work has emerged recently that addresses potential strategies to facilitate helpseeking among college-age men. Davies, Shen-Miller, and Isacco (2010) proposed a "Men's Center" approach that emphasizes a holistic approach to working with this population. Shen-Miller, Isacco, Davies, St. Jean, and Phan (2013) demonstrated that this approach may be effective in reducing men's risk of negative physical and psychological health outcomes.

## Counseling Issues Specific to Men

According to APA (2018), sexism is ingrained into the construction of masculinity for boys and men. From an early age, boys are taught that there are often consequences, and even punishments, for acting in a manner that violates masculine gender norms; These consequences may be physical, verbal, or emotional, and attempt to shame or degrade men for behaving in ways that are considered female (APA, 2018). Within the sporting context, it is not uncommon for teammates, coaching staff, etc. to use expressions like "don't be such a girl," or "man up" (Etzel, 2009). Unfortunately, these comparisons to girls and women can be damaging and problematic (APA, 2018), especially within hypermasculine contexts like college athletics. The quandary for male student-athletes is that despite experiencing great stress, they are expected to remain strong, stoic, and resilient (Wahto, Swift, & Whipple, 2016), which includes concealing their own struggles and rejecting beneficial treatments.

In order to conform to traditional masculinity ideology, men will suppress their softer feelings and instead discuss external matters, participate in physical activities or "good-natured" joking, and seek advice from friends instead of addressing these emotions directly (APA, 2018). This idea of being vulnerable is in direct conflict with masculinity, and by its very definition of exposing oneself to possible harm or damage can been seen as synonymous with weakness, a trait that men are taught to avoid at all costs. However, being vulnerable and open are integral parts of the therapeutic process, which can make it difficult for male student-athletes to fully engage in and benefit from counseling. Etzel (2009) reported that some male student-athletes fake the therapeutic process in order to get cleared, meet the requirements of their time in counseling, appease the counselor, or whatever the motivation may be, all in an effort to return to play without having to truly disclose any of their personal feelings or struggles. Males may be unwilling to disclose the extent of their pain, especially if it comes from a childhood trauma or tragedy, because they have been taught that to do so is a sign of weakness (APA, 2018). The use of explicit goal setting with men can be beneficial to reduce ambiguity and encourage engagement (APA, 2018). Additional strategies (APA, 2018) include making simple shifts in language like "coaching" or "discussing" and using less jargon in the effort to create a more comfortable environment for male student-athletes.

The socialization of boys and men plays a crucial role in the development of male identities and the behavior associated with those identities. For many men, aggression and violence are learned as methods for managing interpersonal conflict (APA, 2018). Research shows that men who adhere to strict male role norms run a greater risk to commit higher levels of intimate partner violence and sexual violence towards women (APA, 2018). Additionally, men with these values tend to aggress more against both men and women who violate traditional gender role norms (APA, 2018). One study indicated male student-athletes being responsible for one third of all sexual assaults on college campuses (Locke & Mahalik, 2005). The same report (Locke & Mahalik, 2005) concluded traditional masculinity norms coupled with alcohol use were stronger predictors of sexually aggressive behavior than athletic involvement alone.

Jessica Luther's book *Unsportsmanlike Conduct* (2016) broke down the culture of college athletics to argue that it is not only acceptable, but expected, that male student athletes will be violent and sexually aggressive. Unfortunately, many universities have been found to do what is necessary to ensure that their revenue-producing athletes remain eligible regardless of their personal conduct. Counselors must consider the underlying causes of aggression in male student-athletes as manifestations of pain and emotions they have been taught not to disclose, while also holding them responsible for their actions and providing new strategies for emotion management (APA, 2018).

Although men are more likely to be perpetrators of physical and sexual violence, it is also important to remember that men are also victims of violence at the hands of both men and women perpetrators. Men in these circumstances often experience significant obstacles when reporting intimate partner violence, mostly related to gender-based stereotypes (APA, 2018). This is especially true for male student-athletes, and counselors should remain alert to signals suggesting the possibility of victimization.

## Gender and the Therapeutic Process

Research has shown that expectations from the counselor and for the counseling process are different for female and male student-athletes. According to López and Levy (2013), female student-athletes placed greater emphasis on personal commitment to the counseling process while male student-athletes cared more about counselors being direct and providing quick solutions. Alternatively, female student-athletes had lower expectations in regard to the counselors level of expertise (López & Levy, 2013). Unsurprisingly, female athletes were far more willing to pursue help from a sport psychologist while their male counterparts chose, instead, to seek help from more familiar sources like friends, family, and coaches (López & Levy, 2013). Regarding consultation related strictly to performance enhancement, the same study reported male student-athletes to be more likely than their female peers to prefer consultants of the same gender, and also of the same race, ethnicity, culture, etc. (López and Levy, 2013). Counselors can use these research findings to make minor modifications in style in order to be optimally effective with men and women student-athletes.

It is important to note, however, that student-athletes expressed their belief that counselors' familiarity with the sport and the athletic experience was a far more important consideration than counselor gender in their evaluation of their counseling experiences (López & Levy, 2013). In other words, self-awareness, skill, *and* knowledge are all key ingredients that comprise the three-legged stool of multicultural competence (Pedersen, 2003).

# Conclusion

This chapter used the lens of gender to explore the student-athlete's experience in counseling. In order to provide effective treatment to men and women student-athletes, counselors need to understand how gender-based stereotypes impact the way their clients are perceived by themselves and others. Likewise, counselors must be aware of disparities in mental health diagnoses and help-seeking behaviors. Finally, counselors should understand how their own attitudes and experiences regarding gender influence their work. If these conditions are met, "Lou" will be in good hands and can look forward to making positive gains in counseling.

# Discussion Questions

1. How might your concept of gender stereotypes influence your work with Lou? Depending upon whether Lou is male or female, would your conceptualization of the presenting problem (angry outbursts and emotional dysregulation) change? What about your diagnostic impressions of Lou?

2. A gender-competent counselor working with "Louise" would take care to facilitate an exploration of her internalized messages about what it means to be an athlete. Louise's conflictual relationship with her doubles' partner might be a source of significant stress for her, and she may benefit from developing some strategies to address their conflict with assertive communication so that this relationship can become a support resource for her. What strategies might be helpful?

3. A gender-competent counselor working with "Louis" would be sensitive to the possibility that he may not feel comfortable sharing his fears of losing at tennis as a threat to his self-concept as an athlete and as a man. The counselor should take care to provide Louis with the space to stay within his emotional comfort zone until he feels safe enough to express his vulnerability more directly.

# References

American Psychological Association, Boys and Men Guidelines Group. (2018). *APA guidelines for psychological practice with boys and men.* Retrieved from http://www.apa.org/about/policy/psychological-practice-boys-men-guidelines.pdf

American Psychological Association. (2017). *Guidelines for psychological practice with women and girls.* (draft)

Asher, M., Asnaani, A., & Aderka, I. M. (2017). Gender differences in social anxiety disorder: Areview. *Clinical Psychology Review, 56,* 1–12. doi:10.1016/j.cpr.2017.05.004

Beasley, M., Thompson, T., & Davidson, J. (2003). Resilience in response to life stress: The effects of coping style and cognitive hardiness. *Personality and Individual Differences, 34*(1), 77–95.

Bringer, J. D., Brackenridge, C. H., & Johnston, L. H. (2002) Defining appropriateness in coach-athlete sexual relationships: The voice of coaches. *Journal of Sexual Aggression, 8*(2), 83–98.

Brown, G. T. (Ed.). (2014). *Mind, body and sport—Understanding and supporting student-athlete mental wellness.* Indianapolis: National Collegiate Athletic Association. Retrieved from http://www.ncaapublications.com/productdownloads/MindBodySport.pdf

Davies, J. A., Shen-Miller, D. S., & Isacco, A. (2010). The men's center approach to addressing the health crisis of college men. *Professional Psychology: Research and Practice, 41*(4), 347–354. http://dx.doi.org/10.1037/a0020308

Etzel, E. F. (Ed.). (2009). *Counseling and psychological services for college student-athletes.* Morgantown, WV: Fitness Information Technology.

Hardin, M., & Greer, J. D. (2009). The influence of gender-role socialization, media use and sports participation on perceptions of gender-appropriate sports. *Journal of Sport Behavior, 32*(2), 207–226.

Koivula, N. (2001). Perceived characteristics of sports categorized as gender-neutral, feminine and masculine. *Journal of Sport Behavior, 24*(4), 377–393.

López, R. L., & Levy, J. J. (2013). Student athletes' perceived barriers to and preferences for seeking counseling. *Journal of College Counseling, 16*(1), 19–31. http://doi.org/10.1002/j.2161-1882.2013.00024.x

Luther, J. (2016). *Unsportsmanlike conduct: College football and the politics of rape.* Brooklyn, NY: Akashic Books.

Mahalik, J. R., Good, G. E., Tager, D., Levant, R. F., & Mackowiak, C. (2012). Developing a taxonomy of helpful and harmful practices for clinical work with boys and men. *Journal of Counseling Psychology, 59*(4), 591–603. http://doi.org/10.1037/a0030130

McGuire, L. C., Ingram, Y. M., Sachs, M. L., & Tierney, R. T. (2017). Temporal changes in depression symptoms in male and female collegiate student-athletes. *Journal of Clinical Sport Psychology, 11*, 337–351.

O'Neill, J. M. (2008). Summarizing 25 years of research on men's gender role conflict using the Gender Role Conflict Scale: New research paradigms and clinical implications. *The Counseling Psychologist, 36(3)*, 358–445.

Owen, J., Wong, Y. J., & Rodolfa, E. (2009). Empirical search for psychotherapists' gender competence in psychotherapy. *Psychotherapy: Theory, Research, Practice, Training, 46*(4), 448–458. doi:10.1037/a0017958

Parsons, E. M., & Betz, N. E. (2001). The relationship of participation in sports and physical activity to body objectification, instrumentality, and locus of control among young women. *Psychology of Women Quarterly, 25*, 209–222.

Pedersen, P. B. (2003). Increasing the cultural awareness, knowledge, and skills of culture-centered counselors. In F. D. Harper, J. McFadden, F. D. Harper, J. McFadden (Eds.), *Culture and counseling: New approaches* (pp. 31–46). Needham Heights, MA, US: Allyn & Bacon.

Rangeon, S., Gilbert, W., & Bruner, M. (2012). Student athlete wellness: Gender perspectives. *Journal of Coaching Education, 5*(1), 83–113.

Salk, R. H., Hyde, J. S., & Abramson, L. Y. (2017). Gender differences in depression in representative national samples: Meta-analyses of diagnoses and symptoms. *Psychological Bulletin, 143*(8), 783–822. doi:10.1037/bul0000102

Sallaup, T. V., Vaaler, A. E., Iversen, V. C., & Guzey, I. C. (2016). Challenges in detecting and diagnosing substance use in women in the acute psychiatric department: A naturalistic cohort study. *BMC Psychiatry, 16*, 1–7. doi:10.1186/s12888-016-1124-y

Shen-Miller, D. S., Isacco, A. , Davies, J. A., St. Jean, M., & Phan, J. L. (2013). The men's center approach: Ecological interventions for college men's health. *Journal of Counseling & Development, 91*, 499–507. doi:10.1002/j.1556-6676.2013.00123.x

Sidor, A., Baba, C. O., Marton-Vasarhelyi, E., & Chereches, R. M. (2015). Gender differences in the magnitude of the associations between eating disorders symptoms and depression and anxiety symptoms. Results from a community sample of adolescents. *Journal Of Mental Health, 24*(5), 294–298. doi:10.3109/09638237.2015.1022250

Steinfeldt, J. A., Zakrajsek, R., Carter, H., & Steinfeldt, M. C. (2011). Conformity to gender norms among female student-athletes: Implications for body image. *Psychology of Men & Masculinity, 12*(4), 401–416. http://doi.org/10.1037/a0023634

Tao, K. W., Owen, J., Pace, B. T., & Imel, Z. E. (2015). A meta-analysis of multicultural competencies and psychotherapy process and outcome. *Journal Of Counseling Psychology, 62*(3), 337–350. doi:10.1037/cou0000086

Vandello, J. A., & Bosson, J. K. (2013). Hard won and easily lost: A review and synthesis of theory and research on precarious manhood. *Journal of Men and Masculinity, 14(2)*, 101–113. doi:10.1037/a0029826

Wahto, R. S., Swift, J. K., & Whipple, J. L. (2016). The role of stigma and referral source in predicting college student-athletes' attitudes toward psychological help-seeking. *Journal of Clinical Sport Psychology, 10*(2), 85–98. Retrieved from http://web.a.ebscohost.com/ehost/pdfviewer/pdfviewer?vid=2&sid=b6324b86-7b2b-4abe-a3b9-cf3cad6042ec%40sessionmgr4007

Watson, J. (2006). Student-athletes and counseling: Factors influencing the decision to seek counseling services. *College Student Journal, 40*(1), 35.

Wong, Y. J., Steinfeldt, J. A., LaFollette, J. R., & Tsao, S. (2011). Men's tears: Football players' evaluations of crying behavior. *Psychology Of Men & Masculinity, 12*(4), 297–310. doi:10.1037/a0020576

Zamboanga, B. L., Horton, N. J., Leitkowski, L. K., & Wang, S. C. (2006). Do good things come to those who drink? A longitudinal investigation of drinking expectancies and hazardous alcohol use in female college athletes. *Journal of Adolescent Health, 39*(2), 229–236. http://doi.org/10.1016/j.jadohealth.2005.11.019

# 12

# Sexual Orientation and Gender Identity Issues in Counseling College Student-Athletes

*Mary Jo Loughran*

## CASE STUDY: JUSTIN

Dr. Leah Condor is a psychologist on the counseling center staff at State University, an NCAA Division I member with a student population of approximately 8,000. About one half of Dr. Condor's caseload at the center is comprised of student-athletes. Dr. Condor identifies as White, female, cisgender, and heterosexual. When Dr. Condor joined the counseling center staff approximately 10 years ago, she headed a committee that was charged with making the center more welcoming of sexual minority diversity. Under her leadership, the center revised its intake forms to remove the forced choice option for gender. The waiting room materials now include some LGBTQ-friendly magazines and the artwork around the center includes photographs of same-gender and opposite gender dyads. The counseling center now offers an LGBTQ support group, which Dr. Condor co-facilitates with one of the centers psychology interns. Dr. Condor's office door is adorned with a "Safe Space" sign with a rainbow flag, the universally recognized symbol for LGBTQ pride.

Dr. Condor's first appointment on a Tuesday morning in early October is Justin. Justin attends State on a full athletic scholarship, without which he could not afford the tuition. He identifies as biracial and is a sophomore placekicker on the football team. Justin entered "Male" on the intake form under the gender question. Under Reason for Referral, Justin wrote, "thinking about quitting school." Justin was referred to the counseling center by the football team's athletic trainer after Justin missed two practices in the same week with the excuse that he "wasn't feeling it" on those days.

Dr. Condor introduced herself to Justin at their initial appointment. As is her practice with all new clients, she explained confidentiality to Justin and included the specific circumstances that would require her to break confidentiality, including threats of imminent harm to self or others, as well as disclosures regarding child abuse or elder abuse (Dr. Condor also discussed the specific confidentiality pertaining to student-athletes, e.g., explaining that she would not disclose any information to members of the Athletics administration without explicit written permission. She explained that during their initial meeting she would ask many questions in an effort to identify the key counseling issues and to determine how to be the most helpful. She then asked Justin, "What are your preferred pronouns?" to which Justin replied "he and him are fine." Dr. Condor noticed that Justin appeared to be slightly more relaxed than he had seemed in the waiting room.

Dr. Condor then asked Justin where he would like to begin, and he became mildly distraught and began to cry quietly. He reported that he had recently been through a breakup and that the split had caught him completely off guard. Dr. Condor was careful not to make any assumptions regarding the gender of Justin's former partner. She nodded empathically to Justin and stated simply, "you are going through a rough time that you didn't see coming. Can you tell me more about the relationship?" Justin asked Dr. Condor if she was sure that their conversation would not leave the room and when she reassured him that this was the case, Justin shared that the breakup was with his boyfriend (Neal) of more than a year. Neal and Justin had been high school classmates and teammates on their HS football team and had begun dating in the summer after their graduation. Neal attended a large university out of state, was not a college athlete, and had become very active in his campus LGBTQ community. During their first year apart from one another, Justin and Neal texted every day and spoke on the phone as often as Justin's demanding class, practice, and game schedule would allow. Justin hadn't told anyone at State about Neal, including his teammates or his coaches. Justin usually remained quiet when the locker room banter included talk of sex and dating or when the occasional homophobic comment or joke was made. Dr. Condor inquired about Justin's assessment of the prevailing attitudes toward sexual minority issues on his team. Justin replied that it was pretty mixed, e.g., some of his teammates made frequent antigay jokes, but he perceived that the majority of his teammates didn't care one way or the other. Also, he noticed that several teammates, including Will, the team captain, actively discouraged homophobic or misogynistic talk or attitudes.

Dr. Condor asked about other social supports in Justin's life. He shared that he had come out to his parents during the previous winter break and that they had responded by telling Justin that they had always thought that he was gay, and that they loved him and supported him. Several years earlier, Justin had also come out to his best high school friend, Monica, who reacted very positively.

At the conclusion of their intake interview, Dr. Condor and Justin agreed to meet again the next week to work on developing coping strategies for dealing with the breakup with Neal and to assist in the decision-making process regarding whether to stay in school.

---

Counselors working with student-athletes invariably will encounter members of the lesbian, gay, bisexual, transgender, and queer (LGBTQ) community in their practice and should be equipped to deliver competent, ethical, and effective assessment and treatment to this population. This chapter explores the issues surrounding work with sexual minority student-athletes and provides guidance for choosing and implementing affirmative interventions.

Understanding and using the appropriate descriptive terminology is an essential first step in acquiring multicultural competence in this area. Sex and gender are sometimes used interchangeably, when in fact they describe different concepts. Sex refers to the category of male or female that is assigned at birth based upon a baby's external genitalia. Gender, on the other hand, is a socially constructed concept and refers to the individual's self-identification with the characteristics typically labeled by society as either male or female. Individuals whose sex and gender are in alignment are considered to be cisgender, while those with non-aligning sex and gender are described as transgender or gender nonconforming (TGNC). Sexual orientation refers to the gender or genders of the person to whom one is sexually or romantically attracted and, for each person, is usually considered to be situated on a continuum between exclusively heterosexual and exclusively homosexual. Gender identity refers to an individual's experiences of themselves as male, female, neither, both, or fluid. Gender expression is the manner in which people opt to present themselves to the public.

To make matters more complicated, even the very notion of sorting people into categories based on these constructs is limiting and controversial in the gender scholarly literature. Oswalt, Evans, and Drott (2016) emphasized that many more than the typical LGBTQ identities exist and there is considerably more fluidity between and within categories than traditionally thought. Diamond and Rosky (2016) concluded from their exhaustive review of the literature that although sexual orientation is not immutable to intentional change, e.g., through therapeutic attempts to change a same-sex orientation into a heterosexual orientation, there is nonetheless scientific evidence to support the occurrence of shifting attractions and self-defined sexual orientation for some men and women (although certainly not all) over the course of a lifetime.

Collegiate athletics, by contrast, is comprised of strictly-defined categories, e.g., Men's and Women's teams. The challenge of using these categories with individuals for whom labels may be an emotionally charged issue is important to acknowledge a priori in the discussion of best practices for working with LGBTQ student-athletes.

In the US and around the world, there has been a dramatic, rapid shift in attitudes toward LGBTQ persons over the course of the past generation. Unheard of only a few decades ago, there is now a strong plurality in support of marriage equality, adoption rights for same-sex couples, nondiscrimination policies in housing and the workforce, and open military service (Flores, 2014). The shift in attitude has coincided with members of the LGBTQ community living openly at home, in the workplace, and in every other sector of society.

Likewise, changing social attitudes have had an impact on the world of athletics, although it can be argued that the pace in this arena is somewhat slower and more uneven than on other sociocultural fronts. For example, an all-time high publicly identified LGBTQ 56 athletes and three coaches competed in the 2016 Summer Olympic Games in Rio (Outsports, 2016). This showing is perhaps slightly less impressive when considering that it represents only a small fraction of the 11,238 total Olympians competing in those games (Olympic Games, 2017). In the professional ranks, disclosure of LGBTQ identities among professional athletes has been slow in coming, particularly in men's sports (Hine, 2016). The high-profile disclosures of football player Michael Sam and basketball's Jason Collins in 2013 were thought by many to signal the breaking down of professional sports' closet door; but surprisingly, a flurry of other male professional athletes did not follow. Women's professional sports are slightly more inclusive of sexual orientation diversity in comparison to men's sports. Although the list is not long, there are self-identified lesbian players in professional basketball, soccer, golf, and tennis.

On the collegiate level, 32 self-identified LGBTQ athletes and coaches won conference titles in men's and women's sports in 2016–17 (Outsports, 2017). Despite these important gains, LGBTQ collegiate athletes still face challenges when attempting to navigate the landscape of intercollegiate athletics. LGBTQ individuals continue to experience discrimination and sometimes open acts of hostility or even violence simply for expressing their authentic selves openly.

## Attitudes in the Athletic Culture

### *Sexual Orientation*

LGBTQ individuals in collegiate athletics have historically encountered both widespread homonegativity, defined as negative feelings, attitudes, and behavior directed toward no-dominant sexual orientations, and heterosexism, defined as discrimination against nonheterosexual orientations based on the assumption that heterosexuality is superior (Wolf-Wendel, Toma, & Morphew, 2001; Cunningham, 2015). A 2011 survey confirmed that LGBTQ student-athletes generally experienced a more negative climate than their heterosexual peers, with subsequent adverse impact on both their athletic identities and academic success. In another survey, Greim (2017) found that the presence of an LGBTQ teammate or coach mitigated student-athletes' perceptions of the campus athletic climate regarding attitudes toward the sexual minority community.

Athletic departments are generally perceived to be more conservative than other departments on the college campus, espousing values of conformity over individual expression and aggression over sensitivity. The result is an environment, in which sometimes even slight variation from the norm is frowned upon at best, and openly condemned at worst. Open sexual orientation diversity in athletic departments is the exception rather than the rule (Cunningham, 2010). Anecdotal evidence suggests that some LGBTQ athletes do not feel safe enough to disclose their identities to their coaches or teammates or to administrators and may go to great lengths to remain closeted (Jacobson, 2002). In fact, Anderson (2011) coined the term "homohysteria" to describe the phenomenon of straight and nonstraight team members' fearful reaction to having their own sexual orientation questioned if their LGBTQ teammate comes out.

There is variation, however, in attitudes toward sexual minority student-athletes. At the present time, the picture is slightly more encouraging for sexual minority women student-athletes than it is for men. In general, women collegiate athletes tend to be more embracing of sexual orientation diversity than their male counterparts (Parrillo, Glazer, & Kuhn, 2008). Similarly, female sexual minority collegiate athletes tend to be viewed more positively than males by others, e.g., athletic trainers (Ensign, Yiamouyiannis, White, & Ridpath, 2011), coaches (Vargas-Tonsing & Oswalt, 2009; Oswalt & Vargas, 2013), and teammates (Mullin, 2016). Worthen (2014) found in a campus climate survey that being a male student-athlete was a significant predictor of anti-LGBTQ attitudes.

Athletic ability is another interesting factor found to be predictive of the treatment an athlete will receive upon minority sexual orientation disclosure. Anderson & Bullingham (2015) found that LGBTQ athletes with high "athletic capital," e.g., greater value to the team's success, encountered greater acceptance and inclusion by their teammates than those with lesser athletic prowess.

The pervasiveness of homonegativity in the athletic culture has been well documented (Kettman, 1998; Jacobson, 2002; Baird, 2002). One example of homonegative behavior includes the use of slurs such as "sissy" and "faggot" by coaches directed toward players to motivate or to chastise inadequate play (Anderson, 2005). Another example is the practice of "negative recruiting," in which a coach intimates that rival teams attempting to recruit a promising high school athlete are populated by lesbian coaches, lesbian players, or both (Sandoval, 2003). A third example of insidious homonegativity in sports occurs in many colleges across the country where veteran members of an athletic team haze the first year players by requiring them to watch or participate in same-sex sexual activity (Allan & Madden, 2012; Chin & Johnson, 2011).

Sexism and misogyny, both historical mainstays in the athletic culture, underlie the concept of homonegativity. Anderson (2005) argued that homosexuality threatens the dominant patriarchy and in order to be characterized as sufficiently masculine, males must eschew all things associated with femininity. Boys learn early in life that displaying interests, behaviors, or emotions deemed to be feminine results in being labeled "girly," "sissy," or subsequently, "gay." Success in many sporting endeavors for both male and female athletes frequently is the result of being stronger, faster, tougher, and more dominant than their opponents, all qualities that are traditionally masculine. As a result, the prevailing attitudes of those belonging to the athletic culture tend to support the notion that the masculine is the ideal. Anderson (2005) called this idealization of masculinity "hegemonic," which is based upon the notion that the dominant culture legitimizes its position by obtaining the support of those below it. In other words, even those individuals who do not conform to the stereotypes of the athlete as macho participate in the glorification of masculinity and the oppression of femininity.

Scholars have studied gender roles in sport for the past several decades. Hardin and Greer (2009) explored the concept of gender-appropriate sports, that is, sports that typify traditional masculine values and those that reflect traditional feminine values. In general, contact sports and those requiring aggressive behaviors tend to be viewed as masculine, while noncontact sports and those dominated by women tend to be viewed as feminine. Hall and LaFrance (2012) posited that the violation of established gender norms, particularly by men, is seen by many to be an indicator of homosexuality and is often met with homophobic responses by others. It is reasonable, then, to conclude that student-athletes who compete in sports that violate traditional gender norms may find their sexual orientation called into question.

The pressure for male athletes to conform to traditional masculinity stereotypes is overt and strong. For female athletes, the picture is a bit more complicated. By their very participation in sports, female athletes defy the feminine stereotype. The traditional feminine gender role requires women to be soft, nurturing, and noncompetitive, all antithetical to the demands of collegiate athletics. Despite the fact that the number of women participating in intercollegiate athletics has skyrocketed from 32,000 in 1982 to more than 217,000 in 2016–17 (National Collegiate Athletic Association [NCAA], 2017), many women athletes continue to experience conflict regarding gender role expectations. Researchers studying gender roles in female athletes have consistently found that these women tend to view themselves as more masculine than their nonathlete counterparts (Miller & Levy, 1996). For many women, however, this is actually a positive experience. Young and Bursik (2000) found in a sample of women athletes that a masculine self-concept was positively related to higher levels of self-esteem and identity achievement. On the other hand, Krane, Choi, Baird, Aimar, and Kauer (2004) concluded from a series of focus group interviews with female athletes that women who participated in collegiate sports experienced both feelings of empowerment and feelings of marginalization due to their differences from nonathlete women.

Although men in athletic environments tend to be generally negative in their attitudes toward LGBTQ individuals, women tend to have more complex responses. Wolf-Wendel, Toma, and Morphew (2001) interviewed student-athletes, coaches, and athletic administrators at several NCAA Division I universities. Their findings revealed that in contrast to men, women tended to have a higher level of acceptance toward LGBTQ persons. At the same time, however, women in athletic environments went to greater lengths to distance themselves from the perception that they may have a lesbian orientation. Baird (2002) posited that the pervasiveness of the perception that all female athletes are suspect in their sexual orientation is another vestige of sexism, designed to deter women from participating in sports and thereby preserving a greater share of the available resources for the male athletes. In summary, athletic culture is characterized by an emphasis on the traditionally male values of strength, dominance, and conformity, and tolerance of behaviors or identities that vary from the prescribed majority is limited. This appears to be the case across the board but more overtly so for men than for women.

## Gender Identity

As previously stated, gender identity describes one's sense of where they lie on the male-female spectrum. Gender identity may be consistent with the sex assigned at birth (cisgender) or inconsistent with the sex assigned at birth (transgender or gender nonconforming). While encountering discrimination and negativity similar to their lesbian, gay, and bisexual peers, transgender and gender nonconforming (TGNC) collegiate-athletes also may be faced with other unique challenges, including regulations pertaining to locker room/bathroom use and regulation-based barriers to their ability to compete in a manner consistent with their gender identity. Sports teams at all levels of competition are organized with the presumption of a gender binary; men's and women's teams and collegiate athletics are no different. The NCAA's current policy concerning TGNC athletes dictates that a medical diagnosis, e.g., gender identity disorder or gender dysphoria, must be present in order to receive an exception to the restriction of competition based on sex-at-birth status (NCAA, 2011).

## Best Practices in Counseling LGBTQ Collegiate-Athletes

There is little argument that participation in collegiate athletics is stressful. Individuals in Divisions I, II, and III must balance the competing physical, academic, and social demands that accompany their student-athlete status, all while maintaining a grueling class, practice, and competition schedule. When these stresses are superimposed upon navigating the developmental tasks of emerging adulthood, the possible need for mental health counseling is understandable. In their study of Division I student-athletes, Kern et al. (2017) reported that 62.6% of their study participants self-reported that mental health issues had a negative impact on their athletic performance.

Sexual minority college students are prompted to seek mental health services for the same wide variety of reasons as affects the rest of the population, most frequently these include anxiety, depression, and relationship issues. The codes of ethics for all helping professions mandate that counselors practice within the bounds of their competence. Hence, helping professionals who work with LGBTQ collegiate-athletes must at the very least be competent in understanding the needs of each client within the context of their multiple identities, e.g., athlete, college student, and as a member of the sexual minority community.

In addition to the requisite knowledge base and skill set needed for work with student-athletes from the general population, there are specialized topic areas pertinent to work with LGBTQ-identified clients, among the most critical of these are identity development, psychological risk factors, counselor self-awareness, and advocacy.

## *Identity Development*

Counselors working with LGBTQ student-athletes must be knowledgeable about developmental issues pertaining to identity acquisition of sexual minority individuals. Numerous identity models have evolved that outline the process by which individuals come to understand and embrace their self-concept regarding sexuality, gender, and sexual orientation. Early scholarly work in this area largely embraced a "stage model" of identity development (Cass, 1979). These models posited universal and sequential stages in which individuals would travel from a dominant culture identification through predictable steps during which erupting conflict between one's self-concept and one's lived experience would be sequentially resolved until ultimately arriving at a place of embracing and celebrating an LBGTQ identity. Bilodeau and Renn (2005) criticized stage models as being overly simplified and not taking into account the complex and often nonlinear experience of many individuals engaging in LGBTQ identity exploration. These authors further argued that another limitation of many models is their assumption of a desired, universally shared endpoint to the process of identity formation. This implication disregards the principle that development is lifelong and that helping professionals would be wise to consider the influence and interplay of all aspects of an individual's life, including gender, sexuality, race, social relationships, etc. As opposed to identifying a healthy "endpoint" of development, counselors should focus instead on assisting clients to maximize health and well-being at every point in life.

## Psychological Risk Factors

Historically, research studies suggested that sexual minority emerging adults were at higher risk of psychological distress than their heterosexual, cisgender peers (Shepler & Perrone-McGovern, 2016). Recently, however, as methodological and analytic strategies have improved, a more complex picture has emerged, suggesting that the risks encountered by sexual minority youth are actually mitigated by the presence of social support and the availability of affirmative role models. Just as the presence of positive influences can decrease mental health risks, so too can negative experiences have a deleterious impact on health and health behaviors.

Numerous studies have explored the mental health and substance use risks encountered by sexual minority college students. It appears that life experiences and other contextual factors are highly influential in determining the emotional well-being of LGBTQ youth and emerging adults. Dermody, Marshal, Burton, and Chisolm (2016) found evidence supporting the relationship between anti-LGBTQ victimization and heavy episodic drinking in sexual minority adolescents. Similarly, sexual minority student-athletes were found in one large sample study to have greater mental health risks than straight student-athletes. The same study also reported greater substance abuse risk in LGBTQ student-athletes, although this risk was mediated by mental health (Kroshus & Davoren, 2016).

## Counselor Self-Awareness and Knowledge

Arguably the most important step in gaining competence to work effectively and ethically with LGBTQ individuals requires that helping professionals examine and address their own biases and internal homonegativity. Pachankis and Goldfried (2013) used the term *heterocentrism* to describe the error that some counselors make in assuming that all clients have a heterosexual orientation or that the experiences of heterosexuality can be generalized to persons of all sexual orientations and identities. For example, the counselor must be careful not to assume that an LGBTQ identity is the reason for seeking mental health services and must not under any circumstances attempt to change that identity. On the other hand, ignoring the client's LGBTQ identity, however well-intentioned, can also be harmful because the student-athlete may perceive this topic to be out-of-bounds. LGBTQ-competent counselors communicate their commitment to creating a safe space for their client in multiple ways, including by tending to the language on forms and in the intake interview. The use of open-ended questions without assumptions communicates to the client that the counselor does not presume a majority culture identity. For example, rather than inquiring, "Do you have a boyfriend/girlfriend," the counselor may simply ask, "Tell me about your dating life." Likewise, the counselor may ask student-athletes what pronouns they prefer when referring to themselves.

In addition to examining biased attitudes toward members of the sexual minority community, counselors also need to explore their own privilege related to their identities as members of the dominant culture. Heterosexual privilege encompasses the status of being able to share one's dating or romantic relationship with others without the fear of rejection or discrimination. Singh (2016) also referred to the need for the exploration of *cis-privilege*, that is, the societal advantages afforded to cisgender persons to the detriment of TGNC people. This author suggested that counselors should begin by engaging in self-reflection about their own histories regarding gender, including recollections of their experiences and conceptualization of gender and its role in the development of their worldviews. Through this effort, counseling can move beyond simple affirmation and toward broader societal change, a process this author referred to as liberation.

Another important consideration for counselors working to gain competence in this area is to seek basic foundational knowledge about issues related to sexuality and gender. Although the counselor needs to ask questions to understand the specific circumstances of every client's life, including history, social supports, and symptoms/resources, it is not the client's responsibility to educate the counselor about basic knowledge regarding sexuality and identity. This knowledge can be gained through reading, attending educational workshops and through supervision and consultation.

The avoidance of sexual orientation-based discriminatory behavior within the therapeutic relationship is critical but insufficient in work with LGBTQ collegiate athletes. Skerven & de St. Aubin (2015) argued that helping professionals also must work to actively validate the experiences of their clients. This may include exploring the client's experiences of identity-based discrimination and acknowledging the impact that social context can have on emotional and physical health. The American Psychological Association (APA, 2012) issued 21 separate guidelines for psychological practice with LGBTQ clients. These guidelines underscore the importance of both understanding and communicating the understanding of minority sexual orientation as nonpathological and as a normal variant of human sexuality.

Theorists have advanced our understanding of identity development among many minority communities, including LGBTQ individuals. One consistent hallmark of optimal health and well-being involves the integration of one's LGBTQ identity into the rest of the self-concept. For many individuals, identity integration may mean "coming out" to the people in their social network and for this disclosure to be embraced and celebrated.

## Therapeutic Issues

LGBTQ student-athletes present with a number of therapeutic challenges unique to their life circumstances and others that are common across their age cohort. LGBTQ college students sometimes struggle to find supportive peer networks and student-athletes in this community are no exception. LGBTQ student-athletes may be further hampered in this regard by the demanding time commitments required by collegiate athletics. Counselors working with LGBTQ student-athletes should be sure to inquire about social support, both within the team and outside of the athletic sphere. Counselors also should be knowledgeable about campus and online resources dedicated to building social supports.

Counselors must be sensitive to the stress, anxiety, and pitfalls inherent in the coming out process. Is the athlete "out" to teammates? Coaches? Roommates? Parents? Friends? The decision to come out to teammates, coaches, and athletic administrators is a highly personal one and the counselor can provide assistance with the decision-making process by providing a safe space for the student-athlete to explore the pros and cons of making this disclosure. Kashubeck-West, Szymanski, and Meyer (2008) recommend assisting LGBTQ clients to develop positive coping strategies in the event that they encounter oppressive treatment by others. For the LGBTQ student-athletes who find themselves in a highly homophobic environment, effective counseling may involve assisting in the exploration of changing environments, e.g., transferring to a more welcoming and inclusive school.

Similar to their majority culture peers, LGBTQ student-athletes will at times experience angst in their romantic lives that bring them to counseling. Pachankis and Goldfried (2013) encourage counselors to be knowledgeable about the unique characteristics of same-gender romantic relationships. LGBTQ student-athletes and their partners may struggle to negotiate the challenges that arise from the absence of proscribed culturally-reinforced gender roles. It is critical that the counselor avoid pathologizing the relationship or reinforcing antiquated stereotypes based upon outdated ideas about sexual minority culture.

Romantic entanglements between teammates are another unique challenge that may occur. The counselor in this situation may need to assist the student-athlete(s) in establishing and navigating the boundary issues that will inevitably surface both on the athletic field and within the relationship. Potential strategies may include teaching assertive communication and conflict resolution skills, so that personal issues do not interfere with athletic performance or team dynamics.

Kashubeck-West, Szymanski, and Meyer (2008) encouraged helping professionals to consider internalized heterosexism in their work with LGBTQ individuals. Internalized heterosexism is defined as the adoption and incorporation of societal oppression toward sexual minorities in one's self-concept, with accompanying feelings of shame and diminished self-worth. LGBTQ student-athletes with high levels of internalized heterosexism may need to explore their experiences of negative treatment related to their identities and the impact these experiences may have had on them. Interventions to combat internalized heterosexism will most likely be multi-pronged, focusing on remediating harm to the individuals' self-concepts and assisting them to make changes in their environment.

Just as it is important for the counselor from a majority culture background not to assume similarity to their clients, the same applies to LGBTQ-identified helping professionals. Sexual orientation and gender identity may be central aspects of a person's self-concept, but they are not the only ones. The counselor who presumes to know all that there is to know about a client because of a shared identity runs the risk of failing to truly listen to the details of the client's story. By the same token, it can also be helpful to the student-athlete to know that the counselor understands from a personal standpoint the process of sexual minority identity formation.

Similar to the guidelines for working with LGBTQ clients, APA also issued guidelines for psychological practice with TGNC people (APA, 2015). These 16 aspirational guidelines were subcategorized into (1) foundational knowledge and awareness, (2) stigma, discrimination, and barriers to care, (3) lifespan development, (4) assessment, therapy, and intervention, and (5) research, education, and training. Guideline #1 implores the counselor to understand that gender is a non-binary construct and that gender identity may or may not be in alignment with the sex assigned to a person at birth. Mizock and Lundquist (2016) identified several categories of therapeutic missteps committed by counselors working with TGNC clients. Similar to the therapeutic blunders cited by LGBTQ clients, the missteps identified by TGNC clients included attributing all of the client's difficulties to their gender identity, pathologizing TGNC identity, and failing to recognize the impact of societal bias on the individual's mental health.

Counselors working with TGNC student-athletes need to be knowledgeable about NCAA rules related to gender and eligibility, including those pertaining to testosterone as a banned substance. For the Female-to-Male (FTM) transgender person, testosterone is frequently taken to suppress estrogen production and to promote masculinization, e.g., facial/body hair growth, voice deepening, thus allowing the body's characteristics to more closely align with the self-concept. Transgender student-athletes may need assistance in decision-making regarding whether to delay hormone treatment until sport retirement.

## *Advocacy*

In addition to working with individual LGBTQ student-athletes, helping professionals should consider expanding their efforts to work toward changing the athletic environment to promote greater inclusion of sexual minority athletes, coaches, administrators, and fans. Singh (2016) argued that it is the counselor's responsibility to advocate for societal change on behalf of TGNC individuals.

Organized efforts have been launched to support sexual minority inclusion efforts at the collegiate level. In 2016, former collegiate football player Eric Leushen cofounded (with LGBTQ diversity consultant Nevis Caple) the organization "SportSafe," whose mission it is to promote inclusion for all athletes across collegiate and professional athletics (LGBT SportSafe Inclusion Program, 2017). Currently there are more than 30 university members. Counselors working in a collegiate athletic system should consider encouraging athletic administrators to make visible efforts to be inclusive of all forms of diversity, including sexual orientation and gender identity.

## Discussion Questions

1. How might Justin's experience of homonegativity at State U be different if he were a woman rather than a man? What does Dr. Condor need to know about these gender-based differences in order to be effective in working with Justin?

2. What role does Justin's LGBTQ identity play in the difficulties he is experiencing? How does the culture of State U's athletic department contribute to Justin's struggles? How would you discuss these issues if you were working with Justin?

3. Justin has disclosed his LGBTQ identity to some people, but not others. How does his being "in the closet" with his teammates impact Justin? What steps would you take to ensure that your personal attitudes toward LGBTQ individuals would not be harmful to Justin?

4. How might Dr. Condor's LGBTQ advocacy activities on campus benefit Justin? How would you engage in LGBTQ advocacy in the State U athletic department? How would you encourage Justin to advocate for himself?

# References


Allan, E. J., & Madden, M. (2012). The nature and extent of college student hazing. *International Journal of Adolescent Medicine and Health, 24*(1), 1–8.

American Psychological Association. (2012). Guidelines for psychological practice with lesbian, gay, and bisexual clients. *American Psychologist, 67*(1), 10–42.

American Psychological Association. (2015). Guidelines for psychological practice with transgender and gender nonconforming people. *American Psychologist, 70*(9), 832–864.

Anderson, E. (2005). *In the game: Gay athletes and the cult of masculinity.* Albany: State University of New York Press.

Anderson, E. (2011). The rise and fall of western homohysteria. *Journal of Feminist Scholarship. 1*(1), 80–94.

Anderson, E., & Bullingham, R. (2015). Openly lesbian team sport athletes in an era of decreasing homohysteria. *International Review for the Sociology of Sport, 50*(6), 647–660.

Baird, J. A. (2002). Playing it straight: An analysis of current legal protections to combat homophobia and sexual orientation discrimination in intercollegiate athletics. *Berkeley Women's Law Journal,* 31–67.

Bilodeau, B. L., & Renn, K. A. (2005). Analysis of LGBT identity development models and implications for practice. *New Directions for Student Services, 2005*(111), 25–39.

Cass, V. C. (1979). Homosexual identity formation: A theoretical model. *Journal of Homosexuality, 4*(3), 219–235.

Chin, J. W., & Johnson, J. (2011). Making the team: Threats to health and wellness within sport hazing cultures. *International Journal of Health, Wellness & Society, 1*(2), 29–38.

Cunningham, G. B. (2010). Predictors of sexual orientation diversity in intercollegiate athletic departments. *Journal of Intercollegiate Sport, 3,* 256–269.

Cunningham, G. B. (2015). Creating and sustaining workplace cultures supportive of LGBT employees in college athletics. *Journal of Sport Management, 29,* 426–442.

Dermody, S. S., Marshal, M. P., Burton, C. M., & Chisolm, D. J. (2016). Risk of heavy drinking among sexual minority adolescents: Indirect pathways through sexual orientation-related victimization and affiliation with substance-using peers. *Addiction 111*(9), 1599–1606. doi: 10.1111/add.13409

Diamond, L. M., & Rosky, C. J. (2016). Scrutinizing immutability: Research on sexual orientation and U.S. legal advocacy for sexual minorities. *The Journal of Sex Research, 54*(3–4), 363–391. doi: 10.1080/00224499.2016.1139665

Flores, A. R. (2014). National trends in public opinion on LGBT rights in the United States. *The Williams Institute.* Retrieved from williamsinstitute.law.ucla.edu/wp-content/uploads/POP-natl-trends-nov-2014.pdf

Greim, R. D. (2017). You can play, but can you be yourself? How LGBT and non-LGBT student-athletes perceive the climate of NCAA Division I athletic departments. *Dissertation Abstracts International Section A, 77.*

Hall, J., & LaFrance, B. (2012). "That's gay": Sexual prejudice, gender identity, norms, and homophobic communication. *Communication Quarterly, 60*(1), 35–58.

Hardin, M., & Greer, J. D. (2009). The influence of gender-role socialization, media use, and sports participation on perceptions of gender-appropriate sports. *Journal of Sport Behavior, 32*(2), 207–226.

Hine, C. (2016, June 25). As LGBT rights progress, why do gay athletes remain in the closet? *The Chicago Tribune.* Retrieved from http://www.chicagotribune.com/sports/ct-gay-athletes-stay-in-closet-spt-0626-20160624-story.html

Kern, A., Heininger, W., Klueh, E., Salazar, S., Hansen, B., Meyer, T., & Eisenberg, D. (2017). Athletes connected: Results from a pilot project to address knowledge and attitudes about mental health among college student-athletes. *Journal of Clinical Sport Psychology, 11*, 324–336.

Krane, V., Choi, P. Y. L., Baird, S. M., Aimar, C. M., & Kauer, K. J. (2004). Living the paradox: Female athletes negotiate femininity and muscularity. *Sex Roles, 50*(5/6), 315–328.

Kroshus, E., & Davoren, A. K. (2016). Mental health and substance use of sexual minority student-athletes. *Journal of American College Health, 64*(5), 371–379.

LGBT SportSafe Inclusion Program. (2017). *Making the world of sport safe for all.* Retrieved from http://lgbtsportsafe.com/

Miller, J. L., & Levy, G. D. (1996). Gender role conflict, gender-typed characteristics, self-concepts, and sport socialization in female athletes and non-athletes. *Sex Roles, 35*(1/2), 111–122.

Mizock, L., & Lundquist, C. (2016). Missteps in psychotherapy with transgender clients: Promoting gender sensitivity in counseling and psychological practice. *Psychology of Sexual Orientation and Gender Diversity, 3*(2), 148–155.

National Collegiate Athletic Association. (2011). *Office of Inclusion.* Retrieved from http://www.ncaa.org/about/resources/inclusion

National Collegiate Athletic Association. (2017). Sport sponsorship, participation and demographics search [Data file]. Retrieved from http://web1.ncaa.org/rgdSearch/exec/main

Oswalt, S. B., & Vargas, T. M. (2013) How safe is the playing field? Collegiate coaches' attitudes towards gay, lesbian, and bisexual individuals. *Sport in Society, 16*(1), 120–132. doi: 10.1080/17430437.2012.69040

Oswalt, S. B., Evans, S., & Drott, A. (2016). Beyond alphabet soup: Helping college health professionals understand sexual fluidity. *Journal of American College Health, 64*(6), 502–508.

Outsports. (2016). A record 56 out LGBT athletes compete in Rio Olympics: The Rio Olympics has 56 publicly out LGBT athletes, the most ever for an Olympics. Retrieved from https://www.outsports.com/2016/7/11/12133594/rio-olympics-teams-2016-gay-lgbt-athletes-record.

Outsports. (2017). 32 college athletes, coaches won conference titles this year: It was a banner year on the court and field. Retrieved from https://www.outsports.com/2017/6/2/15721682/32-lgbt-college-athletes-coaches-won-conference-titles-this-year

Olympic Games. (2017). *Rio 2016.* Retrieved from https://www.olympic.org/rio-2016

Pachankis, J. E., & Goldfried, M. R. (2013). Clinical issues in working with lesbian, gay, and bisexual clients. *Psychology of Sexual Orientation and Gender Diversity, 1*(S), 45–48. doi: 10.1037/2329-0382.1.S.45

Sandoval, G. (2003, January 24). Going behind the back: College recruiters raise issue of sexual orientation. *The Washington Post,* D1.

Shepler, D., & Perrone-McGovern, K. (2016). Differences in psychological distress and esteem based on sexual identity development. *College Student Journal, 50*(4), 579–589.

Skerven, K., & de St. Aubin, E. (2015) Internalized homonegativity and the double bind for lesbians: Those with higher need perceive more barriers to mental health treatment. *Journal of LGBT Issues in Counseling, 9*(1), 17–35. doi:10.1080/15538605.2014.997331

Worthen, M. F. (2014). Blaming the jocks and the Greeks? Exploring collegiate athletes' and fraternity/sorority members' attitudes toward LGBT individuals. *Journal Of College Student Development, 55*(2), 168–195. doi:10.1353/csd.2014.0020

Wolf-Wendel, L. E., Toma, J. D., & Morphew, C. C. (2001). How much difference is too much difference? Perceptions of gay men and lesbians in intercollegiate athletics. *Journal of College Student Development, 42*(5), 465–479.

Young, J., & Bursik, K. (2000). Identity development and life plan maturity: A comparison of women athletes and nonathletes. *Sex Roles, 43*(3/4), 241–254.

# 13

# Meeting Student-Athletes Where They Are: Counseling and Psychological Services for College Student-Athletes of Diverse Racial, Ethnic, and Socioeconomic Backgrounds

*Angel Brutus and Shameema Yousuf*

## CASE STUDY: ANDY

Andy is a first-generation college student who is a member of a blended family. Andy's parents have heritages that differ from one-another (mother is German and father is African-American). Her parents divorced during Andy's junior year of middle school resulting in both parents remarrying by her senior year of high school. Andy and her mother moved to Germany to be with her maternal family, where she commenced her high school years and continued her schooling. She is bilingual and has dual citizenship. She is on full scholarship as a member of an NCAA Division I tennis team and is the only team member referred to as a student of color. Andy often declines invitations from team members to attend outings or social activities due to the additional costs associated with events. Her teammates accuse Andy of being anti-social and she has recently learned that the coaching staff has advised team members to increase attempts toward being more inclusive to strengthen team cohesion. Prior to college, Andy participated in tennis programs within her hometown that targeted under-represented populations in addition to representing her local high school situated in an urban community. Her collegiate coach is the first she has encountered who was not affiliated with programming designed to target students of color. Andy's mother has encouraged her to pursue counseling services to assist in dealing with difficulties Andy has described pertaining to feeling isolated, homesick, and having decreased interest in playing her sport. Her father has verbalized distrust of her college coach's interests in ensuring Andy feels welcomed and further cites the possibility of her coach being vested in Andy's athleticism while negating any other potential contributions to the team's success.

Culturally-informed, effective service provision for student-athletes from diverse backgrounds is an ethical responsibility for every counselor. Developing multicultural competence to work with this population requires a dual understanding of the unique identity-related needs of racial, ethnic, and SES minorities and athletes. It is incumbent upon counselors to understand that acquiring familiarity with the knowledge bases pertinent to these identities is a necessary, but not sufficient step in multicultural competence development. In addition, counselors must consider the individual presenting concerns, historical contexts, and environmental forces that each student-athlete brings into the helping relationship. Failing to do so increases the risk of over-relying on assumptions or stereotypes associated with social identities. In short, counselors must strive to capture the essence of meeting diverse student-athletes where they are in their process of help seeking.

Counseling student-athletes of diverse backgrounds requires the adoption of a worldview perspective that recognizes the many environmental, systemic, interpersonal, and intrapersonal factors that influence the collegiate experience (Parham, 2009). It is imperative to understand the contextual background of each client in order to avoid the trap of stereotyping or expecting student-athletes to confirm stigmas attached to their respective social identity groups (Brutus, 2016; Steele, 2014; Harrison, 2012). Further, counselors should consider how individual student-athlete experiences of athletic identity intersect with other salient aspects of identity to operate as a multifaceted, fluid process (American Psychological Association [APA], 2017; Brutus, 2016; Stone, 2012).

The availability of personal counseling is a necessary ancillary service for student-athletes across NCAA divisions, sport types, and backgrounds. The counselor and student-athlete relationship must be supported by high levels of trust, understanding, acceptance, vulnerability and authenticity. Such facilitative factors can only be guaranteed when counselors take an honest approach to becoming aware of one's own biases and perspectives that have the potential to hinder the helping process. By embracing a worldview perspective, providers set the stage to engage in a more individualized therapeutic relationship with each student-athlete, in the current moment, with a specified set of concerns that can be fluid and ever-changing (APA, 2017; Parham, 2009).

Within the therapeutic relationship, counselors should consider how the student-athlete's race, ethnicity, socioeconomic, and international status influence the provider-client relationship. Likewise, counselors also should examine how their own race, ethnicity, SES and domestic status influences the relationship and are well-advised to continuously explore how these influential forces come into play in the counseling process. By adopting a client-centered approach in conjunction with a worldview perspective regarding diverse backgrounds, helping professionals create an environment that affords opportunities for the student-athlete to serve as the expert on their respective collegiate experiences while the helping professional adopts a supportive role facilitated by an ecological approach to counseling.

## Defining the Constructs

Race, ethnicity, socioeconomic status (SES), and international student status are inter-relational constructs that necessitate in-depth understanding. These constructs require attention not afforded to the length of this chapter, therefore it is highly recommended that helping professionals pursue due diligence to increase their understanding of the social and historical processes that have contributed to development of theories related to racial formation, recognition of ethnicity as being separate from race, and the experiences influencing both constructs in conjunction with socioeconomic status and international student status. The following operational definitions provide further understanding of these constructs in pursuit of meaningful, working relationships with student-athletes of diverse backgrounds.

Race is operationally defined as a social construct used to categorize individuals based on familial lineage. Historically, race has been viewed as a biological construct based on phenotypic characteristics, giving way to influencing identity categorization within social and historical processes. Racial categorization has been used as a process of selection, which imparts social and symbolic meaning to perceived physical differences (i.e., skin color, hair texture). In essence, race is a social construct and not a biological one (Bell, 1976; Chadderton, 2013; Hylton, 2013; Leonardo, 2009; Omi & Winant, 2015; Tajfel, 1981; Yosso, 2002). The historical context of racial categorization in the United States has implications for how this country collects demographic data and allocates its resources accordingly. The helping professions have historically broached the topic of race as a stand-alone identity. More recent movements have begun to recognize the malleable and fluid nature of race as a social construct that intersects with many other identities, all of which correlate with notable disparities between and among groups regarding access to mental health services (APA, 2017). Race salience, defined as the degree of importance individuals assign to that characteristic, has a long history of influencing racialized group members' perceptions and experiences of inferiority, superiority, oppression, privilege, and access to power (Omi & Winant, 2015).

Critical race theory (CRT) emerged in the 1980s as a multidisciplinary effort to explain the persistence of racism despite widespread perceptions of societal progress toward its elimination (Harris, 2012). Briefly, CRT posits that racism in the US persists because it is embedded into American institutions in order to preserve the privileges that are afforded to white society (Bell, 1976; Hylton, 2013). CRT presumes homogeneous racial categorization as a fixed variable as opposed to a more fluid form of identity (Chadderton, 2013; Leonardo, 2009; Yosso, 2002). Members of marginalized racial groups have expressed disparities in the realms of education, employment, and sociopolitical representation that persist at the forefront of concerns while navigating these different social contexts (Abrams & Moio, 2009; Dimock, Kiley, & Suls, 2013; Hylton, 2013; Fasching-Varner, Reynolds, Albert, & Martin, 2014; Steele, 2014). These disparate experiences do not disappear upon arrival onto a college campus. In fact, felt disparities can be heightened when exposed to a number of different identity primers and cues that perpetuate negative stigmas.

Increased exposure to stigma for racialized minority group members has resulted in increased risk of exclusion and discrimination (Crenshaw, 1989; Hylton, 2013; Steele & Aronson, 1995). One tenet affiliated with Bell's (1976) *Rules of Racial Standing* suggested that the discriminatory experiences of minority groups tend to be discounted unless validated by those in the majority. In other words, racism and classism are self-perpetuating forces that persist because change requires those with privilege to give it up, the prospect of which is difficult at best (Bell, 1976; Guillermo-Wann & Johnston, 2012; Hylton, 2013). Steele and Aronson (1995) extended this concept and proposed the existence of stereotype threat, referring to the preoccupation with having a negatively stigmatized social identity that is highly influenced by situational and environmental cues, also called identity contingencies.

Social Identity Theory (Tajfel, 1978) posited that individuals' behaviors are influenced by their social group membership, including race. According to this theory, members of "in groups" derive a stronger sense of identity by denigrating members of "out groups." Studies exploring the influence of identity contingencies within environments such as employment, educational, and political arenas have demonstrated significant influence on participants' behaviors and psychological outcomes (Hughes, Kiecolt, Keith, & Demo, 2015).

Research studies exploring racial identity have been hampered methodologically by attempting to categorize the myriad of racial groupings used to organize individuals along this dimension. Social psychology studies conducted in recent years have used anywhere from three to over 50 different racial categories (AAA,

2009; Barbujani, 2005; Forman, Lewis, & Wailoo, 2013; Phillips, Odunlami, & Bonham, 2007). Again, as providers work with student-athletes of diverse racial backgrounds, it is critically important to consider the many implications of such a fluid and malleable aspect of identity (Brutus, 2016).

Ethnicity is a concept that emerged in the early 20th century through the study of immigration and the resultant social paradigms of cultural pluralism (retention of indigenous identity while existing among other groups) and assimilationism (adjusting and absorbing the culture of a group). Later definitions were refined during the post-civil rights era with attempts to assign status based hyphenated groups (i.e., Italian-American, African-American, Asian-American) to signify cultural descent, ancestry, and kinship that has the potential to influence such lifestyle experiences as religion, language, beliefs, and cuisine, among other values-based factors (Omi & Winant, 2015; Root, 1990; Shih & Sanchez, 2009). This paradigm has been criticized for downplaying the dimensions of political-economic, national, and racialized corporealities of race as a social construction, and also has been used as an indicator of how close in proximity a group or individual remains with regard to euro-centricity (Parham, 2009).

Socioeconomic status (SES) refers to the distribution of occupational status and income, the availability of goods and services, access to desirable resources, educational attainment, and opportunity to garner purchasing power on an individual and group level within a societal structure (Williams & Rucker, 1996). SES can be viewed as a three-tiered model comprised of (1) structural and material factors; (2) the effects of inequality and relative perceived status; and (3) the persistent reproduction of hierarchies of power and privilege resulting in the subjective perception of social status and social class within society (APA, 2007).

International student status refers to students who "have crossed a national or territorial border for the purpose of education and are now enrolled outside their country of origin." (International, 2017). In the case of international student-athletes, they may do so in pursuit of academic and athletic ambitions concurrently (Lee & Opio, 2011). International student-athletes typically are admitted on F1 visa status and are categorized by government as "non-resident alien" in the United States. That is, they are foreigners who are allowed a temporary stay under the conditions of their visa.*

## Ethical Obligations and Considerations

The counseling relationship serves to empower student-athletes to enhance their wellness, mental health, performance, educational, and career goals. Further,

---

* For more in-depth information on international student-athletes, see Chapter 14.

helping professionals' judgments greatly impact student-athletes' lives (American Counseling Association [ACA], 2014; APA, 2002). As part of the core professional values symbolizing ethical commitment to diverse individuals and groups, providers are obligated to

- embrace a multicultural approach to support the dignity, worth, potential, and individual differences of people within their social and cultural contexts;

- practice competently and ethically;

- safeguard the provider/student-athlete relationship; and

- support the promotion of social justice.

All of these tenets are the drivers for the conceptual framework in support of autonomy, beneficence, nonmaleficence, justice, fidelity, integrity, respect for people's rights and dignity, as well as veracity (ACA, 2014; APA, 2002). Working within the sport culture presents the counselor with the opportunity to serve in a variety of settings and roles, whether within the athletic department, campus counseling center, or as an outside contractor. Regardless of practice setting, counselors are obligated to prioritize student-athletes' needs and solely act with their best interests in mind (Mintz & Zito, 2017).

In the process of conceptualizing student-athletes' presenting concerns, counselors must proactively pursue increased self-awareness in their interactions with the student-athlete (Scott, Tinsley, Ng, Withycombe, & Poudevigne, 2017). By actively developing cultural awareness, providers must consistently consider the student-athletes' individualized backgrounds when developing treatment plans and selecting interventions. Addressing such diverse needs requires an increased contextual understanding of the environments that diverse student-athletes must navigate during their collegiate experiences.

## NCAA Demographics

As counselors gain increased understanding of the demographic representation of student-athletes across NCAA divisions and sport-types, it is important to know how the NCAA defines and records population characteristics. The *NCAA Race and Gender Demographics Database* (NCAA, n.d.) categorizes only nine racial and ethnic identities for its faculty, staff, administration, and student-athlete populations:

1. *American Indian/Alaskan Native.* Person of origin in North America who maintains cultural identification through affiliations with a tribe or recognized community.

2. *Asian.* Person originating from far East, Southeast Asia, or Indian subcontinent.

3. *Black/Non-Hispanic.* Person with origins in any black racial groups of Africa, except Hispanic origin.

4. *Hispanic/Latino.* Person with Puerto Rican, Mexican, Cuban, South or Central American, or other Spanish heritage or cultural origin regardless of race.

5. *White, Non-Hispanic.* Person with origins from original European, North African, or Middle Eastern origins, except those with Hispanic origin.

6. *Native Hawaiian/Pacific Islander.* Person with origins in Guam, Hawaii, Samoa, or other Pacific Islands.

7. *Two or More Races.* Person with origins from one or more ethnicities.

8. *Other.* Person unable to identify with any of the above categories.

9. *Non-Resident Alien.* Person not a citizen or national of the US in this country via visa or temporary status without rights to remain indefinitely.

According to the *NCAA Race and Gender Demographics Database* (NCAA, n.d.), the data provided to the NCAA by its member institutions regarding the above race and ethnicity category definitions has been notably variable and inaccurate. The result is considerable confusion in the attempts to collect accurate longitudinal data related to race, ethnicity, and international status. This is symbolic of the inherent complexities involved in using a homogenous paradigm to describe the intersectional-identity experiences of student-athletes. The above is one of many examples of the limited opportunity to self-identify or describe one's own identity to provide more accurate demographic information. Nonetheless, the following provides a snapshot of how the athletic culture, from a racial and ethnic background, is populated across NCAA divisions and sport-types.

**Athletic department demographics.** According to the NCAA database for the 2016–2017 academic year, 85.7% of athletic directors self-identified as White, while the remaining percentage of directors were 10.3% Black, 2.2% Hispanic/Latino, and less than 1% all other self-identified racial and ethnic categories. When Historically Black Colleges and Universities (HBCUs) are excluded from the calculations, the percentages shift to 89.5% White, 6.4% Black, 2.3% Hispanic/Latino, and less than 1% remains for all other self-identified categories. Diving deeper into the demographic characteristics of other administrative positions—such as assistant or associate athletic directors (87.2% White), coaches, head athletic trainers (91.1% White), academic advisors (73% White), life skills coordinators (74.8% White), senior women administrators (87.1% White), presidents (88.8% White), and chancellors (87% White)—there is a similar trend of disproportionate numbers of White representation in decision-making roles compared to the diverse demographic makeup of the student-athlete populations across NCAA divisions and sport-types (NCAA, n.d.).

**Student-athlete demographics.** The same database capturing athletic department demographics also presents student-athletes' and head coaches' racial, ethnic, and international status for the 2016–2017 academic year. According to the database, the following sports consist of student-athletes and head coaches who self-identify as White across all three divisions: baseball (81.4% student-athletes vs over 90% of head coaches), basketball (42% student-athletes vs. over 80% of head coaches), football (51% student-athletes vs. over 90% of head coaches), lacrosse (85% student-athletes vs. over 90% of head coaches), soccer (60% student-athletes vs. over 80% of head coaches), tennis (57% student-athletes vs. over 80% of head coaches), track (63% student-athletes vs. over 80% of head coaches), and volleyball (71% student-athletes vs. over 80% of head coaches). Despite the fluctuating percentages of diverse representation across sport-types, the coaching position remains dominant in the White racial category, and more specifically White males (NCAA, n.d.). Counselors should remain aware of the implications for establishing a sense of autonomy, connectedness, and value with regard to the collegiate experience—particularly, that of student-athletes who identify with minority social identity categories, such as race. Sociopolitical narratives of oppression, marginalization, and negative stigmas can influence, the ways student-athletes manage their relationships with coaches, staff, faculty, and administrators.

For athletes who self-identify similarly with the demographics of their coaching staff and administrators, counselors should also remain aware of the potential for the presence of operating from a lens of privilege, defined as the inherent advantages given to members of the dominant culture. Counselors must be careful not to assume that category membership translates to privilege. However, by remaining aware of this possibility, they can help facilitate meaningful dialogue with student-athletes from all backgrounds.

## Brief Examples of Stigmas and Stereotypes of Various Groups

Sport is a microcosm of the larger society. A predominant narrative exists maintaining that sport is free of prejudice, discrimination, racism, and classism and there is the pretense of colorblindness and equitable treatment for the love-of-the-game. Student-athletes from diverse backgrounds must navigate problems related to inequality in an atmosphere that denies its existence. Counselors must encourage student-athletes' attempts to reconcile the false narrative by strengthening racial, ethnic, socioeconomic, or international status identities. Counselors must also acknowledge and explore the stereotypes and stigmas attached to members of diverse groups (APA, 2017).

Stereotype is defined as "rigid clusters of isolated and simplified social/cultural characteristics conjoined into a single imagined identity, that is then used to label a social group and assess their [its] character" (Parezo, 2000, p. 42). Stigma associates people to a set of unwanted and pejorative characteristics that form a stereotype, and subjects those being stigmatized to discrimination. Stereotype threat impacts cognitive and emotional resources through salience of a stereotype or stigma, salience of membership in the stigmatized group, and salience of desires to perform well in the performance domain (Steele & Aaronson, 1995; Stone, 2012). Below are a few examples of stigmas and stereotypes associated with four outlined sociocultural groups.

**Stereotypes of student-athletes.** Student-athletes are negatively stereotyped as academically inferior to their classmates (Beilock & McConnell, 2004; Hodge, Burden, Robinson, & Bennett, 2008; Hodge, Harrison, Burden, & Dixson, 2008; Sailes, 1993; Simons, Bosworth, Fujita, & Jensen, 2007; Wininger & White, 2008) despite comparable or higher graduation rates compared with the general student body (Hosick, 2014). They are often labeled "dumb jock" and "class punk" and perceived as receivers of unmerited privileges. Further, Black male athletes have reported encounters where they feel even more pressure to prove they belong in the classroom setting when compared to their White athlete peers who are perceived as receiving greater leniency and forgiveness from professors and classmates (Comeaux, 2010; Steele, 2011; Stone, 2012). Female athletes have also reported perceived gender-based disparities in the classroom setting (Brutus, 2016; Stanley & Robbins, 2011).

**Stereotypes of racial groups.** Within the sporting context, White athletes are often described by media as being skillful and intelligent whereas Black athletes are depicted as animalistic and athletic in nature. For many, this narrative perpetuates the assumption of Black athletes having low intelligence that transcends the sporting domain and carries over into the academic setting (Comeaux, 2012; Harrison & Lawrence, 2004; Hodge, Burden, Robinson & Bennett, 2008; Steele & Aaronson, 1995). The same is true for White athletes who are stigmatized as not having athletic abilities when compared to their Black sport-peers (Stone, Lynch, Sjomeling, & Darling, 1999). Similarly, student-athletes with African heritage, e.g., Kenyan, are espoused to have superior speed, further exaggerating assumptions regarding natural abilities and discounting hard work or effort as contributors to achieving sport-performance goals. Similarly, student-athletes of mixed heritage are often miscategorized by others and are frequently assumed to deal with identity crises or to have inherent athletic ability if portions of their heritage is of African descent when in fact for some, racial identity is viewed as a fluid category depending on the context and environment (APA, 2017; Brutus, 2016; Owens & Massey, 2011). For these student-athletes, hard work is underestimated and instead is attributed to being inherently athletically gifted (Brutus, 2016).

**Stereotypes of ethnic groups.** Numerous ethnicity-based stereotypes persist in and outside of athletic spheres. Native American people frequently have been portrayed as blood-thirsty savages as sports team mascots, perpetuating dominant culture hegemony. Likewise, South Asian-American men have faced characterizations of being terrorists, geeky, or effeminate (Cheng, 1996). Hispanic and Latino(a) populations have been stereotyped as having occupational interests that are agricultural, service-oriented, and labor-intensive, discounting any interest in professional skill level vocations. Hispanic and Latino communities often are portrayed as animalistic, violent, and sexually aggressive. Finally, macroaggressive sentiments are heavily present in media coverage concerning immigrant and migrant communities.

**Stereotypes of socioeconomic groups.** Mainstream media frequently portray people of low SES as dirty, aggressive, inbred, unkempt, poor, unintelligent, stupid, and lacking in ambition, talent and morals. Lack of resources, inadequate educational training, scant parental support, and limited access to successful role models are stated reasons for these collectively held stereotypes attached to individuals with low SES backgrounds (Haycock & Jerald, 2002; Rothstein, 2004; Toporek & Pope-Davis, 2005). Differences in standardized test scores attributed to disparate educational experiences further perpetuates the stereotype that strong academic and intellectual capabilities are uncommon within low SES communities despite the underrepresentation of individuals from resource-poor environments in the norming of these standardized assessments (Plous, 2003).

## Identity Priming

Student-athletes from diverse backgrounds encounter multiple cues in their day-to-day lives on campus that raise their awareness of differences from others in their environment. The concept of priming one's identity incorporates the presence of a stimulus that activates implicit memory effects and may result in individuals behaving in ways that confirm stereotypes. Stimuli, or cues, can take various forms: interpersonal interactions (verbal and nonverbal), environmental signs or symbols, location, and sensory triggers (Schrobsdorff, Ihrke, Behrendt, & Hermann, 2012; Steele, 2011). For example, an individual's identity can be primed by merely completing intake paperwork as they seek counseling services. By answering the demographic questions pertaining to race and ethnicity, student-athletes from diverse backgrounds may be reminded of negative stereotypes associated with minority populations.

Systemically, identity primers are rife in the academic setting. While undergoing standardized testing, completing demographic information may prime racial and ethnic identity. Submitting travel letters to instructors primes student-athletes' athletic identity. Course requirements to purchase supplemental supplies or books primes the identity of low SES student-athletes. Requirements for English language proficiency and off-campus internship completion are both identity primers for international student-athletes.

Similarly, identity primers can be evident in the sport setting. The racial and ethnic composition of the team may be a primer for minority student-athletes. The emphasis on talent versus hard work or effort primes athletic identity. Even the playing of the U.S. National Anthem ceremony during competitions serves as a reminder to international student-athletes of their minority status, as well as the status of marginalized populations being at the forefront of conversations surrounding Anthem protests.

Student-athletes encounter identity primers in the academic sphere as well. Racial and/or ethnic priming may take the form of academic advisors encouraging minority students to register for less rigorous courses. Academic support services for student-athletes housed separately from those for nonathletes reinforce the stereotype of athletes as academically inferior. SES identity priming may surface in the limited hours of operation for campus-based counseling offices and cafeterias. These limited hours frequently conflict with sport and class schedules, resulting in the need for higher priced alternative meal options or the inability to make use of other needed student services.

Within the sporting domain, environmental identity primers abound. For example, spectators' use of "mugshot" fatheads depicting likenesses of athletes during competitions conveys the subtle message that minority student-athletes are criminals. The public display of team-based grade point averages reminds student-athletes of their status as athlete-over-student. Likewise, campus sales of athletic gear with an athlete's jersey number to support the department and not the athlete exploits the lower SES of some student-athletes.

Elsewhere on campus, student-athletes of diverse backgrounds may experience discrimination and inequitable treatment in their interpersonal interactions with faculty, staff, and students (Lapchick, 2015). Academically, instructors may teach from material developed from a hegemonic history or approach that perpetuates privileged status of historically "dominant" groups, which magnifies racial and ethnic disparities. Instructors' uses of illustrative examples not typically afforded to low-resource populations are hurtful to lower SES students. Nonathlete classroom peers who decline opportunities to partner with student-athletes for group work based on the dumb-jock stereotype convey negativity toward their student-athlete peers. In the sport setting, these issues may present as coaches who address those of the dominant cultural group, while ignoring those of the minority status, or student-athletes from lower SES groups being excluded from informal social team gatherings.

## Applied Setting Considerations

Counselors working with student-athletes from diverse backgrounds in race, ethnicity, and SES, must consider the impact of the campus climate, broadly defined as the collective attitudes, cultural norms, and welcoming of diversity by members of the organization (Hart & Fellabaum, 2008). Help-seeking behaviors can be significantly affected by the institution's campus climate, both positively and negatively.

**Potential stressors.** Counselors must consider the student-athletes' presenting concerns within the context of the systemic, environmental, and interpersonal stressors they encounter on a day-to-day basis (APA, 2017). Social identity characteristics have the potential to be facilitative or detrimental to the student-athlete, depending upon the meaning and significance they are assigned by the individual. Counselors have the opportunity to work with student-athletes to identify and explore how aspects of social identity contribute to overall well-being.

Group belongingness is a psychological experience that can further contribute to the lived experiences of student-athletes on campus (Abrams & Hogg, 1988; Steele, 2011; Tajfel, 1981). Student-athletes from diverse backgrounds need to experience environments where their needs are met and their values supported. When messages from one's environment conflict with self-identity, the result may be counterproductive emotions, cognitions, or behaviors (Haslam, 2015; Steele, 2011). Likewise, discrepancies or perceived threats to one's individual and/or group identity have been found to influence behavior and performance where the social stigma has been assigned (Brutus, 2016; Harrison, 2012; Steele, 2011; Stone, 2012). Stereotype threat provides an additional lens for counselors observing and understanding how student-athletes navigate spaces when engaging with others, including non-sport peers, faculty, staff, and administrators (Haslam, 2015; Hogg & Terry, 2014).

When a student-athlete encounters identity stereotypes and subsequent threats to identity, there is potential for behavioral responses that can either hinder or facilitate performance (Steele, 2011). Either way, this process requires minority student-athletes to expend considerable mental energy to disprove stigmas through increased vigilance, heightened awareness of one's minority status, as well as disengagement to avoid confirming held stereotypes (Brutus, 2016; Comeaux, 2012; Harrison, 2012; Steele & Aaronson, 1995). Counselors who are aware of this behavioral response to the phenomenon of stereotype threat can approach athlete concerns for underperformance—in both sport and academic domains—with increased understanding of how to incorporate stereotype lift from a strengths-based approach.

Student-athletes who are members of underrepresented racial groups have reported micro- and macro-aggressive experiences. Brief examples include verbal comments regarding the physical characteristics of Black women (i.e., hair, buttocks, weight), instructors' seemingly surprised responses to demonstrated intelligence or academic astuteness as abnormal representation of one's racial group (Solórzano, 2014), overt questioning of one's heritage due to racial or ethnic ambiguity (Brutus, 2016), or extensive monitoring of activities attended by racial minorities, such as fraternities or sororities (Solórzano, 2014). Further, academic integrity and intellectual prowess frequently are scrutinized in members of minority racial, ethnic, and SES groups (Comeaux, 2012; Harrison, 2012; Lee & Opio, 2011; Steele & Aaronson, 1995).

Counselors working to assist student-athletes' development of effective coping skills must validate these experiences as they are presented, especially with an understanding of the potential presence of internalized oppression that can manifest in devaluing the higher education experience (Brown, Rosnick, & Segrist, 2017). Despite the legal removal of school segregation, to date, US schools remain socially segregated by class, race and ethnicity (National Center for Educational Statistics, 2016). To understand the vivid experiences of how the student-athlete perceives their collegiate environment, the counselor must create opportunities to facilitate exploration of the shared content, associated feelings, and assigned meanings of student-athletes' interactions with the system and its people (Carkhuff, 2000).

Student-athletes have faced opposition by stakeholders regarding their decisions to participate in public protests of oppressive acts towards marginalized communities of color. Counselors must recognize the psychological benefits of participation in social justice activities and for this reason are well advised to advocate for their clients' rights in this situation (Tibbetts et al., 2017).

For student-athletes with limited financial resources outside of those provided by their respective athletic department budgets, seeking counseling services may present a financial burden. As counselors consider making treatment recommendations, the student-athlete's access to resources supported by the department of athletics, campus student services, and community-based services must be taken into consideration. When possible, the removal of barriers to accessing services based on financial limitations can be addressed by offering professional services for little or no financial return, such as sliding scale and/or pro bono meetings on a limited basis (ACA, 2014; Koocher & Keith-Spiegel, 2008).

All too often, student-athletes are limited in their help-seeking choices as a result of financial barriers, including campus-based services with maximum session limits, community-based providers within or outside of insurance networks, or associated out-of-pocket expenses, such as copays, deductibles, and co-insurances.

Another complicating factor involves the need to sacrifice access to specialized services by working with a provider who may not have specific training or contextual understanding of the sport culture and performance requirements. Access to providers with expertise in the many intersecting identities functioning in academic settings, sporting domains, and interpersonal relationships on college campuses is critical to the overall well-being of diverse student-athletes.

Religious and spiritual beliefs may also be an area of concern for student-athletes from diverse backgrounds. It is incumbent upon the counselor to understand and discern how the student-athlete places meaning on religion and spirituality, particularly when they come into conflict with the majority culture. Understanding how student-athletes' beliefs and practices are culturally-relevant to their self-defined identity and the subsequent implications for supporting or diverging from the family system's values are critical for the counselor to explore with clients. College-aged individuals during this emerging adult stage of development are often navigating multiple identity development stages and religious/spiritual identity may be one such aspect. At a time when the student-athlete is subject to numerous social influences—e.g., coaches, athletic directors, teammates, academic support team, deans, multiple professors, athletic trainers, strength coaches—there may be conflicting messages regarding the appropriate expression of religious and spiritual beliefs. Often-times, teams participate in religious or spiritual activities before games or meals, and for student-athletes from under-represented backgrounds on their respective teams, the counseling space can serve as an opportunity to create an environment that promotes autonomy and supportive identity exploration. Rather than pathologizing the potential threat to having a sense of belonging, the counselor has an opportunity to facilitate meaningful dialogue that establishes a relationship of trust, understanding, and therapeutic alliance.

Another key stressor for international and lower SES student-athletes concerns personal finances (Lee & Rice, 2007). These student-athletes may not be able to afford to engage in social events or expensive meal outings with their teammates and may experience stress of limited meal options available to student athletes after their late-night training.

Help-seeking carries the threat of stigma among many non-dominant cultural groups, which may result in an underutilization of services (Sue & Sue, 1999, Tilliman, 2007). Counselors working with student-athletes should direct their efforts toward destigmatizing the counseling process, beginning as early as the orientation process. In addition, it is essential that counselors be aware of possible biases such that they do not interpret student-athletes' silence to signify all is well (Wei, Liao, Heppner, Chao, & Ku, 2012).

Although similar to other marginalized student populations, diverse student-athletes experience some unique stressors and behavioral responses. Sociocultural stressors have potential effects on students' mental health and adjustment (Popp, 2007). Cultural shock, financial stress, prejudicial discrimination, and stereotyping are stressors that can reinforce isolation, alienation, lack of self-esteem, and emotions of anger, anxiety and depression. Maladaptive coping mechanisms may become pronounced if student-athletes are unsupported and left to find their own way. For example, disenfranchised student-athletes may withdraw from social engagements and feel alienated in their interactions with the environment, system, and interpersonal relationships. As with the general student college population, the isolation and personal stress may intensify (Chen, 1999) when they experience value and lifestyle conflicts with majority culture, particularly when seeking help is seen as a last resort (Sue & Sue, 1991, Tilliman 2007).

Cultural shock is conceptualized as stress associated with the transition from one's home culture to a significantly different environment (Winkelman, 1994). It may manifest as disorientation or anxious confusion (Furnham, 2015). Cultural shock is a particular concern for students where incompatibility in values is noted (Idowu, 1985; Williamson, 1982). For minority and international student-athletes, differences in the philosophy of education and customs may cause stress, especially when unrecognized or unaddressed by academic and coaching staff (Liberman, 1994; Lee & Opio, 2011). The resulting effects on mental well-being can be significant.

Counselors should be sensitive to the potential that their student-athlete clients may be experiencing isolation and exclusion. Leaving friends behind and traveling across the world may leave international students experiencing social loss as they enter the United States. The same may be true for a student-athlete leaving their neighborhoods where low SES is prevalent. Homesickness and the feeling of isolation are common reactions to student-athletes' attempts to adapt to a new environment (Sandhu, 1995; Lee & Rice, 2007; Lee & Opio, 2011). For some, being a first-generation college student presents added pressure to perform well, as the value of athletic participation becomes linked to the ability to give back to the family and community. Being seen as the one who survived or made it can create a sense of responsibility (known as survivor's guilt) to represent an entire group in addition to the collegiate-team. Counselors must understand the collectivist underpinnings inherent with this experience and not discredit or devalue the weight associated with the pressure to perform. Counselors may wish to explore the roots of financial stress and provide support in seeking financial assistance, affordable housing, and food options that serve to meet student-athletes' needs within the parameters of NCAA compliance guidelines.

Stigmatization and stereotyping of their cultural identities coupled with the experience of prejudicial discrimination may derail the healthy adjustment of student-athletes. Minority student-athletes may develop and foster maladaptive coping strategies that augment their overall stress level, resulting in internalized and externalized anger, feelings of helplessness, negativity toward the mainstream dominant culture, and emotional difficulties (Chen, 1999). There also may be a history of disparate underuse of behavioral or mental health services. Contributing factors to the underuse of services are many and include distrust of Western approaches to treatment, cultural mistrust, linguistic differences, history of misdiagnosis, and the failure to understand presenting needs of people of color. Additionally, some student-athletes may fear that seeking treatment may jeopardize their sport status or signify failure (Alegría et al., 2008; Breaux & Ryujin, 1999; Chang & Yoon, 2011; Whaley, 2001; Edberg, Cleary, & Vyas, 2011; Sue & Sue, 1991; Tilliman, 2007).

## Supporting Student-Athletes' Presenting Needs

Fostering positive student-athlete experiences requires institutions to take responsibility for cultivating a culture of acceptance by rejecting negative stereotypes and stigmas. Faculty, staff, athletic departments, student affairs, and counseling departments should collaborate to construct and enforce guidelines to inform cultural competence in working with diverse student-athletes. Counselors are ethically bound and morally responsible to attend to the needs of student-athletes seeking behavioral and mental health services. It is incumbent upon providers to understand the dangers of misdiagnosis and over-pathologizing of behavioral symptoms when, for some diverse cultures, the responses are within a normalized stress-response (Dow, 2011).

Counselors must be cognizant of the student-athletes' experiences of negative stigmas, stereotypes, aggressions (micro- and macro-), and financial, systemic, and environmental barriers to thriving on college campuses. Further, counselors must recognize the presence of a power-differential in the counseling setting and how issues involving power and privilege may play out in the counseling setting. Serving in a role of advisor, facilitator, and advocate can assist the counselor to meet the student-athlete where they are in their process. Another important step is for counselors to validate the potential presence of mistrust by demonstrating cultural humility characterized by a willingness to renounce privilege and engage in openness to learning from the student-athlete's culture as opposed to learning about their culture and needs (Miike, 2012).

Counselors are encouraged to adopt a strengths-based approach. A hallmark of this approach involves acknowledging diverse student-athlete challenges and at the same time understanding ways they have positively addressed life's issues. Extracting examples of strength from their family system, community, and sporting experiences highlights an inherent capability to thrive under pressure. By focusing on strengths, counselors can begin to understand how student-athletes can move toward achieving optimal functioning and well-being during the college experience (Seligman & Csikszentmihalyi, 2000).

Active support from multiple systems can promote a sense of resilience both inter- and intra-personally (Theron, Theron, & Malindi, 2012). Diversity training for staff is necessary to promote continued engagement in the environment. Provisions should be made to assist student-athletes of diverse racial, ethnic, socio-economic, and international backgrounds adjust to campus life by soliciting their ideas on how they believe their needs can be met. In addition, providing opportunities for additional extracurricular activities that allow student-athletes to maintain their values and identities will support their wellbeing and may provide additional opportunities for belongingness and inclusion.

## Conclusion

The traditional model of individual counseling may not be enough for this group of college students. Counselors have the opportunity to serve as an integral member of the larger team of individuals charged with the care of student-athletes. Counselors must consider and take advantage of opportunities to learn more about various organizational and environmental obstacles that student-athletes navigate daily. By understanding and witnessing the campus climate from an intersectional lens, counselors can truly facilitate culturally-relevant therapeutic relationships to support the overall well-being of diverse student-athlete clientele. It is incumbent for counselors to remain aware of personal biases and consider the power and privileges associated with one's group belonging. Furthermore, counselors must be cognizant of the underpinnings and implications associated with stigmas and stereotypes, while considering one's proximal relation to dominant culture. With a multicultural awareness and perspective of diverse groups, the counselor-student-athlete relationship may be enriched with trust, truly making a difference in the effectiveness of counseling services for student-athletes.

## Discussion Questions

1. Consider the case of Andy. In what circumstances might you expect Andy to experience reminders of her minority status? What identity primers must Andy confront in the classroom? At tennis practice? In social settings?

2. What are some of the stressors Andy is experiencing due to her status as an athlete? As an international student-athlete? What about as a student-athlete of color? What are some of the barriers that may prevent Andy from seeking the help she needs to address these issues?

3. What would you need to keep in mind in order to provide strength-based, culturally competent counseling for Andy? How might you advocate for Andy to help her to get her needs met in the classroom? On her team? In the athletic department? In the US?

# References


Abrams, D., & Hogg, M. A. (1988). Comments on the motivational status of self-esteem in social identity and intergroup discrimination. *European Journal of Social Psychology, 18*(4), 317–334.

Abrams, L. S., & Moio, J. A. (2009). Critical race theory and the cultural competence dilemma in social work education. *Journal of Social Work Education, 45*(2), 245–261. doi:10.5175/JSWE.2009.200700109

Alegría, M., Chatterji, P., Wells, K., Cao, Z., Chen, C., Takeuchi, D., Jackson, J., & Meng, X. (2008). Disparity in depression treatment among racial and ethnic minority populations in the United States. *Psychiatric Services, 59*(11), 1264–1272.

American Counseling Association. (2014). *ACA Code of Ethics.* Alexandria, VA: Author.

American Psychological Association (2002). *Guidelines on multicultural education, training, research, practice, and organizational change for psychologists.* Washington, DC: Author.

American Psychological Association, Task Force on Socioeconomic Status. (2007). *Report of the APA Task Force on socioeconomic status.* Washington, DC: American Psychological Association.

American Psychological Association. (2017). *Multicultural guidelines: An ecological approach to context, identity, and intersectionality.* Retrieved from http://www.apa.org/about/policy/multicultural-guidelines.pdf

Barbujani, G. (2005). Human races: Classifying people vs understanding diversity. *Current Genomics, 6*(4), 215–226.

Bell, Jr., D. A. (1976). Racial remediation: An historical perspective on current conditions. *Notre Dame Law, 52*(5), 5–29.

Beilock, S. L., & McConnell, A. R. (2004). Stereotype threat and sport: Can athletic performance be threatened? *Journal of Sport & Exercise Psychology, 26*, 597–609.

Breaux, C., & Ryujin, D. H. (1999). Use of mental health services by ethnically diverse groups within the United States. *Clinical Psychologist, 52*, 4–15.

Brown, D. L., Rosnick, C. B., & Segrist, D. J. (2017). Internalized racial oppression and higher education values: The mediational role of academic locus of control among college African American men and women. *Journal of Black Psychology, 43*(4), 358–380.

Brutus, A. L. (2016). *Minority, Student, and Athlete: Multiracial Division I College Athletes' Stereotype Threat Experiences* (Doctoral dissertation, The University of the Rockies).

Carkhuff, R. R. (2000). *The art of helping.* (8th ed.). Amherst, MA: Human Resource Development Press, Inc.

Chadderton, C. (2013). Towards a research framework for race in education: Critical race theory and Judith Butler. *International Journal of Qualitative Studies in Education, 26*(1), 39–55. doi:10.1080/09518398.2011.650001

Chang, D. F., & Yoon, P. (2011). Ethnic minority clients' perceptions of the significance of race in cross-racial therapy relationships. *Psychotherapy Research, 21*(5), 567–582.

Cheng, C. (1996). "We choose not to compete": The "merit" discourse in the selection process, and Asian and Asian American men and their masculinity. In C. Cheng (Ed.), *Research on men and masculinities series, 9. Masculinities in organizations* (pp. 177–200). Thousand Oaks, CA: Sage Publications.

Chen, C. P. (1999). Professional issues: Common Stressors among international college students: research and counseling implications. *Journal of College Counseling, 2*, 49–65.

Comeaux, E. (2010). Racial differences in faculty perceptions of collegiate studentathletes' academic and post-undergraduate achievements. *Sociology of Sport Journal, 27*(4), 390–412.

Comeaux, E. (2012). Unmasking athlete microaggressions: Division I studentathletes' engagement with members of the campus community. *Journal of Intercollegiate Sport, 5*(2), 189–198.

Crenshaw, K. (1989). Demarginalizing the intersection of race and sex: A Black feminist critique of antidiscrimination doctrine, feminist theory and antiracist politics. *University of Chicago Legal Forum, 140*, 139–167.

Dimock, M., Kiley, J., & Suls, R. (2013, August 22). *King's dream remains an elusive goal: Many Americans see racial disparities. Pew Research Center.* Retrieved from http://pewrsr.ch/16R4azG

Dow, H. D. (2011). Migrants' mental health perceptions and barriers to receiving mental health services. *Home Health Care Management & Practice, 23*(3), 176–185.

Edberg, M., Cleary, S., & Vyas, A. (2011). A trajectory model for understanding and assessing health disparities in immigrant/refugee communities. *Journal of Immigrant and Minority Health, 13*(3), 576–584.

Fasching-Varner, K. J., Reynolds, R. E., Albert, K. A., & Martin, L. L. (Eds.). (2014). *Trayvon Martin, race, and American justice: Writing wrong.* Rotterdam, Netherlands: Sense. doi:10.1007/978-94-6209-842-8

Forman, T., Lewis, E., & Walu, K. [Emory JWJI] (2013, April 22). *Exploring the race and difference initiative at Emory University: Current research on race and difference* [Video file]. Retrieved from https://www.youtube.com/watch?v=xkm7xS-kUVw

Furnham, A. (2015). Culture Shock. Why is culture shock so common, surprising and hurtful? *Psychology Today.* Retrieved from https://www.psychologytoday.com/blog/sideways-view/201512/culture-shock

Guillermo-Wann, C., & Johnston, M. P. (2012, November). Rethinking research on multiracial college students: Toward an integrative model of multiraciality for campus climate. Paper presented at the 2nd bi-annual Critical Mixed Race Studies Conference, Chicago, IL.

Harris, A. P. (2012). Critical race theory. *International Encyclopedia of the Social & Behavioral Sciences.* Retrieved from http://works.bepress.com/angela_harris/17/

Harrison, K. (2012). "Don't call me a studentathlete": The effect of identity priming on stereotype threat for academically engaged African American college athletes. *Basic and Applied Social Psychology, 34*(2), 99–106. doi:10.1080/01973533.2012.655624

Harrison, C. K., & Lawrence, S. M. (2004). College students' perceptions, myths, and stereotypes about African American athleticism: A qualitative investigation. *Sport, Education and Society, 9*(1), 33–52.

Hart, J., & Fellabaum, J. (2008). Analyzing campus climate studies: Seeking to define and understand. *Journal of Diversity in Higher Education, 1*(4), 222.

Haslam, A. [The British Psychological Society]. (2015, February 26). *Social Identity and the new psychology of mental health.* DCP Annual conference 2014: Division of clinical psychology. Standing up and speaking out: Clinical psychology and social context [Video file]. Retrieved from https://www.youtube.com/watch?v=TWWZd8lrraw

Haycock, K., & Jerald, C. (2002). Closing the achievement gap. *Principal, 82*(2), 20–23.

Hodge, S. R., Burden, J. Jr., Robinson, L., & Bennett, R. A., III. (2008). Theorizing on the stereotyping of Black male student-athletes: Issues and implications. *Journal for the Study of Sports and Athletics in Education, 2*(2), 203–226.

Hodge, S. R., Harrison, L., Jr., Burden, J., Jr., & Dixson, A. D. (2008). Brown in Black and White—Then and now: A question of educating or sporting African American males in America. *American Behavioral Scientists, 51*(7), 928–952.

Hosick, M. B. (2014). Student-athletes earn diplomas at record rates: Graduation Success Rate jumps two points, virtually every demographic improves. *NCAA.* Retrieved from http://www.ncaa.org/about/resources/media-center/news/student-athletes-earn-diplomas-record-rate

Hughes, M., Kiecolt, K. J., Keith, V. M., & Demo, D. H. (2015). Racial identity and well-being among African Americans. *Social Psychology Quarterly, 78*(1), 25–48. doi:10.1177/0190272514554043

Hylton, K. (2013, November 11). *What is critical race theory and what is it doing in a nice field like sport and leisure?* [Video file]. Retrieved from https://www.youtube.com/watch?v=9urhrbVGIsI

Idowu, A. I. (1985), Counseling Nigerian students in United States colleges and universities. *Journal of Counseling & Development, 63,* 506–509.

International (or internationally mobile) students. (2017). *UNESCO.* Retrieved from http://uis.unesco.org/en/glossary-term/international-or-internationally-mobile-students

Koocher, G. P., & Keith-Spiegel, P. (2008). *Ethics in psychology: Professional standards and cases* (3rd ed.). New York, NY: Oxford University Press.

Lapchick, R. E. (2015). *The racial and gender report card.* Retrieved from www.tidesport.org/reports.html.

Lee, J., & Opio, T. (2011). Coming to America: Challenges and difficulties faced by African student athletes. *Sport, Education and Society, 16*(5), 629–644.

Lee, J., & Rice, C. (2007). Welcome to America? International student perceptions of discrimination. *Higher Education: The International Journal of Higher Education and Educational Planning, 53*(3), 381–409.

Leonardo, Z. (2009). *Race, whiteness, and education.* New York, NY: Routledge.

Liberman, K. (1994). Asian student perspectives on American university instruction. *International Journal of Intercultural Relations, 18,* 173–192.

Miike, Y. (2012). "Harmony without uniformity": An Asia centric worldview and its communicative implications. In L. A. Samovar, R. E. Porter, & E. R. McDaniel (Eds.), *Intercultural communication: A reader* (12th ed., pp. 36–47). Belmont, CA: Thompson.

Mintz, M., & Zito, M. (2017). Ethical issues in sport psychology. In J. Taylor (Ed.), *Assessment in applied sport psychology.* (pp. 47–57). Champaign, IL: Human Kinetics.

National Collegiate Athletic Association. (n.d.). *Diversity research: NCAA race and gender demographic database.* Retrieved from http://www.ncaa.org/about/resources/research/diversity-research

Omi, M. A., & Winant, H. [UC Berkeley AAADS]. (2015, February 4). *Racial formation in the United States: Introduction to the 3rd edition talk given at the University of California Berkley campus* [Video file]. Retrieved from https://www.youtube.com/watch?v=yawU5yhHGug&feature=youtu.be

Parezo, N. J. (Spring 2000). American Indian stereotypes: Persistent cultural blindness. Red Ink Magazine, 9(2), 41–55.

Parham, W. (2009). Raising the bar: Developing an understanding of athletes from racially, culturally, and ethnically diverse backgrounds. In M. B. Andersen (Ed.), *Sport psychology in practice.* (pp. 201–215). Champaign, IL: Human Kinetics.

Phillips, E. M., Odunlami, A. O., & Bonham, V. L. (2007). Mixed race: Understanding difference in the Genome Era. *Social Forces; A Scientific Medium of Social Study and Interpretation, 86*(2), 795–820. doi:10.1093/sf/86.2.795

Plous, S. (2003). The psychology of prejudice, stereotyping, and discrimination: An overview. *Understanding prejudice and discrimination,* 3–48.

Popp, N. (2007). International student-athlete perception of college sport and its effect on adjustment to college. *Electronic Theses and Dissertations. Paper 1142.*

Root, M. P. P. (1990). Resolving "other" status: Identity development of biracial individuals. *Women and Therapy, 9,* 185–205. doi:10.1300/J015v09n01_11

Rothstein, R. (2004). Wising up on the black-white achievement gap. *Education Digest, 70*(4), 27–36. Retrieved from http://web.ebscohost.com/ehost/delivery?sid=232d51fd-f474a00-915a-5c45c15126a9

Sailes, G. A. (1993). An investigation of campus stereotypes: The myth of Black athletic superiority and the dumb jock stereotype. *Sociology of Sport Journal, 10*(1), 88–97.

Sandhu, D. S. (1995). International student populations and needs assessment. In S. D. Stabb, S. M. Harris, & J. E. Talley (Eds). *Multicultural needs assessment for college and University student populations* (pp. 2003–223). Springfield, IL: Charles Thomas Publisher.

Schrobsdorff, H., Ihrke, M., Behrendt, J., Hasselhorn, M., & Herrmann, J. M. (2012). Inhibition in the dynamics of selective attention: An integrative model for negative priming. *Frontiers in psychology, 3,* 491.

Scott, L. F., Tinsley, T. M., Ng, K., Withycombe, J. L. & Poudevigne, M. (2017). Diversity in sport psychology assessment. In J. Taylor (Ed.), *Assessment in applied sport psychology* (pp. 59–86). Champaign, IL: Human Kinetics

Seligman, M., & Csikszentmihalyi, M. (2000). Positive psychology: An introduction. *American Psychologist, 55*(1), 5–14.

Shih, M., & Sanchez, D. T. (2009). When race becomes even more complex: Toward understanding the landscape of multiracial identity and experiences. *Journal of Social Issues, 65*(1), 1–11. doi:10.1111/j.1540-4560.2008.01584.x

Simons, H. D., Bosworth, C., Fujita, S., & Jensen, M. (2007). The athlete stigma in higher education. *College Student Journal, 41*(2), 251–273.

Solórzano, D. G. [UC Davis School of Education]. (2014, May 8). *Using the tools of critical race theory and racial microaggressions to examine everyday racism.* Presented at the UC Davis School of Education Distinguished Educational Thinkers and the Critical Consciousness Speaker Series [Video file]. Retrieved from https://www.youtube.com/watch?v=6JU4294fZNA

Stanley, C. T., & Robbins, J. E. (2011). Racial identity and sport: The case of a bi-racial athlete. *International Journal of Sport & Exercise Psychology, 9*(1), 64–77. doi:10.1080/1612197X.2011.563127

Steele, C. M. (2011). *Whistling Vivaldi: How stereotypes affect us and what we can do.* New York, NY: W.W. Norton & Company.

Steele, C. [Family Action Network]. (2014, December 10). *Whistling Vivaldi: How stereotypes affect us and what we can do.* Presentation to the Family Action Network [Video file]. Retrieved from https://www.youtube.com/watch?v=-YbE3ljT3t4

Steele, C. M., & Aronson, J. (1995). Stereotype threat and the intellectual test performance of African Americans. *Journal of Personality and Social Psychology, 69*(5), 797–811. doi:10.1037/0022-3514.69.5.797

Stone, J. (2012). A hidden toxicity in the term "studentathlete": Stereotype threat for athletes in the college classroom. *Wake Forest Journal of Law & Policy, 2,* 179–533.

Stone, J., Lynch, C. I., Sjomeling, M., & Darley, J. M. (1999). Stereotype threat effects on Black and White athletic performance. *Journal of Personality and Social Psychology, 77*(6), 1213–1227. doi:10.1037/0022-3514.77.6.1213

Sue, D. W., & Sue, D. (1999). *Counseling the culturally different: Theory and practice.* 5th ed. New York: John Wiley & Sons.

Tilliman, D. G. (2007). The utilization of counseling by the international student population on U.S. college and university campuses. *Counselor Education Master's Theses, 106.*

Tajfel, H. (1978). Social categorization, social identity and social comparison. In H. Tajfel (Ed.), *Differentiation between social groups: Studies in the social psychology of intergroup relations.* (pp. 61–76). London, England: Academic Press.

Tajfel, H. (1981). *Human groups and social categories: Studies in social psychology.* Cambridge, MA: Cambridge University Press.

Theron, L. C., Theron, A. M., & Malindi, M. J. (2012). Toward an African definition of resilience: A rural South African community's view of resilient Basotho youth. *Journal of Black Psychology, 39*(1), 63–87.

Tibbetts, E., Longshore, K., Cropper, R., Lipsky, S., Brutus, A., Bonura, K., & Galli, N. (2017). Supporting the athlete in society: Athlete activism. *SportPsych Works, 5*(3), 1–2.

Toporek, R. L., & Pope-Davis, D. B. (2005). Exploring the relationships between multicultural training, racial attitudes, and attributions of poverty among graduate counseling trainees. *Cultural Diversity and Ethnic Minority Psychology, 11*(3), 259.

Wei, M., Liao, K. Y., Heppner, P. P., Chao, R. C., & Ku T. Y (2012). Forbearance coping, identification with heritage culture, acculturative stress, and psychological distress among Chinese international students. *Journal of Counseling Psychology, 59*(1), 97–106.

Whaley, A. L. (2001). Cultural mistrust and mental health services for African Americans: A review and meta-analysis. *The Counseling Psychologist, 29*(40), 513–531.

Williams, D. R., & Rucker, T. (1996). Socioeconomic status and the health of racial minority populations. In *Handbook of diversity issues in health psychology* (pp. 407–423). Springer, Boston, MA.

Williamson, G. (1982). Impediments to health for the foreign student. *Journal of the American Health Association, 30*, 189–190.

Wininger, S., & White, T. (2008). The dumb jock stereotype. To what extent do student-athletes feel the stereotype? *Journal for the Study of Sports and Athletics in Education, 2*(2), 227–238.

Winkelman, M. (1994). Cultural shock and adaptation. *Journal of Counseling & Development, 73*(2), 121–126.

Yosso, T. J. (2002). Toward a critical race curriculum. *Equity and Excellence in Education 35*(2), 93–107. doi:10.1080/713845283

# 14

# Understanding International Student-Athletes in the American Collegiate Sport System

*Marc Cormier*

## CASE STUDY: ALEX

Alex is an outstanding ice-hockey player and first year member of Puck State University (PSU) hockey team, a Division 1 NCAA program located in the northeastern United States. Originally from Sweden, Alex was heavily recruited and decided to join PSU because of its academic and athletic reputations. Her team has several other international athletes, but all are from nearby Canada. While it was never her dream to play elite-level hockey, Alex and her parents jumped at the opportunity to receive a full athletic scholarship. Alex is an intelligent, hard working, and focused student who has always taken school seriously. However, her entire education has been in Swedish, and while she understands and can speak English, she has some anxiety about an all-English education and environment.

Although Alex arrived a month before school began, throughout the first semester she felt lost around campus. She established several friendships on her team and also met a handful of other students in her residence hall and classes. With the onset of the hockey season, however, Alex could no longer find the time to socialize with her non-athlete friends.

Despite being a first-year student, Alex earned a starting spot on her hockey team and was given a lot of top-line minutes. However, she did not play particularly well in the early months of the season. Her coaches were concerned about her poor play but remained optimistic and patient. They addressed this with her and she assured them that she simply needed to adjust to new coaching philosophies and what she calls "a North American approach" to hockey. They also noticed that she often looked sad and appeared isolated from the rest of her team. She usually warmed up alone and often did not participate in team outings (e.g., movies nights, bowling, dinners). Her roommate told the coaches that she typically stays in her room or works in the library and that she also calls home at least once every few days.

The coaches had several conversations with Alex about her poor play and threatened to decrease her playing time until she can demonstrate on-ice improvements. Alex worried that her scholarship would be in jeopardy and she would no longer be able to afford the high international tuition at PSU, forcing her to return home. She also struggled to adjust to the U.S. university system and English instruction. Alex loved her major (physics) and was managing quite well in statistics, chemistry, and other science-based courses. However, she was often lost in large lecture courses. Although she understands English, she finds that her instructors speak quickly and rarely check to make sure everything is being understood.

Following the winter holiday, the coaching staff recommended that Alex visit Dr. Sue, the psychologist for PSU athletics. Alex was reluctant at first and didn't know what to expect. She arrived early to complete the intake paperwork and wore neutral clothing with no team logos. Dr. Sue noticed that while Alex seemed engaged, she did not say much and mostly nodded her head in agreement. She rarely made eye contact, frequently scanned the room, and picked at her fingernails for the majority of the session. When asked about reasons for visiting, Alex answered, in broken English, that her coaches did not think she was playing well enough and were concerned about some of her academic performance. She also acknowledged feeling homesick and lonely despite being surrounded by friends and teammates. Alex reported feeling tremendous pressure and had begun questioning her decision to attend PSU. Although she still loved to play hockey, she admitted to feeling it had become more like an obligation or "job" than an enjoyable activity. Alex admitted that she does not feel "at home" on campus. She reported calling her parents regularly, which is quite expensive, but claims that it is "worth the money" since they provide her an opportunity to vent and talk about something other than hockey. The first session ended positively, with Alex agreeing to return on a weekly basis. As she rose to leave, Alex asked Dr. Sue if she could bring a translator to her next session, just in case.

In recent years, increasing numbers of international student-athletes have populated American colleges and universities (National Collegiate Athletic Association [NCAA], 2018). According to the NCAA, over 17,000 international student-athletes are currently enrolled and competing in the NCAA at the Division I, II, and III levels. Helping professionals must understand the unique circumstances surrounding international student-athletes in order to assist them in their adjustment to U.S. intercollegiate athletics.

Kim and Sax (2009) recommended against a "one size fits all" approach to working with college students, and this advice is particularly apt as it pertains to interactions with international student-athletes. Different groups have different needs, many of which play an important role in determining their overall college experience. Upon their arrival to the United States, international students face many challenges in adjusting to living and learning in their new environment. Adjustment difficulties may depend on individual country of origin, race and ethnicity, language proficiency, and overall cultural, political, and even religious beliefs (Constantine, Anderson, Berkel, Caldwell, & Utsey, 2005). International student-athletes also may come from countries with vastly different cultural importance placed on sport. Such dramatic differences in development systems require the athlete to make significant adjustments upon their arrival in the US, the burden of which may lessen with a counselor's assistance.

A successful transition to the U.S. college experience is essential to international students' overall well-being. For instance, satisfaction with the college experience is linked to higher rates of academic success, which may result in post-graduate education, and even athletic honors (Yukselturk & Yildirim, 2008). Further, Russell, Thomson, and Rosenthal (2008) found that international students (nonathletes, in this case) reported overall satisfaction with health and counseling services on university campuses, although cultural background influenced satisfaction with these services.

These results are encouraging, however, there is a paucity of research devoted to international student-athletes' experience, which may challenge helping professionals' ability to deliver effective services. For example, the literature fails to identify specific social and cultural factors that may influence mental health needs and services. This chapter bridges that gap and explores the common issues arising from being an international student-athlete. An attempt is made to describe international student-athletes (i.e., what portion of total student-athletes they represent, what sports they commonly play), followed by an exploration of the common struggles associated with being an international student-athlete.

## Who Are International Student-Athletes?

Following the events of September 11, 2001, all international students were required to register for a personal tracking number known as Student & Exchange Visitor Information Service (SEVIS). Other regulation changes included tougher visa rules to get in and out of the country and closer tracking of students through computerized systems (Chapman, 2003). These new processes allowed the United States government to monitor all international students and, as a consequence, made it challenging for many (athletes and nonathletes) to travel outside the country during their time in the US (holidays, conferences, tournaments, etc.). Initially, the number of international students applying to study in the United States dropped dramatically (Gilman & Shulz, 2004), yet recently, we have observed a resurgence in the overall international student-athlete population (NCAA, 2018). Today, international student-athletes represent nearly 4% of the total collegiate athlete population across all divisions, with the majority competing at the Division I level (NCAA, 2018). It is possible that this increase is due to a number of factors, including (1) the attractiveness of an American education, (2) the caliber of NCAA sport, and (3) aspirations of participating in the professional ranks. As Brown and Mazzarol (2009) suggested, a U.S. education is a marketable product, often used to attract elite international athletes.

An examination across collegiate sports demonstrates that foreign born student-athletes not only excel on their adopted NCAA teams, but frequently represent their home country's Olympic or national team. According to the NCAA (2016), over 1,000 incoming, current, or former NCAA student-athletes competed at the 2016 Olympic games in Brazil, representing a total of 107 countries and 223 member institutions. Among that group were gold medalists Katinka Hosszu (Hungary/University of Southern California/Swimming), Derek Drouin (Canada/Indiana University/Track & Field), and Nicco Campriani (Italy/West Virginia University/Rifle). Further, numerous foreign-born stars in the National Hockey League (Canadians Jonathan Towes and Duncan Keith; Austrian Thomas Vanek) and National Basketball Association (Canadian Andrew Wiggins and Australian Ben Simmons) trace their roots to the NCAA ranks.

This population is, of course, not divided evenly across all sports. Many sports have a significant international student-athlete population whereas others are primarily domestic athletes. For instance, an investigation of Division I teams in 2013–2014 (Notte, 2017) revealed that nearly one third of male and female tennis players are not native to the US. Many other sports are comprised of a large proportion of international student-athletes, including men's (21%) and women's (26.9%) ice hockey, men's and women's skiing (17.9%), women's golf (15.8%), and men's soccer (12.2%). International student-athletes tend to assume central positions on their teams, are regular starters, and are more likely to take active team leadership roles (i.e., team captain), particularly when they hail from a culturally close country to the US (Han, 2008). This suggests that cultural similarities may be critical factors to the overall transitional experience, adjustment, and perhaps success, of the international athlete.

## Common Struggles

International student-athletes encounter a unique set of circumstances. As athletes, they must deal with the typical athletic transitions from high school to university competition. However, as cross-cultural visitors, they must also adjust socially and culturally to their new environments. They face the demands of studying at a new educational system that is likely different from their own, often using a language that is not their native tongue. They may also experience a number of other barriers that make their experiences unique compared to their domestic teammates. Specifically, sport psychology professionals should consider the following five burdens faced by international student-athletes.

### *Homesickness and Loneliness*

Loneliness is a common feeling experienced by all human beings at certain times in life. It is, of course, more likely to occur under times of extended absences from one's home and support networks (Wiseman, 1997). Specifically, social loneliness involves a lack of involvement with peers who share one's worldview, and often is characterized by boredom and a sense of exclusion (Weiss, 1973). In crossing international borders for the purpose of education and/or athletic pursuits, individuals leave their families, social networks, and often, the familiar comforts of their home countries and native cultures. Newly arrived international students may suddenly find themselves suffering from social isolation or relationship deficit at a time when they need more than the usual support (Wiseman, 1997). As Grinberg and Grinberg (1989) stated, "one ceases to belong to the world one left behind and does not yet belong to the world in which one has nearly arrived" (p. 23). International students may feel lost, both figuratively and literally, with added feelings of isolation and anxiety (Brislin & Yoshida, 1994). Often, the physical and cultural environment is very different with new social norms and customs and many international students may feel extremely uncomfortable and find this adjustment very difficult. While some research (Trendafilova, Hardin, & Kim, 2010) has suggested that international student-athletes experienced high levels of satisfaction in team social contribution and team integration, it remains a challenge for coaches or sport psychology professionals to create an environment where all members' cultural needs are met and they feel integrated within the group. In short, the context that international student-athletes enter creates a perfect storm for the development of profound personal loneliness (Sawir, Marginson, Deumert, Nyland, & Ramia, 2008).

Unlike domestic student-athletes who have the luxury of staying connected to family and friends by cell phones, trips home during holidays, and low(er)-cost airfare, international student-athletes must rely on alternative means, such as email, video chat, infrequent (and expensive) phone calls, and social network mechanisms (i.e., Facebook, Instagram, Twitter). Admittedly, these are a significant improvement when compared to the student-athlete experience 20 years ago, where the only means of communication was the telephone. Yet, even the most advanced communication technology fails to provide feelings of physical proximity. Student-athletes benefit from various forms of support: emotional, tangible, informational, and companionship support, which acts as either a main effect (i.e., social networks provide individuals with regular, positive, stable experiences) or as a buffering effect (i.e., social networks may help eliminate stress by providing a positive environment) (Cohen & Willis, 1985). While technology may provide an individual with the ability to communicate with support networks, create dialogue, and offer emotional assistance, it simply cannot mimic physical proximity or companionship. A commonly cited solution to loneliness is to simply "call home," however, for some, overseas phone charges may not be supported by their monthly budget (Sawir et al., 2008). Similarly, time zone issues may also add an element of difficulty, as in our case study, Alex. Therefore, finding personal support from one's parents or siblings may not always be possible. For others, email and video chat have become a critical way of keeping in touch with families and friends. However, for those whose loved ones do not have regular Internet access, the isolation becomes even more of a burden. As a result, many international students have a difficult time keeping regular contact with their distant loved ones, further perpetuating feelings of homesickness and loneliness. Finally, given the prevalence of extended breaks in the United States (i.e., Thanksgiving, Christmas, spring break, Easter), many international students may at times find themselves alone or isolated on college campuses. Although it is common for local student-athletes to invite their international teammates for holidays, it is never a guarantee. Many sports also require its athletes to return to campus shortly after a holiday, thus making it less cost-effective for foreign-born athletes to pay travel costs during peak travel season for a few days over holiday breaks. Therefore, scheduled breaks from the school year may actually cause increased feelings of loneliness. As a result, many international student-athletes may divest from their family and friends at a much earlier stage than their domestic peers, perhaps leading to potential unhealthy relationships or experiences to "fill the void" (Sawir et al., 2008).

Typically, universities provide support for international students that are intended to facilitate the cultural transition and provide optimal academic and social adjustments. Throughout the year, student government and/or athletic departments host orientation programs designed to familiarize new students with various campus activities, support services, and cultural events. These may include cultural-specific events (i.e., Spanish Nights), weekly club meetings, cultural conferences, or "world-wide mixers" where all students on campus are invited to mingle with peers and share their culture and heritage. As is common with the student-athlete experience, campus organizations and events are rarely a priority and go unattended. Due to busy schedules (i.e., training camps, practice, travel, tutoring, team meetings), student-athletes rarely have time to invest in transitional social activities. Therefore, despite efforts to provide international students with adjustment assistance to celebrate diversity and combat feelings of loneliness and isolation, international student-athletes are often left even more on the outside looking in.

Perhaps the biggest advantage of being a student-athlete is team membership and thus, an (almost) guaranteed social network. Team building activities, training camps, and team retreats provide student-athletes with opportunities to socialize with members of their team and to build strong interpersonal trust and connections (Prapavessis, Carron, & Spink, 1996). These activities may even provide an international student-athlete an opportunity to share his/her difficulties with a group, thus encouraging empathy from teammates, coaches, and staff. In many cases, teammates also live together in residence halls and off-campus housing, which can foster strong friendships and social support. Even domestic student-athletes have referred to teammates as family, due to the proximity, time spent together, and similarity of struggles (Rees & Hardy, 2000). In some cases, however, relationships with teammates may not satisfy the desired depth of interaction. While teammates may be convenient acquaintances due to physical proximity, some students may require a more intense connection or the ability to connect with someone outside their sport. This is particularly apparent in the United States as many international students revealed disappointment at the underdevelopment of empathic relationships with domestic students (Lee, Maldonado-Maldonado, & Rhoades, 2006). Therefore, it may be advantageous for international student-athletes to seek social relationships with other students from their home country.

## Culture Shock

Youngsters often grow up idolizing and cheering for their favorite collegiate teams, with many having dreams of one day wearing those sacred colors in a Rudy-like significance. Similarly, many youths grow up understanding the impact of collegiate sports and recognizing that it represents significant status in the athletic and non-athletic domains. While some see it as a stepping-stone to a lucrative professional career, others may simply view it as an opportunity to attend the university free of charge. Though amateur in status, collegiate sports dominate national television and thus, domestic students are exposed to its purpose and importance early in their lives. Consider then the athlete who has not grown up watching televised collegiate sports and knows nothing of their cultural significance. Due to the technological advances associated with the Internet, few foreign-born athletes remain totally ignorant to the existence of the NCAA, but their lack of awareness of its cultural significance may impede their transition. Similarly, many international student-athletes bring an entirely different background in sport and are products of different development systems. Many come from countries where intercollegiate sport is an entirely foreign concept, thus necessitating an adjustment period to facilitate the student-athlete's understanding of the intercollegiate system's financial and social significance. Incoming international athletes have to acclimate to the social and political cultures of an American college campus, but perhaps more importantly, to the sport culture as well.

Once in the US, international student-athletes often feel overwhelmed by differences in values, lifestyle, food, habits, and academic demands (Sawir et al., 2008). Many student-athletes may view their experience on an NCAA team as a unique cultural adventure and enjoy the overall experience. Others may be highly uninterested in assimilating and may even regard American culture on campus as obnoxious or unpleasant. Some may also refrain from discussing any political or religious beliefs out of fear of alienation, ridicule, or even persecution. Accordingly, this social reticence may make it more difficult to create meaningful social bonds with peers and/or teammates. International student-athletes may also refrain from joining social groups out of fear of rejection.

During their formative years, athletes around the world are exposed to different youth sport models and coaching styles. Some countries (e.g., Canada, the United Kingdom, Australia, United States) have well-publicized long-term development models (LDADs), designed to increase the likelihood of positive experiences in sport and encourage life-long participation (Fraser-Thomas, Cote, & Deakin, 2005). Conversely, some Romanian or Russian gymnasts are known to come from auto-cratic (or even abusive) coaches during the early developmental stages (Coakley, 2015). Popp, Hums, and Greenwell (2009) revealed that domestic student-athletes found college sport to focus more on competition than their international counterparts. Therefore, an athlete entering the NCAA with certain expectations may require significant time to adjust to a new coaching climate that is vastly different from that which they are accustomed. American sport culture, particularly at the collegiate level, socializes athletes toward winning and reinforces this outcome with praise, honor, and publicity (Eitzen & Sage, 2009). International student-athletes will need to adjust to the intense competitive nature of American collegiate sport. This may come as a shock to an athlete who arrives and is expected to "play to win" if that individual views collegiate sport participation as little more than just a sporting endeavor, leading them to focus more on nonathletic pursuits, a difference that may create division among teammates (Popp et al., 2009).

## Financial Burdens

Both American and international student-athletes share common stressors, such as family-related pressures, academic pressures, social pressures, and even financial burdens (Cheng, Leong, & Geist, 1993). However, perceptions of financial stress might differ between domestic and international athletes. According to the National Center for Education Statistics (2015), the average annual cost for an American student to attend a private university is $37,990 whereas in-state public institutions, the average student will pay $18,632. International students on the other hand will pay similar living costs, but tuition fees are often double that of domestic students. For students who are fortunate enough to receive financial compensation for participation in sport (i.e., scholarship), financial concerns are generally lower. However, it is important to realize that only full scholarships include tuition waivers, dormitory rooms, meal plans, and small stipends for living expenses. Partial scholarships only include some portion of the above. In these cases, they may not cover book fees, transportation costs, or any extra costs of living. Due to the high tuition rates, international students must rely heavily on receiving athletic scholarships, otherwise, in many cases, they would not be able to attend an American institution or participate at the NCAA level. Perhaps this is why there are far more international student-athletes at the Division I level, where scholarships are most often awarded. Even with a scholarship, many international student-athletes must rely on additional financial support in order to live comfortably (i.e., travel costs during holidays, moving expenses, furniture). The majority of international students can bring very few material possessions with them to the US, therefore they will need to purchase many new items upon their arrival. Clearly, finances may be the source of significant stress in international student-athletes.

To further complicate matters, athletic scholarships in the US are all on a one-year renewable basis. In other words, student-athletes are never guaranteed to have funding for the entirety of their education. While it may be nice to receive a "full ride" offer from a Division 1 school, scholarships can be removed and given to a higher-performing teammate or top-level recruit. This leaves the student-athletes to either fend for themselves financially or return to their home country due to lack of income. Reasons for athletic scholarship removal may include unsatisfactory performance, academic failures, breaking team rules, or even criminal charges. Therefore, athletes who are on scholarship are under a tremendous amount of pressure to perform up to expectations in sport while simultaneously achieving in the classroom to keep their scholarships and remain in the United States. This can be particularly stressful for student-athletes in highly demanding academic and/or athletic programs since failure to meet performance expectations may result in removal of financial assistance. This pressure can become increasingly problematic since most international student visas do not permit students to work in the United States while they are studying. Therefore, many international students are completely dependent on scholarship funding with few opportunities to make more money.

## Language Barriers

Similar to issues of homesickness and loneliness, language barriers can be an extremely difficult obstacle to overcome because many international students are not linguistically proficient in English (Constantine et al., 2005). Discomfort about speaking English may impede interactions with their new community, their professors, coaches, and teammates to fulfill their basic needs. Furthermore, student-athletes may feel pressure to read, write, and speak English. However, English fluency can be extremely difficult to master, particularly in a short amount of time. This can become a major contributing factor to high levels of stress and increased feelings of isolation (Grayson & Meilman, 2006).

Furthermore, awareness of having an accent or being difficult to understand may lead many international student-athletes to shy away from interacting with American students. This can be especially detrimental during the early stages of transition as they may be struggling to get their bearings around campus. Early in the transition, international student-athletes may struggle with simple, everyday tasks such as going to the grocery store or buying a cell phone. Difficulty communicating with peers and neighbors will make this transition especially difficult. In order to help relieve these early stressors, teams should assign new student-athletes a mentor or "big brother/sister" to facilitate this transition. The veteran teammate will likely be more patient and understand the struggle more than complete strangers. When possible, efforts should be made to assign international student-athletes as mentors, thus increasing the likelihood of empathy.

In addition to transitioning to campus, language barriers are particularly apparent and stressful in the classroom. Having to adjust to a second language makes coursework more difficult and may complicate interactions with professors and peers. Not only are international student-athletes struggling to understand the professor speak, but they are likely to also express difficulties approaching professors or academic advisors to seek extra help. As mentioned earlier, student-athletes are already under tremendous pressure to perform well in the classroom in order to keep their eligibility and scholarship hopes intact.

Finally, language barriers may also hinder athletic development and the ability to implement coaching feedback or communicate with teammates. It has been well documented in popular media (Kaplan, 2017) that in team sports with larger international contingencies (i.e., hockey, soccer), language barriers can make communication among teammates difficult, thus hindering teamwork. Some players have developed easy-to-learn code words (e.g., Heads up. Chip. Over. Pressure.) to facilitate communication, but this requires significant practice and awareness. Similarly, international students-athletes may struggle to understand instruction from coaches and teammates or experience difficulty comprehending verbal interactions with other members of the support staff (e.g., athletic trainers, student managers, helping professionals). These language barriers may prevent student-athletes from approaching these individuals, therefore making it increasingly difficult to seek help and improve. It may take international student-athletes months or even longer to approach members of the support staff due to embarrassment or discomfort. As mentioned earlier, language difficulties are often a source of embarrassment, particularly for shy individuals. It is important for all members of the athletic support staff to be conscious of this fact and to initiate frequent casual interactions with international student-athletes. This will increase the likelihood of more timely help seeking when needed.

## Interconnectedness of Struggles

Many of the common struggles mentioned above are important concepts for helping professionals to understand, and it is also crucial to acknowledge how these barriers are connected and may impact one another. For instance, a lack of financial resources could result in international student-athletes' inability to visit their home countries, families, and friends during holiday vacations, thereby perpetuating feelings of homesickness and loneliness. Furthermore, financial limitations could also result in the inability to purchase a car. While this may not seem like a necessity for most college students, many campuses and college towns are not easily accessible without this means of transportation. This may force the athlete to live in a central location of campus, near parties, commotion, and little opportunity to focus on schoolwork. Similarly, some educational experiences, e.g., seminar classes requiring extensive discussion, may perpetuate feelings of culture shock. Although these are just two examples of the interconnectedness of struggles, helping professionals should be aware that the above-mentioned struggles rarely operate in a vacuum and may even increase the likelihood of others occurring. For many international student-athletes, it is likely that adjustment struggles are perpetuating other barriers.

Helping professionals must first be aware of these additional struggles and must also be knowledgeable of the resources available to facilitate international student-athletes' successful transition to their new environments.

# Recommendations for Practice

## *Education*

Education is critical for helping professionals as they assist international student-athletes in navigating the American collegiate system. The requisites for being a physically, mentally, and emotionally healthy and successful international student-athlete are complex. In order to best serve this population, helping professionals must be aware of their day-to-day challenges and be skilled at connecting them to the appropriate resources on campus or beyond.

## *Flexibility and Patience*

Helping professionals should be flexible and creative when offering programming, counseling, and advising sessions. For instance, one must be mindful of an international student-athlete's hectic schedule or lack of transportation (e.g., Alex). Helping professionals should therefore be open to meeting after normal business hours, on site (pre- or post-practice), and/or scheduling longer (or more frequent) meetings due to language difficulties.

## *Maintaining a Network*

It is also advantageous for helping professionals to maintain a network of current/former international student-athletes who may serve as mentors. This can be especially useful for incoming athletes who require tangible support (i.e., assistance with visas, social security, accommodation, health insurance, and cell phones). Student-athlete alumni can be guides and may also teach new students how to balance their academic and athletic demands in the American educational system. It may also be useful to keep a list of faculty, administrators, and advisors outside the athletic department who specialize in working with international student-athletes. Meeting with each of these individuals will increase a helping professional's trust in making a particular referral.

## *Educating Others*

It is important to arrange opportunities for faculty and coaches to talk about international student-athletes. This may help reduce the tensions between the two worlds (academics and athletics) of the athlete. Many campus professionals may be oblivious to the challenges they face and the fact that they are very different from both the general student population and general student-athlete population. Therefore, by educating faculty and staff or providing them with helpful reading materials, they may be more empathic and help facilitate the transition process.

## Conclusion

This chapter outlined the common struggles facing international student-athletes. These individuals encounter many of the standard barriers of other minority populations (LGBTQ, first-generation, racial minorities, etc.) while facing other challenges unique to their status as non-U.S. citizens. It is important for helping professionals to understand these additional barriers and to develop strategies to assist them in being successful athletically and academically.

## Discussion Questions

1. How should Dr. Sue help Alex explore the roots of her loneliness to determine the types of social support that she is missing? What concrete steps could she suggest Alex take to gain social support in her immediate environment?

2. Student visas prohibit international students from working beyond the university assistantships. Although she is on an athletic scholarship, her travel expenses home for holidays and her frequent phone communications with her family are very expensive. How can Dr. Sue assist Alex in coping with her difficult financial situation? What resources might she suggest to assist her?

3. What other campus resources should Dr. Sue suggest to help Alex cope with her language-related academic struggles? What about the language barriers on the ice?

## References

Brislin, R., & Yoshida, T. (1994). *Intercultural communication training: An introduction.* Thousand Oaks, CA: Sage

Brown, R., & Mazzarol, T. (2009). The importance of institutional image to student satisfaction and loyalty within higher education. *Higher Education, 58,* 81–95.

Cheng, D., Leong, F. T. L., & Geist, R. (1993). Cultural differences in psychological distress between Asian and Caucasian American college students. *Journal of Multicultural Counseling and Development, 21,* 182–190.

Chapman, D. (2003). Chalking up global lessons: MBA programs: Tougher U.S. visa rules keep foreign students away. *The Atlanta Journal and Constitution, 12,* 126–140.

Coakley, J. (2015). *Sport in society: Issues and controversy* (11th ed.). New York, NY: McGraw-Hill.

Cohen, S., & Willis, T. A. (1985). Stress, social support, and the buffering hypothesis. *Psychological Bulletin, 98*, 310–357.

Constantine, M., Anderson G., Berkel, L., Caldwell, L., & Utsey, S. (2005). Examining the cultural adjustment experiences of African international college students: A qualitative analysis. *Journal of Counseling Psychology, 52*, 57–66.

Eitzen, D. S., & Sage, G. H. (2009). *Sociology of North American sport.* Boulder, CO: Paradigm Publishers.

Fraser-Thomas, J. L., Côté, J., & Deakin, J. (2005). Youth sport programs: An avenue to foster positive youth development. *Physical Education and Sport Pedagogy, 10*, 19–40.

Gilman, V., & Shulz, W. (2004). U.S. schools losing foreign talent, *Education, 82*, 67–70.

Grayson, P. A., & Meilman, P. W. (2006). *College mental health practice.* New York, NY: Routledge.

Grinberg, L., & Grinberg, R. (1989). *Psychoanalytic perspectives on migration and exile.* New Haven, CT: Yale University Press.

Han, J. Y. (2008). Stacking and leadership patterns of NCAA international student-athletes: Theoretical implication to globalization/Americanization. *Dissertations Abstracts International, 69*, 3492A.

Kaplan, E. (2017, November 2). Lost in translation: How players bridge hockey's language barriers. *ESPN.* Retrieved from http://www.espn.com/nhl/story/_/id/21236032/nhl-lost-translation-how-players-bridge-hockey-language-barrier

Kim, Y., & Sax, L. (2009). Student-faculty interaction in research universities: Differences by student gender, race, social class, and first-generation status. *Research in Higher Education, 50*, 437–459.

Lee, J., Maldonado-Maldonado, A., & Rhoades, G. (2006). The political economy of international student flows: Patterns, ideas, and propositions. *Higher Education: Handbook of Theory and Research, 21.*

Medalie, J. (1981). The college years as a mini-life cycle: Developmental tasks and adaptive options. *Journal of American College Health, 30*, 75–79.

National Center for Education Statistics. (2018, January 25). *Fast facts.* Retrieved from https://nces.ed.gov/fastfacts/display.asp?id=76

National Collegiate Athletics Association (2016, August 25). *2016 Rio Olympics: Current NCAA students-athletes competing by school.* Retrieved from https://www.ncaa.com/news/ncaa/article/2016-07-28/2016-rio-olympics-ncaa-olympic-student-athletes-school

National Collegiate Athletics Association (2018, January 2). *International student-athletes.* Retrieved from http://www.ncaa.org/student-athletes/future/international-student-athletes

Notte, J. (2017, May 28). These are the U.S. sports scholarships most likely to go to foreigners. *Market Watch.* Retrieved from https://www.marketwatch.com/story/these-are-the-sports-where-foreigners-get-the-most-us-athletic-scholarships-2017-05-11

Popp, N., Hums, M. A., & Greenwell, T. C. (2009). Do international student-athletes view the purpose of sport differently than United States students-athletes at NCAA Division 1 universities? *Journal of Issues in Intercollegiate Sports, 2*, 93–110.

Prapavessis, H., Carron, A. V., & Spink, K. S. (1996). Team building in sport. *International Journal of Sport Psychology, 27*, 269–285.

Rees, T., & Hardy, L. (2000). An examination of the social support experiences of high-level sports performers. *The Sport Psychologist, 14*, 327–347.

Russell, J., Thomson, G., & Rosenthal, D. (2008). International student use of university health and counseling services. *Higher Education, 56*, 59–75.

Sawir, E., Marginson, S., Deumert, A., Nyland, C., & Ramia, G. (2008). Loneliness and international students: An Australian study. *Journal of Studies in International Education, 12*, 148–180.

Trendafilova, S., Hardin, R., & Kim, S. (2010). Satisfaction among international student-athletes who participate in the National Collegiate Athletic Association. *Journal of Intercollegiate Sport, 3*, 348–365.

Weiss, R. (1973). *Loneliness: The experience of emotional and social isolation.* Cambridge, MA: MIT Press.

Wiseman, H. (1997). Far away from home: The loneliness experience of overseas students. *Journal of Social and Clinical Psychology, 16*, 277–298.

Yukselturk, E., & Yildirim, Z. (2008). Investigation of interaction, online support, course structure and flexibility as the contributing factors to students' satisfaction in an online certificate program. *Journal of Educational Technology & Society, 11*, 51–65.

# 15

# Ethics and Counseling Practice with College Student-Athletes

*Jack C. Watson II, Edward F. Etzel,*
*Jamie L. Shapiro, and Robert C. Hilliard*

## CASE STUDY: DR. SMITH

Dr. Smith is a professor of sport and exercise psychology in the exercise and sport science department at U Tech. This job is a perfect fit for her because of her kinesiology based training, and her background as a former All-American gymnast. One day, Dr. Smith is contacted by her former coach at State U (located in a different state). The coach wants to know if Dr. Smith could start working with an athlete at State U who "could use a sport psychologist because she need lots of mental help." The coach tells Dr. Smith that recently, this athlete has appeared more down at practice than in the past and has not been meeting performance expectations. The coach tells Dr. Smith that the athlete's father passed away shortly before the season started and the athlete has recently gone through a breakup of a long-term relationship.

The coach has heard of sport psychology, believes that Dr. Smith could be of some assistance to the athlete, via telephone or email, and hopes that she will be able to help her before the conference championships next week. She is concerned that the athlete is not coping well with her losses and that it is impacting her performance. During the conversation, the coach states that she is not sure if the athlete wants to work with a sport psychologist, but states that she could "certainly make the athlete take part in this endeavor if it will help." The coach also believes that if Dr. Smith is successful with this athlete that she would be able to get her work as a sport psychologist with several other athletic teams at State U.

Ethical practice in college counseling, psychotherapy, and consultation is the foundation of principled, high-quality service provision. Because of the numerous and often frequent challenges that helping professionals who work with college student-athlete clients are likely to encounter, it is essential that they be ethically well versed. The central premise of ethical practice is to do no harm to the athletes being served. Those helping professionals who work within intercollegiate athletics or who see clients from athletic departments recognize that this special setting and culture offer a set of regular, sometimes unique threats to ethical practice connected to various consultative "undercurrents" (Etzel & Watson, 2007). A counselor will no doubt come across frequent opportunities to do harm to clients—often in simple, unintentional ways (e.g., breaches of confidentiality, multiple relationships). Helping professionals who provide consultation to student-athletes must be able to recognize these ethically challenging dilemmas as they evolve, and be able to resolve these situations in a responsible and competent manner. In this chapter, the term "helping professional"will be used to describe the variety of practitioners who work with college student-athletes in one or more helping capacities. Examples of these professionals are counselors, psychologists, and sport psychology consultants, as well as sports medicine professionals. Helping professionals may also be supervised graduate students from any of the abovementioned domains engaging in practica and internships. All of these professions have their own ethics codes (e.g., Association for Applied Sport Psychology [AASP], 2011; American Counseling Association [ACA], 2014; American Psychological Association [APA], 2017).* Although practitioners from allied  professions have their own codes of ethics to be educated on and follow, all of the ethical issues discussed in this chapter are generally applicable to licensed professionals, as well as professionals in training.

## Ethical Challenges and Ethics Codes

On any given day, helping professionals who work with student-athletes can encounter circumstances that test their values-based thinking and behavior in the workplace. Even the most experienced professional's ethical mettle is tested by these often spontaneous, unpredictable, and sometimes complex turns of events. Regrettably, many of the responses to these situations are not at all clear cut or particularly easy to make. Within the mix of collegiate and athletic cultures, some decisions may be obviously right or wrong (e.g., whether or not to engage in an intimate relationship with a client), or may be less obvious (e.g., sharing information with a coach about an athlete referred for sport performance issues). One thing is certain: ethically challenging situations will occur again and again when working with this population.

---

* Because two of the authors of this chapter are licensed psychologists, we have chosen to primarily make use of the APA code.

Clearly, the decisions that helping professionals must make can have a great impact upon the well-being of the clients with whom they are working, as well as on their individual reputations and the collective reputation of their profession. Consequently, it is essential that helping professionals be aware of and knowledgeable about the code(s) of ethics of their profession(s), as well as willing and able to make sometimes multifaceted ethical judgments.

## Codes

Ethics codes can be considered a set of guidelines or overarching principles that direct the behavior of individuals in line with the fundamental values of an organization or group (Bersoff, 1995). These codes serve as guides to protect the public by helping members resolve the moral problems they face. The current codes of ethics in psychology and applied sport psychology are comprised of an introduction, preamble, general principles, and ethical standards (AASP, 2011; APA, 2017). The initial "preambles" and general "principles" of codes are "aspirational" in nature, designed to encourage members to hold themselves to the highest possible level of behavior, and are useful to ethical decision making (APA, 2017). In contrast, ethical "standards" are designed to more specifically guide member thinking and behavior in an enforceable manner across a wide variety of professional situations.

In addition to ethics codes, helping professionals must be aware of federal and state laws relevant to mental health practice in the jurisdiction in which they are practicing. They should also be aware of the institutional or organizational policies of the setting in which they work (i.e., the university, athletic department, specific team). While knowing the laws, ethics, and institutional policies is essential for protecting the public and the professional, a sole focus on these prescribed ("dos") and proscribed ("don'ts") behaviors can cause a professional to worry more about risk management, or avoiding liability, versus doing the greatest good for the public and the profession. Aoyagi and Portenga (2010) distinguish between such principle ethics, which seek to answer the question, "what shall I do?", and virtue ethics, which incorporate the character and values of the professional above and beyond minimizing harm. Virtue ethics, or positive ethics, seek to answer the question, "who shall I be?" In addition to abiding by principle ethics, Aoyagi and Portenga (2010) recommend that helping professionals in sport and performance psychology remember to focus on virtue, or positive ethics, to provide the best services possible.

Ideally, helping professionals should be able to integrate their personal values with the values of the profession. However, there are certainly times when the law, ethics, institutional policies, and one's personal values might conflict. Standards 1.02 and 1.03 of the APA ethics code (2017) address this and state that professionals should "clarify the nature of the conflict, make known their commitment to the

Ethics Code, and take reasonable steps to resolve the conflict consistent with the General Principles and Ethical Standards of the Ethics Code" (p. 4). However, it is important for the helping professional to know that for risk management purposes, the order of consideration for decision making is: law, ethics codes, institutional policies, and personal values. One example of a conflict that could arise in a college setting involves Title IX reporting of sexual harassment or sexual violence. Title IX is a federal law and employees of universities are required to report any complaint of sexual harassment or violence to the Title IX officer. If a student-athlete discloses an incidence of sexual harassment to a helping professional and asks him/her to keep this confidential, there would be a conflict between the law and institutional policy (Title IX) and the ethics code (and potentially one's personal values if wishing to keep this confidential). Upon being hired by a university, a helping professional must clarify these types of exceptions to confidentiality and integrate them into the informed consent process.

## Confidentiality and Privacy

Confidentiality is an agreed-upon standard of professional behavior that obliges a helping professional not to discuss information about a client with anyone. This practice is regarded as the "cornerstone of trust on which the therapeutic relationship is built" (Glosoff, Herlihy, Herlihy, & Spence, 1997, p. 573), and athletes have reported concerns about confidentiality to be a major barrier to help seeking (Moore, 2017). Although confidentiality is a widespread ethical concept, it may or may not also be consistent with the practice of law in some states and provinces.

Helping professionals on campus need to be able to differentiate between confidentiality and privacy, as these both pertain to practice. As noted above, it is important to bear in mind that although confidentiality is typically an ethical standard it may or may not be the law in one's own state or province. In contrast to confidentiality, *privacy* is a fundamental legal right in the United States that limits the extent to which client information is available and communicated with others (Fisher, 2003; Koocher & Keith-Spiegel, 2016). Privacy is central to the Health Insurance Portability and Accountability Act of 1996 (HIPAA) discussed below (United States Department of Health & Human Resources, 2003).

Professionals must be aware of the ethical principles and standards of their profession concerning confidentiality, and they must also understand and follow the laws that pertain to the practice of counseling, psychology, or other allied professions in the jurisdiction in which they practice. If a strong foundation of trust and rapport is lacking, any counseling or psychological relationship or set of interventions, no matter how useful or innovative, would likely be short-lived and ineffective. Helping professionals must therefore recognize the utmost importance of confidentiality and privacy in building and maintaining trusting relationships with individual student-athletes and group/team clients.

**Release of confidential and/or private information.** The Health Insurance Portability and Accountability Act of 1996 (HIPAA) is intended "to assure that individuals' health information is protected while allowing the flow of health information needed to provide and promote high quality health care and to protect the public's health and well-being" (United States Department of Health & Human Resources, 2003). As such, this law protects the transmission of all individually identifiable information related to past, present, or future physical or mental health services, the current provision of mental health services, and the past, present, or future payment for such health services. The HIPAA Privacy Rule permits communication between healthcare providers on existing treatment teams providing collaborative consultations (e.g., from a team physician to department or campus psychologist). Practitioners must make clients aware of their rights under this law and make every effort to protect their information from unintended disclosure.

**Third-party inquiries.** Today's college and athletic environment and cultures pose several potential ethical challenges to consultation with individual athletes and teams. One such challenge involves determining "Who is the client?" In reality, this issue is quite commonly faced in a setting with many so-called "players." For example, a student-athlete may be referred by one or more members of the athletic department staff, including a coach, athletic trainer, team physician, academic advisor, and/or administrator. Further complicating the matter, the athletic department or team may also be paying the salary or fees for the helping professional. As a result, some referral sources or other third parties may believe they are entitled to know any and all information about "their" athlete, especially if it relates to the performance of high-profile or scholarship athletes (Etzel & Watson, 2007). It should not come as a surprise to a helping professional to be asked by a coach in a hallway or on the phone about how Brandon or Brandy is doing. In general, clients provide "informed consent" for their own treatment, with certain exceptions (e.g., threats to self or other; child or elder abuse; court-ordered exceptions). Within such legally binding contacts with clients, information about appointments, personal issues, progress, and so on must remain confidential unless a release of information has been provided by the client. When such arrangements exist with third-party referrals, practitioners should initially clarify their professional roles and responsibilities to each party, as well as the limits to confidentiality before providing any services to the athlete (APA Ethical Principle B and Standards 3.07, 3.11a, 4.02a, 4.02b, 2017). During the initial session with a client, the limits of confidentiality should be reviewed, as well as very specifically what, if anything, the athlete would want to be disclosed to an inquiring, identified third party. For example, a client might agree that a third party such as a head coach can be made aware only of attendance at counseling sessions and no more. If clients want information to be shared, it is necessary to have them sign a written release of information to be kept on record along with the informed consent form, which specifies these limits to confidentiality (APA Ethical Standard 3.10, 2017). Even if the athlete signs a more general release of information, helping professionals are encouraged to disclose as little as possible to designated third parties and only what is relevant to the purposes of the release (APA Ethical Standard 4.04a; Moore, 2003). It is usually constructive to encourage clients to discuss issues directly with concerned third parties. This allows the client to control the amount and type of information they would like to be released.

Student-athletes may be referred by caring but sometimes intrusive "helicopter" parents (i.e., parents that hover around their children and make decisions for them). Indeed, college is sometimes the first time that parents have had to deal with not being privy to their child's health or academic information, not to mention their status as athletes. This can be quite a surprise and source of consternation to caring but uninformed parents of student-athletes who are over the age of 18 and who are therefore no longer legally "minors." Helping professionals in college settings should keep in mind that they may occasionally encounter clients who are below the age of 18. In these rather rare situations, parents and guardians in some jurisdictions may still have a right to know about the helping professional's work with their son or daughter. As coaches do—but often for different reasons—parents will inquire about how their daughter or son is doing: "Are they still coming to see you?" "How can we be helpful?" Helping professionals need to be able to respond in a respectful yet ethical way to an email message or phone call from an athlete's parent or guardian that may jeopardize the confidential relationship with the client. The ethical helping professional needs to be gently assertive to protect the boundaries of client confidentiality, even in the face of sometimes temperamental inquirers. Parents and coaches alike are often well intentioned and trying to be supportive, but may sometimes be part of a student-athlete's problems.

There are also times when coaches or other third parties recognize that the athlete has improved in performance, affect, or attitude and may inquire about what strategies or techniques the practitioner used to help the athlete. Although such inquiries are most likely well intended, professionals should again protect the confidentiality of the consultation, and instead of possibly offending the coach by stating the rules of confidentiality, simply refer the coach or parent to the athlete. For instance, one might say, "I'm glad you've seen that Joe has improved. Perhaps you could ask him what he learned that may have been helpful to him." This would allow the client to make a decision about what information to discuss (Brown & Cogan, 2006).

**NCAA rules.** Reporting of possible National Collegiate Athletic Association (NCAA) rule violations is another unique issue confronting helping professionals working within or for athletic departments. The 2016–17 NCAA Division I "Manual" is 414 pages long (National Collegiate Athletics Association). Although this publication is not a code of ethics per se (ironically, only two pages are devoted to principles of ethical conduct), it is a document that can have occasional influence on the helping professional's work with student-athletes. All athletic department personnel, including psychologists or counselors if they are part of the athletic department staff, must annually sign a statement stating that they will follow NCAA rules and dutifully report any violations to the athletic department compliance office. Ethical dilemmas may emerge from consultations with student-athletes who divulge information about participating in or observing behaviors that may seem to constitute NCAA violations (e.g., practicing for too many hours, gambling).

Helping professionals who work with college athletes, whether members of the athletic department staff or not, should be aware of NCAA rules. When perceived infractions are identified, they should inform student-athletes that these acts are possible NCAA violations, and then work with them to make informed decisions about how to respond, if at all, to the behaviors in question. Helping professionals should be direct with athletic department staff regarding the protection of information related to possible NCAA rule violations, citing the guidance of the APA ethics code, other professional codes, and state law. Per the initial informed consent agreements with clients, helping professionals should treat information as confidential given that the ethics code and the law represent higher standards of practice by which counselors or psychologists must abide (APA Ethical Standards 1.02 and 1.03, 2017; Etzel & Watson, 2007).

**Records.** Appointment histories, detailed clinical records, and miscellaneous notes must be protected. Although different agencies and professionals use differing formats, useful guidance is provided on this subject by Koocher (2005). This critical information should be stored in a safe and secure place (APA Ethical Standards 4.01, 4.02a, 4.02b, 6.01, 6.02, 2017; Moore, 2003). If these records are electronic, they should be password protected and located on a secure computer server. HIPAA guidelines indicate that hard copy files should also be kept in a locked file and behind a locked door. Although there are different practices associated among agencies and states, records are generally kept on average seven to ten years prior to appropriate disposal. Helping professionals must be knowledgeable of all pertinent statutes regarding record storage, release, and disposal in the jurisdiction within which they work.

## Competence

Although all helping professionals would like to believe they are quite competent to serve their clients, this may not be true in reality. Competence takes considerable time, effort, and work to develop. Further, once achieved, competence is not fixed. Practitioners must continually strive to update their knowledge and skills. The ethical standard of competence includes (1) practicing within the boundaries of one's education, training, and supervision; (2) providing services to only those populations with whom one is trained to work; (3) keeping up with new developments in one's field; and (4) knowing when personal problems might interfere with one's work (APA Ethical Standard 2, 2017). Many issues related to competence arise when considering working with an athlete population on campus.

**Professional backgrounds.** Helping professionals working in intercollegiate athletics come from varying backgrounds with different types and levels of training. Because of these training differences, defining competence becomes an important ethical matter when working with this population. Whereas the services provided by these professionals may overlap, there are important distinctions related to their training and expertise. Those individuals using the term "psychologist" or "counselor" within the United States must meet the requirements set forth for that title by their state or the federal government. For example, in the United States, the title "psychologist" is protected in all 50 states and the District of Columbia. In general, "psychologists have a doctoral degree in psychology from an organized, sequential program in a regionally accredited university or professional school" (APA, 2018), and such degrees are most commonly in clinical, counseling, school, or industrial/organizational psychology. The combination of these qualifications and having completed a licensing process within their state allows them to practice psychology within the bounds of their competence. Licensed psychologists are trained in assisting their clients with mental health issues. In light of licensing requirements, some professionals who have earned a terminal degree in applied sport psychology or a related field may not be able to call themselves "sport psychologists" unless they possess a psychologists' license. The exception to this practice is if they are employed as a psychologist by a state or federal government organization, such as a prison system, or on a university faculty, where they would be able to call themselves psychologists only within those settings.

Counselors are in many ways similar to psychologists in terms of training and areas of competence. Although the title "counselor" is not protected in all states, it communicates a high level of professional training and competence. Professional counselors often receive masters and/or doctoral level training from programs in counseling or counselor education and also obtain state licensure. These professionals are trained to provide mental health services to individuals of all ages and backgrounds, but often have different competency areas than psychologists. As with psychologists, licensed professional counselors can bill third-party agencies and can address issues found within the *Diagnostic and Statistical Manual for Mental Disorders*, 5th edition (*DSM-5*; American Psychiatric Association, 2013).

**Credentials.** Student-athletes and athletic department staff may not be clear about the credentials and competencies of helping professionals. Those persons who do not possess the appropriate training in psychology and/or counseling should not use those terms in their professional titles. They should also not allow other people to misrepresent them by referring to them by incorrect titles (e.g., team psychiatrist versus psychologist; media guide bios). Further, they should quickly correct people who do misrepresent them.

The NCAA Sport Science Institute (2017) issued a consensus statement about mental health best practices with student-athletes. In this document, they strongly recommended that anyone providing mental health services to student-athletes should be a licensed professional (e.g., licensed psychologist, licensed professional counselor, licensed clinical social worker, psychiatrist, primary care physician with competencies to treat mental health disorders). Although it may be disappointing to some, individuals who were trained in the traditional sport sciences/applied sport psychology/physical education model of sport psychology and not licensed or credentialed should not be involved in the provision of counseling and therapy to student-athletes, unless they are competent to provide those services and employed by a state university or federal government organization with a job description that calls for the provision of such services. In order to practice within the law and scope of the ethical codes of their professions (e.g., AASP), such professionals must only teach educational sport performance enhancement skills to athlete clients who present with performance enhancement issues. Similarly, those individuals with training specifically in psychology and counseling should be very careful when working with sport performance enhancement issues if they do not have an established competency area within sport (i.e., education, training, and supervision). The Society for Sport, Exercise, & Performance Psychology (Division 47; SSEPP) of the APA (2003) created a proficiency in sport psychology for psychologists who wish to practice sport psychology. This proficiency is not a credential, but a set of recommendations for specialized knowledge and training in the area of sport psychology. SSEPP is currently working on establishing professional practice guidelines for the practice of sport psychology (Division 47 Executive Committee, personal communication, November 28, 2017). If published, these guidelines would define what sport psychologists do and recommend specific professional behaviors and procedures for this area of practice.* Providers must bear in mind that credentials like licensure and other sport-related certifications do not somehow make one competent to work with college student-athletes (Loughran, Etzel, & Hankes, 2014).

---

* To view other APA professional practice guidelines, see http://www.apa.org/practice/guidelines/index.aspx. For a more complete review of the differences in training and services provided by the above professions, see Watson and Etzel (2004).

As discussed above, competency is a continuous and dynamic assessment of many different factors.

**Presenting concerns.** Is one helping professional really competent to do career counseling, brief psychotherapy, crisis intervention, drug and alcohol counseling, trauma therapy, and learning disability testing? Indeed, it can be tempting to try to be all things to all people, and sometimes in a pinch professionals are asked to perform all of these duties. However, doing so regularly is a risky stretch; in some instances it may be unethical and possibly even illegal.

It is therefore imperative that helping professionals know the limits of their competence regarding student-athletes' issues and problems. When in doubt, ethical helping professionals seek supervision from a colleague within a specific area of their work with student-athletes. Ethical professionals must also know what assessment measures and interventions they are trained to use (e.g., a Myers-Briggs Type Indicator, Beck Depression Inventory-2, Beck Anxiety Inventory, and Minnesota Multiphasic Personality Inventory-2) and when to employ or not employ them with clients. When practitioners determine that client needs are outside the boundaries of their professional training and expertise, they should consult with a competent trusted colleague and consider referring the client to another professional who is competent to handle these issues. Having an up-to-date set of consulting and referral resources on hand is a key to providing high-quality service.

**Populations.** Another aspect of competence relates to being sufficiently trained to work with the population requesting services (Watson, Way, & Hilliard, 2017). Although attending to common features that student-athletes share is quite important, it is just as significant for helping professionals to be aware of potential visible and invisible differences among and between these young people (Loughran & Etzel, 2008). Accordingly, an ethical helping professional should have a good working understanding of the factors associated with "age, gender, gender identity, race, ethnicity, culture, national origin, religion, sexual orientation, disability, language, and socioeconomic status" (APA, 2017, p. 4). It is every helping professional's responsibility to gain the competence necessary to work with diverse client populations. When deficits in knowledge or comfort occur, counselors or psychologists should seek education and/or supervision to rectify the situation. Referrals to another professional should be considered when knowledge or attitudinal deficits pose a danger to the client's well-being. Likewise, the client's discomfort with the clinician may also necessitate a referral to another provider.

As described in other chapters in this book, student-athletes are considered by some to be a unique on-campus population. They are also a diverse group of individuals (perhaps the most diverse on campus) and should not be lumped into one category. There is no pill or quick path to become competent to work with college students and athletes. Competence is developed gradually and maintained over time through education, supervised training (by professionals who understand the athletics culture), and through continued education. Other life and work experiences (e.g., participation in athletics and sport) and related work experiences linked to understanding people in context (e.g., counseling service practica and internships; military service) are also seen as useful to the development and maintenance of competence. Mere exposure and acquisition to core clinical and consulting skills (and ideally sport and performance psychology expertise) will not be sufficient for the trainee or professional to do effective work with student-athlete clients and to negotiate the practical and ethical challenges that are part of professional involvement in intercollegiate athletics today. In addition to the ethical requirement of competence, student-athletes have reported major concerns in seeking help related to the practitioners' understanding, or lack thereof, of the collegiate sporting context (López & Levy, 2013; Moore, 2017). If not sufficiently competent to work with the presenting concerns of college students and student-athletes, professionals should refer them to someone with training and competence in the appropriate field (Brown & Cogan, 2006). Since counseling and/or psychology professionals proficient in this area may not be readily available at many colleges, a psychologist or counselor should at very least consult (i.e., via email or phone) with a qualified sport psychology professional regarding the student-athlete's concerns. Such consultations should always be handled in a confidential manner to protect the client's identity and privacy.

In a sense, competence to work in intercollegiate athletics is analogous to developing cultural competence. Sue and Sue (2013) discussed numerous aspects of multicultural counseling. Based on the work of Sue and Torino (2005), among many things, they emphasized (1) the importance of provider roles, boundaries, and processes associated with helpful service provision to clients from diverse backgrounds; (2) understanding their client's and their culture's values; as well as, (3) appreciating the identities linked to the individual in the context of their cultures and the systems within which they come from and function (Sue & Sue, 2013).

**Continuing education.** As noted above, ethical helping professionals should practice only within the confines of their competence and not outside those limits. Further, competence fades over time when providers do not work regularly with college students and/or with athletes. Just like one's computer, the competent provider of merely a few years ago may not be particularly functional without continued 'upgrading'. Thus, providers who aspire to work in the intercollegiate athletics milieu need to gain the requisite experience and must continually hone their skills and expertise for treatment of athlete clients in that unique environment. Although a terminal degree may serve as evidence of initial competence in one's field, the "half-life" of knowledge in sport psychology has been estimated to be approximately eight years (Neimeyer, Taylor, & Rozensky, 2012). Therefore, the ethical professional must make "a life-long commitment to learning and professional growth"

(Watson & Etzel, 2004, p. 58). It is essential that professionals continue their education and training beyond graduate school to ensure that they keep up with the latest developments in the field in order to provide high quality assistance to their student-athlete clients (APA Ethical Standard 2.03, 2017; Watson & Etzel, 2004).

Continued education can be accomplished by attending conferences and lectures, reading, taking additional courses, and regular consultation with colleagues and supervisors. Ethical helping professionals who work with student-athletes would benefit from regularly updating their knowledge about common issues and interventions associated with the lived experiences of college students and student-athletes. Essential topics include the impact of year-round training, injury risk and response, academic demands, learning disabilities, social media use, and the growing incidence of other psychological disorders or concerns common amongst college students (e.g., alcohol and substance use, depression, suicidality, anxiety disorders, disordered eating and eating disorders, and sexual assault sequellae; National Collegiate Athletic Association, 2007; Pérez-Rojas et al., 2017).

**Self-care.** Counseling and psychotherapy work with college students can be quite demanding in its own right. Stressors, including personal life developments, health problems, addictions, traveling with a team, and other issues can take their toll on the mental and physical health of helping professionals. Other issues (e.g., attraction or aversion to clients, staleness, burnout, work conditions, and relationships with others) can negatively influence the quality of work with clients (Koocher & Keith-Spiegel, 2016; Pope & Tabachnick, 1993). As a result, ethical counselors and psychologists need to be self-aware and monitor how their personal and working lives may be influencing their work. When professionals experience impairment related to personal problems, they should seek out assistance and determine whether they should continue or suspend working with clients (APA Ethical Standard 2.06, 2017; Loughran et al., 2014). Ethical helping professionals also have an obligation to approach peers who appear to be "impaired" and, if so, may be jeopardizing their own or their clients' welfare. Many professional organizations (e.g., state counseling and psychological associations) have colleague assistance programs in place to help those in need (Schoener, 2003).

**Overidentification.** In the stimulating and sometimes seductive world of modern intercollegiate athletics, it is easy to get wrapped up in clients' or their teams' performance. Some helping professionals exhibit a need to be seen with these young people, to "hang out" at competitions, to insist on being included in media guides, and/or display athlete photos and team memorabilia in their offices. This phenomenon is similar to parents who "live through" their children and overidentify with their accomplishments. Those who succumb to this inclination risk compromising their objectivity, competence, and professional reputation. Helping professionals must monitor the extent to which they identify with the teams and student-athletes with whom they work. Ethical helping professionals maintain appropriate distance from their student-athletes and resist the temptation to gain special recognition for services or to become enmeshed with student-athletes' teams.

## Multiple Relationships

Multiple relationships exist when a helping professional "is in a professional role with a person and (1) at the same time is in another role with the person, (2) at the same time is in a relationship with a person closely associated with or related to the person with whom the [helping professional] has a professional relationship, or (3) promises to enter into another relationship in the future with the person or a person closely associated with or related to the person" (APA, 2017, p. 6). The major problems associated with multiple relationships include the ability of a person who is in a position of influence (i.e., consultant or counselor) misusing that influence, either knowingly or unknowingly, resulting in harm to clients. Within the fields of counseling and psychology, multiple relationships generally have the potential to distort the working relationship and the consulting process (Pope & Vasquez, 1991). Such relationships are typically frowned upon (Kitchener, 1988). However, exceptions are seen in unusual situations (e.g., emergencies, lack of other resources) and when harm is very unlikely to happen to the client or the professional's work quality and/or objectivity.

Given the consistently negative view of multiple relationships, it may not be surprising to find that licensed counseling and psychology professionals reported more often than nonlicensed professionals that multiple roles are never appropriate and that they had never taken part in multiple role relationships (Watson, Clement, Harris, Leffingwell, & Hurst, 2006). Moreover, the same study also reported significantly higher levels of concern for both the practitioners and clients engaging in multiple role relationships from mental health professionals than nonpractitioners (Watson et al., 2006).

Because of the relatively small number of qualified service providers in sport psychology, many tend to be employed by or around universities where they often both teach and consult with student-athletes (Watson & Etzel, 2004). This suggests a greater than normal chance for the development of multiple relationships with student-athletes and perhaps others involved with athletics. For example, it is not uncommon for a consultant to teach a course that includes a student-athlete from a team that the consultant currently works with, has worked with in the past, or may work with in the future (Loughran et al., 2014). Additionally, psychologists are sometimes approached to provide consultation to coaches and athletic trainers, which can rapidly transform into a request for personal assistance.

When multiple role relationships exist as described by the APA definition above, they often bring with them the potential for uncomfortable and distressing interactions with potentially unconstructive outcomes. Indeed, if both parties are not able to separate the two roles, it is possible for athlete clients to perceive that what happens in one of the relationships may affect the relationship in the other role. For example, a poor grade on an exam could be perceived as the consultant not valuing or supporting the athlete (Watson & Etzel, 2004).

Other possible multiple role relationships in university settings that may affect student-athletes extend beyond that of teacher-consultant. Such roles may include that of consultant-coach. As is the case with the teacher-practitioner multiple role relationship, there are some potential benefits but also many problems that can result from a coach-consultant relationship (Buceta, 1993). One example of a benefit could include the ease with which rapport can be developed. On the other hand, one potential problem might include the loss of trust in both roles due to behavior in one of the domains.

Some recent literature suggests that the onus of responsibility in such multiple role relationships falls upon the helping professional much more so than the student-athlete (Watson et al., 2006; Watson & Etzel, 2004). The major considerations associated with getting involved in or disengaging from such situations need to be the welfare of the client and clarification of the boundaries of the relationship (Watson et al., 2006). To this end, suggestions have been made for the two parties to meet early and frequently to discuss the potential hazards, the creation of open and honest lines of communication, and the limits to public interaction (Watson & Etzel, 2004; Watson et al., 2017).

Although the frequency of multiple role relationships in traditional college counseling and psychology work with student-athletes is unclear, such contacts may be more likely to occur in sport and exercise psychology settings (e.g., on-site consultations with student-athletes). The campus and surrounding community environment present many opportunities to interact with clients in several professional and nonprofessional capacities. It is a small—sometimes very small—world, after all. However, many interactions with clients, students, or others may not be necessarily unethical and damaging to the client and consultant. In fact, Sonne (2004) suggested that there is considerable uncertainty and debate related to so-called "nonsexual" multiple relationships (e.g., loaning a client a self-help book, shaking a client's hand on the way in or out of a counseling session, benign self-disclosures in session, unintentional encounters at games, on the street, or in a store or health service) and other harmless communications and contacts, referred to as "boundary crossings." It is important to distinguish between these "boundary crossings," or "boundary extensions," and "boundary violations." Boundary crossings or extensions are not intended to harm the client and may even benefit the counselor-client relationship. Boundary violations, on the other hand, involve the intentional exploitation of the client's vulnerability, and are likely to cause harm to the client (Welfel, 2016).

## Marketing

Unfortunately, many barriers to service provision exist within sport and intercollegiate athletics. Marketing is an important aspect of working around or reducing barriers, as well as building and maintaining a successful psychology or counseling practice. Whether one is an employee of the intercollegiate athletics department, a member of a counseling service staff, or a private practitioner, it is critical to provide information to student-athletes about the availability and method of accessing counseling and psychological services. Useful guidance on ethical marketing practices for consultants applicable to work in athletics but beyond the scope of this chapter is offered by Hays and Brown (2004) and Lesyk (1998).

Overall, helping professionals need to present their services and themselves in an accurate, positive light to make potential clients and referral sources aware of their services. The ethical standards of both the APA and AASP suggest that practitioners need to make honest and truthful claims about their training and competence, degrees, credentials, affiliations, fees (if any), and services when marketing their services. With this in mind, ethical professionals will be specific as to what degrees and titles they hold. For example, printing "Dr. Jack Smith" on a business card is vague and does not tell clients in what degree or field Dr. Smith was trained. However, "Jack Smith, Ph.D., Licensed Psychologist" is a better representation of what Dr. Smith was trained to do. Further, helping professionals need to be responsible for making sure that their advertisements are truthful and should take steps to correct any misunderstandings related to their marketing.

Several opportunities exist for those who work with student-athletes to network and communicate about themselves and the nature of their services to potential clients and referral sources. For example, preseason, "pre-participation" team meetings are often held for teams at the beginning of the school year during which information is shared about health services, NCAA compliance issues, etc. Coaching staff meetings are sometimes organized by athletic administrators surrounding various topics of concern and could include an overview of available services. Athletic departments and counseling centers typically have web sites on which information about available services can be posted. With the consent of the athletic department compliance office and administration, helping professionals can distribute flyers to student-athletes, coaches, and staff.

Regrettably, in marketing counseling services it has become rather common practice to use the testimonials of former clients, especially when such clients are high-profile student-athletes. Such testimonials may add instant credibility to the practitioner's credentials and are not inherently unethical, but it should be noted that they should be used with great caution. Testimonials should never be solicited by a practitioner and only included in marketing materials if offered without prompting by the former client. Indeed, it is probably most prudent for professionals to avoid testimonials altogether and let satisfied clients provide them, entirely on their own, to prospective clients.

## Unique Service Settings

The unique settings in which helping professionals may be called upon to consult with collegiate student-athletes and their teams also pose several ethical challenges and concerns (Andersen, Van Raalte, & Brewer, 2001). For example, an athlete might wish to speak to a helping professional during practice, on the sidelines during a competition, or perhaps in the strength and conditioning or athletic training rooms. Engaging "face time" at practices (if welcomed by coaches) and being available to a student-athlete needing some immediate assistance is often encouraged to develop relationships (helping professionals need to be aware of NCAA rules that may limit such interactions and should seek consultation from athletic department compliance staff). On campus, a helping professional may also run into student-athletes in the hallways of academic buildings, the student center, or library, where athletes may or may not want to talk about their concerns.

Consulting in these nontraditional settings presents some out of the ordinary ethical challenges to confidentiality. Friends, faculty, fans, other members of the team, and staff or students may recognize the athlete and consultant or may see the athlete seeking consultation, perhaps may even be close enough to hear what is being discussed. In these instances, ethical professionals should always consider the best interests of the client when determining whether the contact should be initiated at all, moved to a more private place, or discontinued. If the need is immediate and brief intervention is warranted, it may be best to continue the conversation in as discreet a manner as possible and possibly schedule a follow-up meeting for a later date. It is also useful to consider that some athletes are more comfortable than others talking to a psychologist or counselor in such settings. In any case, the ethical professional should inquire about an athlete-client's wishes to interact or not interact in these situations at the outset of their work together (Watson & Etzel, 2004).

The opportunity to travel with college teams to and from competitions also presents some ethical challenges unique to work with student-athletes (e.g., confidentiality issues and blurring of boundaries and roles; Andersen et al., 2001; Aoyagi & Portenga, 2010; Brown & Cogan, 2006). When helping professionals travel with a team, they may consult formally or informally on a bus, while waiting for a plane, during team meals, or in hotels. In these potentially awkward situations, practitioners should consider where and how they can best serve the athlete, that is, what is in the client's best interest, taking into account who is around and the perceived comfort level of the client. For example, a hotel lobby with many people present might seem like a better option than a hotel room, which presents its own risks. Although conversation in a hotel room is more private, others may perceive it as a potentially sexual rather than a professional encounter (Moore, 2003).

Traveling with a team likely presents the opportunity to build rapport and may help the professional learn more about team dynamics, including how to better intervene with the team and team members; however, such situations are tricky with much higher potential for ethical challenges to arise than likely would exist during office sessions. If a helping professional does engage in travel, these situations are likely unavoidable; the ethical professional should have a plan for how to handle them should they occur (Brown & Cogan, 2006). For example, a psychologist can discuss with the coach(es) the logistics of the transportation and hotel arrangements prior to the trip, and discuss a plan with them (and/or the team) for how consultation will work while traveling. This way, the coaches and athletes will know what to expect and can address any concerns in advance.

Just as the athletic environment lends itself to nontraditional settings for consultation, it also lends itself to nontraditional lengths of consultations (Etzel & Watson, 2007; Moore, 2003; Watson & Etzel, 2004). Sessions may be formal or informal and may be shorter or longer than the traditional 50-minute session. For example, athletes may want to quickly vent frustration or raise a performance concern on the sidelines, at practice, or when they see the consultant in the hallway. Although such meetings are often unplanned and informal, the ethical professional should keep brief notes of what was discussed, even if only writing a couple of sentences in the client's file (Etzel & Watson, 2007). A consultation could also be quite extensive, depending on the athlete's concern. For example, to prepare for an upcoming game, an athlete might need a consultation that is longer than the traditional 50 minutes. Helping professionals need to be careful about making such arrangements the norm and what that might communicate about their relationship with clients (e.g., overidentification, attraction).

Although there are a variety of sites in which a helping professional may consult with athletes, practitioners usually have an office located somewhere on campus (e.g., at a counseling center, sometimes in athletics facilities). Given options, what is the optimal location for the office? In fact, it is a challenge to find a location that is both confidential and convenient for athletes. An office in athletic facilities may be more accessible to athletes than in a counseling center since athletes spend so much time there. However, there is a high potential for other athletes and coaches to see the athlete walk in or out of an office in an athletic department.

Having an office in a university counseling center typically offers more privacy from coaches and other athletic personnel. On the other hand, it is often less convenient for an athlete to access (Watson & Etzel, 2004) and may hinder athletes from setting and keeping appointments. Further, some athlete clients report feeling uncomfortable in waiting rooms with others who might recognize them. High-profile student-athletes may be particularly reluctant to walk into a counseling center for fear of being seen by others from the campus community and having information that they are receiving counseling somehow "leaked" to others. Clearly, confidentiality is a major concern when it comes to others seeing athletes enter or exit an office.

Helping professionals may also need to be somewhat flexible in terms of the hours they consult with athletes (Watson & Etzel, 2004). Since athletes typically have class during the day and then practice in the afternoon, they may be available only in the evenings to meet with a counselor.

Meeting at a late time can reduce the concern about confidentiality; however, the professional should be cautious since there may not be others around (colleagues, etc.) in case of an emergency (Etzel & Watson, 2007). These types of arrangements also present some risk in terms of the potential for conveying an unintended message to the student-athlete or others (e.g., attraction or special treatment).

Finally, many professionals working in a college setting will likely have to deal with running into clients in the community (Etzel & Watson, 2007). A professional may see a client in the grocery store, mall, coffee shop, restaurant, bar, etc. It can be an uncomfortable situation for both client and professional when each decides whether or not to acknowledge the other. A suggestion would be to wait for the client to acknowledge the helping professional first and to make the contact as brief as possible. As noted earlier, to prevent an uncomfortable and awkward situation, an ethical professional should discuss the possibility of such encounters with clients upfront in their consultations and ask them how, if at all, they would like to be acknowledged in such situations (Etzel & Watson, 2007).

Working in a college athletic environment also presents the possibility of encountering situations involving alcohol, particularly for young professionals or graduate students working with teams. Professionals may also be invited to functions or coaches' meetings at a restaurant where the staff may be drinking. Although being in such social situations can build rapport, particularly with coaches, a helping professional should make smart personal and professional decisions when alcohol is involved. For example, one can offer to be the designated driver so as not to decline an invitation to an event with coaches but still remain professional without the influence of alcohol (Brown & Cogan, 2006).

## Teleconsulting

Current college students are often referred to as being part of generation Z. Individuals within generation Z have commonly been using the Internet from a very young age. They are often considered to be digital natives who are very comfortable with and in many cases prefer communication via social media. For their entire lives, almost limitless information has been readily available to them at any time or place. They are able to listen to music, search the Internet for pertinent information, watch movies/TV, post to social media sites, and text message with friends, often simultaneously. In many ways, this lifestyle has created the expectation that information should always be instantly available to them. In addition to their comfort with and dependence on technology, collegiate student-athletes keep very busy schedules and frequently travel to compete, and therefore they may want to have contact with their consultants while traveling. If they have a desire or need to "meet" with their consultants while on the road, technological advancements make teletherapy options available. In fact, because of their comfort with technology and consistent use of social media for communication, many student-athletes may actually prefer to communicate with a practitioner via technology. However, these options present several ethical issues that practitioners should consider.

Although the idea of teleconsulting with a client may not have been possible 25 years ago, recent technology has made this a viable option. In fact, research has shown that 35% of sport psychology practitioners rated the Internet as moderately to very important to their practices, and noncertified consultants viewed the Internet as more important and reported using it more than those who were certified by AASP (Watson, Lubker, Zakrajsek, & Quartiroli, 2012). Interestingly, respondents to this survey also frequently expressed the belief that the use of the Internet for consulting presents many potential ethical challenges.

Given the above information, helping professionals working with student-athletes may be drawn to use telecommunications options more often in their practices. Such uses for technology may include the marketing and dissemination of information, supervision, collaboration with colleagues, professional development, research, distance learning, referrals, or even consulting itself (Watson & Etzel, 2000; Watson, Schinke, & Sampson, 2014; Watson, Tenenbaum, Lidor, & Alfermann, 2001). However, use of technology for distance consulting is not without its problems. Potential problems include an inability to identify clients' true identities, difficulties establishing a therapeutic relationship when located great distances away, accurately assessing content and affect, the lack of assumed confidentiality with client contact, and the potential for miscommunications and misunderstandings. Another potential legal issue may involve practicing across state lines (beyond the scope of one's license) when consulting with clients in a different area of the country. Helping professionals must undergo appropriate training of consultants to use the Internet effectively. Finally, they must take care to insure the validity of information obtained from their clients with regard to assessments (Watson & Etzel, 2000; Watson et al., 2001; Watson et al., 2014; Watson et al., 2017).

The current ACA (2014) and AASP (2011) codes of conduct, as well as the Joint Task Force for the Development of Telepsychology Guidelines for Psychologists

(2013) and work by Luxton, Nelson, and Maheu (2016), provide guidance for the ethical use of technology. Such considerations might include developing effective intake and consent procedures that collect appropriate information. Helping professionals must also inform the client about the issues associated with telepsychology and how these issues will be handled. For instance, practitioner considerations may include (1) making a determination as to whether one is legally allowed to consult with the client based upon geographic location and licensure restrictions; (2) informing clients that confidentiality cannot be guaranteed (use of client waiver would help with this); (3) making clients aware of traditional consulting hours and the length of response time; (4) taking reasonable steps to confidentially store client information on a server or hard drive; (5) identifying clients and making sure that they are eligible to consent to such services; (6) maintaining knowledge of events local to the client; (7) taking steps to clarify possible misunderstandings; (8) having a backup plan for technology failures (e.g., phone number if one loses connection during video consulting); and (9) dealing only with cases that can realistically be handled appropriately from a distance (e.g., performance anxiety vs. an eating disorder). Finally, helping professionals should be very cautious with the amount of identifiable client information they provide when requesting consultations from colleagues over the Internet, or with specific information and guidance they provide when responding to requests for consultation over the Internet (Behnke, 2007).

## Ethical Decision Making

Although a basic understanding of ethics and the ethics code(s) that impact the practice of helping professionals is important, this information alone will not guarantee that good decisions will be made, even by those individuals with considerable experience or who act with the best of intentions. For this reason, it is important that helping professionals also be familiar with ethical decision-making models that may help them make effective decisions to guide their thinking and action in work with student-athletes.

Based on commonly used models in psychology (Canadian Psychological Association, 2017; Koocher & Keith-Spiegel, 2016), Watson and Etzel (in press) proposed a sequential, 13-step model of ethical decision-making for helping professionals to guide their thinking in times of uncertainty or confusion. The steps of the model:

1. Determine if the dilemma is indeed an ethical issue.

2. Examine all available facts that are relevant to the situation.

3. Consult existing ethical guidelines, laws, and policy statements.

4. Consider factors that might affect the decision, such as biases from self or others.

5. Consult with other professionals in the field (although consultation can occur at any point in this process).

6. Consider the rights and interests of all affected individuals.

7. Identify plausible alternative solutions to the situation.

8. Consider the potential consequences of all possible decisions.

9. Make a decision about how to respond.

10. Implement the decision.

11. Reflect upon and evaluate the results of the decision.

12. Assume responsibility for the consequences of the decision and take corrective steps if necessary.

13. Take appropriate action to prevent the situation from happening again in the future.

## Conclusion

Awareness of the nature and regular ethical challenges involved with working with college student-athletes is essential to responsible, competent service provision to promote the welfare of clients and to do no harm to them. It is critical for helping professionals to understand and consistently apply, to the best of their abilities, the values of their profession as incorporated into the ethical codes they agree to and are expected to follow. In reality, no one is immune from making ethical mistakes—all practitioners will make mistakes during their careers. However, with knowledge, experience, and consultation, most ethical challenges, as identified above, can be sensed in advance and avoided. However, if an ethical mistake is made, it is incumbent upon the ethical practitioner to take reasonable steps to deal effectively with that situation and to keep the best interests of the client in mind while doing so.

## Discussion Questions

1. Who is the client in this case? Is it Dr. Smith's former coach or the athlete? Why is it important for Dr. Smith to clarify the answer to this question to all of the involved parties?

2. Is distance consulting appropriate for the athlete's presenting concerns? What steps could Dr. Smith take to protect the athlete's confidentiality if they are to communicate via telephone, email, or over the Internet?

3. The coach is the former coach of Dr. Smith's (and someone whom Smith may consider a "friend" if they keep in touch a lot). How might their previous affiliations complicate their current working relationship?

4. What steps should Dr. Smith take to ensure that the athlete's participation in the consulting process if voluntary and not being forced upon her by her coach?

# References

American Counseling Association. (2014). *ACA Code of Ethics.* Retrieved from https://www.counseling.org/resources/aca-code-of-ethics.pdf

American Psychiatric Association. (2013). *Diagnostic and statistical manual of mental disorders* (5th ed.). Arlington, VA: American Psychiatric Publishing.

American Psychological Association. (2018). *What is APA's definition of "psychologist"?* Retrieved from http://www.apa.org/support/about-apa.aspx

American Psychological Association. (2017). *Ethical principles of psychologists and code of conduct* (2002, Amended June 1, 2010 and January 1, 2017). Retrieved from http://www.apa.org/ethics/code/index.aspx

American Psychological Association Division 47. (2003). *APA Sport Psychology Proficiency.* Retrieved from http://www.apadivisions.org/division-47/about/sport-proficiency/index.aspx

Andersen, M. B., Van Raalte, J. L., & Brewer, B. W. (2001). Sport psychology service delivery: Staying ethical while keeping loose. *Professional Psychology: Research and Practice, 32,* 12–18.

Aoyagi, M. W., & Portenga, S. T. (2010). The role of positive ethics and virtues in the context of sport and performance psychology service delivery. *Professional Psychology: Research and Practice, 41,* 253–259.

Association for Applied Sport Psychology. (2011). *Ethical Code: ASSP Ethical Principles and Standards.* Retrieved from http://www.appliedsportpsych.org/about/ethics/ethics-code/

Behnke, S. (2007). Ethics and the Internet: Requesting clinical consultations over listserves. *Monitor on Psychology, 38*(7), 62–63.

Bersoff, D. N. (1995). The virtue of principle ethics. *The Counseling Psychologist, 24,* 86–91.

Brown, J., & Cogan, K. (2006). Ethical clinical practice and sport psychology: When two worlds collide. *Ethics and Behavior, 16*(1), 15–24.

Buceta, J. (1993). The sport psychologist/athletic coach dual role: Advantages, difficulties, and ethical considerations. *Journal of Applied Sport Psychology, 5,* 64–77.

Canadian Psychological Association (2017). *Canadian code of ethics for psychologists* (4th ed.). Retrieved from http://www.cpa.ca/docs/File/Ethics/CPA_Code_2017_4thEd.pdf

Etzel, E. F., & Watson, J. C. (2007). Ethical challenges for psychological consultations in intercollegiate athletics. *Journal of Clinical Sport Psychology, 1,* 304–317.

Fisher, C. B. (2003). *Decoding the ethics code: A practical guide for psychologists.* New York: Sage.

Glosoff, H. L., Herlihy, S. B., Herlihy, B., & Spence, E. B. (1997). Privileged communication in the psychologist-client relationship. *Professional Psychology: Research and Practice, 28*, 573–581.

Hays, K. F., & Brown, C. H. (2004). *You're on! Consulting for peak performance.* Washington, DC: American Psychological Association.

Joint Taskforce for the Development of Telepsychology Guidelines for Psychologists (2013). Guidelines for the practice of telepsychology. *American Psychologist, 68*, 791–800.

Kitchener, K. S. (1988). Dual role relationships? What makes them so problematic? *Journal of Counseling and Development, 67*, 217–221.

Koocher, G. (2005). Prototype mental health records. In G. Koocher, J. Norcross, & S. Hill III (Eds.). *Psychologist's desk reference* (2nd ed., pp. 649–652). New York: Oxford University Press.

Koocher, G. P., & Keith-Spiegel, P. (2016). *Ethics in psychology and the mental health professions: Standards and cases* (4th ed.). New York: Oxford University Press.

Lesyk, J. L. (1998). *Developing sport psychology with your clinical practice: A practical guide for mental health professionals.* San Francisco: Jossey-Bass.

López, R. L., & Levy, J. J. (2013). Student athletes' perceived barriers to and preferences for seeking counseling. *Journal of College Counseling, 16*, 19–31.

Loughran, M. J., & Etzel, E. (2008). Ethical practice in a diverse world: The challenges of working with differences in the psychological treatment of student-athletes. *Athletic Insight, 10*(4). Retrieved from http://athleticinsight.com/Vol10Iss4/Ethical.htm

Loughran, M., Etzel, E., & Hankes, D. (2014). Ethical issues in work with collegiate student-athletes. In E. Etzel & J. Watson (Eds.). *Ethical issues in sport, exercise, and performance psychology* (pp. 37–48). Morgantown, WV: Fitness Information Technology.

Luxton, D., Nelson, E., & Maheu, M. (2016). *A practitioner's guide to telemental health: How to conduct legal, ethical and evidence-based telepractice.* Washington, DC: American Psychological Association.

Moore, M. (2017). Stepping outside of their comfort zone: Perceptions of seeking behavioral health services amongst college athletes. *Journal of Issues in Intercollegiate Athletics, 2017 Special Issue*, 130–144.

Moore, Z. E. (2003). Ethical dilemmas in sport psychology: Discussion and recommendations for practice. *Professional Psychology: Research and Practice, 34*, 601–610.

National Collegiate Athletic Association. (2007). *Managing student-athletes' mental health issues.* Indianapolis: Author.

National Collegiate Athletic Association. (2016). *2016–17 NCAA Division I Manual.* Indianapolis, IN: Author.

National Collegiate Athletic Association Sport Science Institute (2017). *Mental health best practices.* Retrieved from https://www.ncaa.org/sites/default/files/HS_Mental-Health-Best-Practices_20160317.pdf

Neimeyer, G. J., Taylor, J. M., & Rozensky, R. H. (2012). The diminishing durability of knowledge in professional psychology: A Delphi poll of specialties and proficiencies. *Professional Psychology: Research and Practice, 43*, 364–371.

Pérez-Rojas, A., Lockard, A. J., Bartholomew, T. T., Janis, R. A., Carney, D. M., Xiao, H., … Hayes, J. A. (2017). Presenting concerns in counseling centers: The view from clinicians on the ground. *Psychological Services, 14,* 416–427.

Pope, K., & Tabachnick, B. (1993). Therapists' anger, hate, fear, and sexual feelings: National survey of therapist responses, client characteristics, critical events, formal complaints, and training. *Professional Psychology: Research and Practice, 24*(2), 142–152.

Pope, K., & Vasquez, M. (1991). *Ethics in psychotherapy and consulting: A practical guide for psychologists.* San Francisco: Jossey-Bass.

Schoener, G. R. (2003). Recognizing, assisting, and reporting the impaired psychologist. In G. Koocher, J. Norcross, & S. Hill III (Eds.), *Psychologist's desk reference* (2nd ed., pp. 620–624). New York: Oxford University Press.

Sonne, J. L. (2004). Nonsexual multiple relationships: A practical decision-making model for clinicians. Retrieved from http://kspope.com/site/multiple-relationships.php

Sue, D. W., & Sue, D. (2013). *Counseling the culturally diverse: Theory and practice* (6th ed.). New York: John Wiley & Sons.

Sue, W., & Torino, G. (2005). Racial cultural competence: Awareness, knowledge, and skills. In R. T. Carter (Ed.), *Handbook of multicultural psychology and counseling* (pp. 3–18). Hoboken, NJ: Wiley.

United States Department of Health & Human Resources. (2003). *Summary of the HIPAA privacy rule.* Retrieved from https://www.hhs.gov/sites/default/files/privacysummary.pdf

Watson, J. C., Clement, D., Harris, B., Leffingwell, T., & Hurst, J. (2006). Teacher- practitioner multiple role issues in sport psychology. *Ethics and Behavior, 16,* 41–59.

Watson, J. C., & Etzel, E. F. (2000, Fall). Considering ethics: Using the Internet in sport psychology. *AAASP Newsletter, 15*(3), 13–16.

Watson, J. C., & Etzel, E. F. (2004). Ethical issues affecting psychologists, counselors and sport psychology consultants' work with collegiate student athletes. *Professional Studies Review, 1,* 49–60.

Watson, J. C. II, & Etzel, E. F. (in press). Ethical and legal issues in sport and performance psychology. *APA Handbook of Sport and Exercise Psychology.* Washington, D.C.: American Psychological Association.

Watson, J. C., II, Lubker, J., & Zakrajsek, R., & Quartiroli, A. (2012). Internet usage patterns and ethical concerns in sport and exercise psychology. *Athletic Insight, 4*(1), 65–78.

Watson, J. C., II, Schinke, R. J., & Sampson Jr., J. P. (2014). Ethical issues affecting the use of telepsychology in sport and exercise psychology. In E. F. Etzel & J. C. Watson II (Eds.), *Ethical issues in sport, exercise, and performance psychology* (pp. 139–150). Morgantown, WV: Fitness Information Technology.

Watson, J. C., II, Tenenbaum, G., Lidor, R., & Alfermann, D. (2001). Ethical uses of the Internet in sport psychology: A position stand. *International Journal of Sport Psychology, 32,* 207–222.

Watson, J. C., II, Way, W. C., & Hilliard, R. C. (2017). Ethical issues in sport psychology. *Current Opinion in Psychology, 16,* 143–147.

Welfel, E. R. (2016). *Ethics in counseling and psychotherapy: Standards, research, and emerging issues* (6th ed.). Boston, MA: Cengage Learning.

# I



# K



# L



# M



# N



# P



# R

# About the Authors

**Mitch Abrams**   Dr. Mitch Abrams is a sport psychologist and an expert in anger and violence in sports. He earned his bachelor's degree in psychology and pre-med studies from Brooklyn College in 1994, master's in applied psychology in 1996, and doctoral degree in clinical psychology in 1998. He authored the book *Anger Management in Sport—Understanding and Controlling Violence in Sports.* Related to this work, Dr. Abrams has also been a pioneer in sexual assault and dating violence prevention, with specific focus on athlete populations in developing the *Abrams Model of Sexual Assault Prevention.*

Dr. Abrams also oversees mental health services for the New Jersey State Department of Corrections as the chief psychologist and clinician administrator for Rutgers University—University Correctional Healthcare. He is a clinical assistant professor in the Department of Psychiatry at Rutgers/Robert Wood Johnson Medical School and has held adjunct faculty positions at Brooklyn College, Long Island University/C.W. Post, and Fairleigh Dickinson University. In addition, he has been in private practice for the past 18 years and is a licensed psychologist in New York and New Jersey.

**Michelle Bartlett**   Dr. Michelle Bartlett, CMPC, is an associate professor of sports and exercise sciences at West Texas A&M University. She received a BS in both biology and psychology from Syracuse University in 2003, an MS and PhD in sport and exercise psychology from West Virginia University, and received her license-eligible clinical training with an MA in community counseling, also from West Virginia University. Dr. Bartlett has been doing applied work with college athletes for over 10 years. Her main research areas are in the domain of athlete anger and aggression. Additionally, she also supervises practitioners seeking Certified Mental Performance Consultant certification and has publications and presentations in the domain of professional development and supervision issues, as well. Presently, she has several publications with Dr. Abrams on athletes and trauma/sexual assault.

Dr. Bartlett retains membership in the American Psychological Association and the Association for Applied Sport Psychology.

**Jessica Bartley**   Dr. Jessica Bartley is the director of the Center for Performance Excellence and a clinical assistant professor in the Sport and Performance Psychology Program at the University of Denver. She is a licensed clinical psychologist and a certified mental performance consultant (CMPC). She also works with collegiate, professional, and Olympic athletes through her private practice, Sport and Performance Excellence Consultants. Jessica is a member of the Society for Sport, Exercise & Performance Psychology, the American Psychological Association, the Association for Applied Sport Psychology, and the International Society for Sport Psychology. Her areas of expertise include mental health with athletes—specifically personality disorders, depressive disorders, anxiety disorders, eating disorders and body image, and substance-related disorders, as well as learning disorders and attention-deficit/hyperactivity disorders. She also addresses performance anxiety, injury and rehabilitation concerns, motivation, and sport transition/retirement after sport in addition to providing assessment and measurement with athletes.

**Angel Brutus**   Dr. Angel Brutus is a member of Mississippi State University's Sports Medicine team, serving as director of counseling and sport psychology. She serves in this role after managing a private practice based in Atlanta, GA, where she provided clinical and sport performance services to individuals, teams, and organizations. Her training includes licensed professional counseling in Georgia, certified rehabilitation counseling, and sport-performance psychology, which gives her the opportunity to provide holistic services based on clients' clinical and performance needs. She serves as coordinator for the Association for Applied Sport Psychology's Race & Ethnicity in Sport Special Interest Group (SIG) and is a member of multiple committees within the Association. In her spare time, she enjoys spending quality time with her three daughters and husband, engaging as a community volunteer with philanthropic organizations targeting at-risk youth, and mentoring students interested in pursuing careers in the helping profession.

**Jennifer Carter**   Dr. Jen Carter's wonderful experience in the sport of swimming drove her to the career of sport psychology. She was the NCAA Division III Swimmer of the Year in 1993 and a Honda Award Winner in 1994. At The Ohio State University (OSU) Wexner Medical Center, Jen is the lead sport psychologist at the Jameson Crane Sports Medicine Institute and clinical associate professor at Psychiatry and Behavioral Health. In this role, she provides mental health and performance psychology counseling to OSU athletes, road warriors, sports medicine patients, clients with body image issues, and individuals in the community. Jen is a counseling psychologist with specialties in sport psychology and eating disorders. She strives to help adults and adolescents achieve peak performance in multiple life domains.

**Daniel B. Charek**  Dr. Daniel B. Charek is currently a postdoctoral fellow specializing in neuropsychology with the UPMC Sports Medicine Concussion Program. Dr. Charek received his bachelor's degree in psychology from the University of Akron in 2009. He then earned his doctoral degree in clinical psychology from the University of Toledo and completed his predoctoral, APA-accredited internship along the neuropsychology track at the Phoenix VA Health Care System in Phoenix, Arizona, in 2016. Dr. Charek's clinical and research interests include sport-related concussion, treatment of concussion, and identification of clinical risk factors relevant to management and recovery.

**Marc Cormier**  Dr. Marc Cormier—a native of Nova Scotia, Canada—received his PhD in sport and exercise psychology from West Virginia University. Currently, he is an assistant professor in the Department of Kinesiology and Health Promotion at the University of Kentucky and serves as the director for the Sport and Exercise Psychology Graduate Program. His primary areas of research include the psychological aspects of sport injury, team cohesion, and mental skills training, and his work has been published in regional, national, and international journals/conference proceedings. In addition to his faculty responsibilities, Dr. Cormier has a 50% appointment in UK Athletics, where he coordinates all counseling and performance psychology services. Dr. Cormier is a certified mental performance consultant (CMPC), a licensed professional counselor, and a member of the United States Olympic Committee's Sport Psychology registry. A former competitive athlete, he continues to enjoy recreational sports such as hockey, cycling, golf, and running.

**Meredith Deal**  Meredith Deal, MS, is a research specialist at the University of Pittsburgh Medical Center and a member of the Chatham University research team recently awarded the NCAA Innovations in Research and Practice Grant. She holds a BS in exercise science from the University of Delaware and an MS in counseling psychology from Chatham University. At Chatham, she was a member of the Gender Research Team and presented research on a variety of topics, including athletic identity, experiences of sexism in female student-athletes, and resilience in adolescent girls, at conferences. With research interests in gender, masculinity, and sexual violence in college athletics, injury recovery, and coach-athlete relationships, she has intentions of pursuing a PhD in counseling psychology. As a former athlete, Meredith played soccer and ran track, in addition to coaching soccer, field hockey, and basketball.

**V. Paul Downey**   V. Paul Downey, EdD, serves as director of the Athletics Study Center at Illinois State University, overseeing the academic and life skills staff. Downey is responsible for the development, implementation, and evaluation of academic and life skills initiatives, including targeting, tutoring, and study hall programs—as well as the career and personal development of student-athletes for the purpose of promoting academic success, retention, and, ultimately, graduation.

Prior to Illinois State, Downey served in multiple capacities at West Virginia University (WVU) including GA, academic advisor, and director of the Coliseum Academic Performance Center. Downey earned his doctorate in Sport and Exercise Psychology from WVU in 2005.

Downey most recently served as chair of the Legislative Services Committee and second term as Region III Director of N4A—The National Association of Academic and Student-Athlete Development Professionals. Downey has been an N4A member for over 10 years, with the last four years on the Board of Directors.

**Edward F. Etzel**   Dr. Edward F. Etzel is a professor of sport and exercise psychology at West Virginia University, where he teaches a number of courses related to applied sport psychology. He is a licensed psychologist in the state of West Virginia. Dr. Etzel is a certified mental performance consultant through the Association for Applied Sport Psychology (AASP), and has served as chair of the ethics committee within AASP. In a previous lifetime, Dr. Etzel was the gold medalist at the 1984 Olympics in Los Angeles in the men's english match rifle event and was a gold medalist in the 1978 World Championships and 1979 Pan American Games.

**Brandon Gillie**   Dr. Brandon Gillie is currently a postdoctoral fellow in UPMC Sports Medicine Concussion Program. Dr. Gillie received his bachelor's degree in psychology from the University of Pittsburgh in 2010. He then earned his doctoral degree in clinical psychology from The Ohio State University and completed his pre-doctoral, APA-accredited internship at the Salem Veteran's Affairs Medical Center in Salem, Virginia in 2016. Dr. Gillie's clinical and research interests include the extent to which markers of self-regulatory capacity predict resiliency and recovery from concussion. He is also interested in the role of mood and anxiety as risk factors for poor outcomes following concussion.

**Deanna Hamilton**   Dr. Deanna Hamilton is an associate professor of graduate psychology at Chatham University in Pittsburgh, PA, where she teaches courses in developmental psychology, psychopathology, and positive psychology. Dr. Hamilton earned her doctoral degree in clinical/developmental psychology from Bryn Mawr College in 2005. She completed her doctoral internship at the University of Pittsburgh Counseling Center and a post-doctoral fellowship at the

Duquesne University Counseling Center. Dr. Hamilton has published research in the areas of positive psychology and well-being, and self-efficacy among graduate student trainees.

**Doug Hankes**   Dr. Doug Hankes is a licensed psychologist and the director of Student Counseling Services at Auburn University. He is in his 14th year as a sport psychologist on the Auburn University Sports Medicine Optimum Performance Sports (OPS) team. He is a fellow and CMPC of the Association for Applied Sport Psychology (AASP). He has served in multiple roles on the Executive Boards of APA Division 47 (Society for Sport, Exercise, and Performance Psychology) and AASP. He is currently listed on the 2016–2020 United States Olympic Committee Sport Psychology Registry.

**Robert C. Hilliard**   Robert C. Hilliard is currently a PhD student in sport and exercise psychology and an MA student in clinical mental health counseling at West Virginia University. He has worked as a counselor and sport psychology consultant with Division I and III student-athletes. He has published articles in the mental health field related to stigma toward help-seeking as well as on topics related to ethics in sport psychology and the psychology of sport injury. His dissertation focuses on stigma and help-seeking behavior in college student-athletes.

**Michael Johnson**   Dr. Mike Johnson is a licensed psychologist and serves as the director of Clinical and Sport Psychology at the University of Arkansas (U of A) in the Department of Athletics—a position he has held since 2013. Dr. Johnson oversees the mental health services for U of A student-athletes and coordinates with other departments (e.g., medical, strength and conditioning) to assure that U of A student-athletes receive optimal mental healthcare.

Prior to joining Arkansas, Dr. Johnson was the sport psychologist at Kansas State University. His other higher-education experiences include being a professor at the University of Tennessee at Chattanooga, Georgia Highlands College, and the University of Texas-Pan American.

Dr. Johnson was a four-year letter winner in swimming at Brown University, where he received his bachelor's degree in economics. He earned his master's degree in educational psychology (sport psychology major, measurement/stats minor) and his PhD in counseling psychology and human systems from Florida State University.

**Anthony P. Kontos**   Dr. Anthony P. Kontos is research director for the UPMC Sports Medicine Concussion Program and associate professor in the Departments of Orthopaedic Surgery and Sports Medicine and Rehabilitation at the University of Pittsburgh. He has specialized in concussion research for 13 years and has 181 professional publications and 290 professional presentations. His research is funded by the *National Institutes of Health (NIH)* and *Department of Defense (DoD)* and focuses on risk factors; neurocognitive/neuromotor effects; psychological issues; treatment; and concussion in military, pediatric, and sport populations. Dr. Kontos is a fellow and past-president of the *Society for Sport, Exercise, & Performance Psychology (APA-Div47)*, and a fellow of the *National Academy of Kinesiology, Association for Applied Sport Psychology*, and *Eastern Psychological Association*. He is also the lead coauthor (with Dr. Collins) of *Concussion: A Clinical Profiles Based Approach to Assessment and Treatment*.

**Sam Maniar**  Dr. Sam Maniar is the president and founder of the Center for Peak Performance, LLC. He works with athletes, sports teams, executives, and organizations to help them achieve peak performance. In his work with amateur, Olympic, and professional athletes, Dr. Maniar has focused on both counseling and performance enhancement interventions. He has worked with the Ohio State Buckeyes, University of Akron Zips, Washington State Cougars, Cleveland Browns, Olympic athletes, and numerous professional athletes from various sports. In addition, he has authored numerous refereed publications related to counseling athletes and coauthored the initial depression guidelines for the *NCAA Sports Medicine Handbook*. He holds a doctorate degree in counseling psychology with a specialization in sport psychology and is a licensed psychologist in the state of Ohio.

**Samantha Monda**  Dr. Samantha Monda is an associate professor of psychology at Robert Morris University in Pittsburgh, PA, and a certified mental performance consultant for KPEX Consulting. A former Academic All-American swimmer at Carnegie Mellon University, Dr. Monda specializes in working with collegiate student-athletes. Dr. Monda is certified by the Association for Applied Sport Psychology (AASP), the National Board for Certified Counselors (NCC), and is a member of the United States Olympic Committee Sport Psychology Registry. She received her PhD specializing in sport and exercise psychology and a master's degree in counseling from West Virginia University, where she worked with the life skills program for WVU Athletics and the Carruth Center for Psychological Services. She has written extensively on issues relating to academic and personal development of student-athletes and has presented her work at the NCAA's Scholarly Colloquium on Intercollegiate Athletics.

**Deborah N. Roche**  Dr. Deborah Roche is a licensed counseling psychologist. She began working with athletes in 1999 during her graduate training, where she performed research and applied work in the athletic department at the University of Buffalo. After graduation, Dr. Roche went on to complete a post-doctoral fellowship at the University of Delaware and was hired there as assistant director for Student Services for Athletes. She worked at Delaware for several years before returning to her hometown in New York and starting her own company, Counseling and Sport Psychology Services. In her practice she works with U.S. National team, collegiate, high school and recreational athletes. She provides performance and clinical work to her clients as well as consultations to coaches and other athletic administrators. In 2017, Dr. Roche joined the Hospital for Special Surgery Women's Sports Medicine staff as a part time consultant providing sport psychology treatment and consultations at their facilities in NYC and Westchester.

**Natalie Sandel**   Dr. Natalie Sandel is a second-year neuropsychology fellow for the UPMC Sports Medicine Concussion Program. She has authored multiple peer-reviewed publications on concussion, and her dissertation research was recently published in the *American Journal of Sports Medicine*. Through her clinical training at institutions such as the Hospital of Pennsylvania, Temple University Hospital, and Children's Hospital of Philadelphia, she has obtained extensive clinical training in the neuropsychological sequelae of developmental and acquired neurological disorders. Dr. Sandel also has her master's degree in business administration.

**Jamie Shapiro**   Dr. Jamie Shapiro is a faculty member in the MA in sport and performance psychology program in the Graduate School of Professional Psychology at the University of Denver. She earned a PhD in sport and exercise psychology from West Virginia University (WVU), an MA in community counseling from WVU, an MS in athletic counseling from Springfield College, and a BS in psychology from Brown University, where she was on the gymnastics team for four years. Dr. Shapiro is a certified mental performance consultant (CMPC), listed on the United States Olympic Committee's Sport Psychology Registry, and a National Certified Counselor (NCC). She is a consultant for Sport & Performance Excellence Consultants based in Denver, CO, and has consulted with youth, collegiate, elite, and Paralympic athletes from a variety of sports.

**Leigh Skvarla**   Dr. Leigh Skvarla, NCC, currently serves as the clinical counselor for the University of Pittsburgh Department of Athletics in partnership with the Western Psychiatric Institute and Clinic of UPMC. She also works with youth, adolescent, and adult performers through KPEX Consulting, and teaches courses as an adjunct instructor at Chatham University. Leigh is a member of the American Psychological Association, the Association for Applied Sport Psychology, and the International Association of Dance Medicine and Science. A proud graduate of Bucknell University and West Virginia University, she has presented research and collaborative workshops at a variety of conferences, and particularly enjoys continuing education related to mental health, stress management, identity development, injury and return to sport, trauma, and professional ethics. An avid exerciser, Leigh is a former gymnast, dancer, and soccer player.

**John P. Sullivan**   John P. Sullivan, PsyD is a sport scientist and clinical sport psychologist with over 20 years of clinical and scholarly experience. He has held appointments within the National Football League (NFL), English Premier League (EPL), the NCAA, the elite military, and law enforcement. Dr. Sullivan is also a visiting scholar and sport scientist at the Queensland Academy of Sport and Queensland University of Technology in Brisbane, Australia. He is a frequent contributor writing on sport science and sports medicine, and his latest efforts have focused on a series of books that distill the latest performance psychology, cognitive science, and neuroscience, related to optimal brain performance and health, entitled *The Brain Always Wins.*

**Ryan Sweeny**   Dr. Ryan Sweeny is the assistant director of the Career Center at the University of Pittsburgh (Pitt). He began his career at Pitt in 2004. Prior to joining the Pitt staff, he was a mental health counselor, a high school teacher, and a coach. In addition to his duties as assistant director, Ryan enjoys working with undecided students.

Ryan holds a BA in psychology, and a Master's and PhD in counseling psychology from the University of Notre Dame, where he also played football.

**Jack C. Watson II**   Dr. Jack C. Watson II is a professor and associate dean in the College of Physical Activity and Sport Sciences at West Virginia University. He has written extensively in the area of professional issues in sport psychology, with a specific focus upon ethical issues associated with applied sport psychology. As a past president of the Association for Applied Sport Psychology, he has also been heavily involved with updating the certified mental performance consultant (CMPC) certification program within the organization. He is a CMPC and a licensed psychologist within the state of West Virginia.

**Shameema Yousuf**   Dr. Shameema Yousuf is an applied sport psychology practitioner, counselor, and founder of *Empower2Perform*, London, UK. She is also employed to lead psychological delivery for the British professional women's soccer team Brighton Hove Albion Football Club in the UK. In practice, she has supported athletes internationally, including in Zimbabwe, where she competed as an elite athlete. She is a certified mental performance consultant for the Association for Applied Sport Psychology (AASP) and currently sits on the diversity and international relations committees for AASP. Dr. Yousuf is also a registered counselor with the

British Association of Counselling and Psychotherapy, a Graduate Member of the British Psychological Society—Division of Sport and Exercise Psychology, and a member of the American Psychological Society—Division 47.

At *Empower2Perform*, Dr. Yousuf works extensively along the athletic development spectrum to elite level. Her key interests are mindfulness and performance, athlete transitions, and cultural diversity in sport, with a practitioner philosophy of performance with wellbeing. Dr. Yousuf is published in peer review journals and educational publications used for Sport Higher Education Curriculum in the UK, is a contributor on topics of performance and athlete wellbeing for a number of local and international media publications, and has appeared on Sky Sport News.

Dr. Yousuf has made a home in London, UK, having been raised in Africa and lived and worked in a few countries internationally. She enjoys and pursues many outdoor activities, explores what London has to offer, and is refining her culinary skills.

# About the Editor

**Dr. Mary Jo Loughran** is a licensed psychologist and a certified mental performance consultant (CMPC) of the Association for Applied Sport Psychology (AASP). She is an associate professor and the program director of graduate psychology at Chatham University in Pittsburgh, Pennsylvania, where she teaches in the PsyD and MS programs in counseling psychology. She joined the Chatham faculty in 2005 and teaches courses in ethics and health psychology.

In 1992, Dr. Loughran completed her PhD in counseling psychology at the University of Pittsburgh, including her doctoral internship at the University of Akron's Counseling & Testing Center. In 2005, Dr. Loughran was awarded her MS in exercise physiology with an emphasis on health and wellness from the University of Pittsburgh.

Dr. Loughran's clinical services career spans the better part of three decades, including 15 years working with collegiate student-athletes in a university counseling center and private practice. Dr. Loughran's research interests include psychology training issues and integrated behavioral and medical healthcare. She has also published research on the psychology of marathon running.